BENDIS & BAGLEY'S BRILLIANT

BENDIS & BRILL

BAGLEY'S GIANT

CREATED & PRODUCED BY

BRIAN MICHAEL BENDIS
& MARK BAGLEY

INKS: JOE RUBINSTEIN
COLORS: NICK FILARDI

LETTERS: CHRIS ELIOPOULOS

EDITOR/PRODUCTION: JENNIFER GRÜNWALD

BUSINESS AFFAIRS: ALISA BENDIS

COLLECTION DESIGNER: PATRICK McGRATH

BRILLIANT VOL. 1. Contains material originally published in magazine form as BRILLIANT #1-5. First printing 2014. ISBN# 978-0-7851-5914-8. Published by MARVEL WORLDWIDE, INC., a subsidiary of MARVEL ENTERTAINMENT, LLC. OFFICE OF PUBLICATION: 135 West 50th Street, New York, NY 10020. Copyright © 2013 Jinxworld, Inc. All rights reserved. Brilliant, its logo design, and all characters featured in or on this issue and the distinctive names and likenesses thereof, and all related indicia are trademarks of Jinxworld, Inc. No similarity between any of the names, characters, persons, and/or institutions in this magazine with those of any living or dead person or institution is intended, and any such similarity that may exist is purely coincidental. ICON and the Icon logos are trademarks of Marvel Characters, Inc. **Printed in the U.S.A.** Manufactured between 2/12/2014 and 3/17/2014 by R.R. DONNELLEY, INC., SALEM, VA, USA.

10 9 8 7 6 5 4 3 2 1

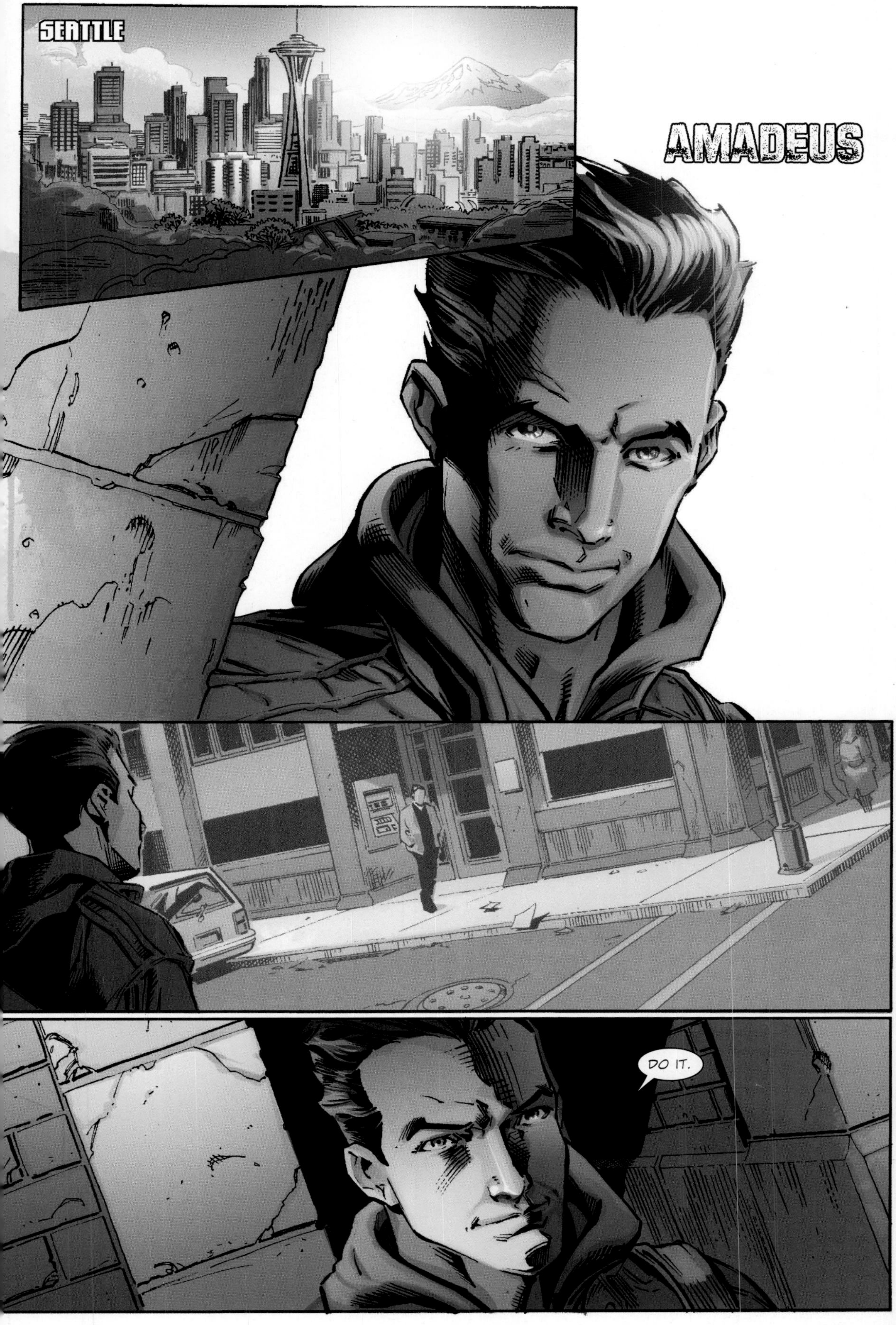
SEATTLE
AMADEUS
DO IT.

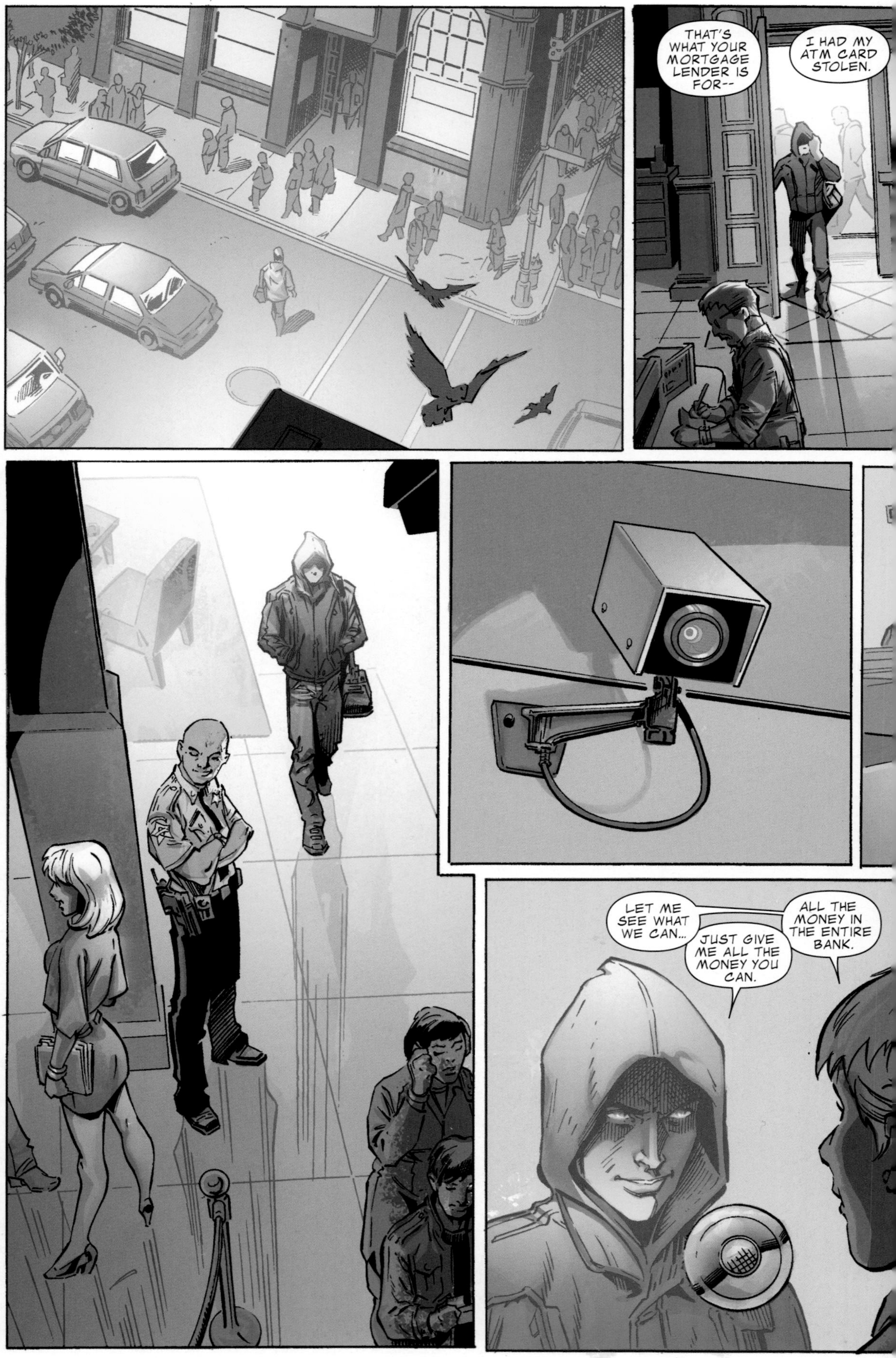
THAT'S WHAT YOUR MORTGAGE LENDER IS FOR--
I HAD MY ATM CARD STOLEN.
LET ME SEE WHAT WE CAN...
JUST GIVE ME ALL THE MONEY YOU CAN.
ALL THE MONEY IN THE ENTIRE BANK.

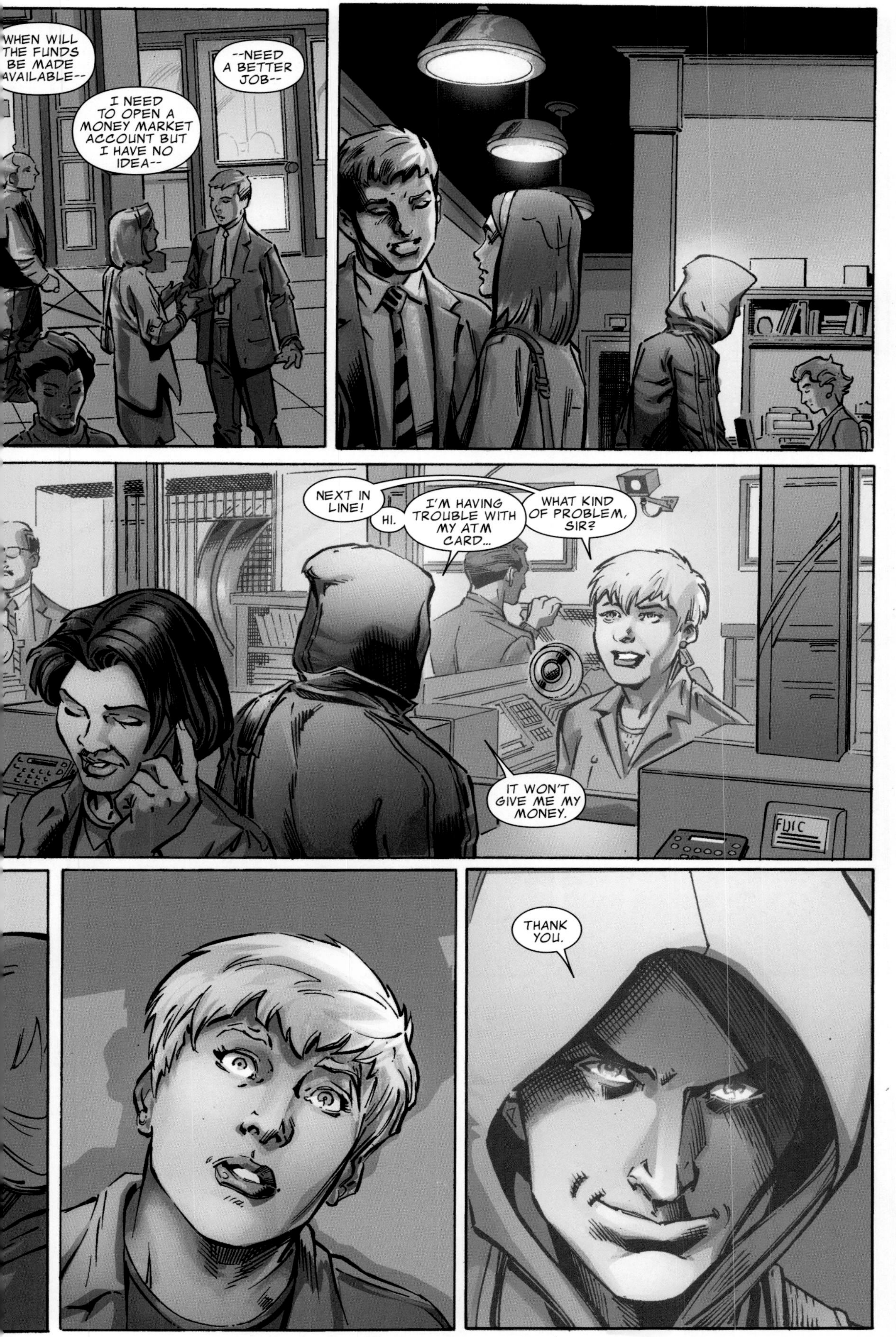
WHEN WILL THE FUNDS BE MADE AVAILABLE--
I NEED TO OPEN A MONEY MARKET ACCOUNT BUT I HAVE NO IDEA--
--NEED A BETTER JOB--
NEXT IN LINE!
HI.
I'M HAVING TROUBLE WITH MY ATM CARD...
WHAT KIND OF PROBLEM, SIR?
IT WON'T GIVE ME MY MONEY.
FDIC
THANK YOU.

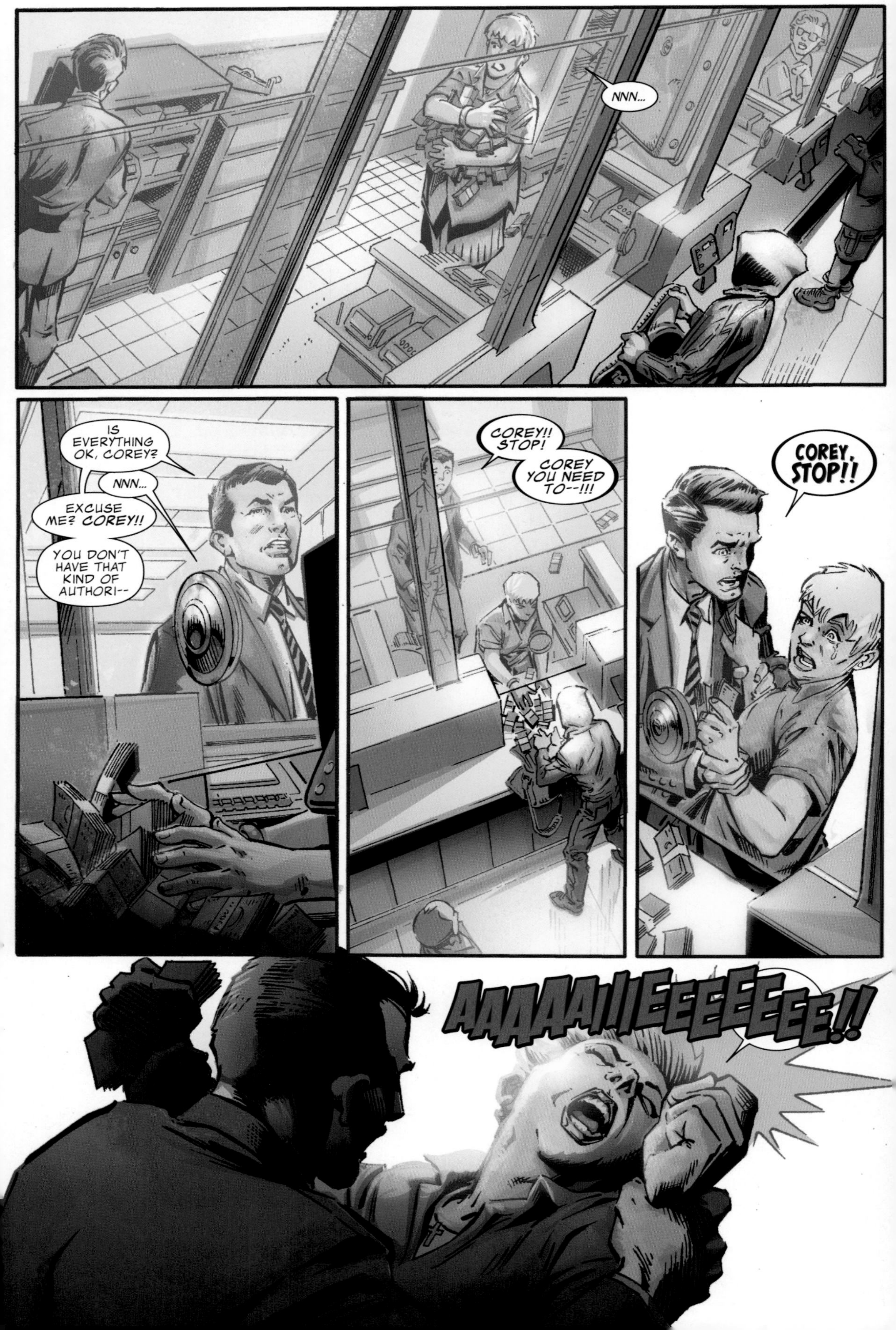
NNN...
IS EVERYTHING OK, COREY?
NNN...
EXCUSE ME? COREY!!
YOU DON'T HAVE THAT KIND OF AUTHORI--
COREY!! STOP!
COREY YOU NEED TO--!!!
COREY, STOP!!
AAAAAIIEEEEEEE!!

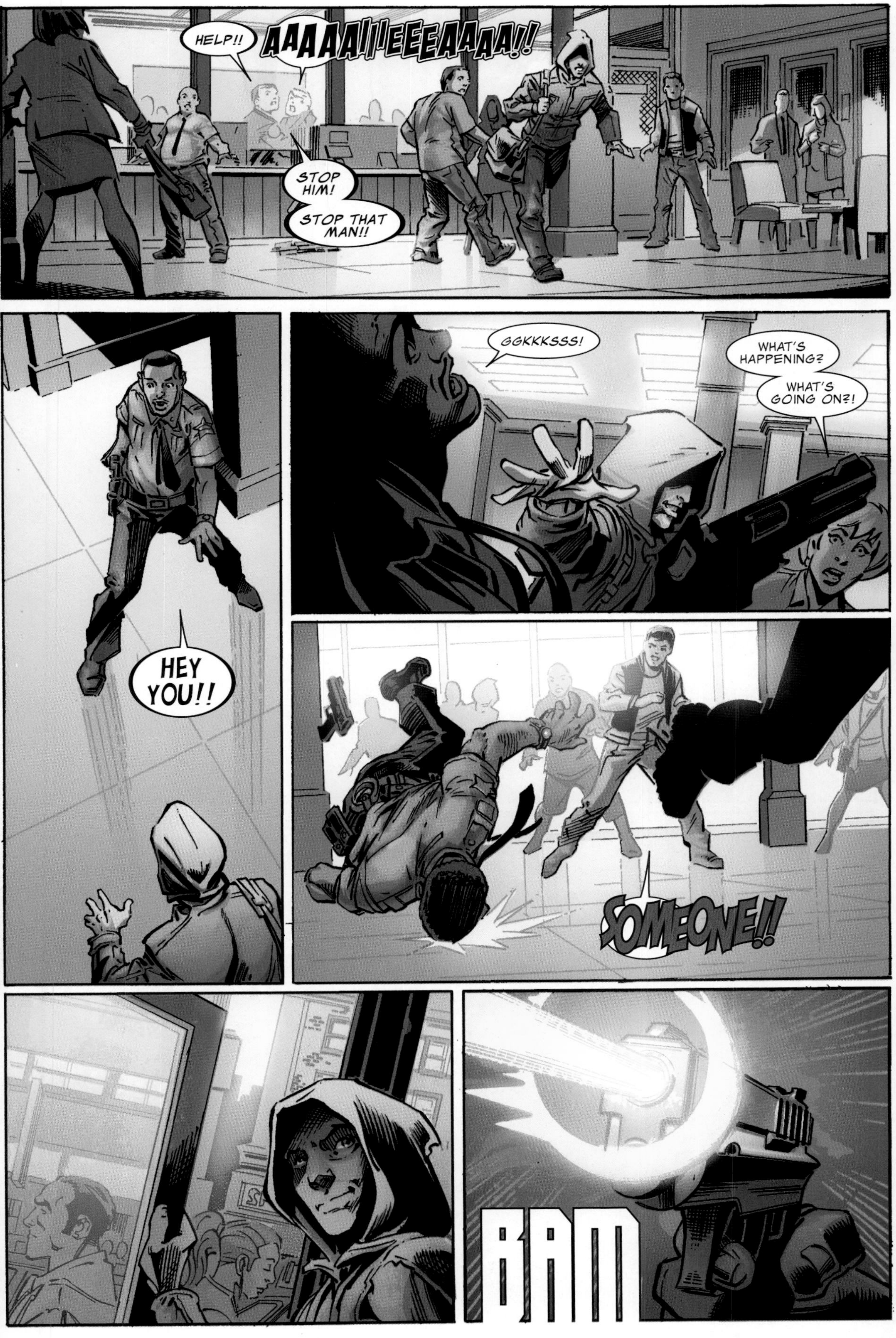
HELP!!
AAAAA!!!EEEAAAA!!
STOP HIM!
STOP THAT MAN!!
HEY YOU!!
GGKKKSSS!
WHAT'S HAPPENING?
WHAT'S GOING ON?!
SOMEONE!!
BAM

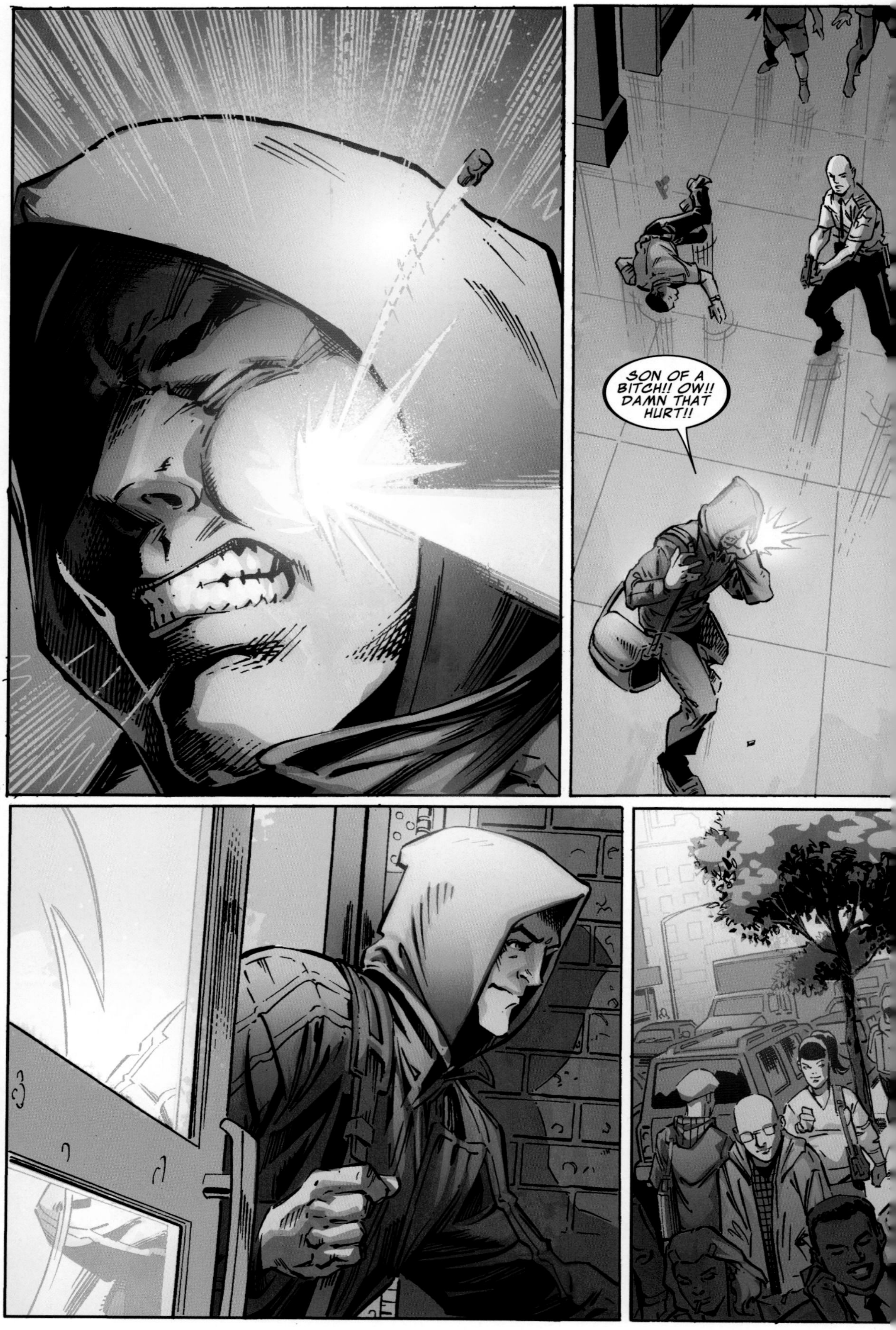
SON OF A BITCH!! OW!! DAMN THAT HURT!!

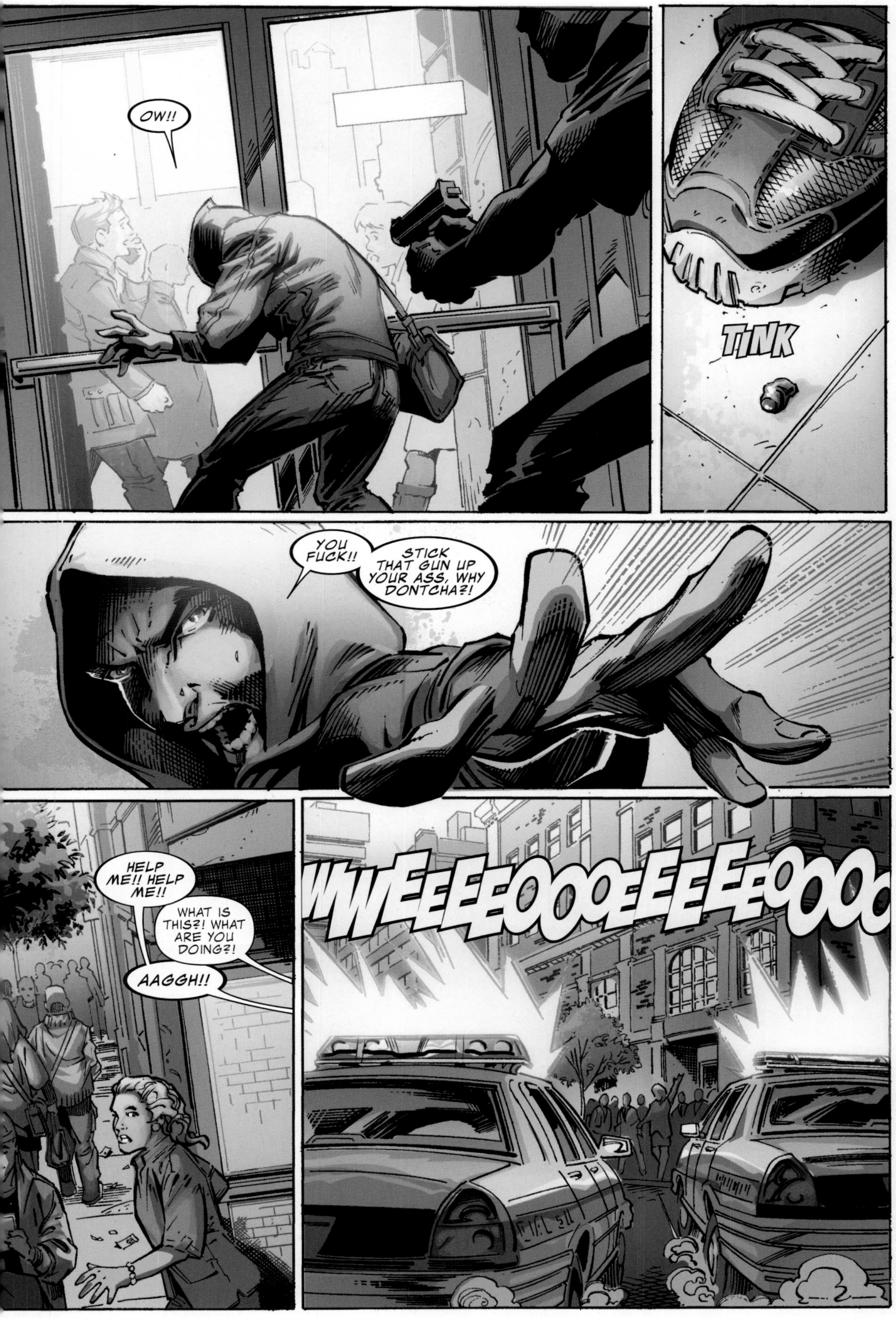
OW!!
TINK
YOU FUCK!!
STICK THAT GUN UP YOUR ASS, WHY DONTCHA?!
HELP ME!! HELP ME!!
WHAT IS THIS?! WHAT ARE YOU DOING?!
AAGGH!!
WWEEEEOOOEEEEOOO

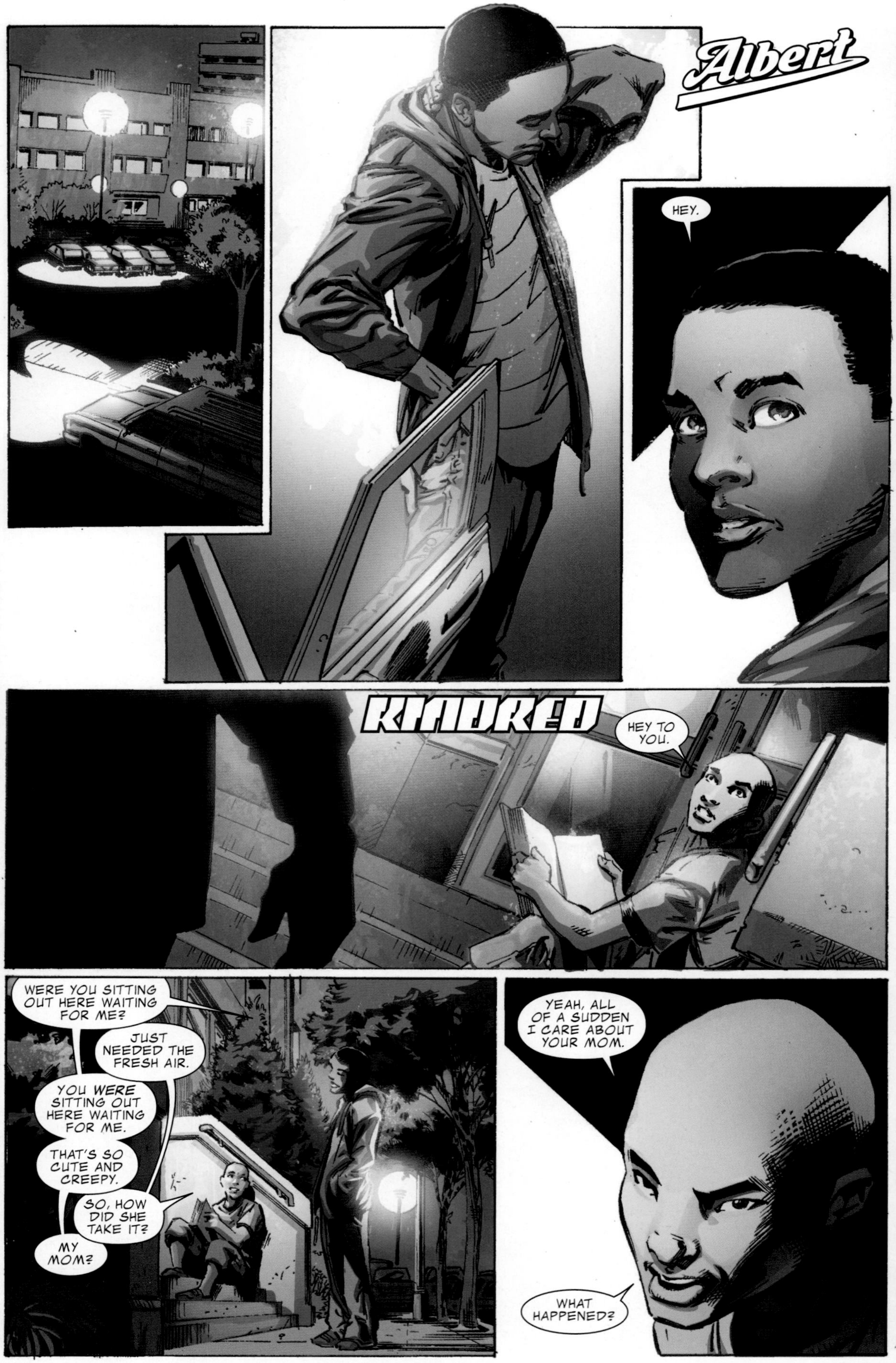
Albert
HEY.
KINDRED
HEY TO YOU.
WERE YOU SITTING OUT HERE WAITING FOR ME?
JUST NEEDED THE FRESH AIR.
YOU WERE SITTING OUT HERE WAITING FOR ME.
THAT'S SO CUTE AND CREEPY.
SO, HOW DID SHE TAKE IT?
MY MOM?
YEAH, ALL OF A SUDDEN I CARE ABOUT YOUR MOM.
WHAT HAPPENED?

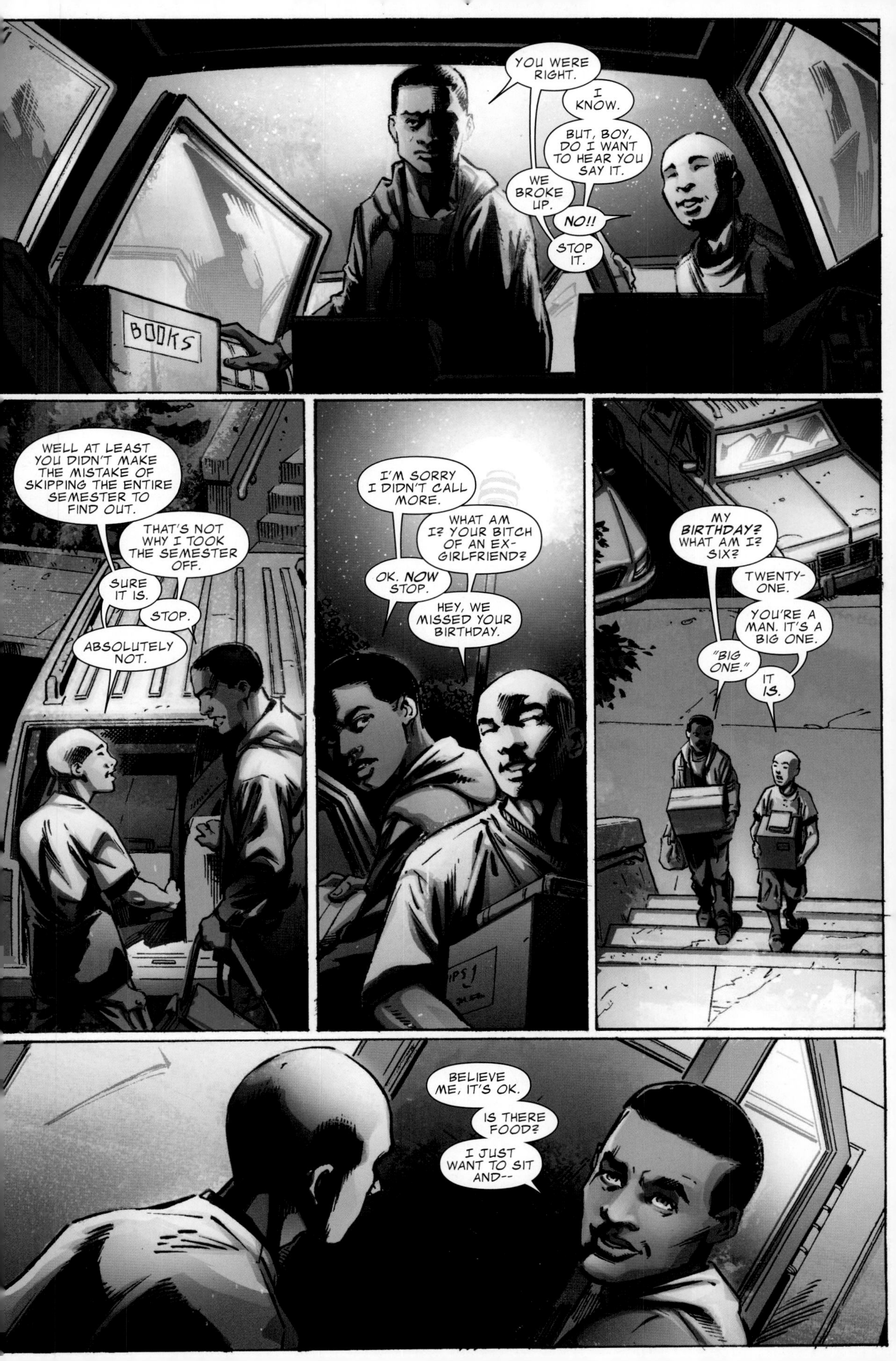
YOU WERE RIGHT.
I KNOW.
BUT, BOY, DO I WANT TO HEAR YOU SAY IT.
WE BROKE UP.
NO!!
STOP IT.
BOOKS
WELL AT LEAST YOU DIDN'T MAKE THE MISTAKE OF SKIPPING THE ENTIRE SEMESTER TO FIND OUT.
THAT'S NOT WHY I TOOK THE SEMESTER OFF.
SURE IT IS.
STOP.
ABSOLUTELY NOT.
I'M SORRY I DIDN'T CALL MORE.
WHAT AM I? YOUR BITCH OF AN EX-GIRLFRIEND?
OK. NOW STOP.
HEY, WE MISSED YOUR BIRTHDAY.
MY BIRTHDAY? WHAT AM I? SIX?
TWENTY-ONE.
YOU'RE A MAN. IT'S A BIG ONE.
"BIG ONE."
IT IS.
BELIEVE ME, IT'S OK.
IS THERE FOOD?
I JUST WANT TO SIT AND--

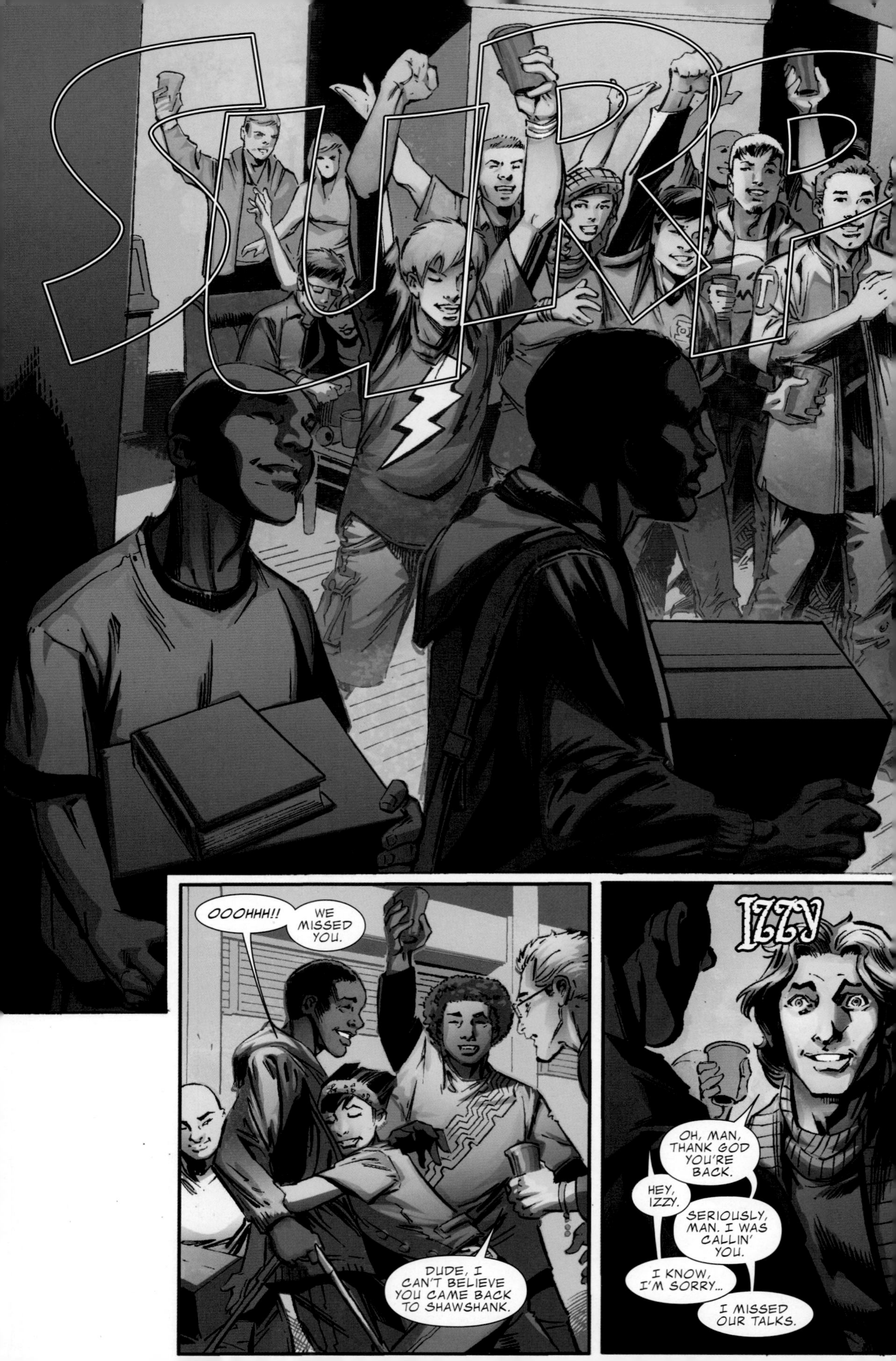
SURP
OOOHHH!!
WE MISSED YOU.
DUDE, I CAN'T BELIEVE YOU CAME BACK TO SHAWSHANK.
IZZY
OH, MAN, THANK GOD YOU'RE BACK.
HEY, IZZY.
SERIOUSLY, MAN. I WAS CALLIN' YOU.
I KNOW, I'M SORRY...
I MISSED OUR TALKS.

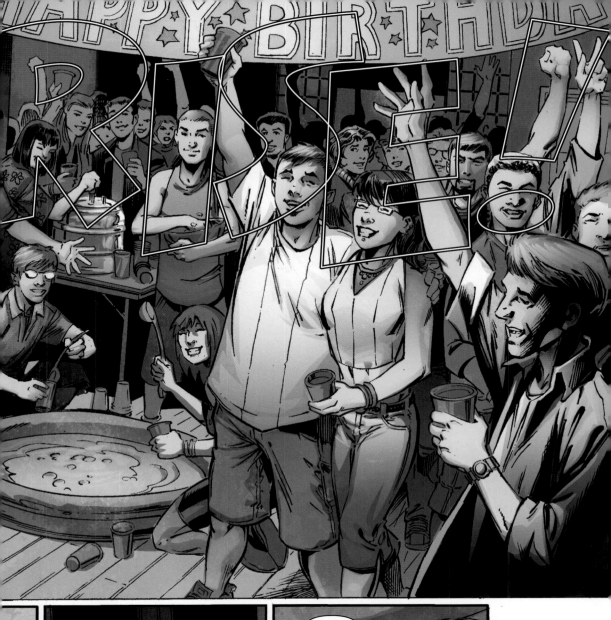

WHEN DID ME AND HIM HAVE TALKS?

HE'S VERY EMOTIONAL.

OH MY GOD, ALBERT! ALBERT!!

HERE WE GO...

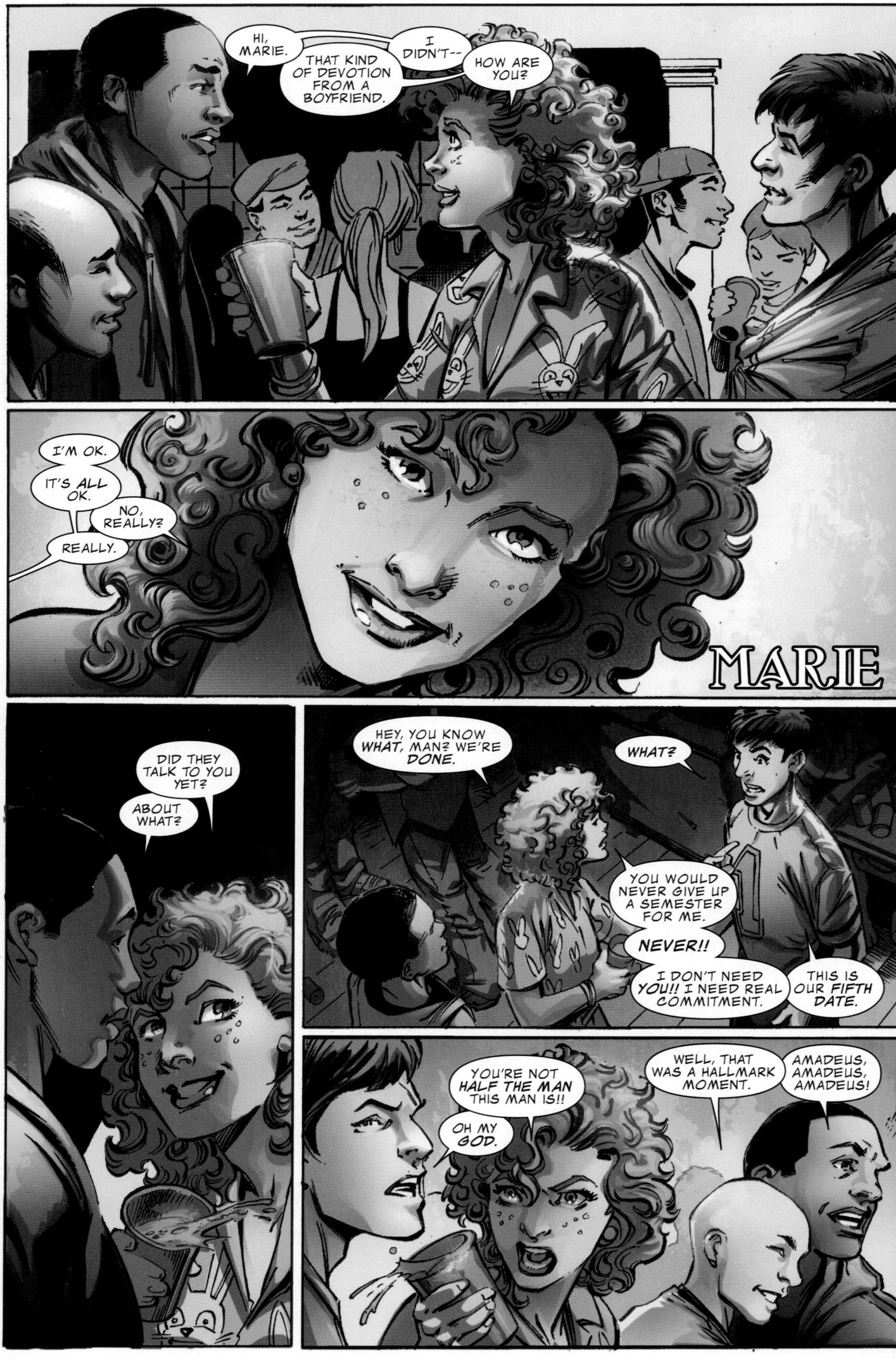

HI, MARIE.
THAT KIND OF DEVOTION FROM A BOYFRIEND.
I DIDN'T--
HOW ARE YOU?
I'M OK.
IT'S ALL OK.
NO, REALLY?
REALLY.
MARIE
DID THEY TALK TO YOU YET?
ABOUT WHAT?
HEY, YOU KNOW WHAT, MAN? WE'RE DONE.
WHAT?
YOU WOULD NEVER GIVE UP A SEMESTER FOR ME.
NEVER!!
I DON'T NEED YOU!! I NEED REAL COMMITMENT.
THIS IS OUR FIFTH DATE.
YOU'RE NOT HALF THE MAN THIS MAN IS!!
OH MY GOD.
WELL, THAT WAS A HALLMARK MOMENT.
AMADEUS, AMADEUS, AMADEUS!

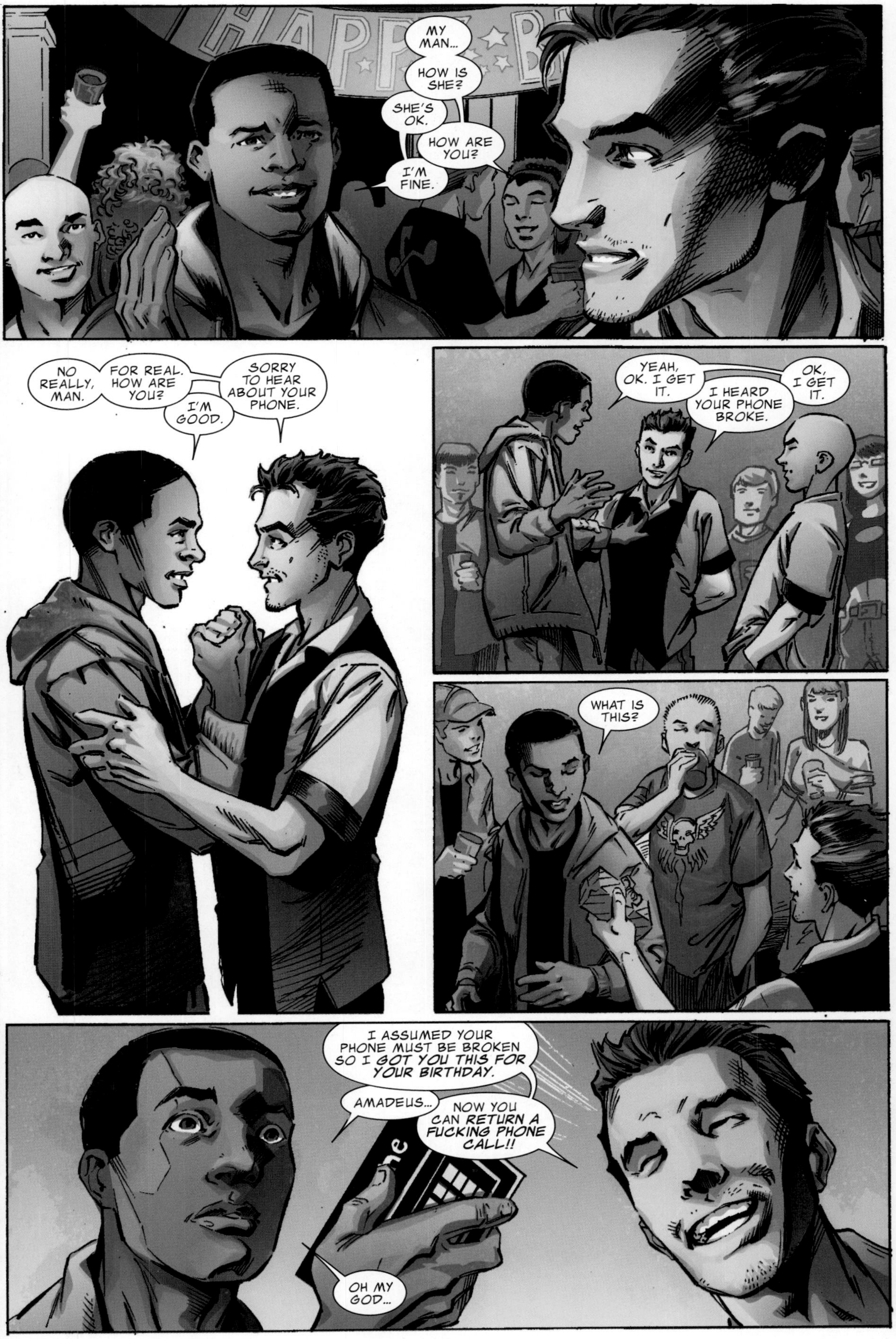
MY MAN...
HOW IS SHE?
SHE'S OK.
HOW ARE YOU?
I'M FINE.
NO REALLY, MAN.
FOR REAL. HOW ARE YOU?
I'M GOOD.
SORRY TO HEAR ABOUT YOUR PHONE.
YEAH, OK. I GET IT.
I HEARD YOUR PHONE BROKE.
OK, I GET IT.
WHAT IS THIS?
I ASSUMED YOUR PHONE MUST BE BROKEN SO I GOT YOU THIS FOR YOUR BIRTHDAY.
AMADEUS...
NOW YOU CAN RETURN A FUCKING PHONE CALL!!
OH MY GOD...

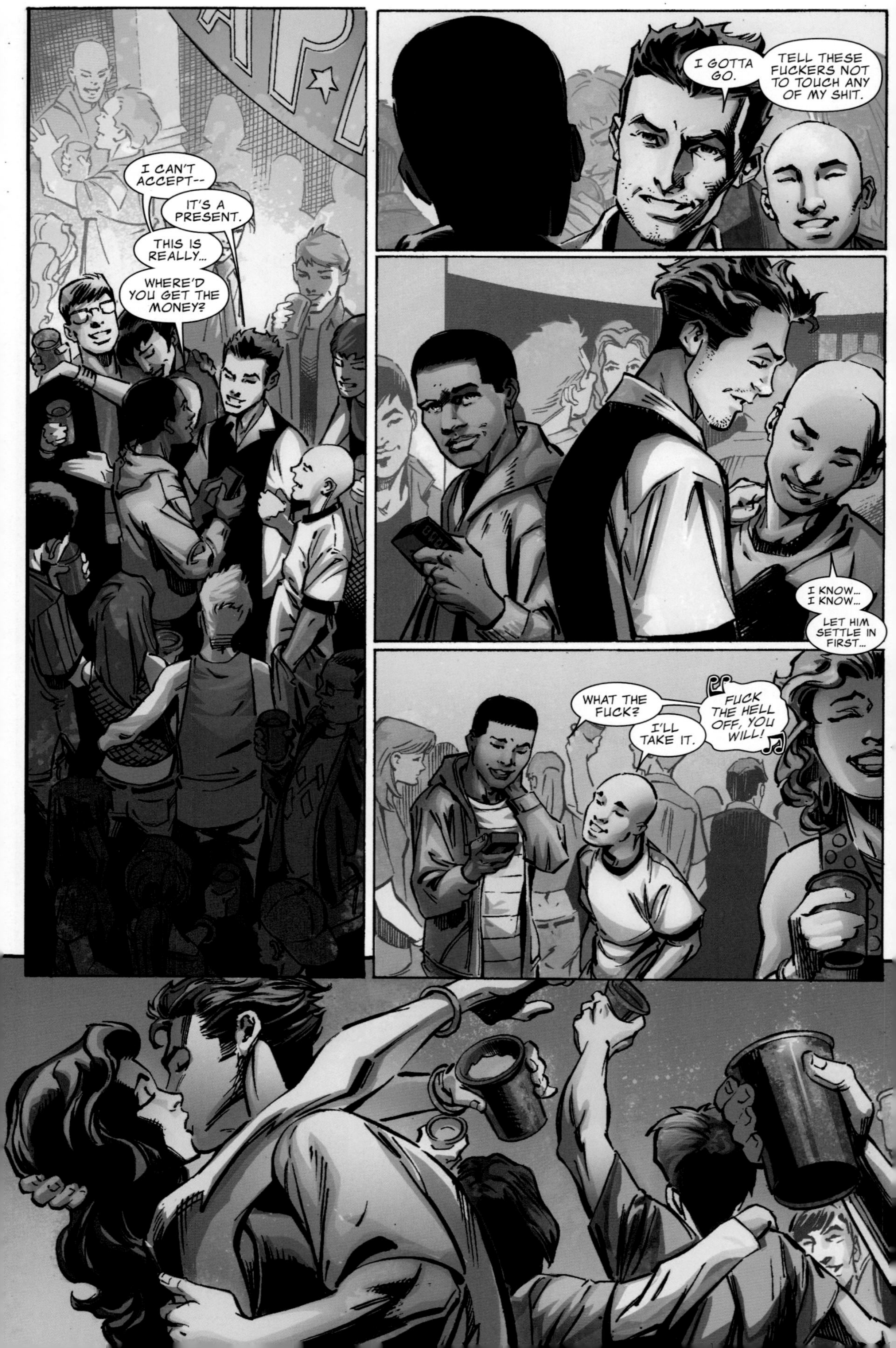
I CAN'T ACCEPT--
IT'S A PRESENT.
THIS IS REALLY...
WHERE'D YOU GET THE MONEY?
I GOTTA GO.
TELL THESE FUCKERS NOT TO TOUCH ANY OF MY SHIT.
I KNOW... I KNOW...
LET HIM SETTLE IN FIRST...
WHAT THE FUCK?
I'LL TAKE IT.
FUCK THE HELL OFF, YOU WILL!

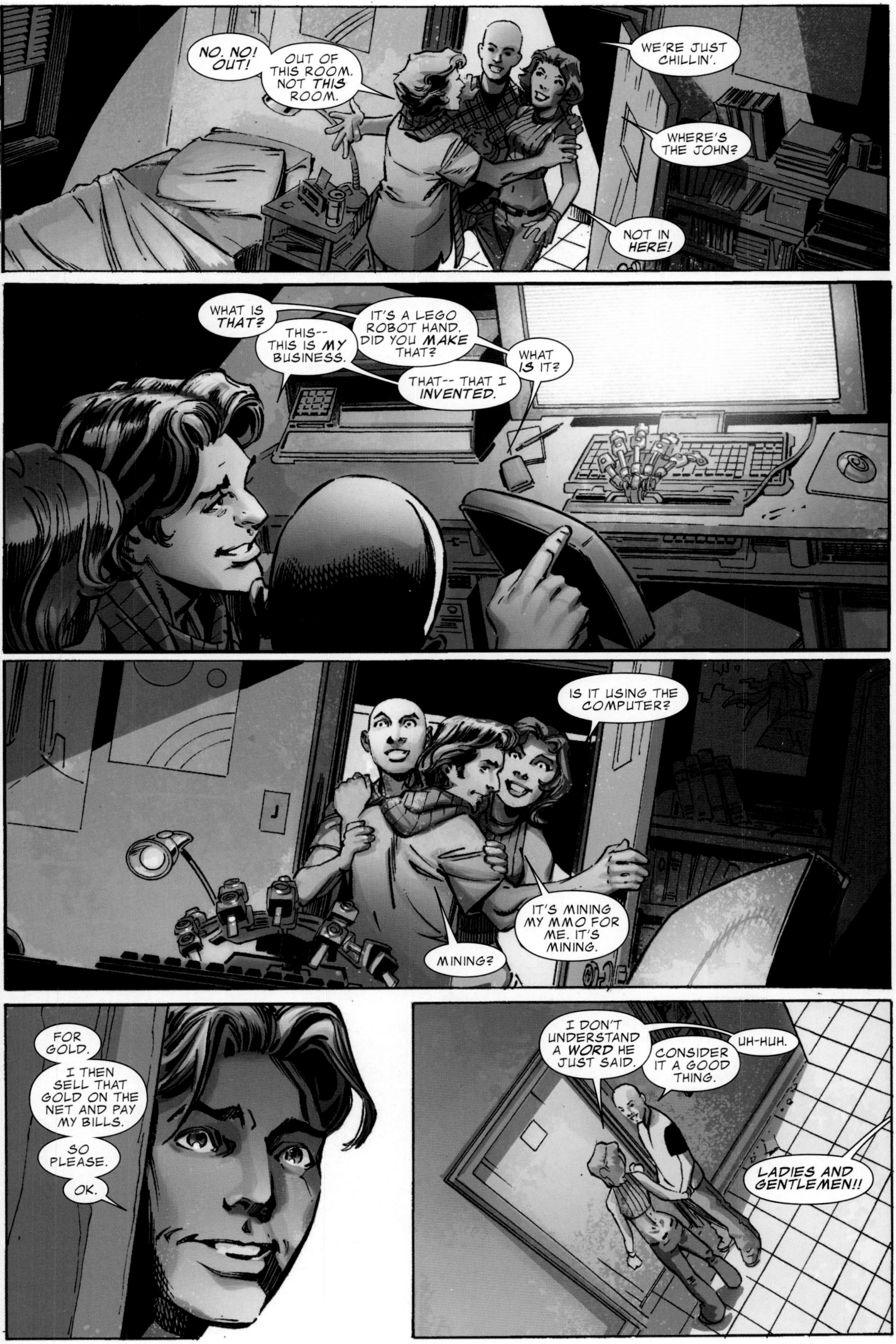
NO. NO! OUT!
OUT OF THIS ROOM. NOT THIS ROOM.
WE'RE JUST CHILLIN'.
WHERE'S THE JOHN?
NOT IN HERE!
WHAT IS THAT?
IT'S A LEGO ROBOT HAND. DID YOU MAKE THAT?
THIS-- THIS IS MY BUSINESS.
WHAT IS IT?
THAT-- THAT I INVENTED.
IS IT USING THE COMPUTER?
IT'S MINING MY MMO FOR ME. IT'S MINING.
MINING?
FOR GOLD.
I THEN SELL THAT GOLD ON THE NET AND PAY MY BILLS.
SO PLEASE.
OK.
I DON'T UNDERSTAND A WORD HE JUST SAID.
UH-HUH.
CONSIDER IT A GOOD THING.
LADIES AND GENTLEMEN!!

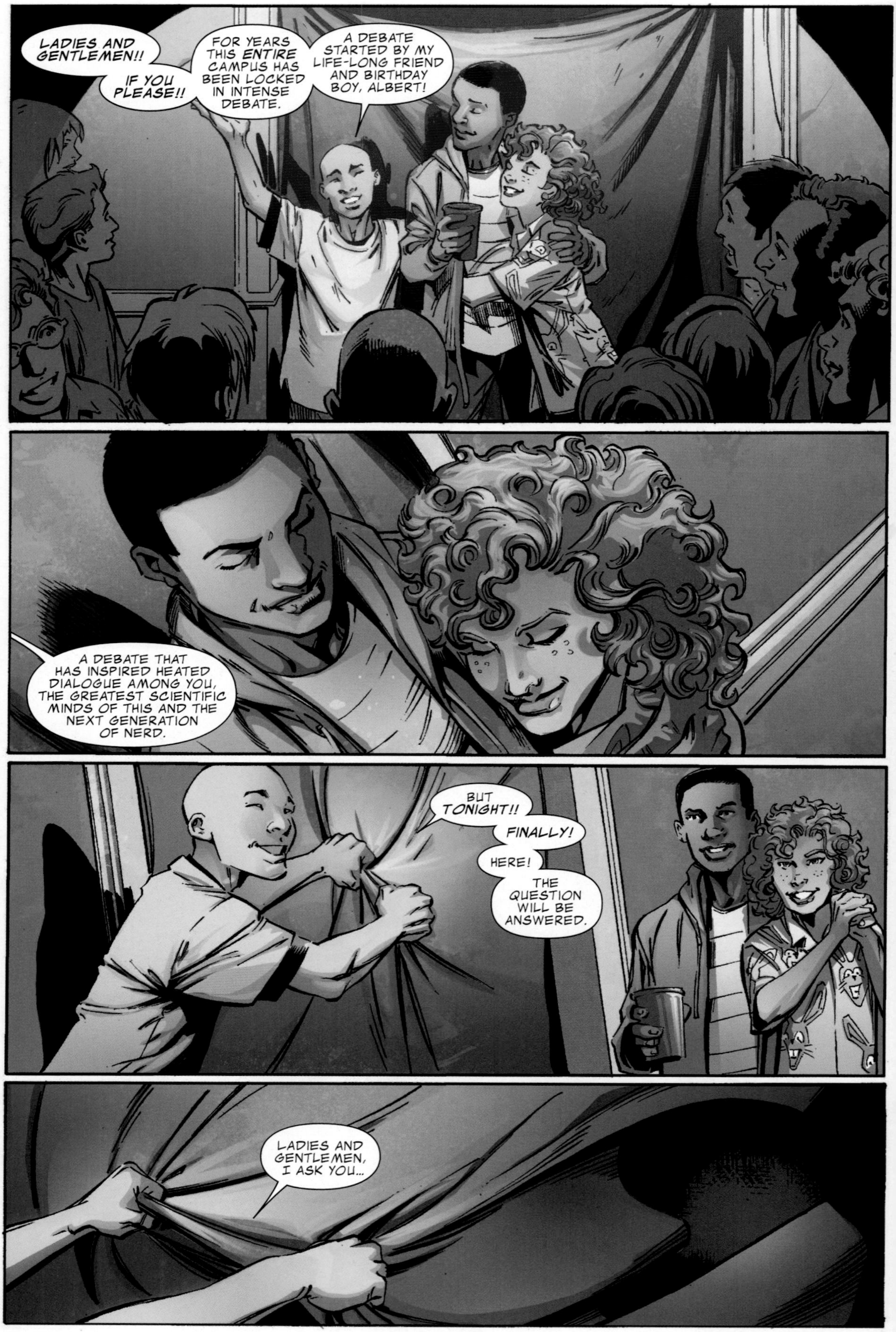
LADIES AND GENTLEMEN!!
IF YOU PLEASE!!
FOR YEARS THIS ENTIRE CAMPUS HAS BEEN LOCKED IN INTENSE DEBATE.
A DEBATE STARTED BY MY LIFE-LONG FRIEND AND BIRTHDAY BOY, ALBERT!
A DEBATE THAT HAS INSPIRED HEATED DIALOGUE AMONG YOU, THE GREATEST SCIENTIFIC MINDS OF THIS AND THE NEXT GENERATION OF NERD.
BUT TONIGHT!!
FINALLY!
HERE!
THE QUESTION WILL BE ANSWERED.
LADIES AND GENTLEMEN, I ASK YOU...

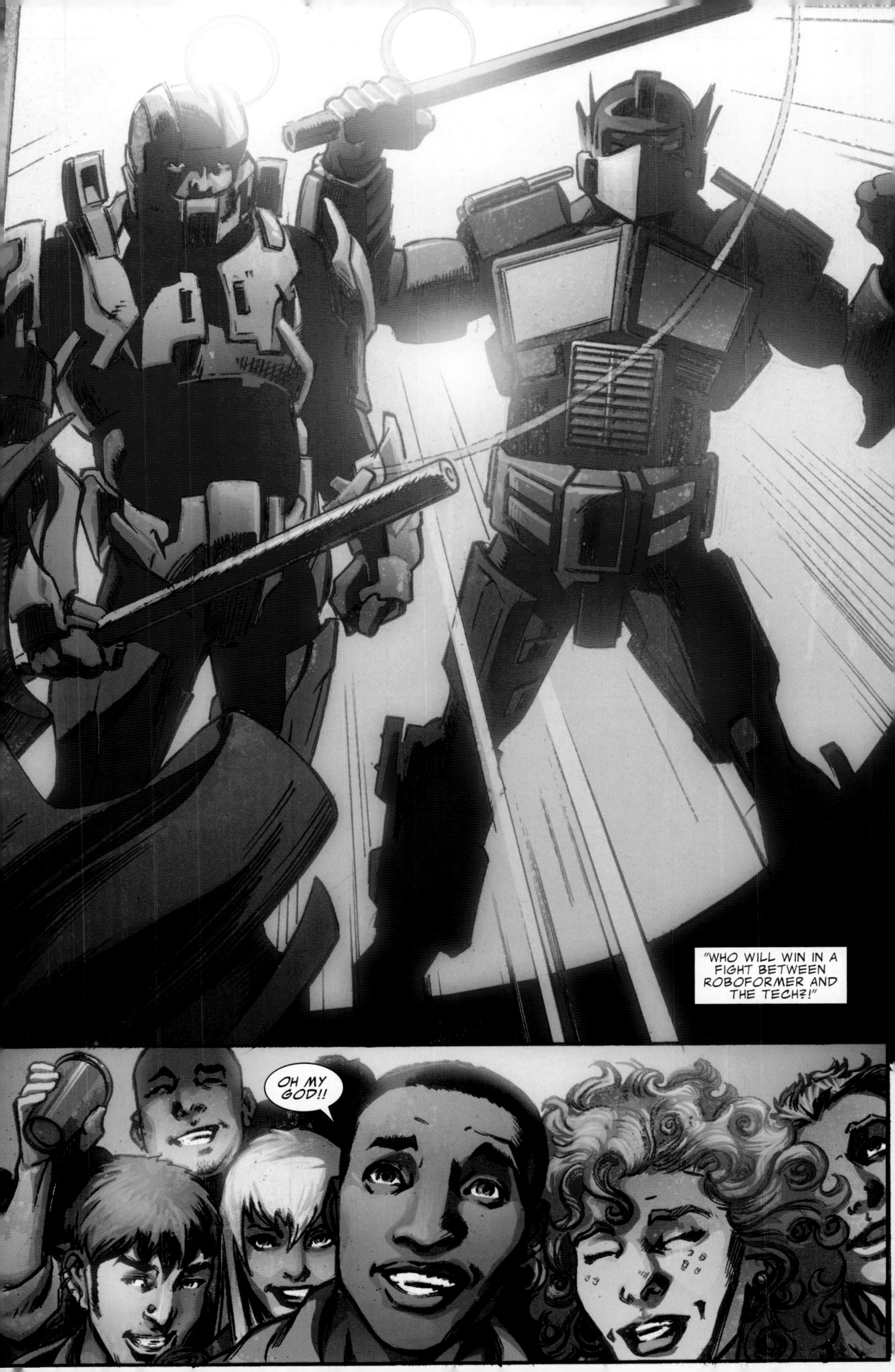
"WHO WILL WIN IN A FIGHT BETWEEN ROBOFORMER AND THE TECH?!"
OH MY GOD!!

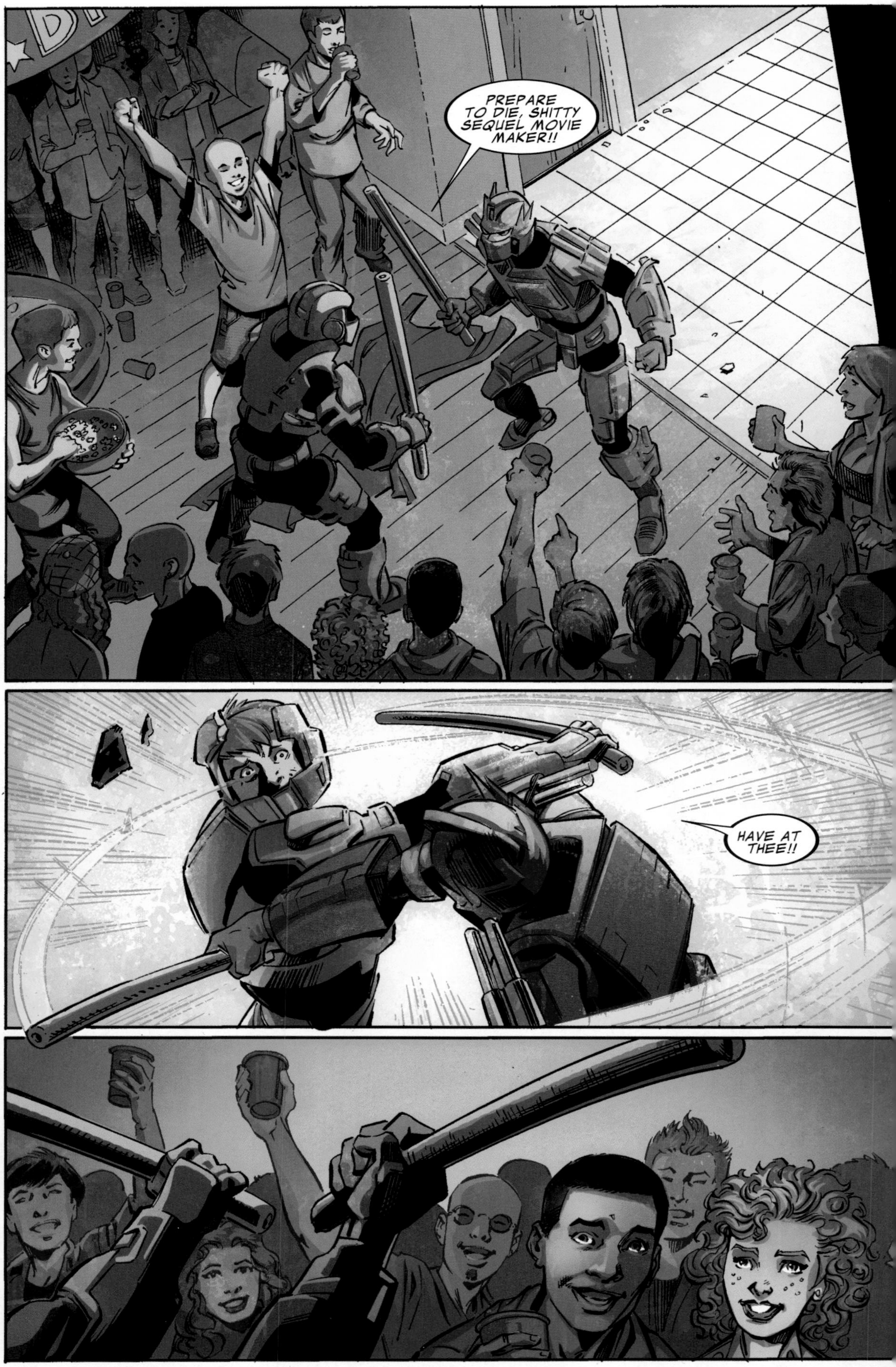
PREPARE TO DIE, SHITTY SEQUEL MOVIE MAKER!!
HAVE AT THEE!!

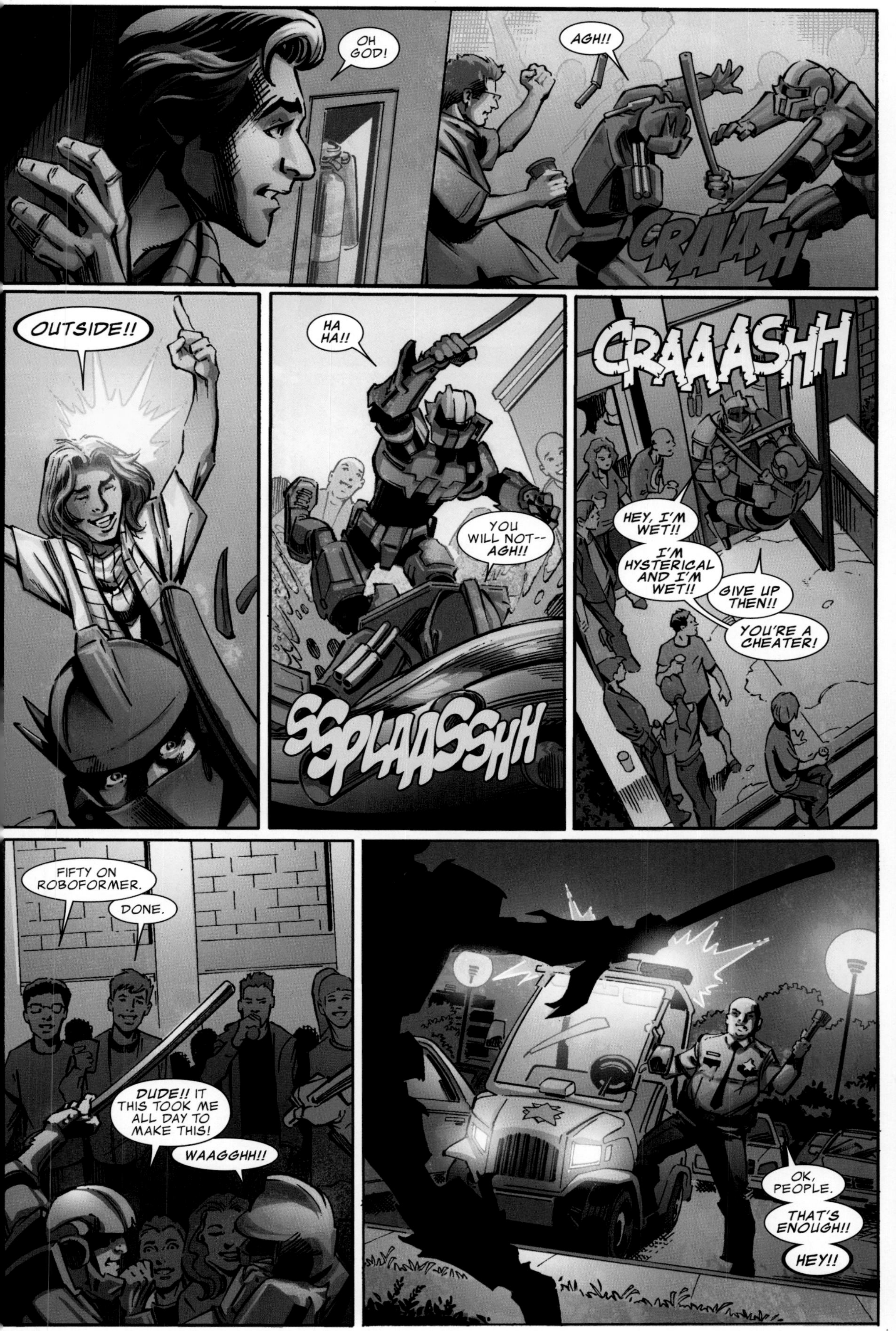
OH GOD!
AGH!!
CRAAASH
OUTSIDE!!
HA HA!!
YOU WILL NOT-- AGH!!
SSPLAASSHH
CRAAASHH
HEY, I'M WET!!
I'M HYSTERICAL AND I'M WET!!
GIVE UP THEN!!
YOU'RE A CHEATER!
FIFTY ON ROBOFORMER.
DONE.
DUDE!! IT THIS TOOK ME ALL DAY TO MAKE THIS!
WAAGGHH!!
OK, PEOPLE.
THAT'S ENOUGH!!
HEY!!

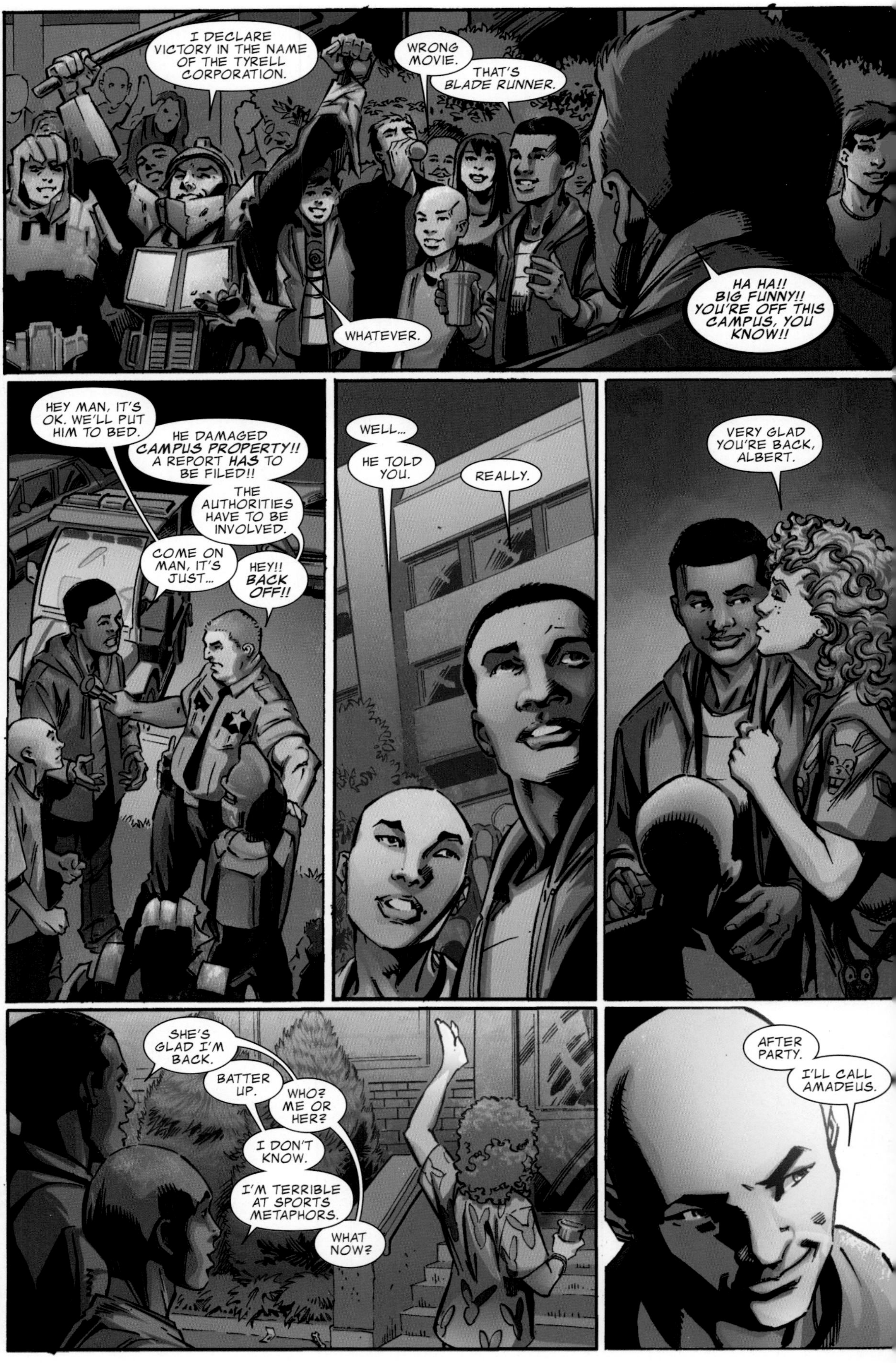
I DECLARE VICTORY IN THE NAME OF THE TYRELL CORPORATION.
WRONG MOVIE.
THAT'S BLADE RUNNER.
WHATEVER.
HA HA!! BIG FUNNY!! YOU'RE OFF THIS CAMPUS, YOU KNOW!!
HEY MAN, IT'S OK. WE'LL PUT HIM TO BED.
HE DAMAGED CAMPUS PROPERTY!! A REPORT HAS TO BE FILED!!
THE AUTHORITIES HAVE TO BE INVOLVED.
COME ON MAN, IT'S JUST...
HEY!! BACK OFF!!
WELL...
HE TOLD YOU.
REALLY.
VERY GLAD YOU'RE BACK, ALBERT.
SHE'S GLAD I'M BACK.
BATTER UP.
WHO? ME OR HER?
I DON'T KNOW.
I'M TERRIBLE AT SPORTS METAPHORS.
WHAT NOW?
AFTER PARTY.
I'LL CALL AMADEUS.

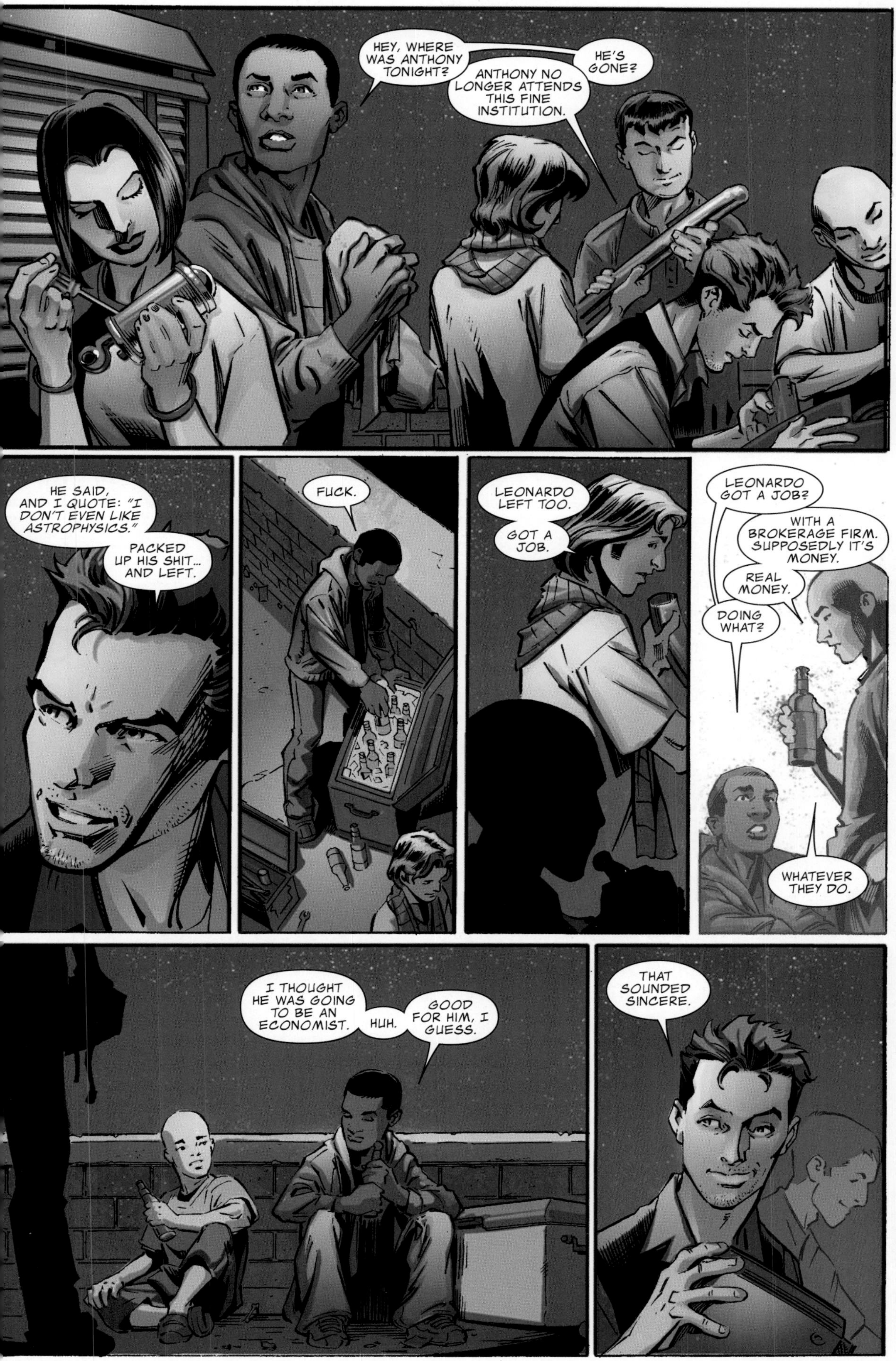
HEY, WHERE WAS ANTHONY TONIGHT?
ANTHONY NO LONGER ATTENDS THIS FINE INSTITUTION.
HE'S GONE?
HE SAID, AND I QUOTE: "I DON'T EVEN LIKE ASTROPHYSICS."
PACKED UP HIS SHIT... AND LEFT.
FUCK.
LEONARDO LEFT TOO.
GOT A JOB.
LEONARDO GOT A JOB?
WITH A BROKERAGE FIRM. SUPPOSEDLY IT'S MONEY.
REAL MONEY.
DOING WHAT?
WHATEVER THEY DO.
I THOUGHT HE WAS GOING TO BE AN ECONOMIST.
HUH.
GOOD FOR HIM, I GUESS.
THAT SOUNDED SINCERE.

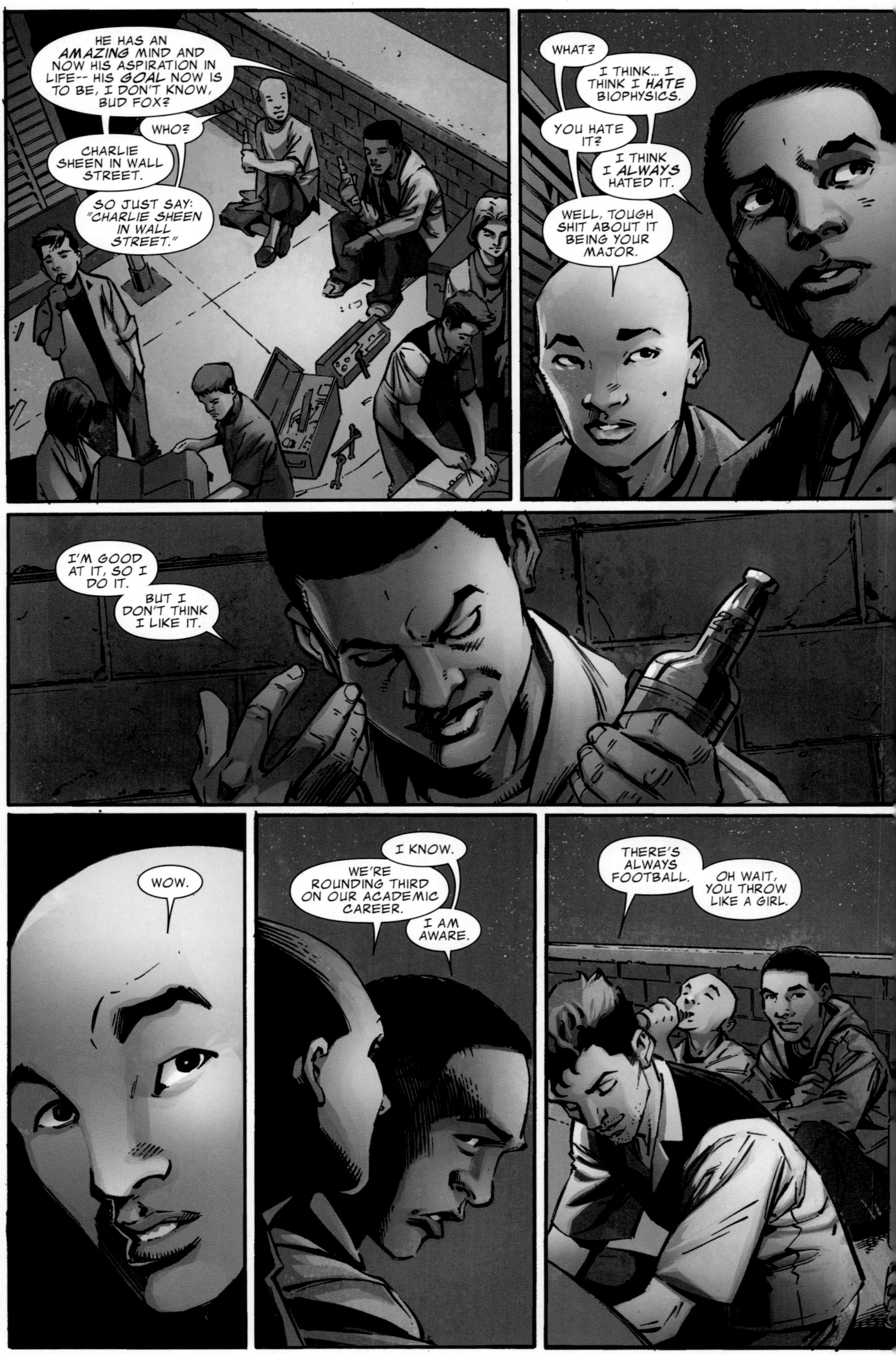
HE HAS AN AMAZING MIND AND NOW HIS ASPIRATION IN LIFE-- HIS GOAL NOW IS TO BE, I DON'T KNOW, BUD FOX?
WHO?
CHARLIE SHEEN IN WALL STREET.
SO JUST SAY: "CHARLIE SHEEN IN WALL STREET."
WHAT?
I THINK... I THINK I HATE BIOPHYSICS.
YOU HATE IT?
I THINK I ALWAYS HATED IT.
WELL, TOUGH SHIT ABOUT IT BEING YOUR MAJOR.
I'M GOOD AT IT, SO I DO IT.
BUT I DON'T THINK I LIKE IT.
WOW.
I KNOW.
WE'RE ROUNDING THIRD ON OUR ACADEMIC CAREER.
I AM AWARE.
THERE'S ALWAYS FOOTBALL.
OH WAIT, YOU THROW LIKE A GIRL.

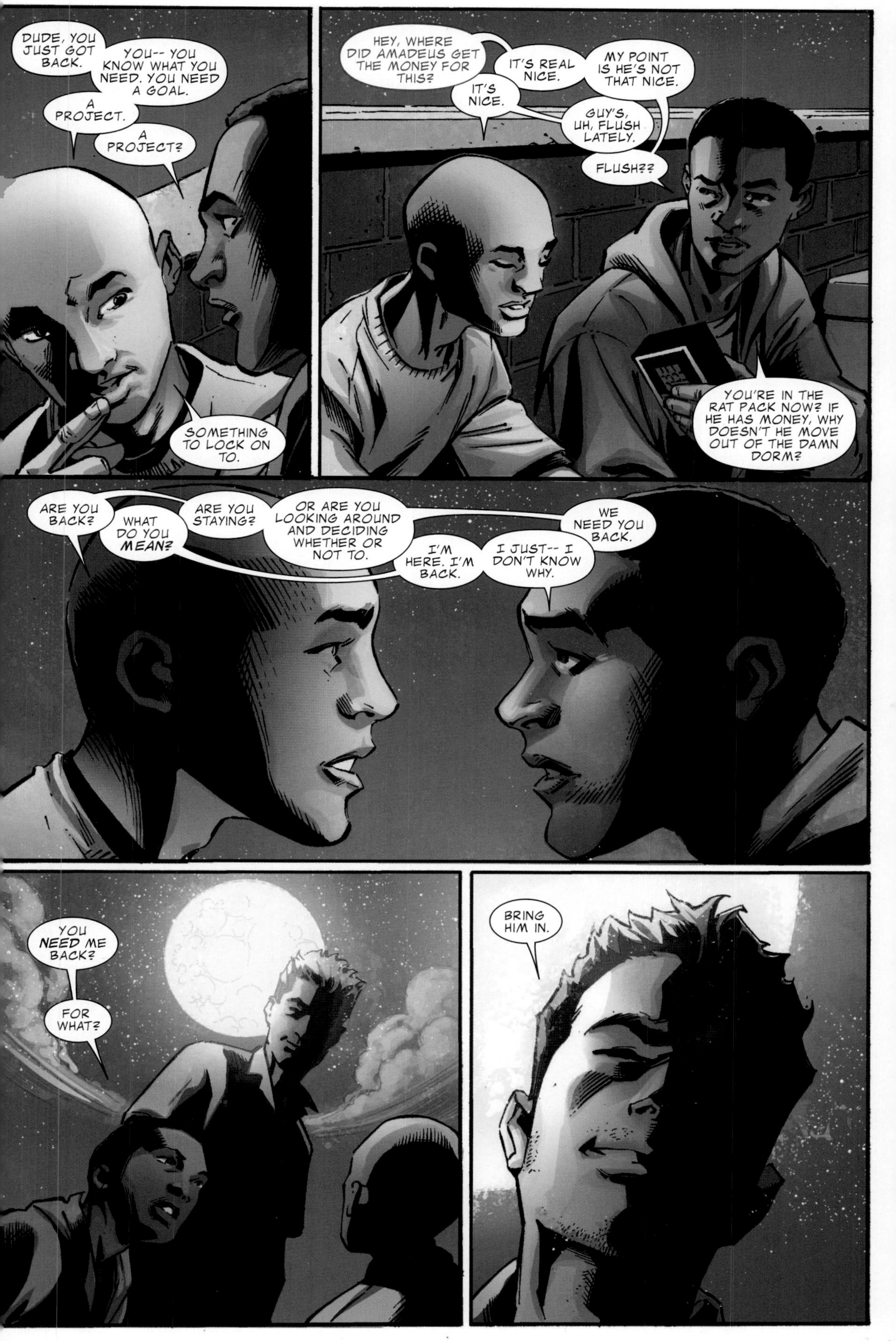
DUDE, YOU JUST GOT BACK.
YOU-- YOU KNOW WHAT YOU NEED. YOU NEED A GOAL.
A PROJECT.
A PROJECT?
SOMETHING TO LOCK ON TO.
HEY, WHERE DID AMADEUS GET THE MONEY FOR THIS?
IT'S NICE.
IT'S REAL NICE.
MY POINT IS HE'S NOT THAT NICE.
GUY'S, UH, FLUSH LATELY.
FLUSH??
YOU'RE IN THE RAT PACK NOW? IF HE HAS MONEY, WHY DOESN'T HE MOVE OUT OF THE DAMN DORM?
ARE YOU BACK?
WHAT DO YOU MEAN?
ARE YOU STAYING?
OR ARE YOU LOOKING AROUND AND DECIDING WHETHER OR NOT TO.
I'M HERE. I'M BACK.
I JUST-- I DON'T KNOW WHY.
WE NEED YOU BACK.
YOU NEED ME BACK?
FOR WHAT?
BRING HIM IN.

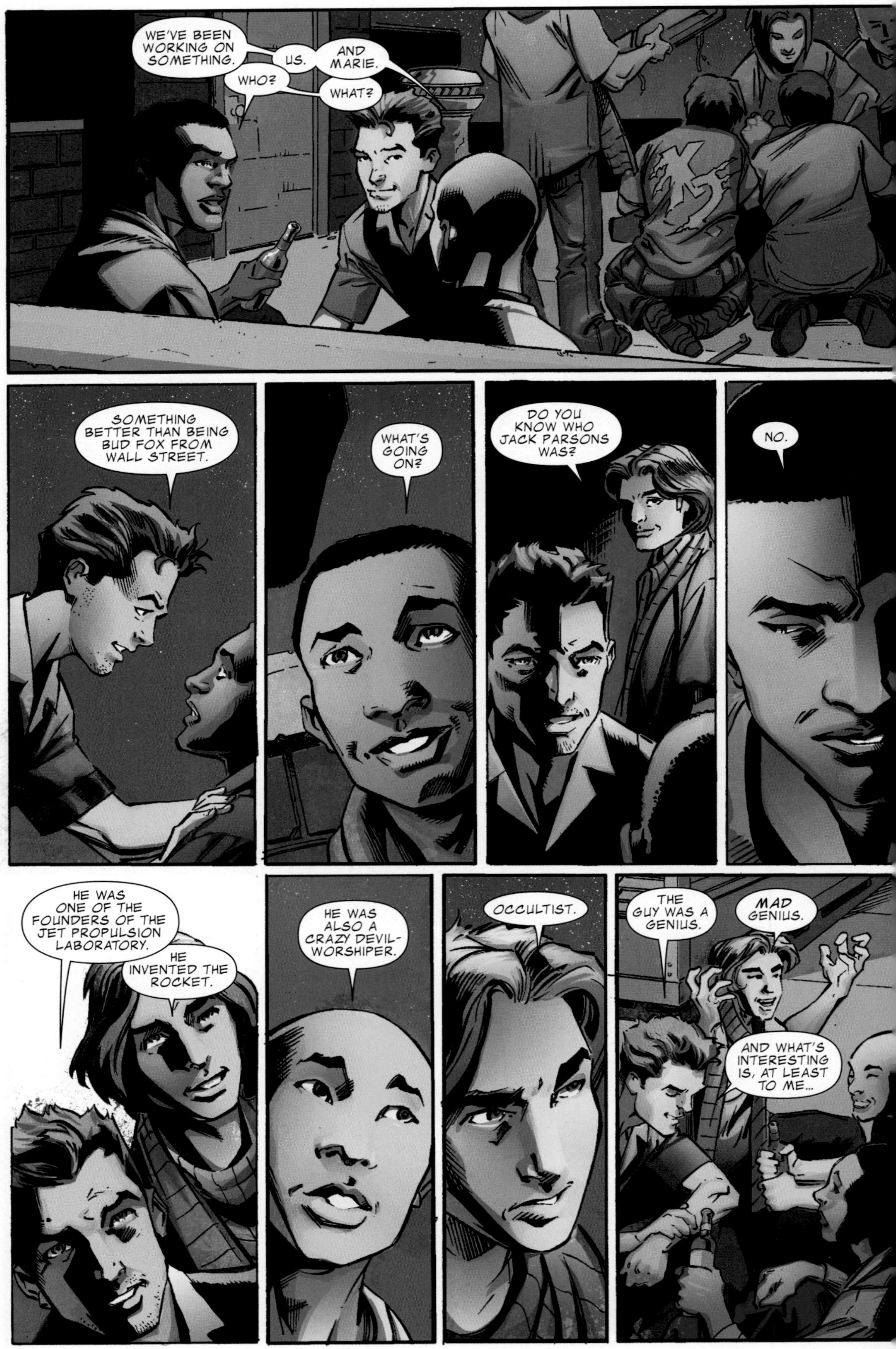
WE'VE BEEN WORKING ON SOMETHING.
US.
AND MARIE.
WHO?
WHAT?
SOMETHING BETTER THAN BEING BUD FOX FROM WALL STREET.
WHAT'S GOING ON?
DO YOU KNOW WHO JACK PARSONS WAS?
NO.
HE WAS ONE OF THE FOUNDERS OF THE JET PROPULSION LABORATORY.
HE INVENTED THE ROCKET.
HE WAS ALSO A CRAZY DEVIL-WORSHIPER.
OCCULTIST.
THE GUY WAS A GENIUS.
MAD GENIUS.
AND WHAT'S INTERESTING IS, AT LEAST TO ME...

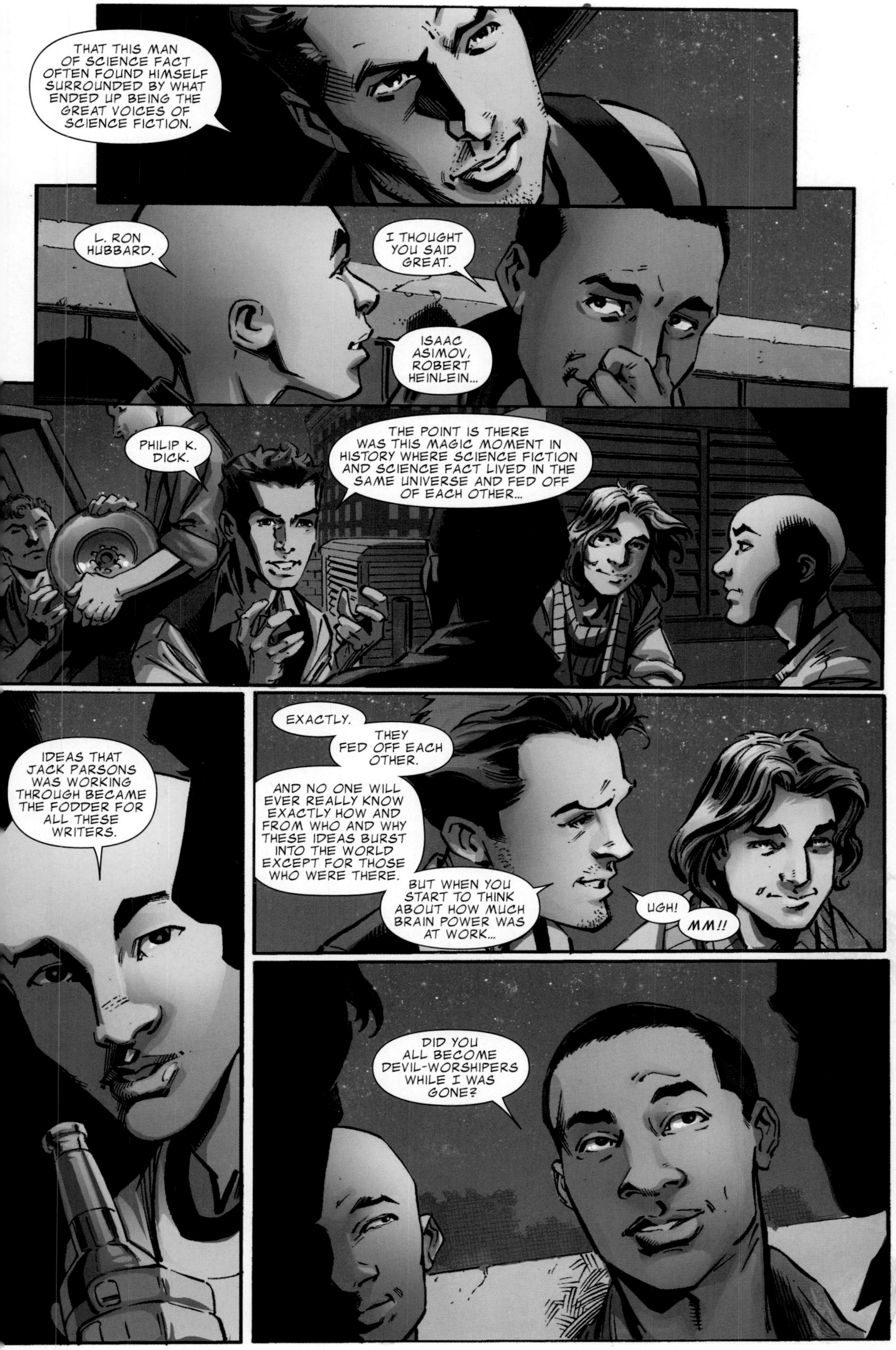
THAT THIS MAN OF SCIENCE FACT OFTEN FOUND HIMSELF SURROUNDED BY WHAT ENDED UP BEING THE GREAT VOICES OF SCIENCE FICTION.
L. RON HUBBARD.
I THOUGHT YOU SAID GREAT.
ISAAC ASIMOV, ROBERT HEINLEIN...
PHILIP K. DICK.
THE POINT IS THERE WAS THIS MAGIC MOMENT IN HISTORY WHERE SCIENCE FICTION AND SCIENCE FACT LIVED IN THE SAME UNIVERSE AND FED OFF OF EACH OTHER...
IDEAS THAT JACK PARSONS WAS WORKING THROUGH BECAME THE FODDER FOR ALL THESE WRITERS.
EXACTLY.
THEY FED OFF EACH OTHER.
AND NO ONE WILL EVER REALLY KNOW EXACTLY HOW AND FROM WHO AND WHY THESE IDEAS BURST INTO THE WORLD EXCEPT FOR THOSE WHO WERE THERE.
BUT WHEN YOU START TO THINK ABOUT HOW MUCH BRAIN POWER WAS AT WORK...
UGH!
MM!!
DID YOU ALL BECOME DEVIL-WORSHIPERS WHILE I WAS GONE?

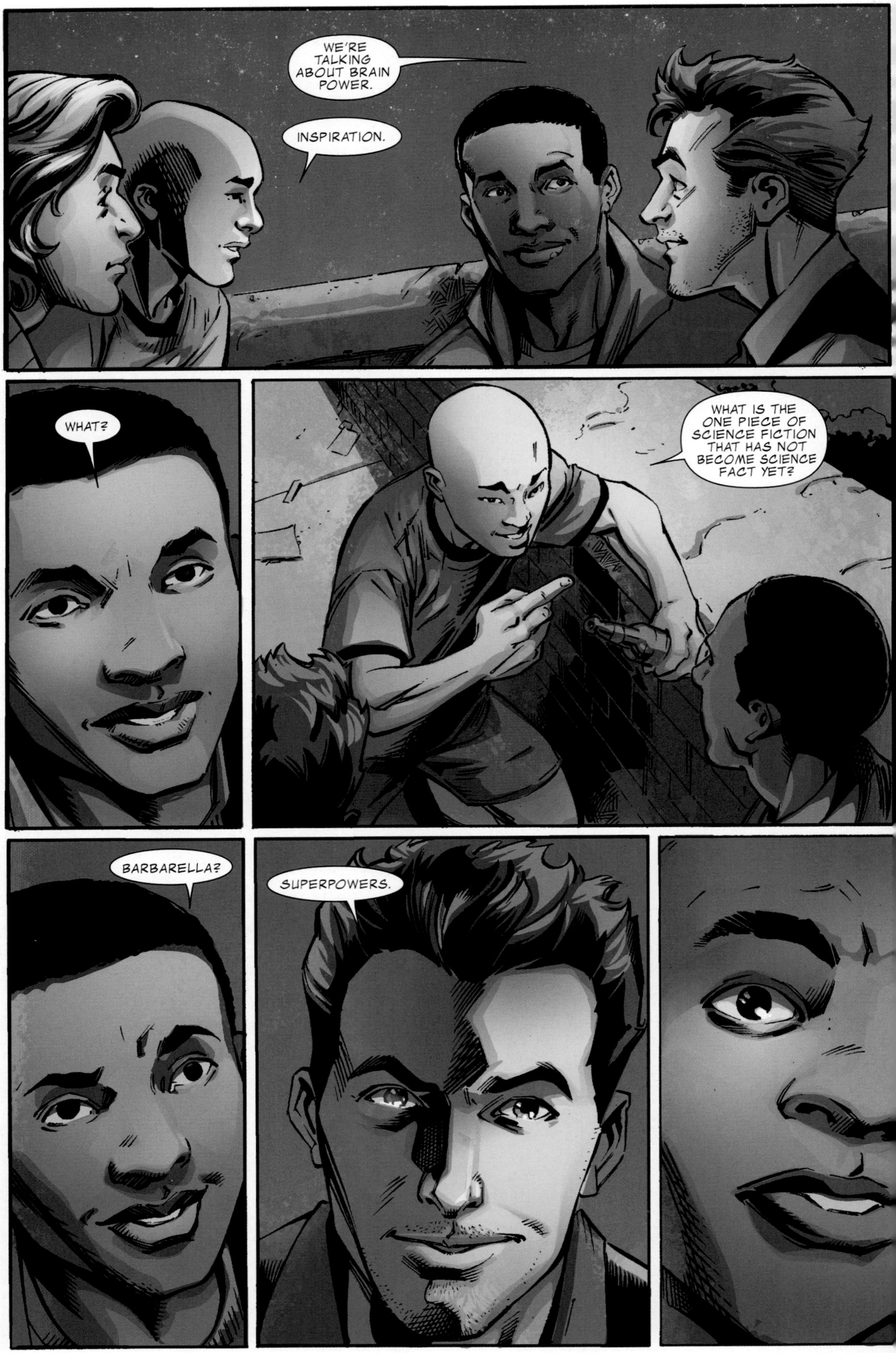
WE'RE TALKING ABOUT BRAIN POWER.
INSPIRATION.
WHAT?
WHAT IS THE ONE PIECE OF SCIENCE FICTION THAT HAS NOT BECOME SCIENCE FACT YET?
BARBARELLA?
SUPERPOWERS.

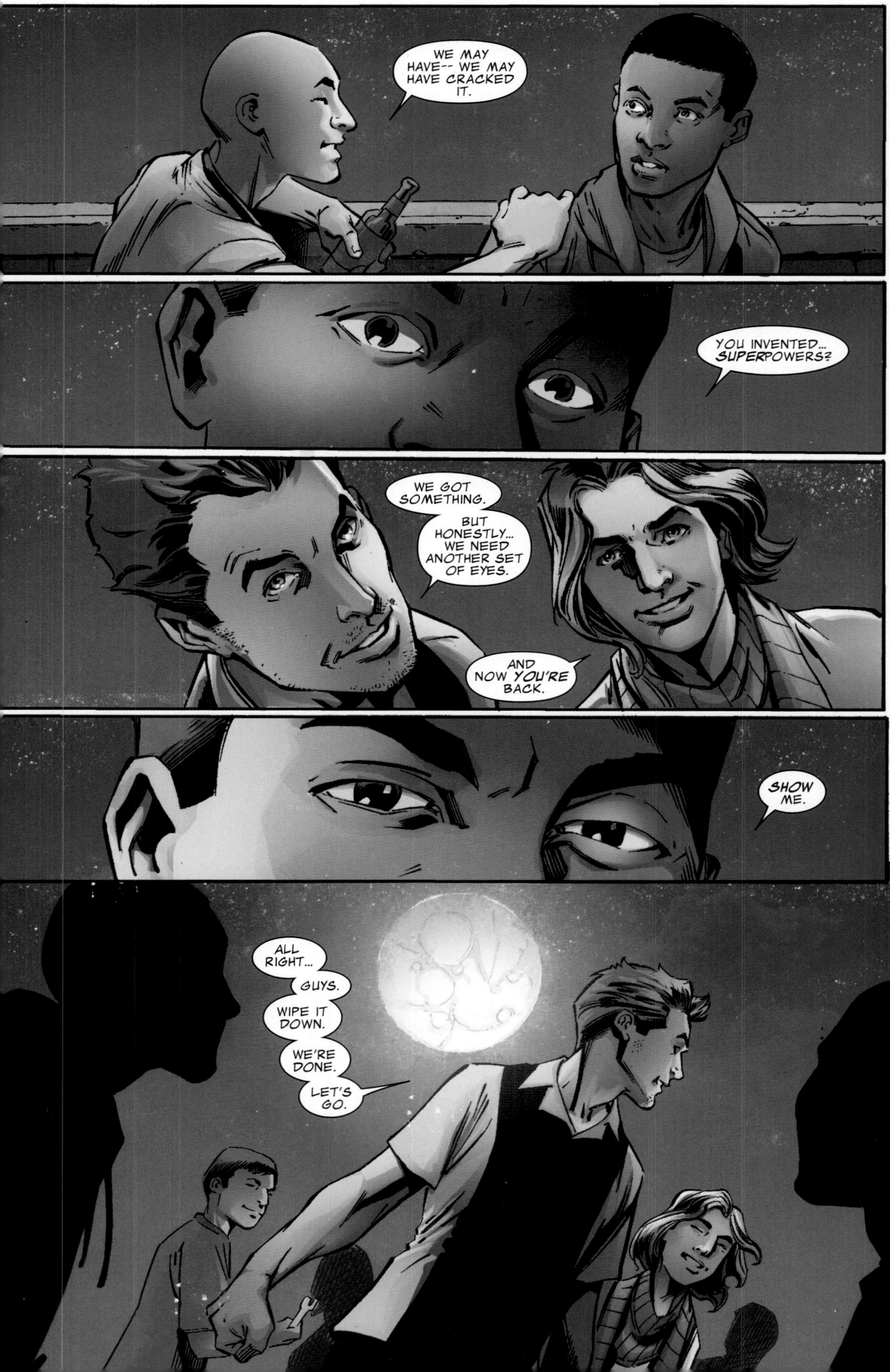

WE MAY HAVE-- WE MAY HAVE CRACKED IT.
YOU INVENTED... SUPERPOWERS?
WE GOT SOMETHING.
BUT HONESTLY... WE NEED ANOTHER SET OF EYES.
AND NOW YOU'RE BACK.
SHOW ME.
ALL RIGHT...
GUYS.
WIPE IT DOWN.
WE'RE DONE.
LET'S GO.

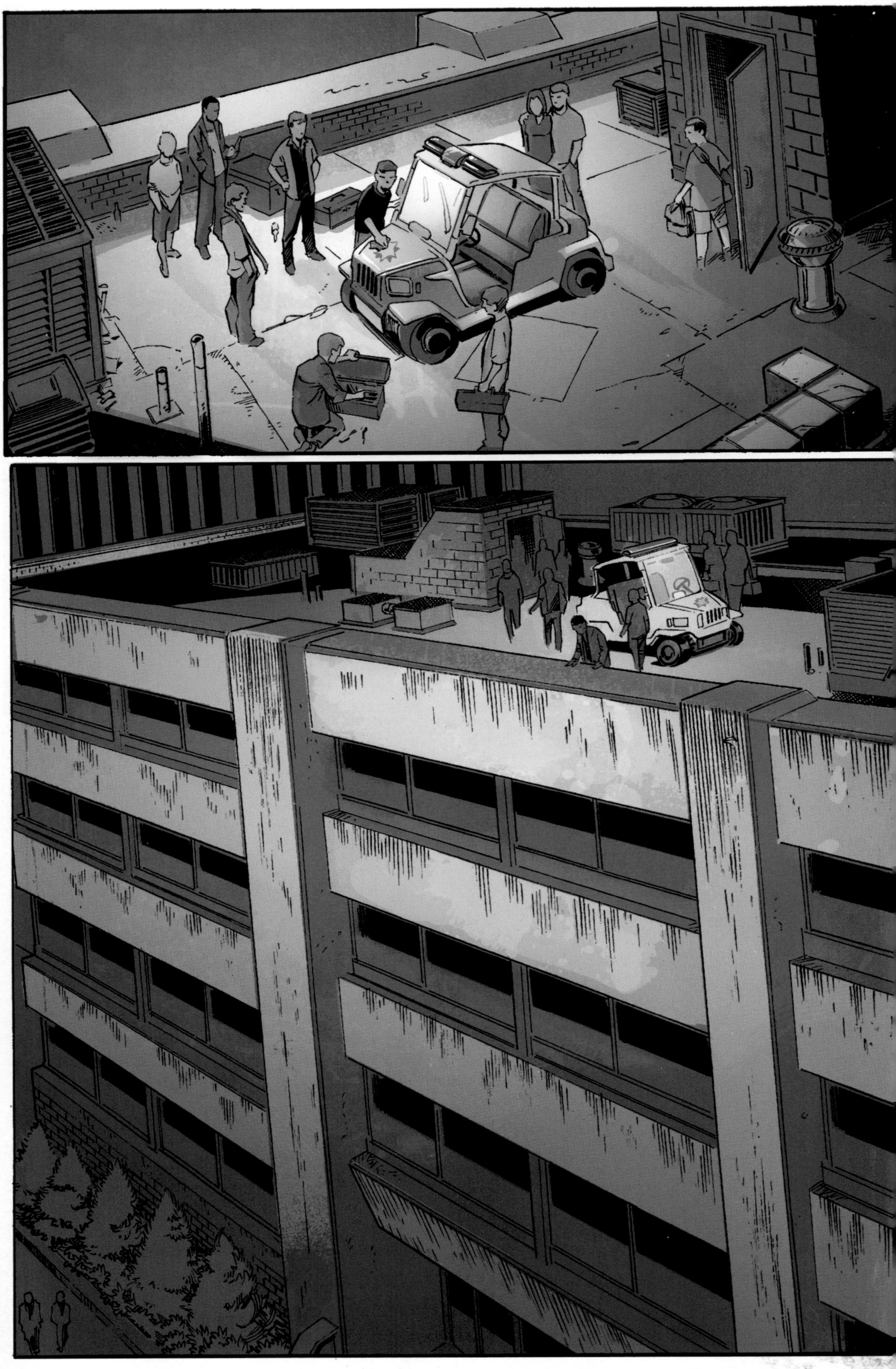

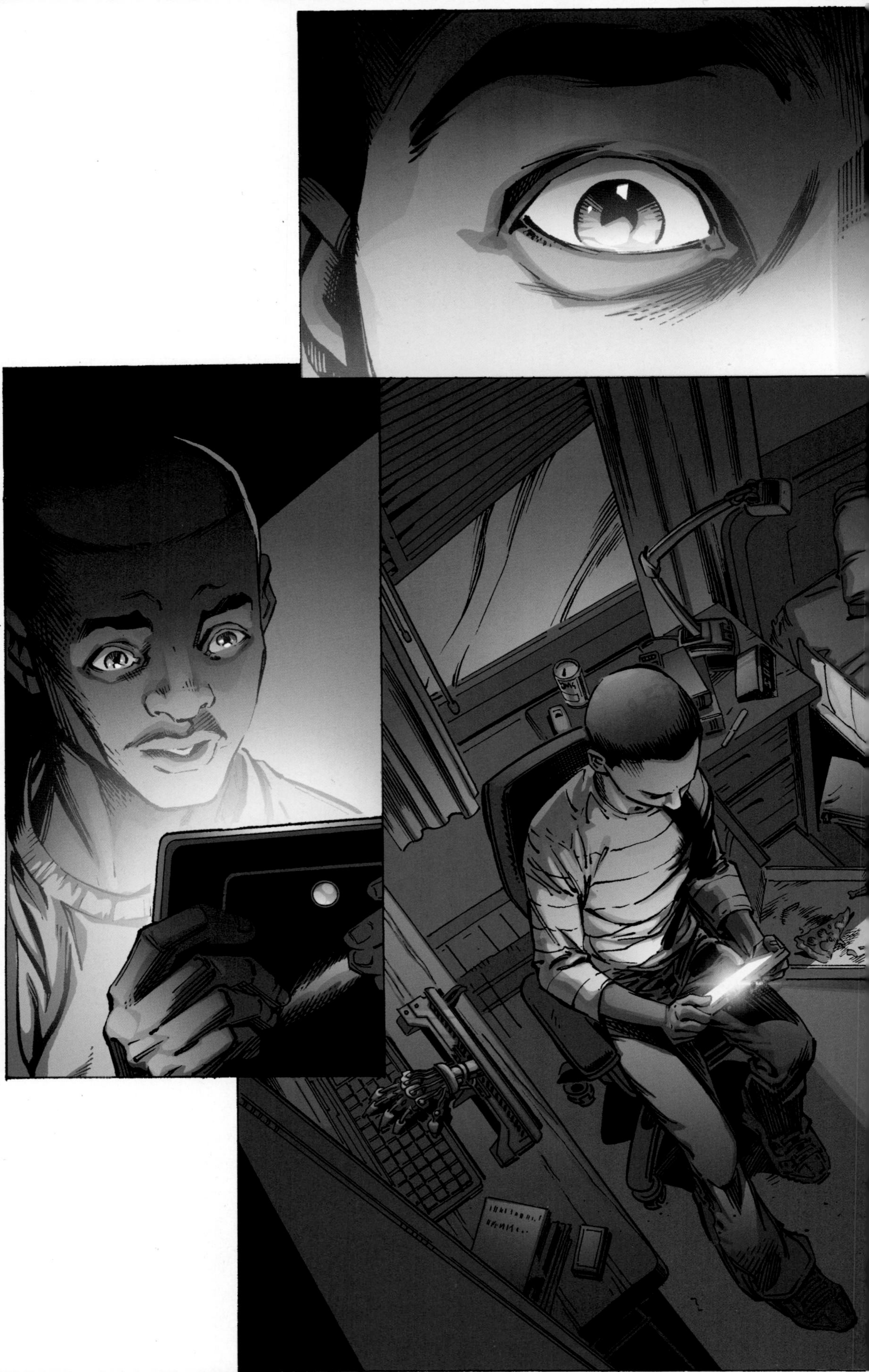

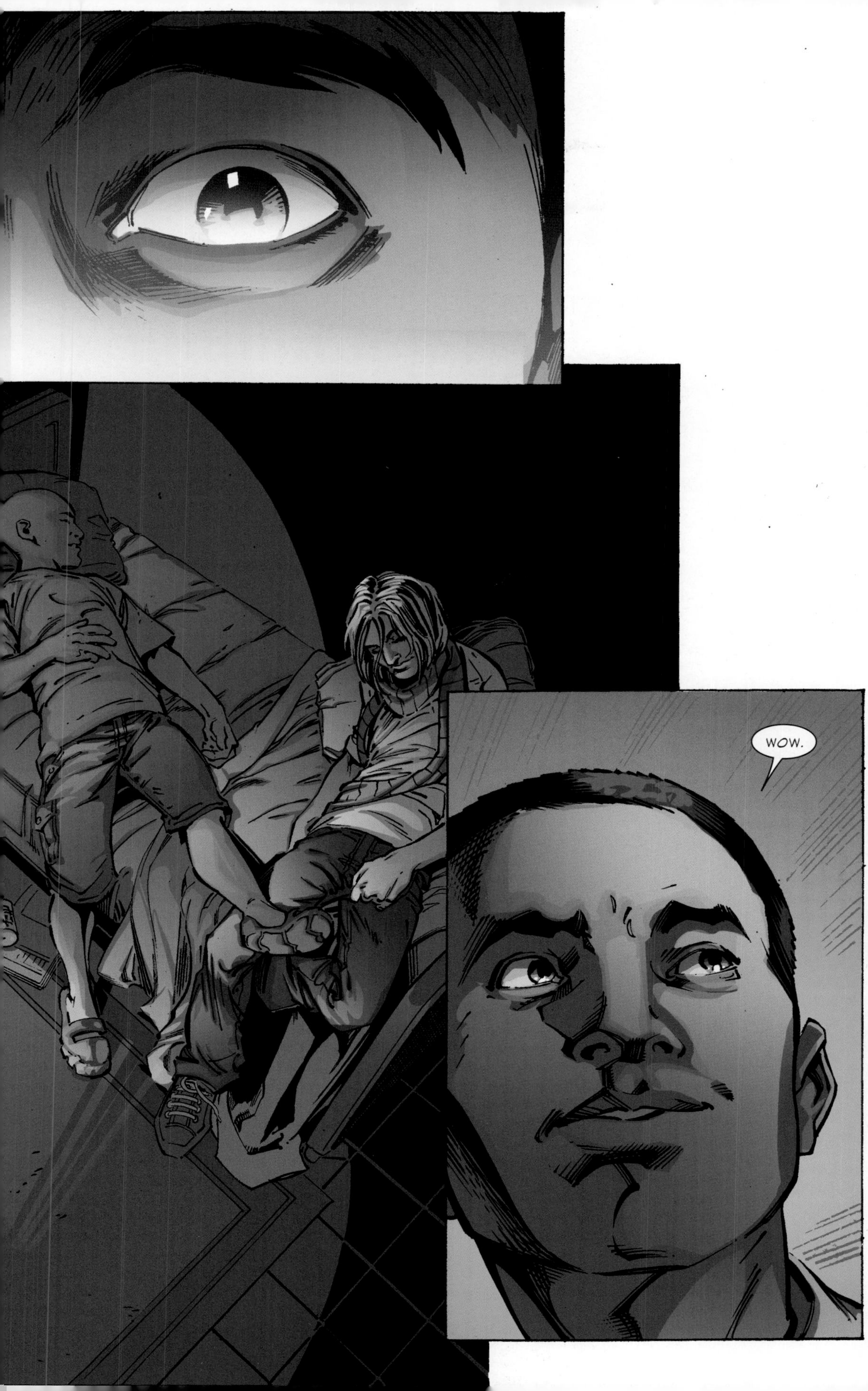
WOW.

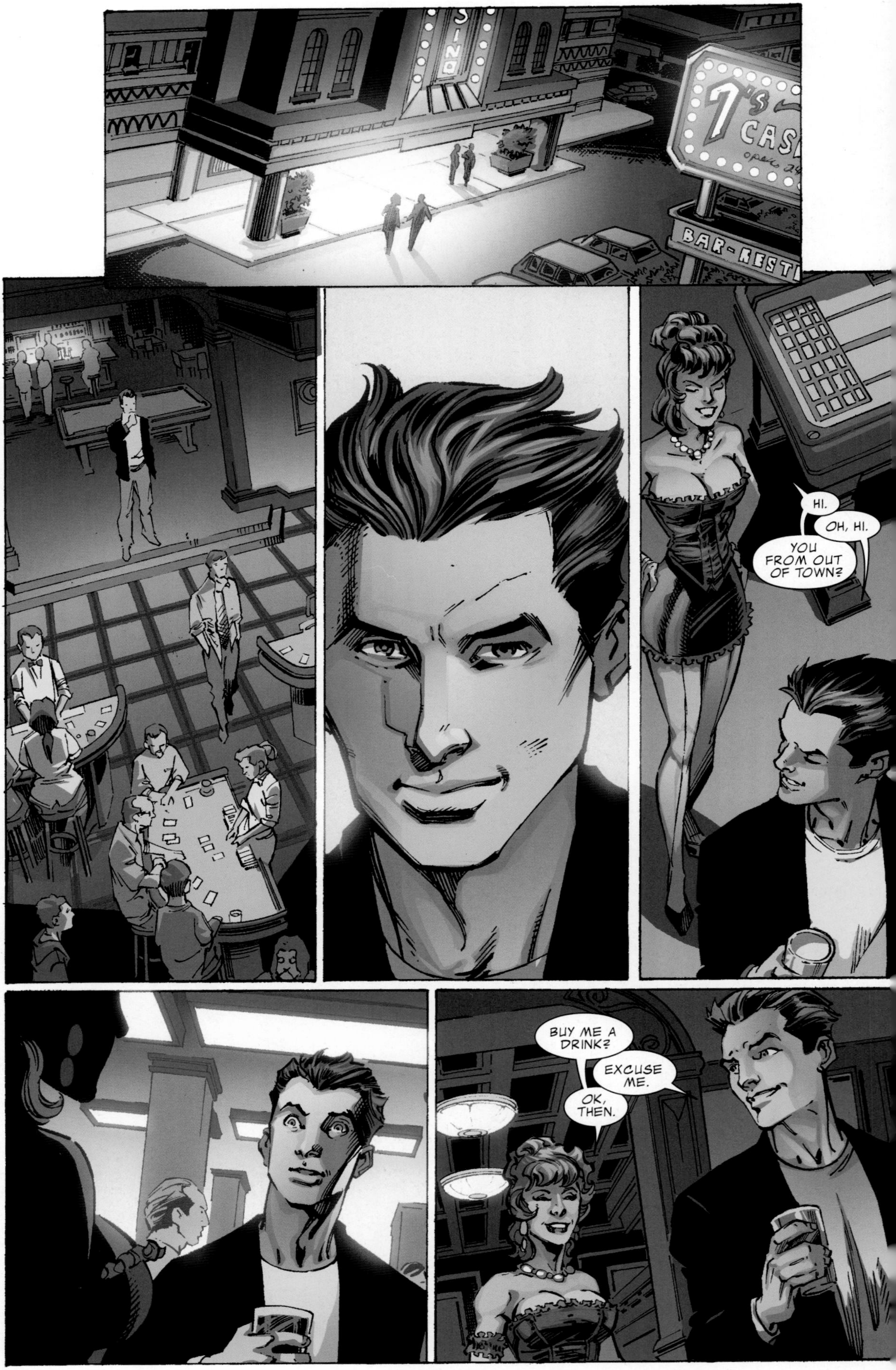
SINO
7's CAS
open 24
BAR-REST
HI.
OH, HI.
YOU FROM OUT OF TOWN?
BUY ME A DRINK?
EXCUSE ME.
OK, THEN.

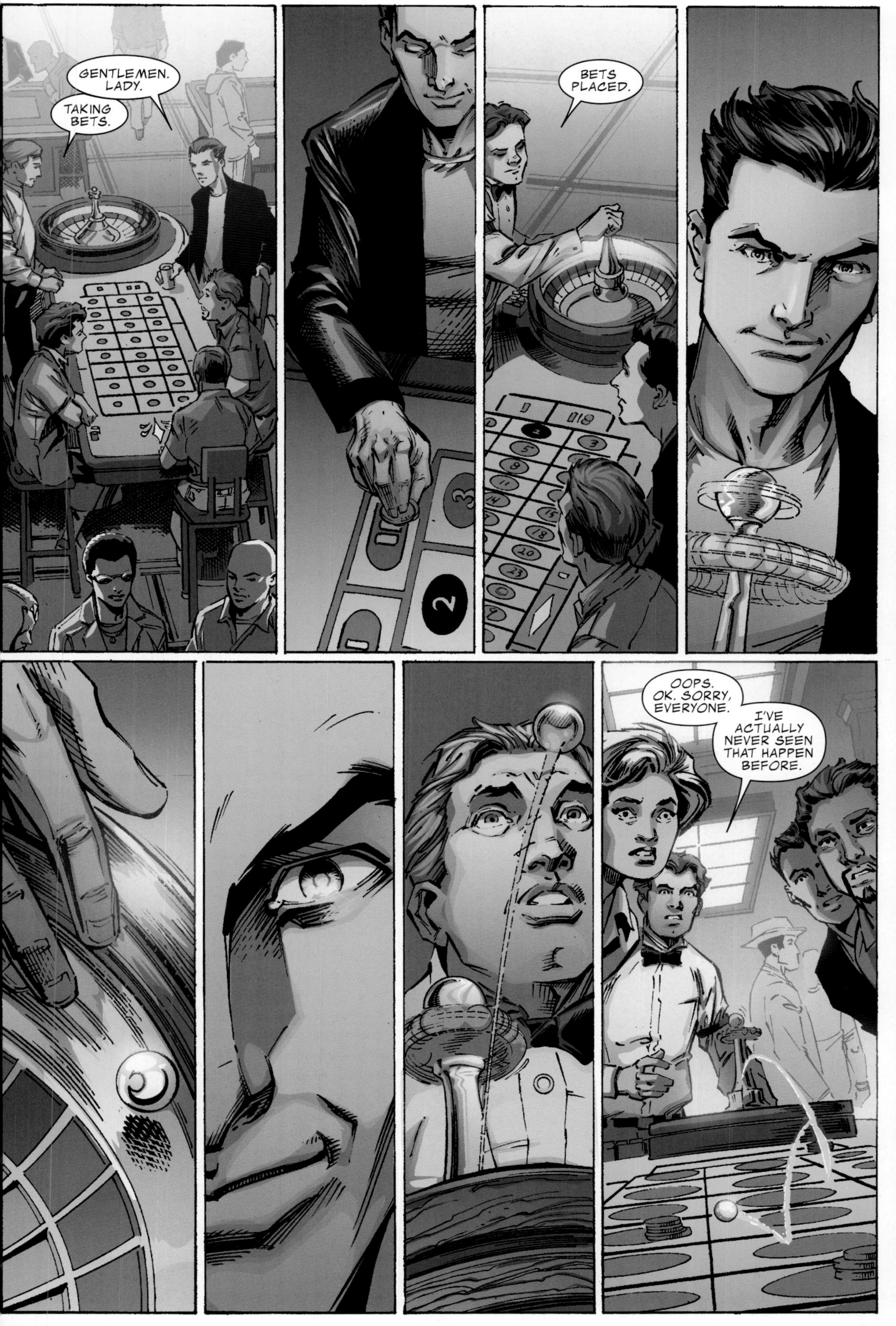
GENTLEMEN. LADY.
TAKING BETS.
BETS PLACED.
OOPS. OK. SORRY, EVERYONE.
I'VE ACTUALLY NEVER SEEN THAT HAPPEN BEFORE.

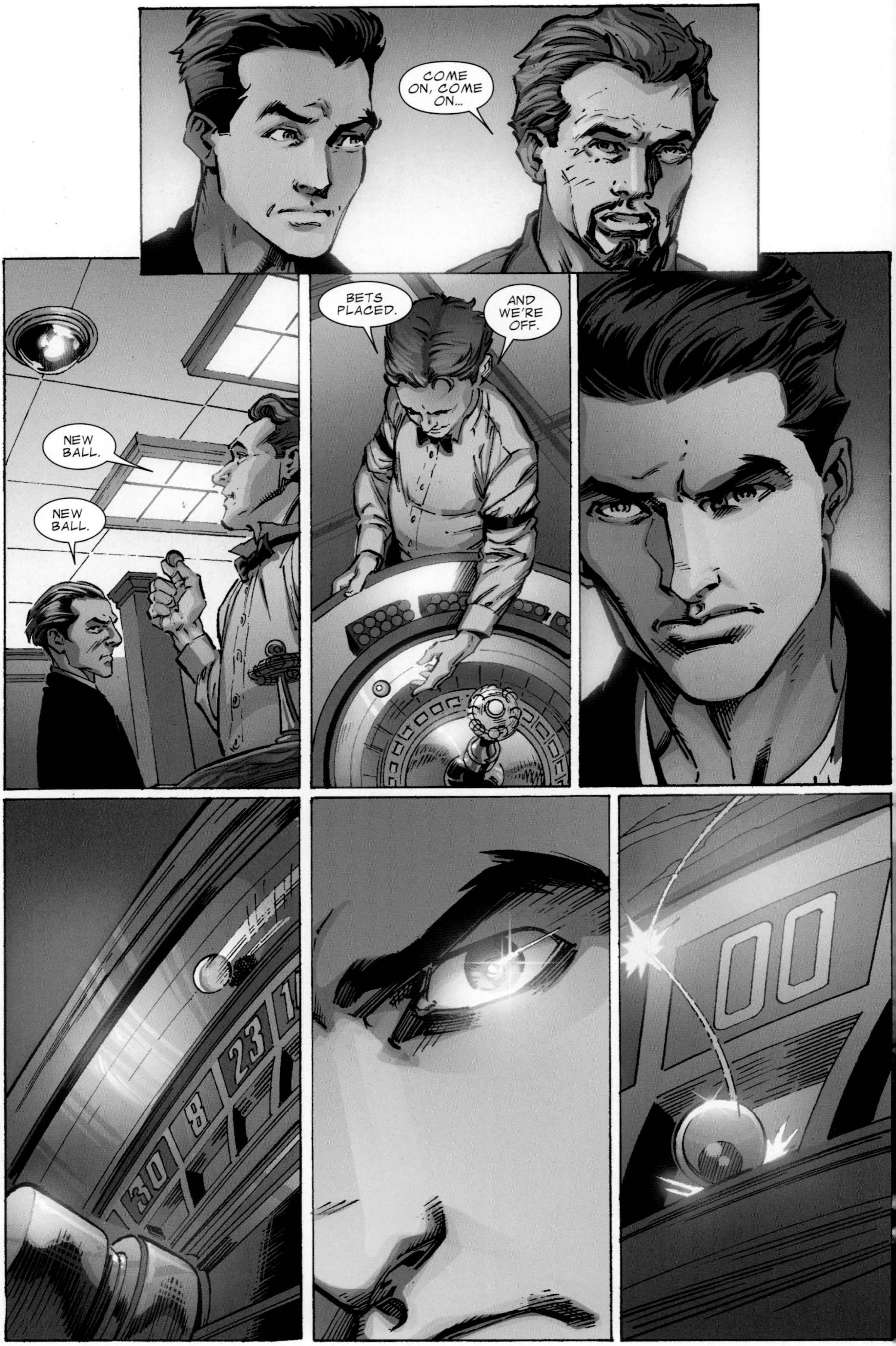
COME ON, COME ON...
NEW BALL.
NEW BALL.
BETS PLACED.
AND WE'RE OFF.
23
8
30
00

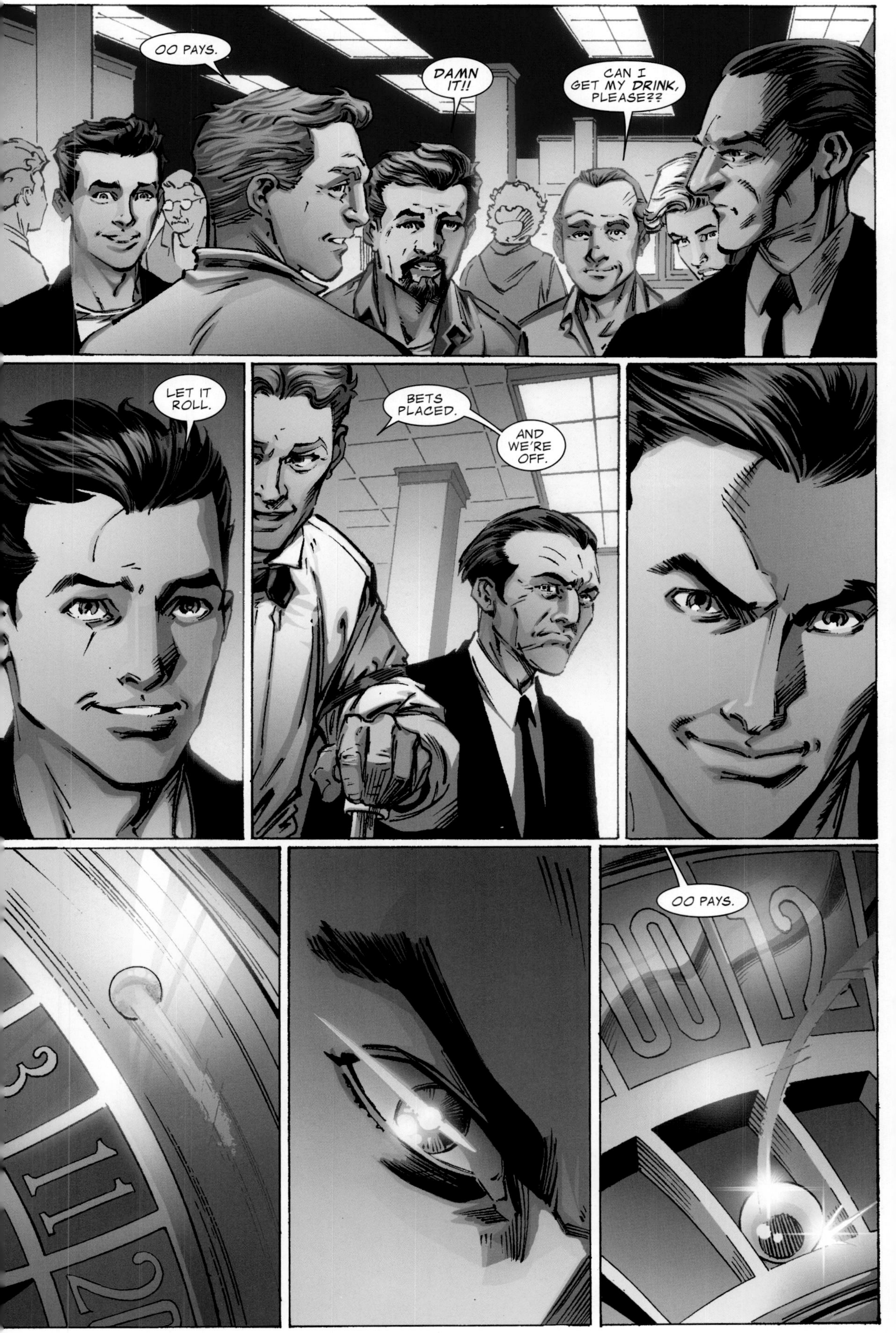
OO PAYS.
DAMN IT!!
CAN I GET MY DRINK, PLEASE??
LET IT ROLL.
BETS PLACED.
AND WE'RE OFF.
OO PAYS.

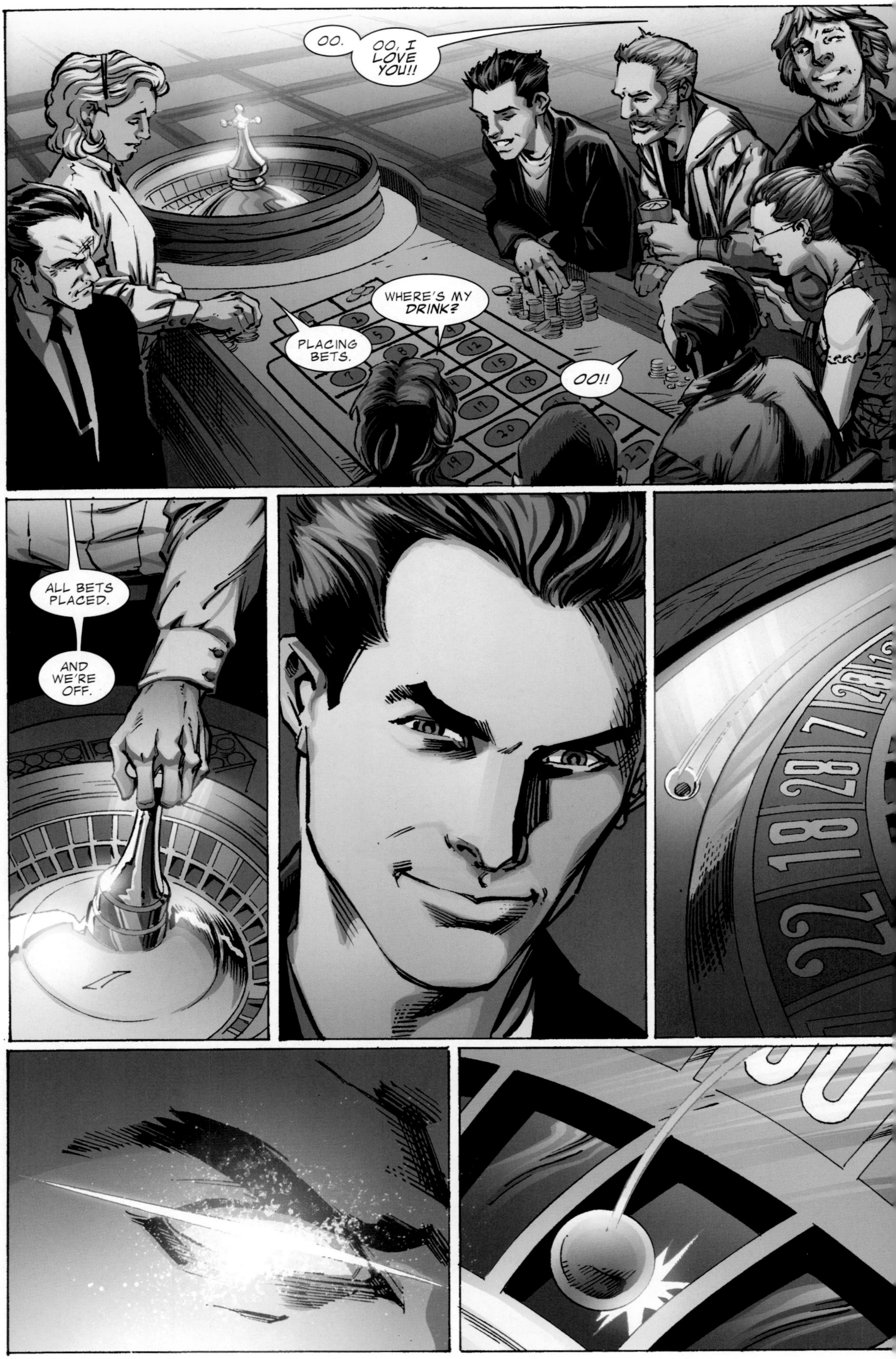
OO.
OO, I LOVE YOU!!
PLACING BETS.
WHERE'S MY DRINK?
OO!!
ALL BETS PLACED.
AND WE'RE OFF.

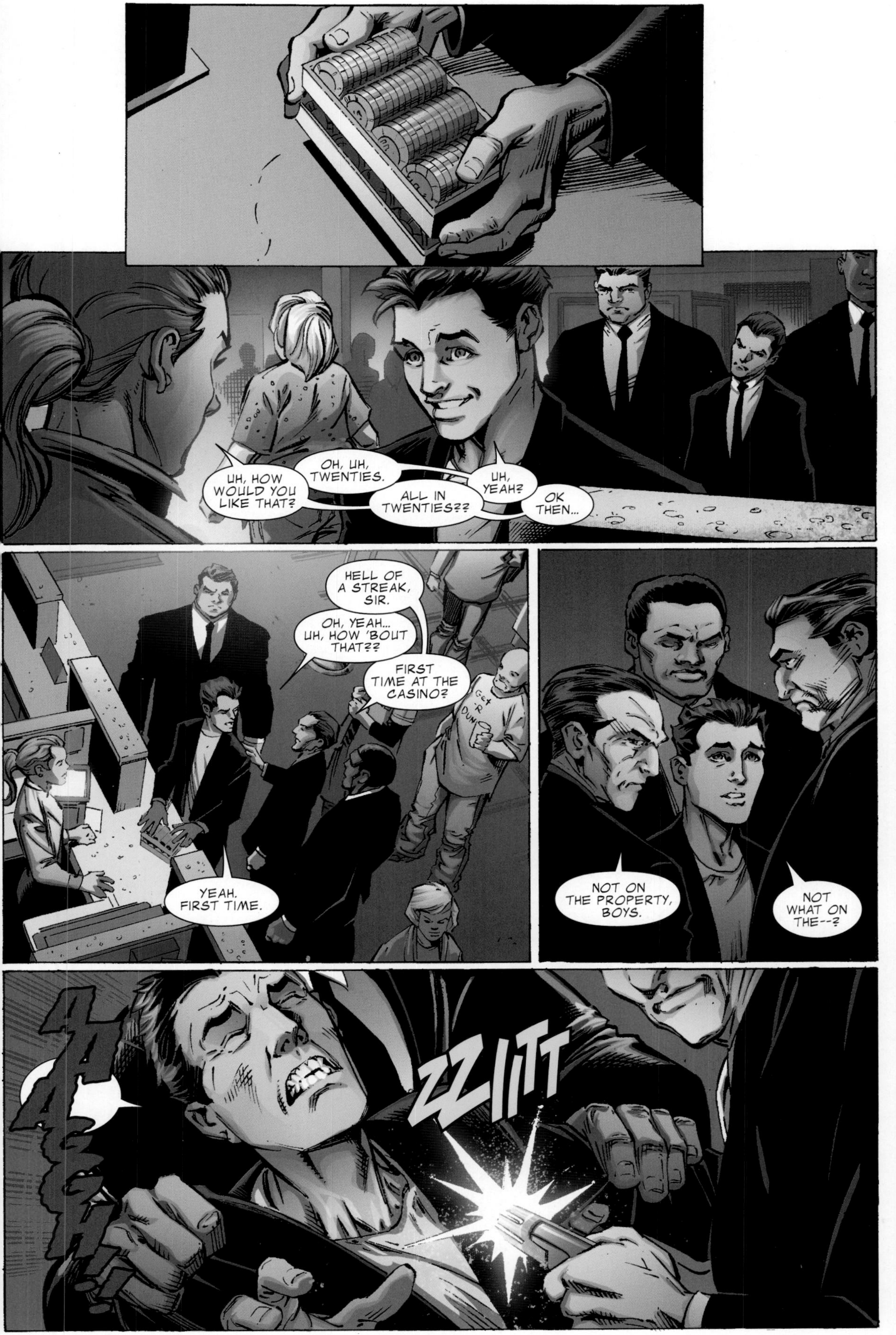
UH, HOW WOULD YOU LIKE THAT?
OH, UH, TWENTIES.
UH, YEAH?
ALL IN TWENTIES??
OK THEN...
HELL OF A STREAK, SIR.
OH, YEAH... UH, HOW 'BOUT THAT??
FIRST TIME AT THE CASINO?
YEAH. FIRST TIME.
NOT ON THE PROPERTY, BOYS.
NOT WHAT ON THE--?
ZZIITT

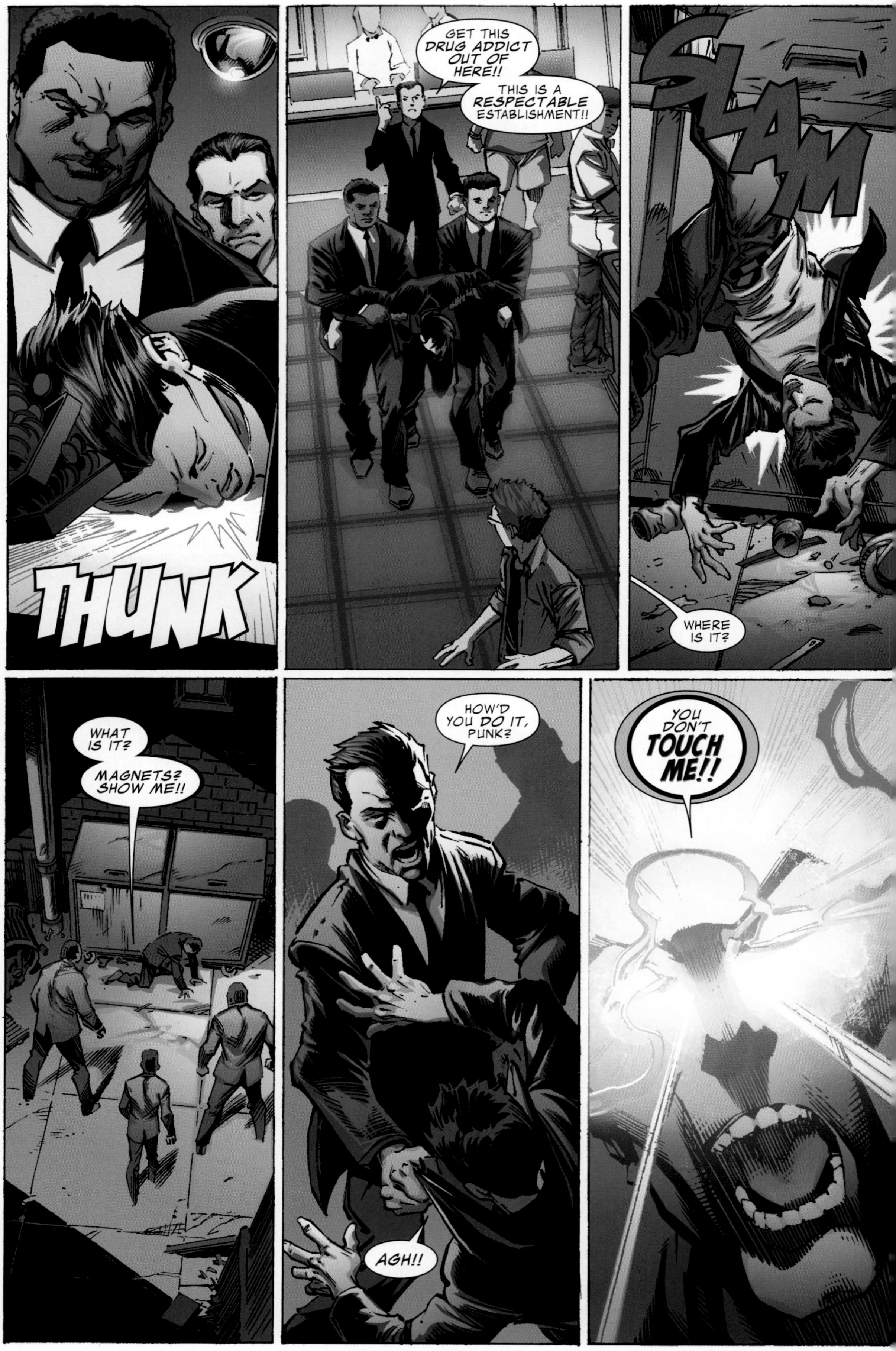
THUNK
GET THIS DRUG ADDICT OUT OF HERE!!
THIS IS A RESPECTABLE ESTABLISHMENT!!
SLAM
WHERE IS IT?
WHAT IS IT?
MAGNETS? SHOW ME!!
HOW'D YOU DO IT, PUNK?
AGH!!
YOU DON'T TOUCH ME!!

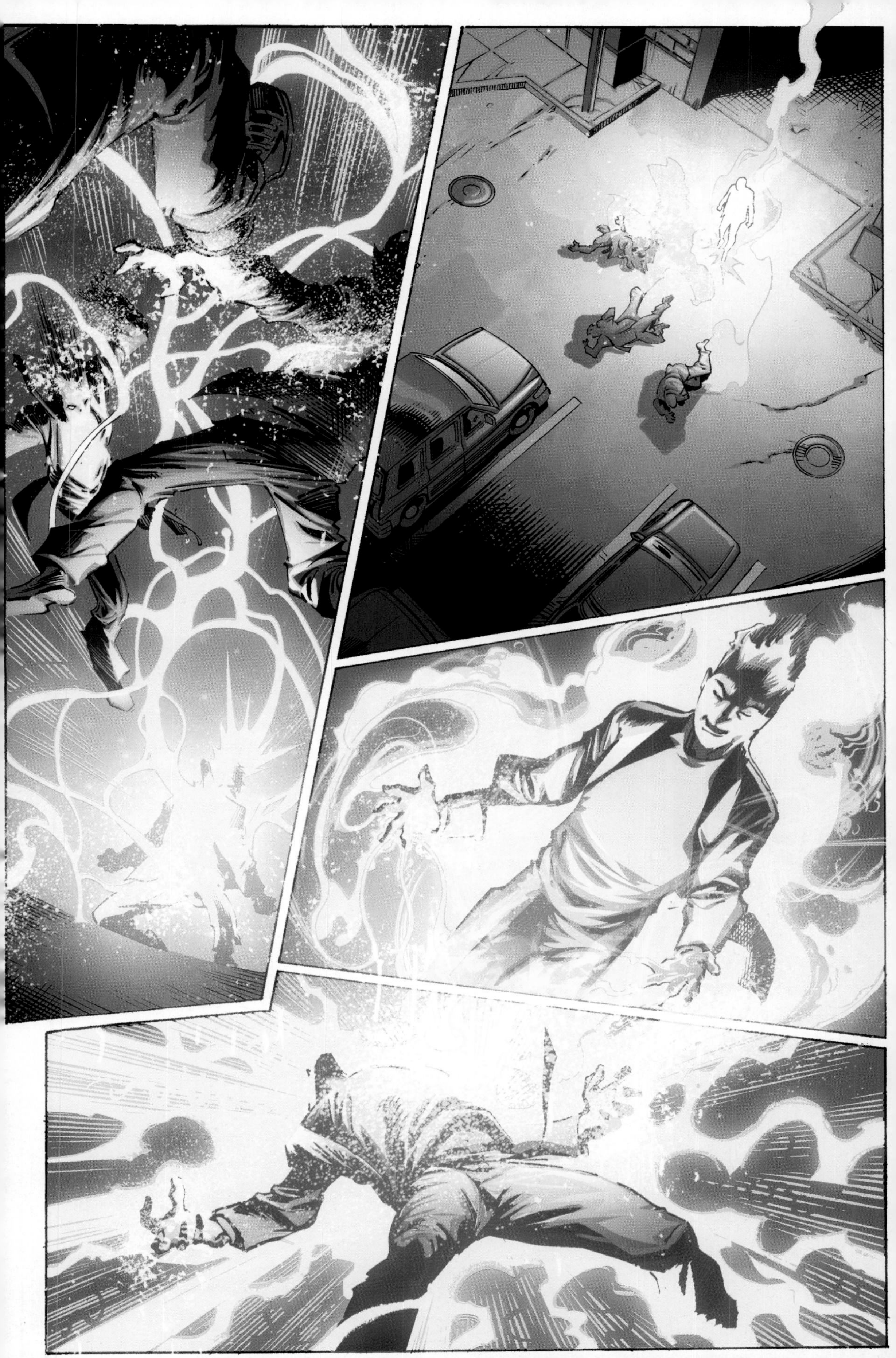

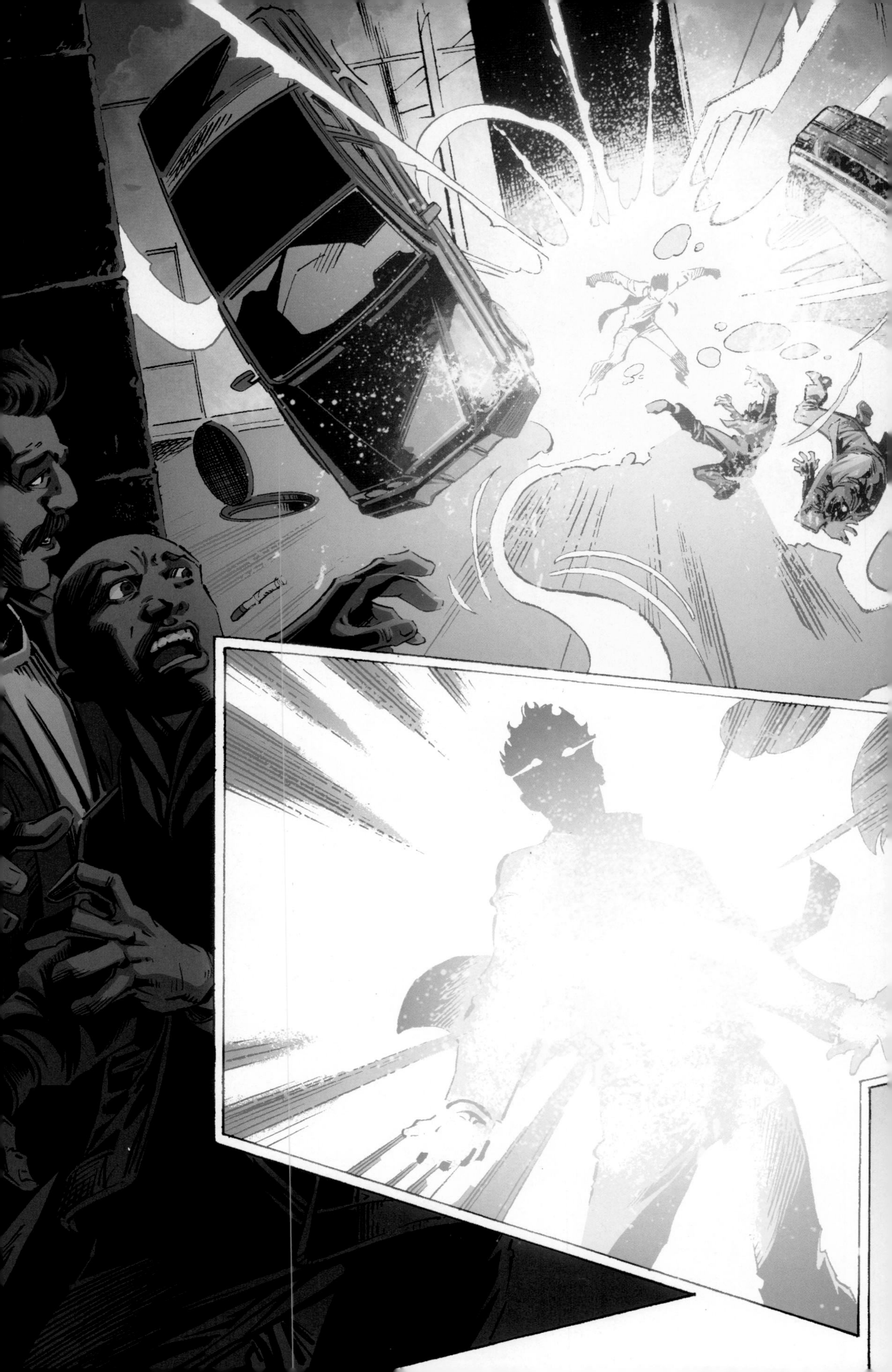

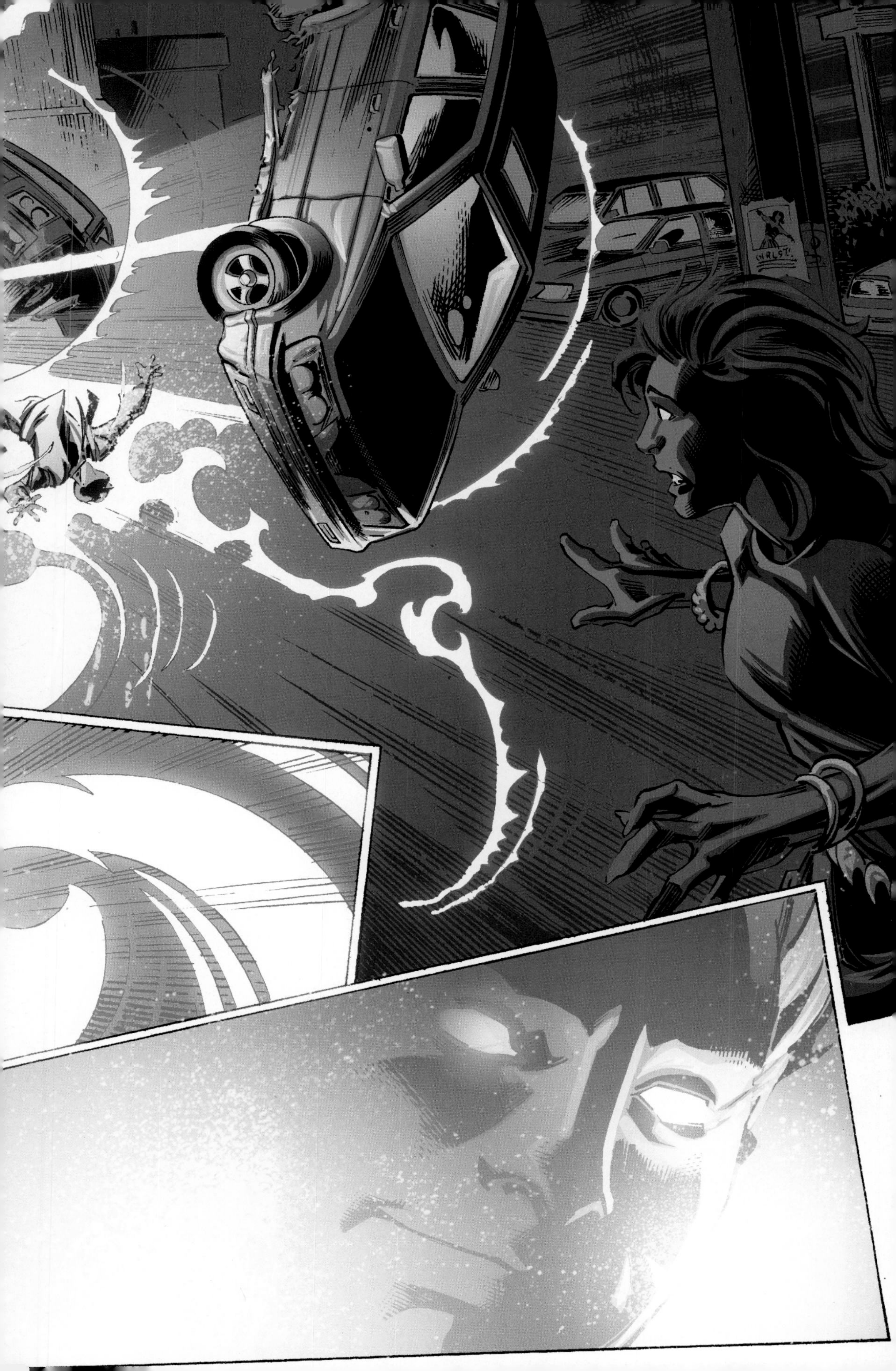

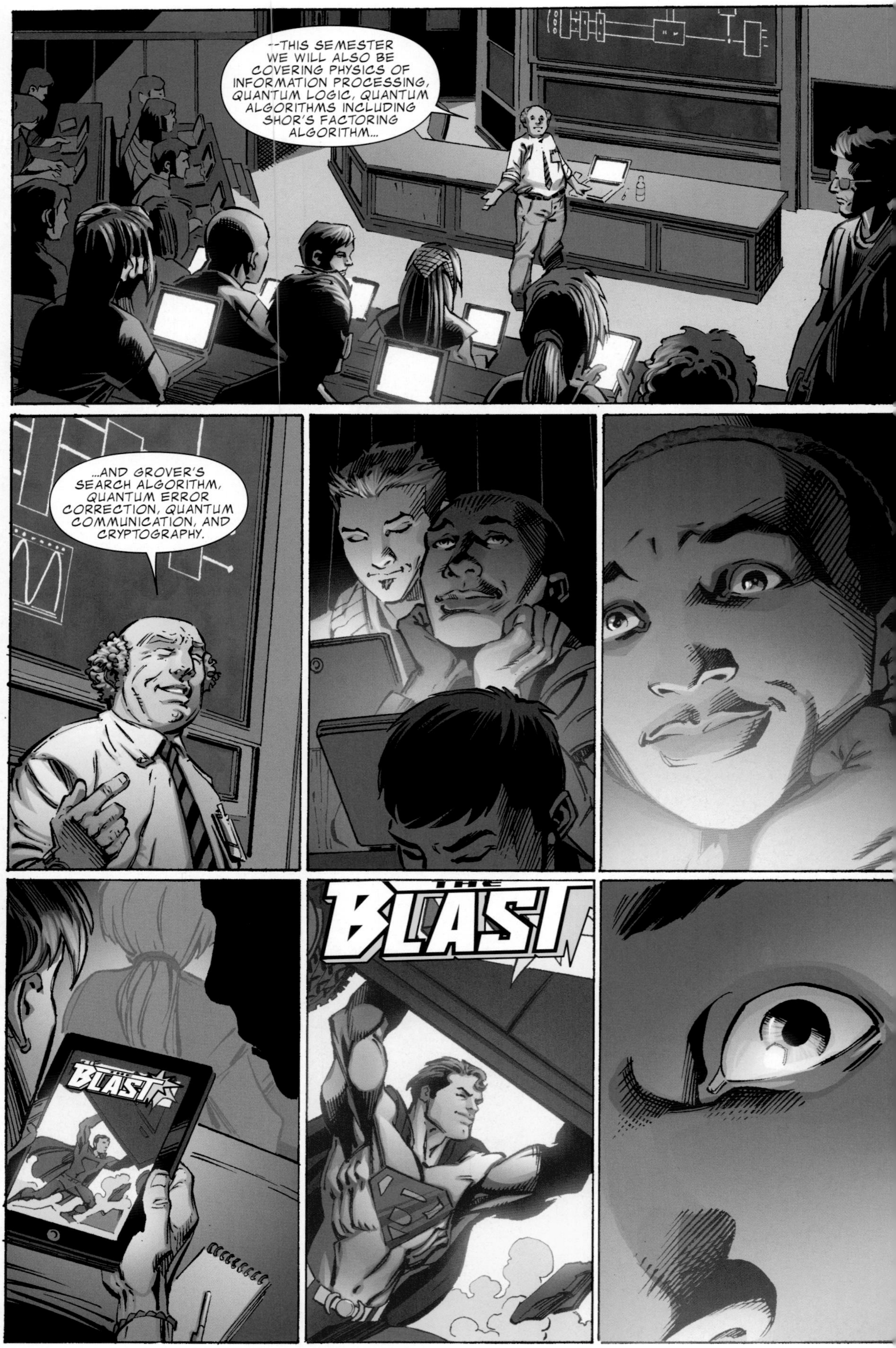
--THIS SEMESTER WE WILL ALSO BE COVERING PHYSICS OF INFORMATION PROCESSING, QUANTUM LOGIC, QUANTUM ALGORITHMS INCLUDING SHOR'S FACTORING ALGORITHM...
...AND GROVER'S SEARCH ALGORITHM, QUANTUM ERROR CORRECTION, QUANTUM COMMUNICATION, AND CRYPTOGRAPHY.
THE BLAST
BLAST
THE BLAST

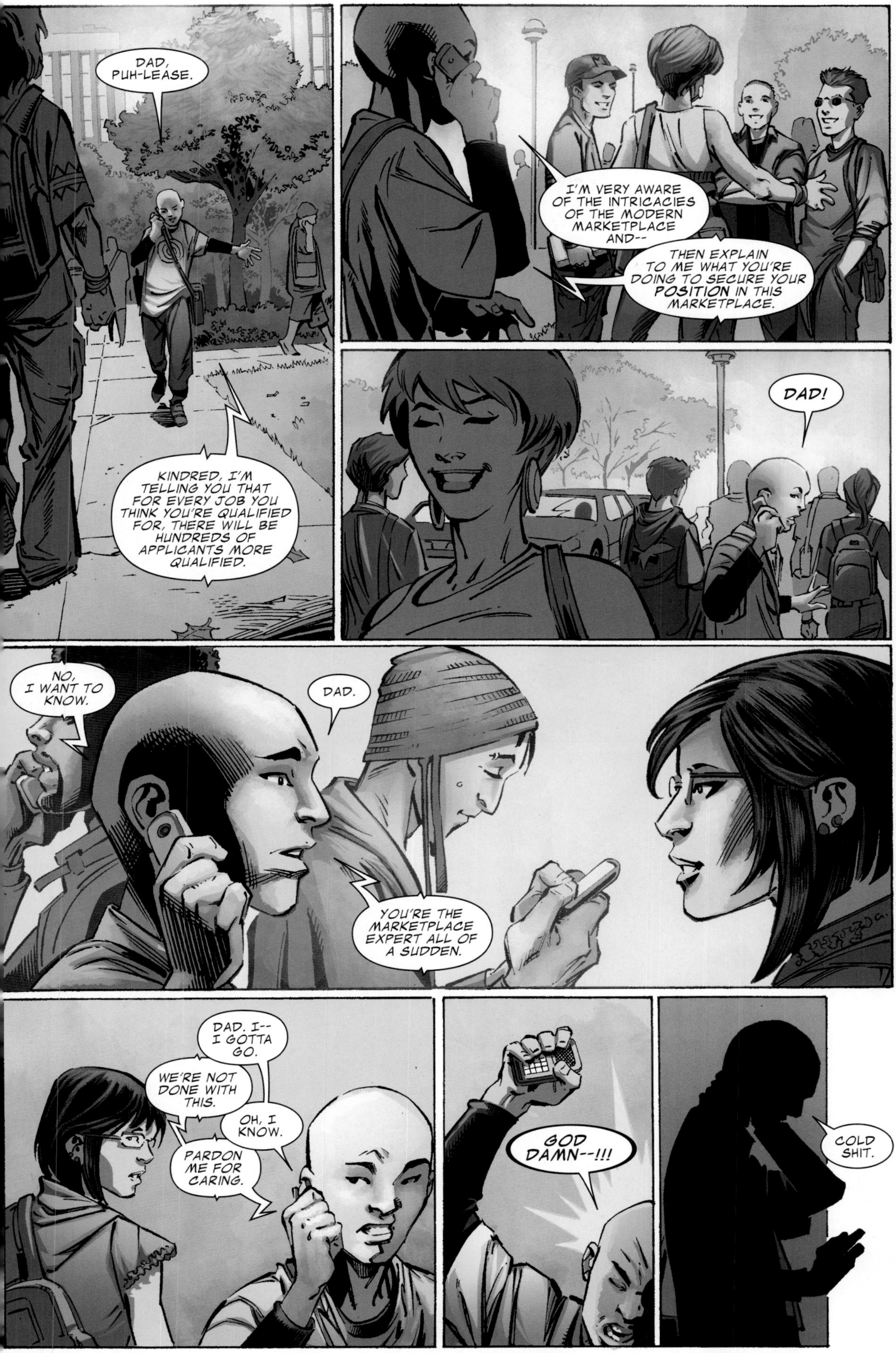
DAD, PUH-LEASE.
KINDRED, I'M TELLING YOU THAT FOR EVERY JOB YOU THINK YOU'RE QUALIFIED FOR, THERE WILL BE HUNDREDS OF APPLICANTS MORE QUALIFIED.
I'M VERY AWARE OF THE INTRICACIES OF THE MODERN MARKETPLACE AND--
THEN EXPLAIN TO ME WHAT YOU'RE DOING TO SECURE YOUR POSITION IN THIS MARKETPLACE.
DAD!
NO, I WANT TO KNOW.
DAD.
YOU'RE THE MARKETPLACE EXPERT ALL OF A SUDDEN.
DAD. I-- I GOTTA GO.
WE'RE NOT DONE WITH THIS.
OH, I KNOW.
PARDON ME FOR CARING.
GOD DAMN--!!!
COLD SHIT.

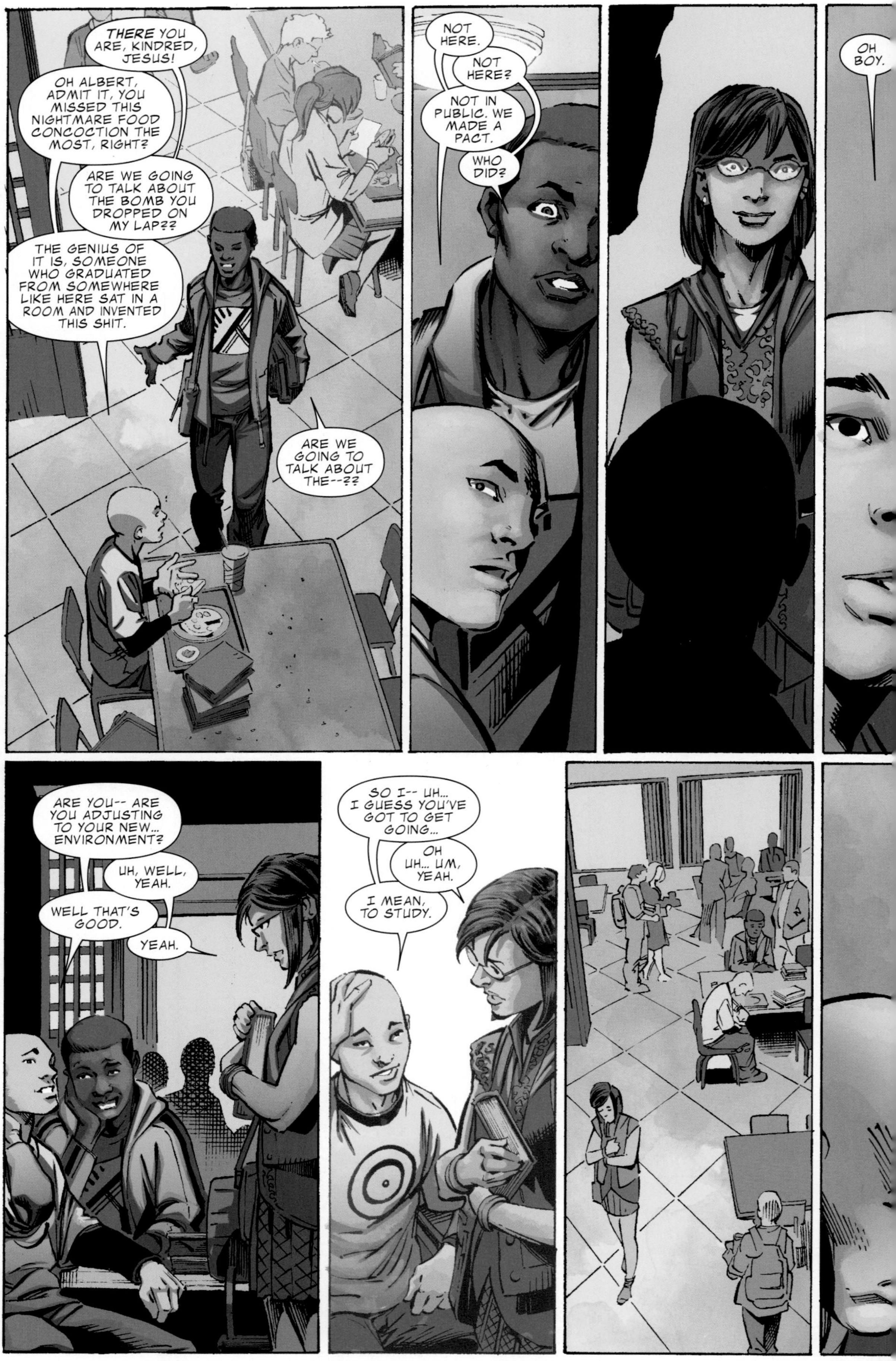
THERE YOU ARE, KINDRED, JESUS!
OH ALBERT, ADMIT IT, YOU MISSED THIS NIGHTMARE FOOD CONCOCTION THE MOST, RIGHT?
ARE WE GOING TO TALK ABOUT THE BOMB YOU DROPPED ON MY LAP??
THE GENIUS OF IT IS, SOMEONE WHO GRADUATED FROM SOMEWHERE LIKE HERE SAT IN A ROOM AND INVENTED THIS SHIT.
ARE WE GOING TO TALK ABOUT THE--??
NOT HERE.
NOT HERE?
NOT IN PUBLIC. WE MADE A PACT.
WHO DID?
OH BOY.
ARE YOU-- ARE YOU ADJUSTING TO YOUR NEW... ENVIRONMENT?
UH, WELL, YEAH.
WELL THAT'S GOOD.
YEAH.
SO I-- UH... I GUESS YOU'VE GOT TO GET GOING...
OH UH... UM, YEAH.
I MEAN, TO STUDY.

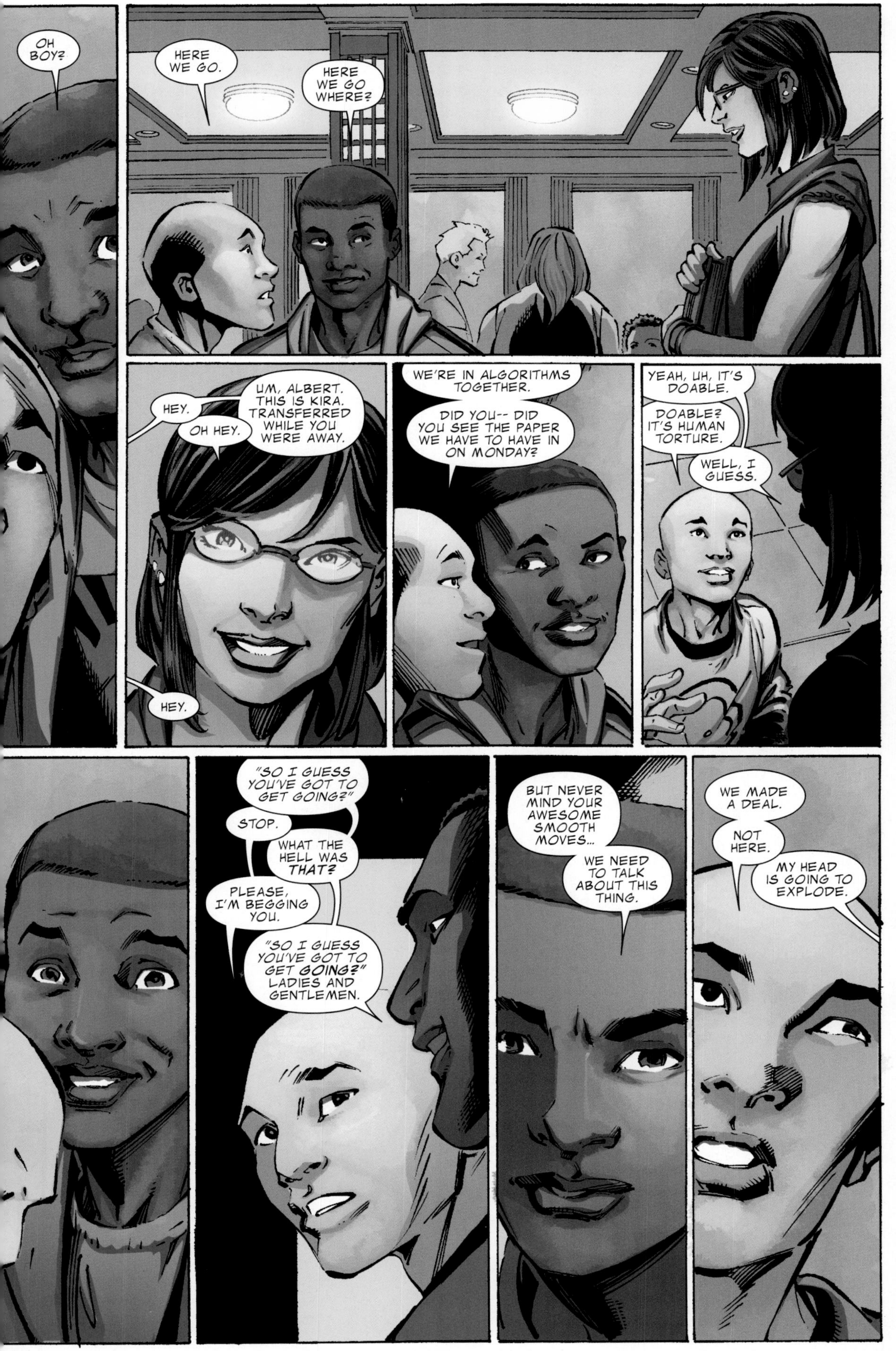
OH BOY?
HERE WE GO.
HERE WE GO WHERE?
HEY.
OH HEY.
UM, ALBERT. THIS IS KIRA. TRANSFERRED WHILE YOU WERE AWAY.
HEY.
WE'RE IN ALGORITHMS TOGETHER.
DID YOU-- DID YOU SEE THE PAPER WE HAVE TO HAVE IN ON MONDAY?
YEAH, UH, IT'S DOABLE.
DOABLE? IT'S HUMAN TORTURE.
WELL, I GUESS.
"SO I GUESS YOU'VE GOT TO GET GOING?"
STOP.
WHAT THE HELL WAS THAT?
PLEASE, I'M BEGGING YOU.
"SO I GUESS YOU'VE GOT TO GET GOING?" LADIES AND GENTLEMEN.
BUT NEVER MIND YOUR AWESOME SMOOTH MOVES...
WE NEED TO TALK ABOUT THIS THING.
WE MADE A DEAL.
NOT HERE.
MY HEAD IS GOING TO EXPLODE.

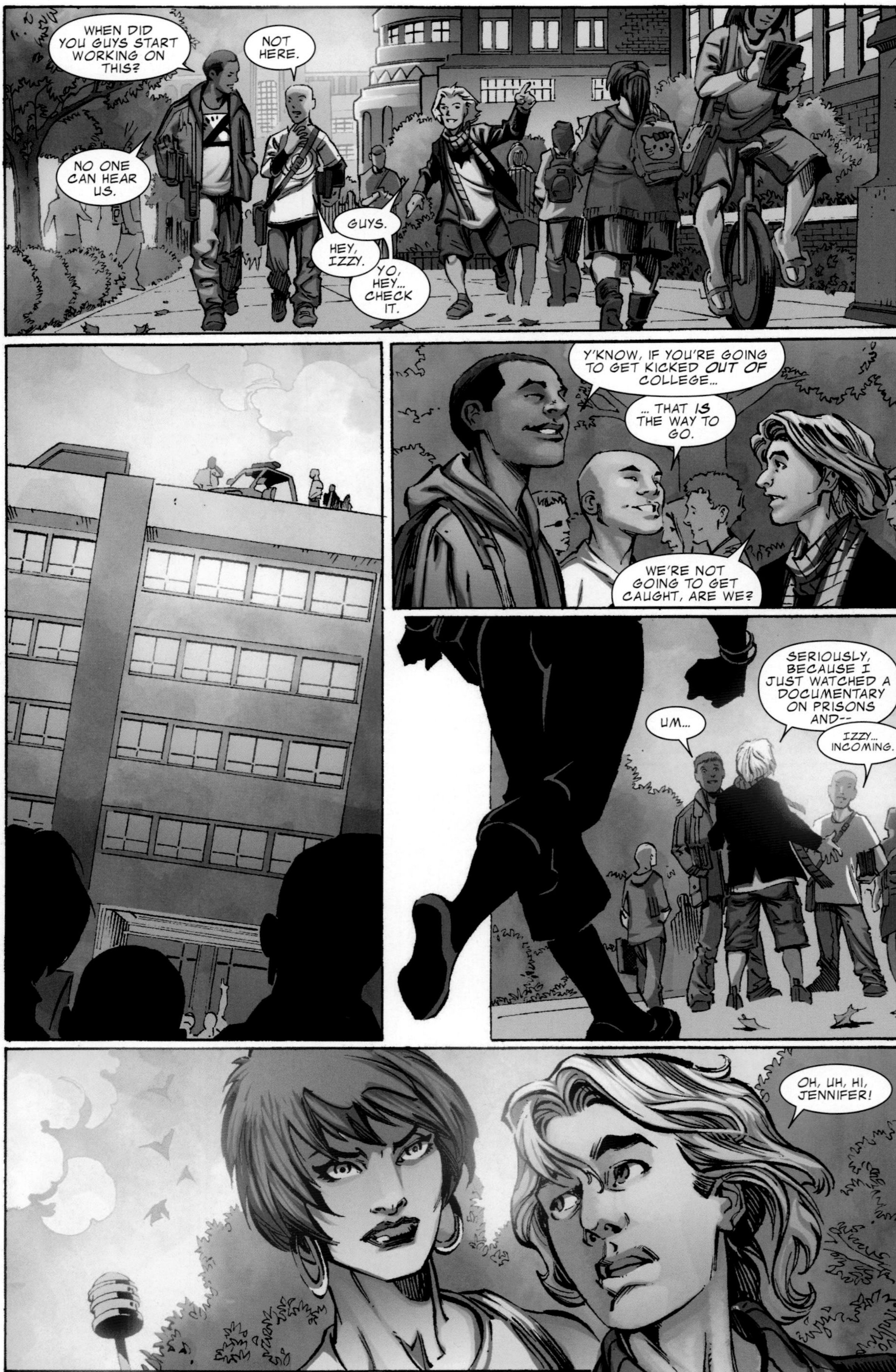
WHEN DID YOU GUYS START WORKING ON THIS?
NOT HERE.
NO ONE CAN HEAR US.
GUYS.
HEY, IZZY.
YO, HEY... CHECK IT.
Y'KNOW, IF YOU'RE GOING TO GET KICKED OUT OF COLLEGE...
... THAT IS THE WAY TO GO.
WE'RE NOT GOING TO GET CAUGHT, ARE WE?
SERIOUSLY, BECAUSE I JUST WATCHED A DOCUMENTARY ON PRISONS AND--
UM...
IZZY... INCOMING.
OH, UH, HI, JENNIFER!

HEY!!

SO, IT ISN'T BROKEN!

UH, YOU TOLD ME WE SHOULD TAKE A BREAK.

SO THAT MEANS YOU CAN'T RETURN A TEXT??!!

YOU TOLD ME WE--

WHEN I TEXT, YOU TEXT BACK!!

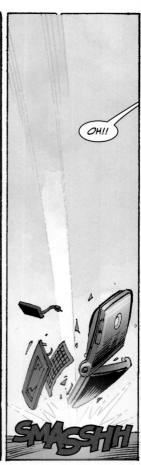

OH!!

SMASSHH

AND THAT'S... WHY YOU DON'T SLEEP WITH THE FACULTY.

SHE BROKE UP WITH ME.

YOU DID HER?

DON'T SLEEP WITH THE FACULTY.

I BELIEVE IT'S IN THE SCHOOL BROCHURES.

IT SHOULD BE.

YOU CLIMBED THAT MOUNTAIN?

IT OCCURS TO ME... IF YOU HAD SUPERPOWERS YOU COULD HAVE STOPPED THAT FROM--

DUDE!

NOT HERE.

DID YOU READ THE--??

NOT HERE!

MARIA IS WAITING FOR US.

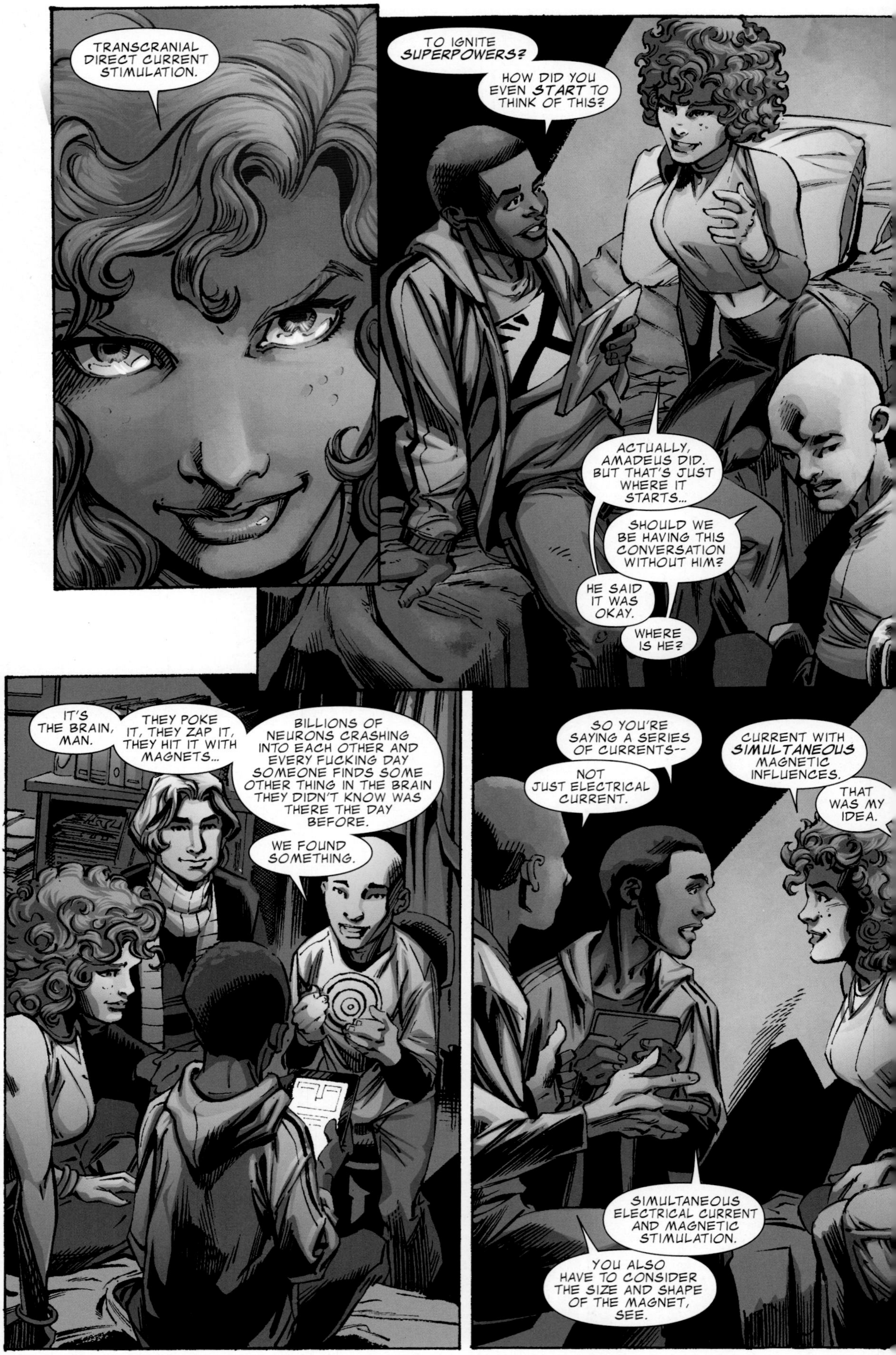
TRANSCRANIAL DIRECT CURRENT STIMULATION.
TO IGNITE SUPERPOWERS?
HOW DID YOU EVEN START TO THINK OF THIS?
ACTUALLY, AMADEUS DID. BUT THAT'S JUST WHERE IT STARTS...
SHOULD WE BE HAVING THIS CONVERSATION WITHOUT HIM?
HE SAID IT WAS OKAY.
WHERE IS HE?
IT'S THE BRAIN, MAN.
THEY POKE IT, THEY ZAP IT, THEY HIT IT WITH MAGNETS...
BILLIONS OF NEURONS CRASHING INTO EACH OTHER AND EVERY FUCKING DAY SOMEONE FINDS SOME OTHER THING IN THE BRAIN THEY DIDN'T KNOW WAS THERE THE DAY BEFORE.
WE FOUND SOMETHING.
SO YOU'RE SAYING A SERIES OF CURRENTS--
NOT JUST ELECTRICAL CURRENT.
CURRENT WITH SIMULTANEOUS MAGNETIC INFLUENCES.
THAT WAS MY IDEA.
SIMULTANEOUS ELECTRICAL CURRENT AND MAGNETIC STIMULATION.
YOU ALSO HAVE TO CONSIDER THE SIZE AND SHAPE OF THE MAGNET, SEE.

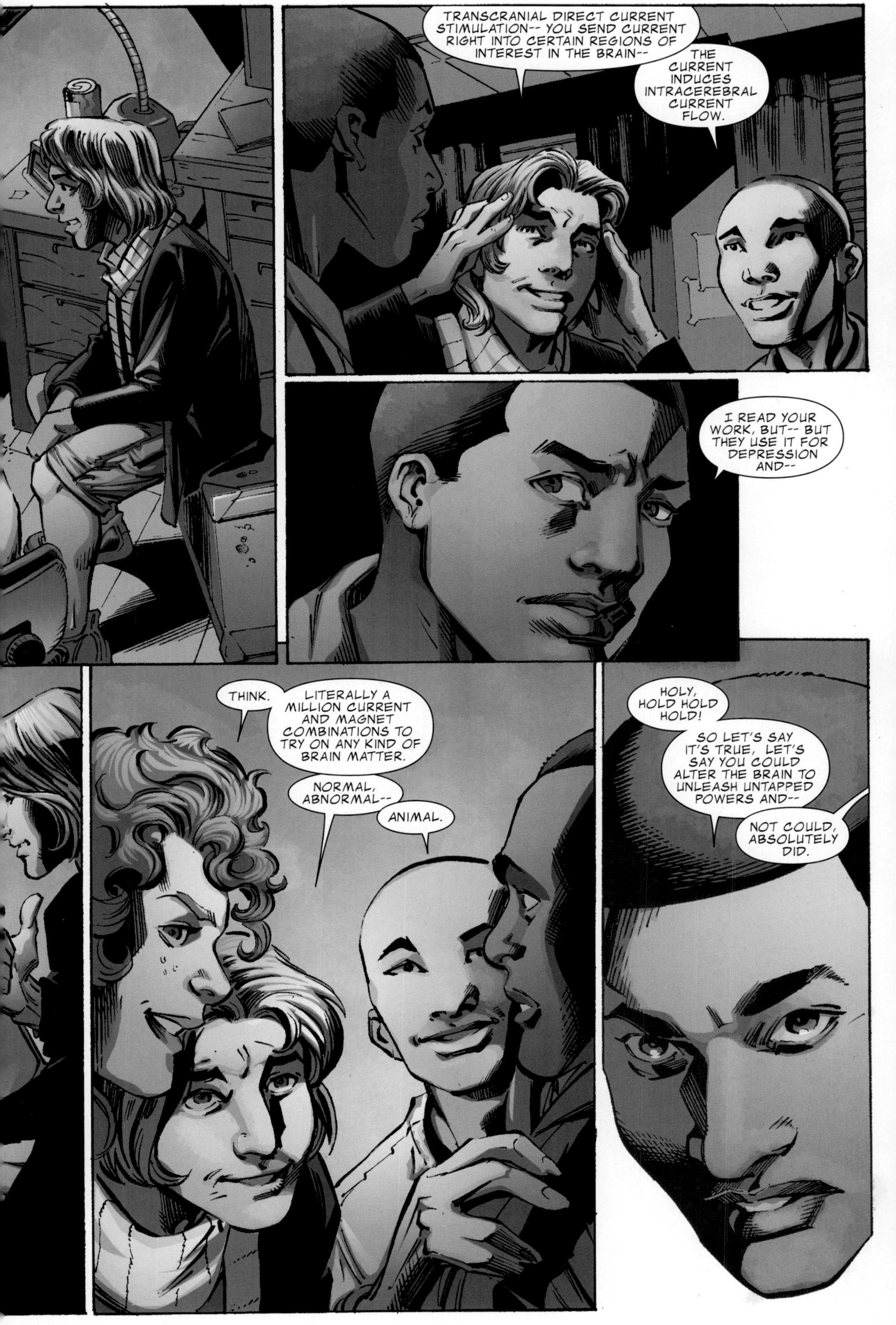
TRANSCRANIAL DIRECT CURRENT STIMULATION-- YOU SEND CURRENT RIGHT INTO CERTAIN REGIONS OF INTEREST IN THE BRAIN--
THE CURRENT INDUCES INTRACEREBRAL CURRENT FLOW.
I READ YOUR WORK, BUT-- BUT THEY USE IT FOR DEPRESSION AND--
THINK.
LITERALLY A MILLION CURRENT AND MAGNET COMBINATIONS TO TRY ON ANY KIND OF BRAIN MATTER.
NORMAL, ABNORMAL--
ANIMAL.
HOLY, HOLD HOLD HOLD!
SO LET'S SAY IT'S TRUE, LET'S SAY YOU COULD ALTER THE BRAIN TO UNLEASH UNTAPPED POWERS AND--
NOT COULD, ABSOLUTELY DID.

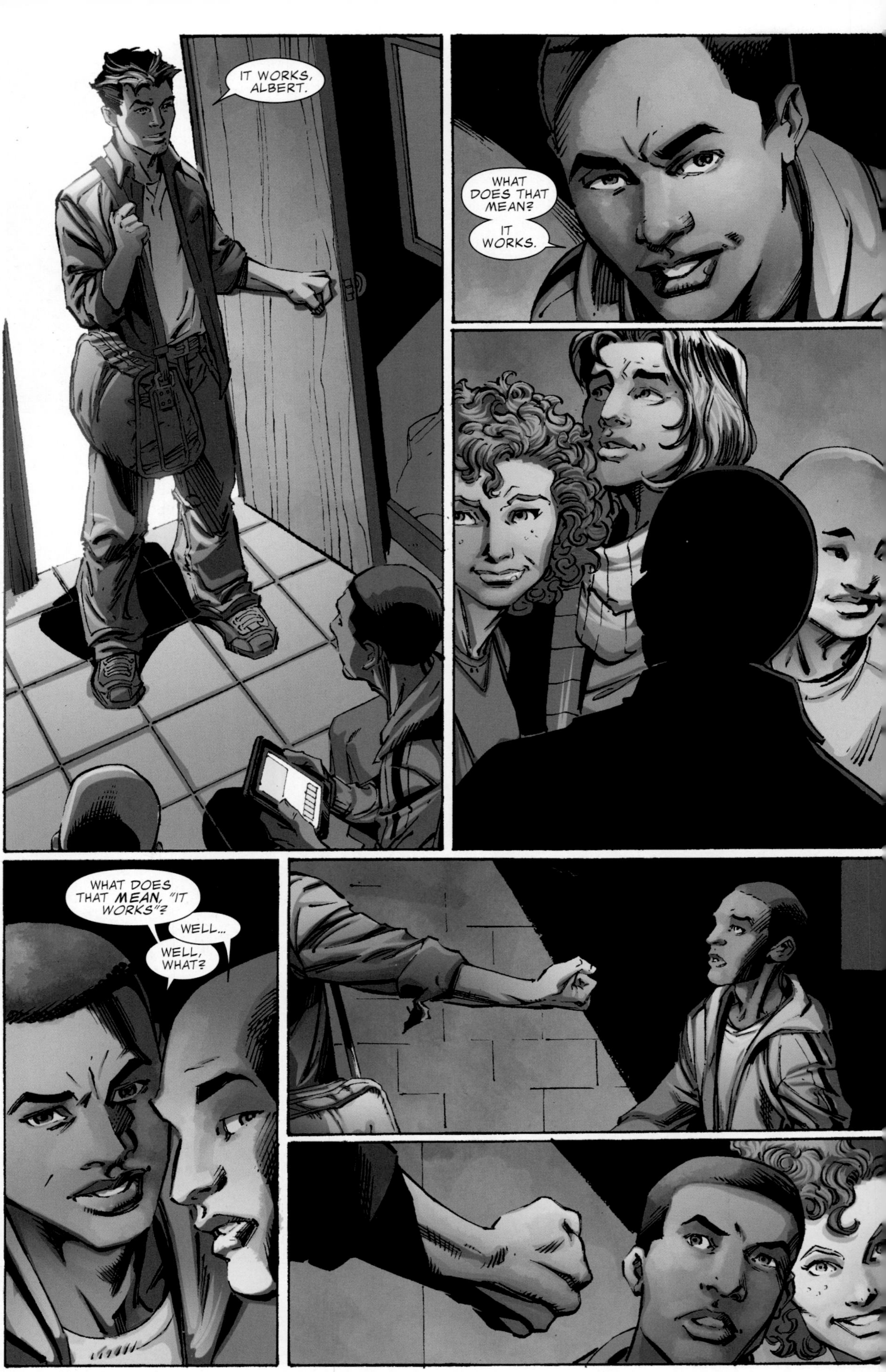
IT WORKS, ALBERT.
WHAT DOES THAT MEAN?
IT WORKS.
WHAT DOES THAT **MEAN**, "IT WORKS"?
WELL...
WELL, WHAT?

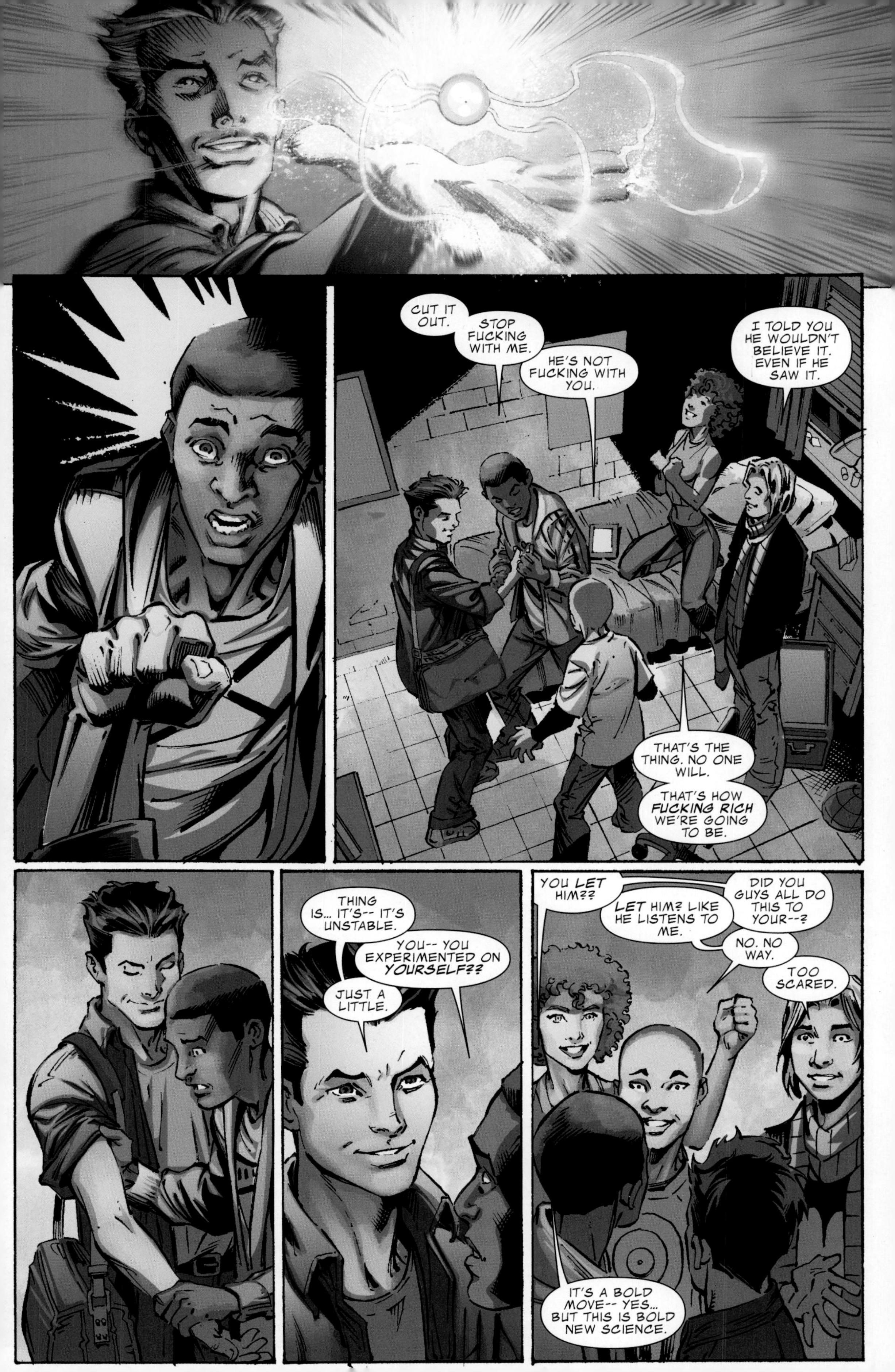
CUT IT OUT.
STOP FUCKING WITH ME.
HE'S NOT FUCKING WITH YOU.
I TOLD YOU HE WOULDN'T BELIEVE IT. EVEN IF HE SAW IT.
THAT'S THE THING. NO ONE WILL.
THAT'S HOW *FUCKING RICH* WE'RE GOING TO BE.
THING IS... IT'S-- IT'S UNSTABLE.
YOU-- YOU EXPERIMENTED ON *YOURSELF??*
JUST A LITTLE.
YOU *LET* HIM??
LET HIM? LIKE HE LISTENS TO ME.
DID YOU GUYS ALL DO THIS TO YOUR--?
NO. NO WAY.
TOO SCARED.
IT'S A BOLD MOVE-- YES... BUT THIS IS BOLD NEW SCIENCE.

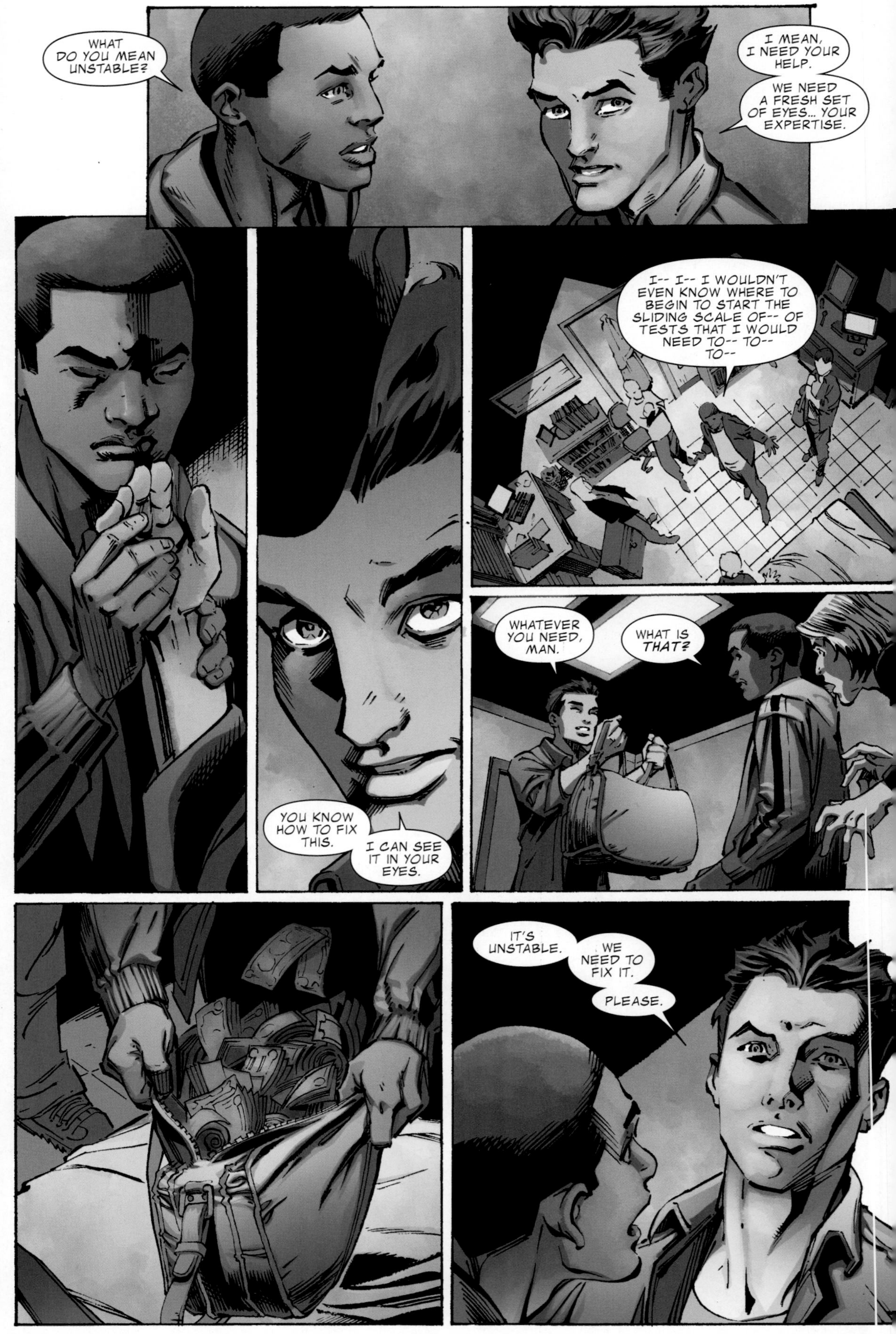
WHAT DO YOU MEAN UNSTABLE?
I MEAN, I NEED YOUR HELP.
WE NEED A FRESH SET OF EYES... YOUR EXPERTISE.
YOU KNOW HOW TO FIX THIS.
I CAN SEE IT IN YOUR EYES.
I-- I-- I WOULDN'T EVEN KNOW WHERE TO BEGIN TO START THE SLIDING SCALE OF-- OF TESTS THAT I WOULD NEED TO-- TO-- TO--
WHATEVER YOU NEED, MAN.
WHAT IS THAT?
IT'S UNSTABLE.
WE NEED TO FIX IT.
PLEASE.

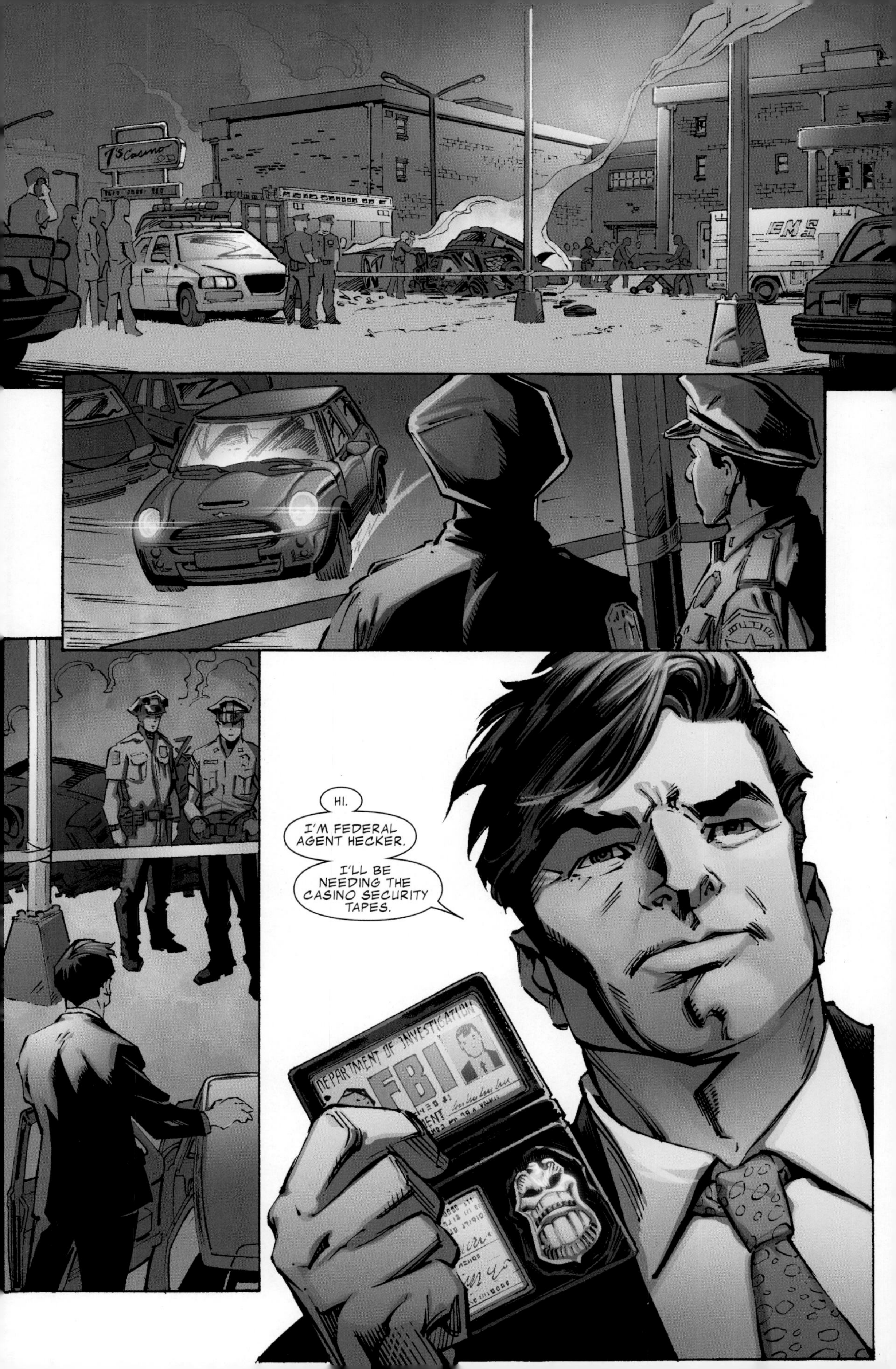

HI.
I'M FEDERAL AGENT HECKER.
I'LL BE NEEDING THE CASINO SECURITY TAPES.
EMS
DEPARTMENT OF INVESTIGATION
FBI

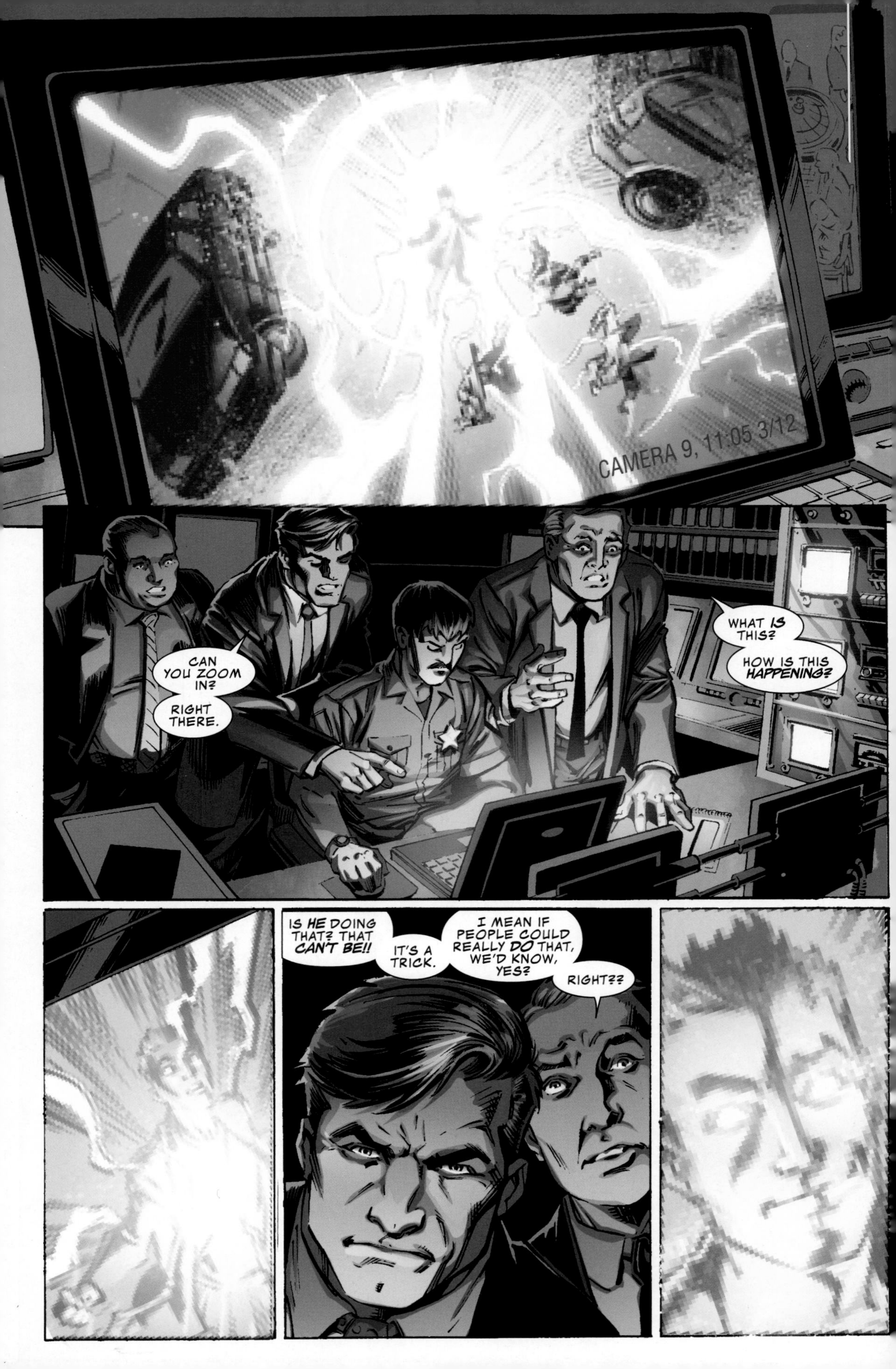
CAMERA 9, 11:05 3/12
CAN YOU ZOOM IN?
RIGHT THERE.
WHAT IS THIS?
HOW IS THIS HAPPENING?
IS HE DOING THAT? THAT CAN'T BE!!
IT'S A TRICK.
I MEAN IF PEOPLE COULD REALLY DO THAT, WE'D KNOW, YES?
RIGHT??

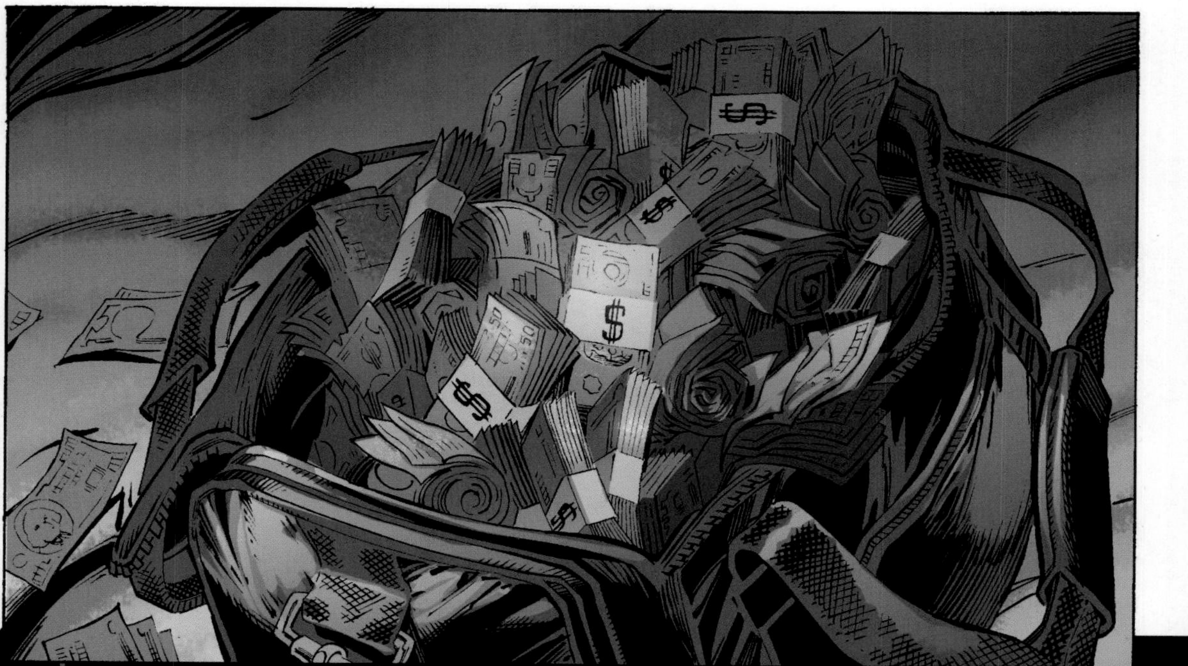

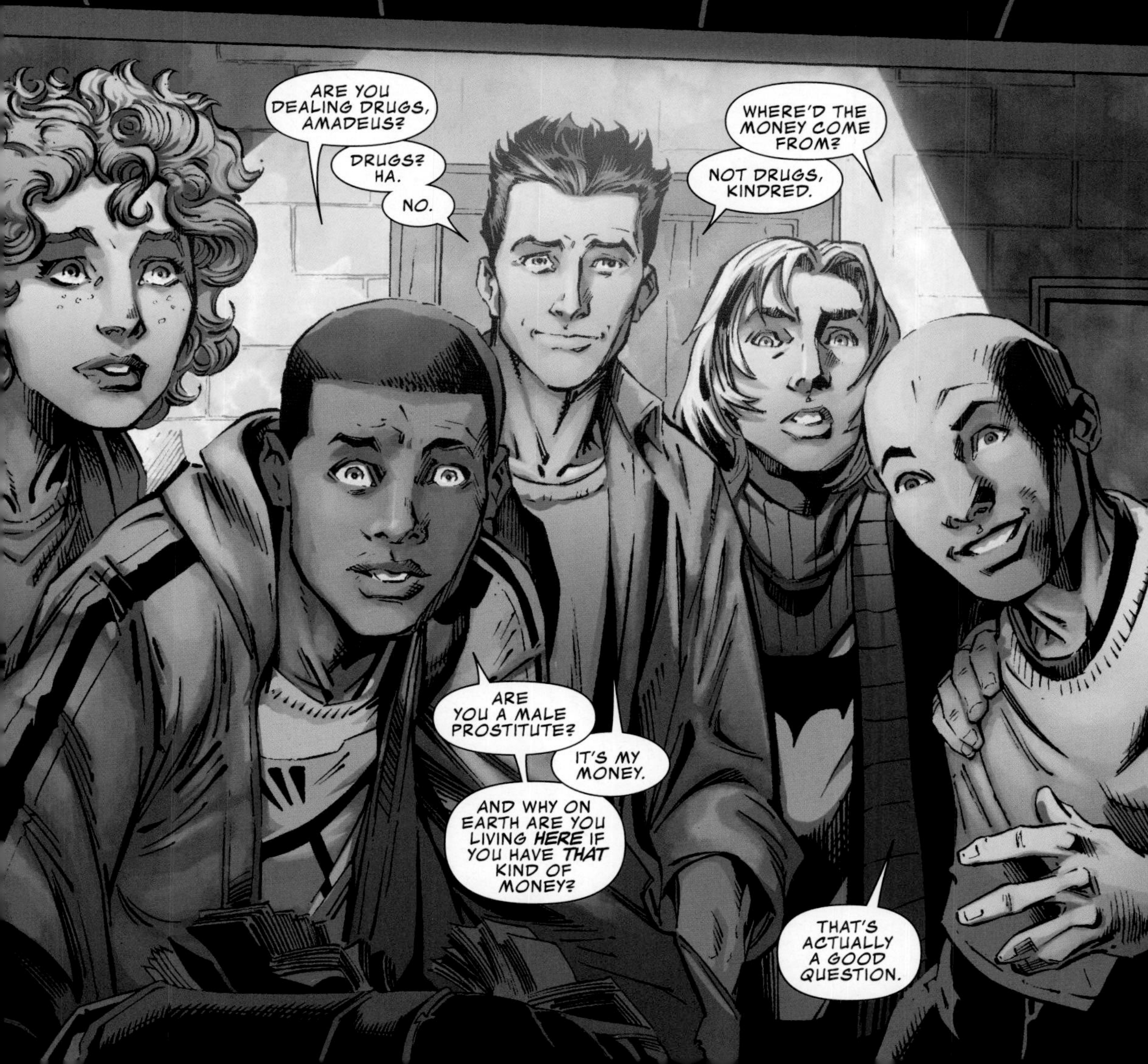
ARE YOU DEALING DRUGS, AMADEUS?
DRUGS? HA.
NO.
WHERE'D THE MONEY COME FROM?
NOT DRUGS, KINDRED.
ARE YOU A MALE PROSTITUTE?
IT'S MY MONEY.
AND WHY ON EARTH ARE YOU LIVING HERE IF YOU HAVE THAT KIND OF MONEY?
THAT'S ACTUALLY A GOOD QUESTION.

WE ARE GOING TO NEED SOME SERIOUS EQUIPMENT, WE CAN'T JUST USE THE SCHOOL STUFF WITHOUT--

WHAT?

I THINK WE ARE GOING TO HAVE TO FIND A PLACE *OFF CAMPUS* TO RUN OUR EXPERIMENTS--

DID YOU STEAL THIS MONEY?

WHAT KIND OF QUESTION IS *THAT*?

ANSWER THE QUESTION. DID YOU *STEAL* THIS MONEY?

OH MY GOD, HE DID.

WHERE'RE YOU GOING?

I DON'T LIKE THIS.

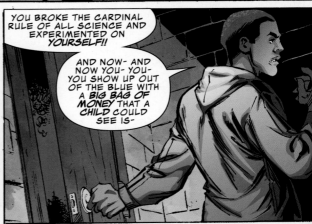

YOU BROKE THE CARDINAL RULE OF ALL SCIENCE AND EXPERIMENTED ON *YOURSELF!!*

AND NOW-- AND NOW YOU-- YOU SHOW UP OUT OF THE BLUE WITH A *BIG BAG OF MONEY* THAT A *CHILD* COULD SEE IS--

DUDE, NO JOKE.

I NEED YOUR HELP.

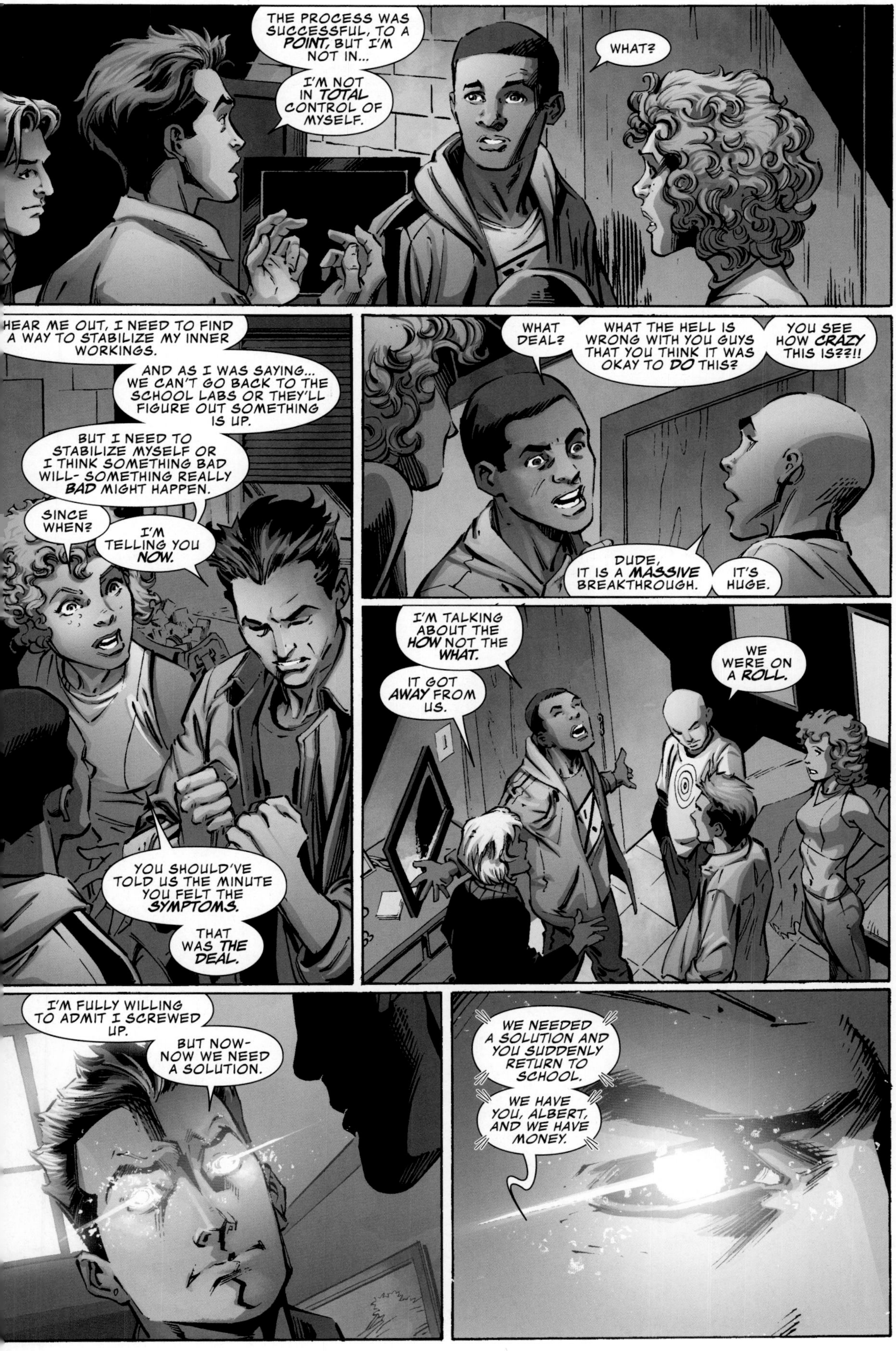
THE PROCESS WAS SUCCESSFUL, TO A POINT, BUT I'M NOT IN...
I'M NOT IN TOTAL CONTROL OF MYSELF.
WHAT?
HEAR ME OUT, I NEED TO FIND A WAY TO STABILIZE MY INNER WORKINGS.
AND AS I WAS SAYING... WE CAN'T GO BACK TO THE SCHOOL LABS OR THEY'LL FIGURE OUT SOMETHING IS UP.
BUT I NEED TO STABILIZE MYSELF OR I THINK SOMETHING BAD WILL- SOMETHING REALLY BAD MIGHT HAPPEN.
SINCE WHEN?
I'M TELLING YOU NOW.
YOU SHOULD'VE TOLD US THE MINUTE YOU FELT THE SYMPTOMS.
THAT WAS THE DEAL.
WHAT DEAL?
WHAT THE HELL IS WRONG WITH YOU GUYS THAT YOU THINK IT WAS OKAY TO DO THIS?
YOU SEE HOW CRAZY THIS IS??!!
DUDE, IT IS A MASSIVE BREAKTHROUGH.
IT'S HUGE.
I'M TALKING ABOUT THE HOW NOT THE WHAT.
IT GOT AWAY FROM US.
WE WERE ON A ROLL.
I'M FULLY WILLING TO ADMIT I SCREWED UP.
BUT NOW- NOW WE NEED A SOLUTION.
WE NEEDED A SOLUTION AND YOU SUDDENLY RETURN TO SCHOOL.
WE HAVE YOU, ALBERT, AND WE HAVE MONEY.

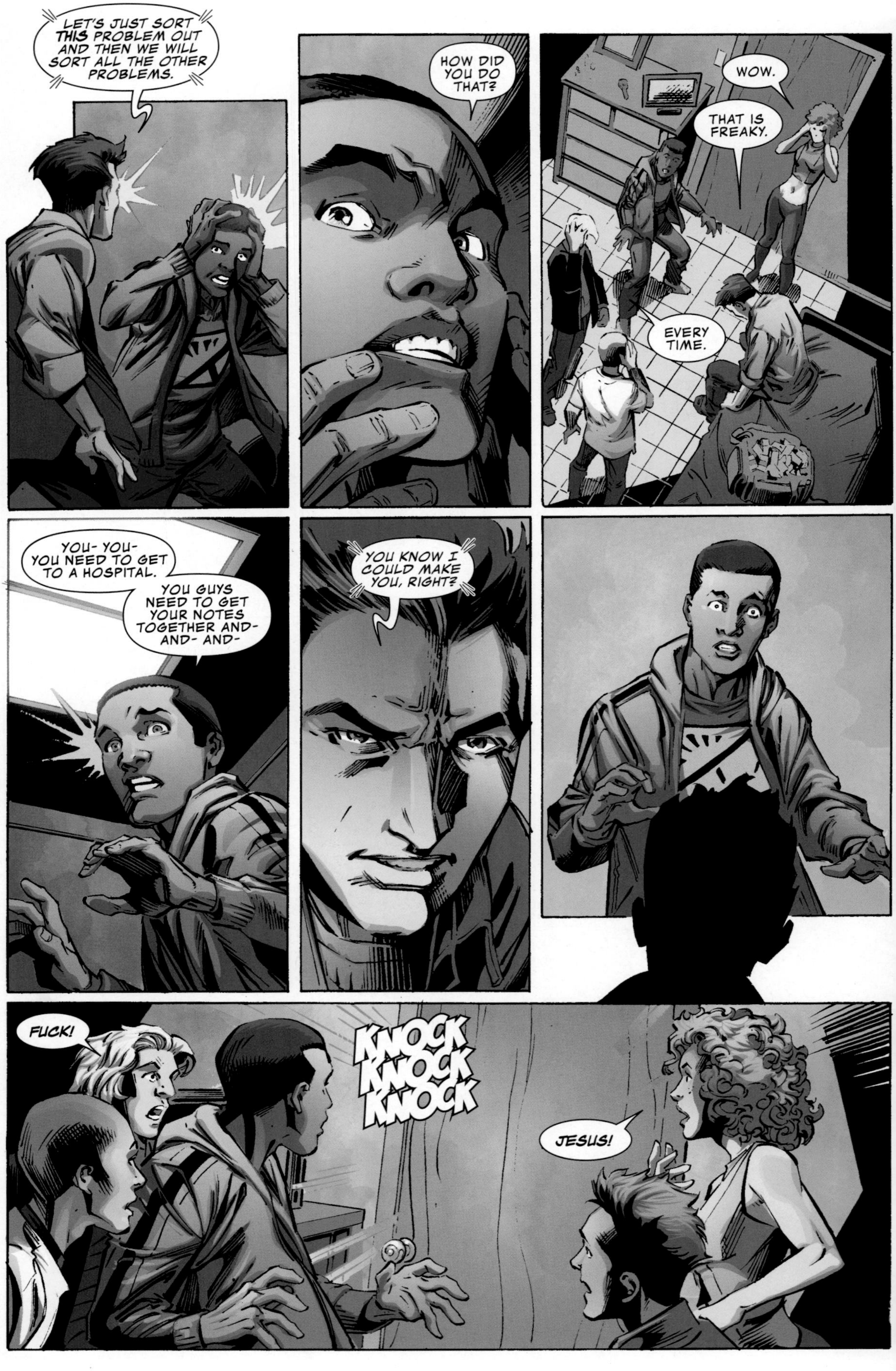
LET'S JUST SORT THIS PROBLEM OUT AND THEN WE WILL SORT ALL THE OTHER PROBLEMS.
HOW DID YOU DO THAT?
WOW.
THAT IS FREAKY.
EVERY TIME.
YOU- YOU- YOU NEED TO GET TO A HOSPITAL.
YOU GUYS NEED TO GET YOUR NOTES TOGETHER AND- AND- AND-
YOU KNOW I COULD MAKE YOU, RIGHT?
FUCK!
KNOCK KNOCK KNOCK
JESUS!

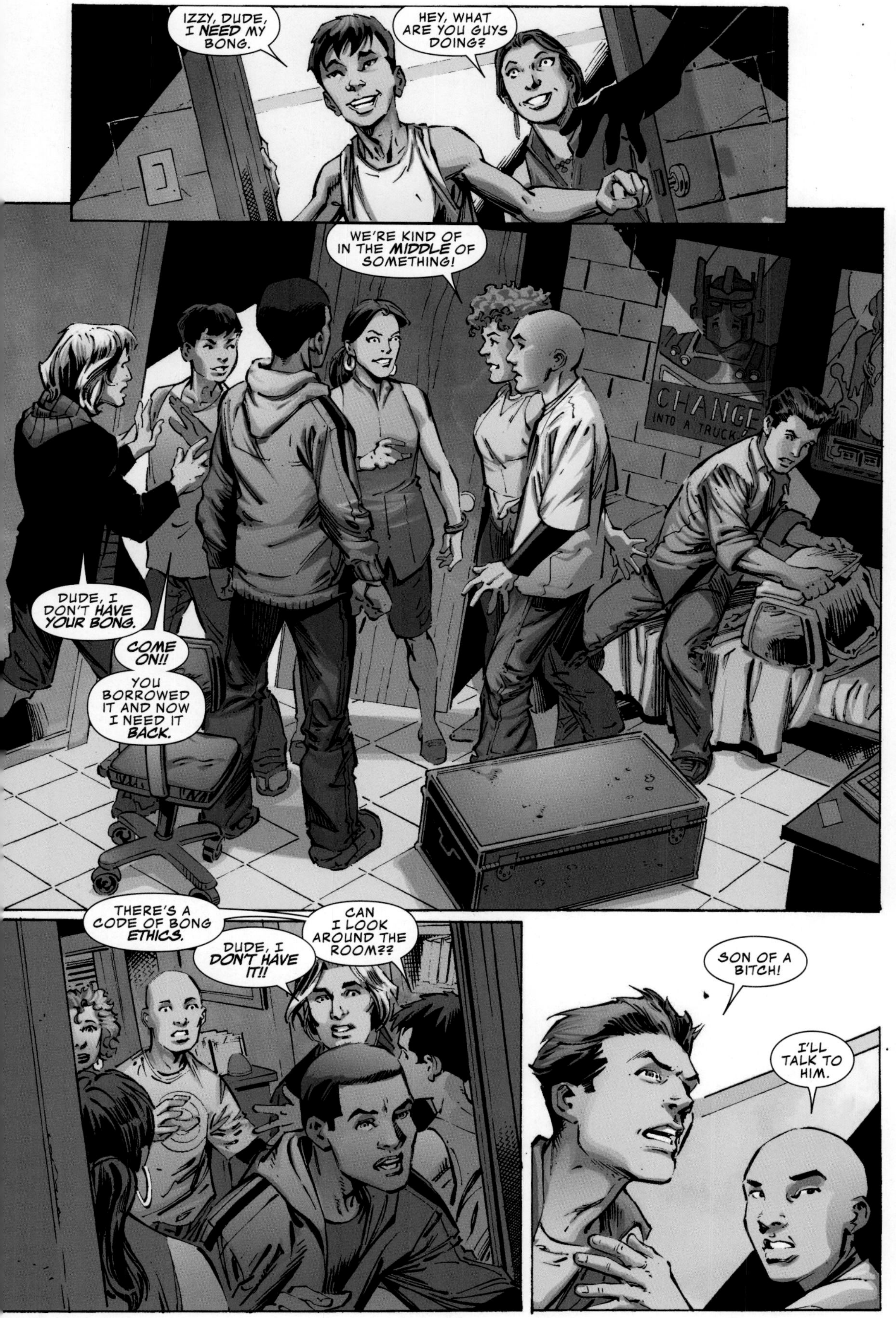
IZZY, DUDE, I NEED MY BONG.
HEY, WHAT ARE YOU GUYS DOING?
WE'RE KIND OF IN THE MIDDLE OF SOMETHING!
CHANGE INTO A TRUCK.
DUDE, I DON'T HAVE YOUR BONG.
COME ON!!
YOU BORROWED IT AND NOW I NEED IT BACK.
THERE'S A CODE OF BONG ETHICS.
DUDE, I DON'T HAVE IT!!
CAN I LOOK AROUND THE ROOM??
SON OF A BITCH!
I'LL TALK TO HIM.

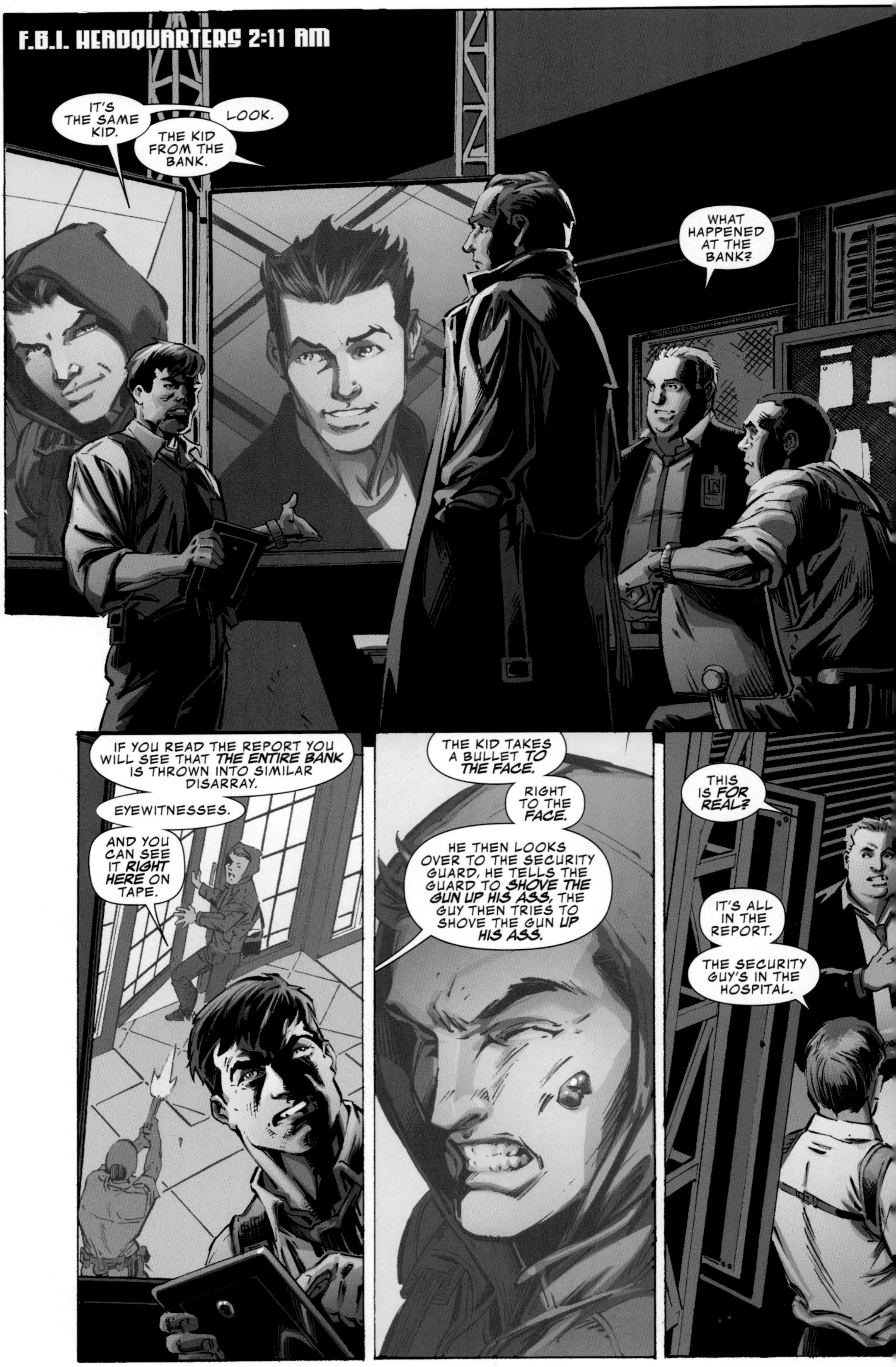
F.B.I. HEADQUARTERS 2:11 AM
LOOK.
IT'S THE SAME KID.
THE KID FROM THE BANK.
WHAT HAPPENED AT THE BANK?
IF YOU READ THE REPORT YOU WILL SEE THAT THE ENTIRE BANK IS THROWN INTO SIMILAR DISARRAY.
EYEWITNESSES.
AND YOU CAN SEE IT RIGHT HERE ON TAPE.
THE KID TAKES A BULLET TO THE FACE.
RIGHT TO THE FACE.
HE THEN LOOKS OVER TO THE SECURITY GUARD, HE TELLS THE GUARD TO SHOVE THE GUN UP HIS ASS, THE GUY THEN TRIES TO SHOVE THE GUN UP HIS ASS.
THIS IS FOR REAL?
IT'S ALL IN THE REPORT.
THE SECURITY GUY'S IN THE HOSPITAL.

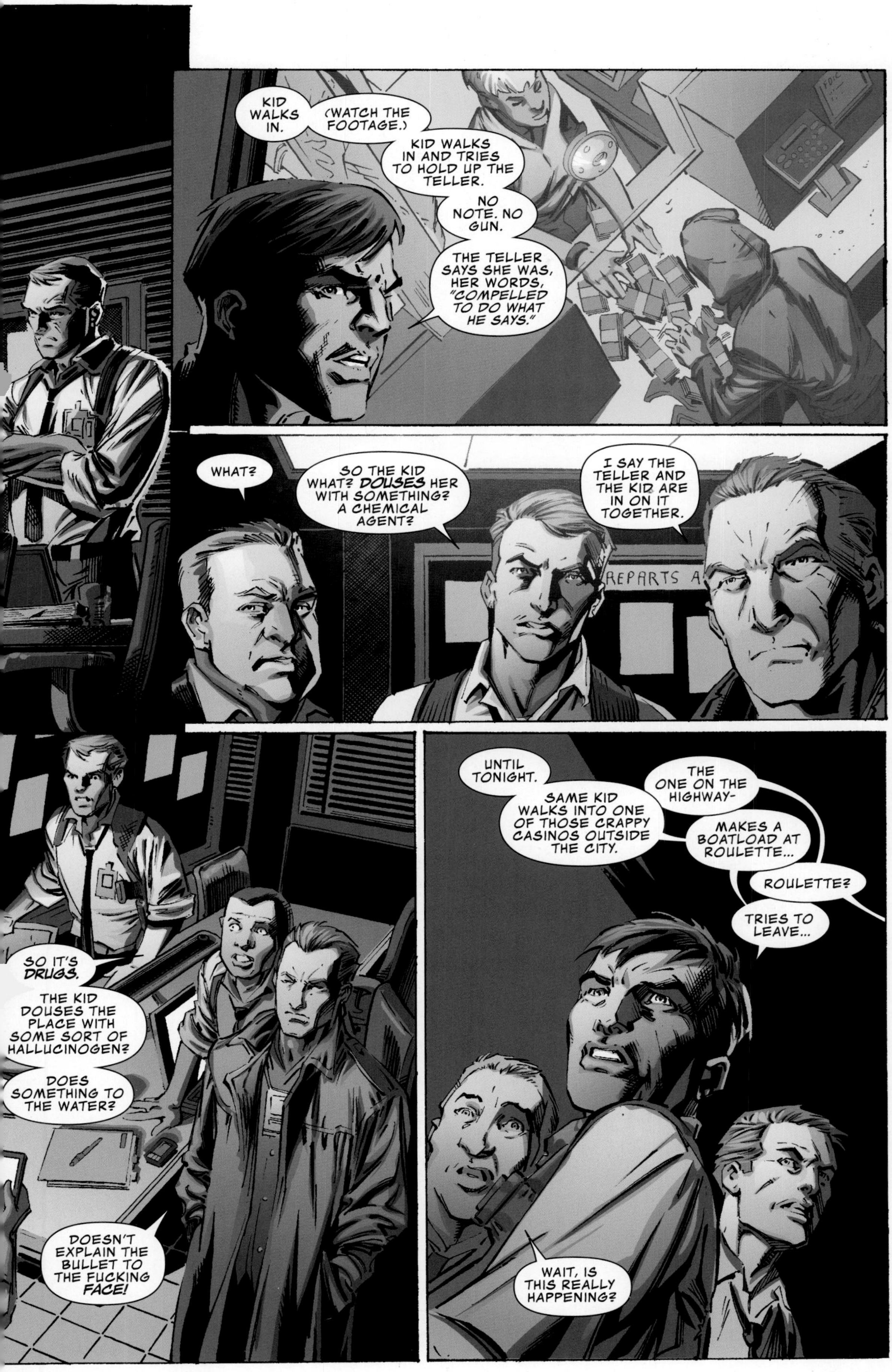

KID WALKS IN.
(WATCH THE FOOTAGE.)
KID WALKS IN AND TRIES TO HOLD UP THE TELLER.
NO NOTE. NO GUN.
THE TELLER SAYS SHE WAS, HER WORDS, "COMPELLED TO DO WHAT HE SAYS."
WHAT?
SO THE KID WHAT? DOUSES HER WITH SOMETHING? A CHEMICAL AGENT?
I SAY THE TELLER AND THE KID ARE IN ON IT TOGETHER.
REPARTS A
SO IT'S DRUGS.
THE KID DOUSES THE PLACE WITH SOME SORT OF HALLUCINOGEN?
DOES SOMETHING TO THE WATER?
DOESN'T EXPLAIN THE BULLET TO THE FUCKING FACE!
UNTIL TONIGHT.
SAME KID WALKS INTO ONE OF THOSE CRAPPY CASINOS OUTSIDE THE CITY.
THE ONE ON THE HIGHWAY-
MAKES A BOATLOAD AT ROULETTE...
ROULETTE?
TRIES TO LEAVE...
WAIT, IS THIS REALLY HAPPENING?

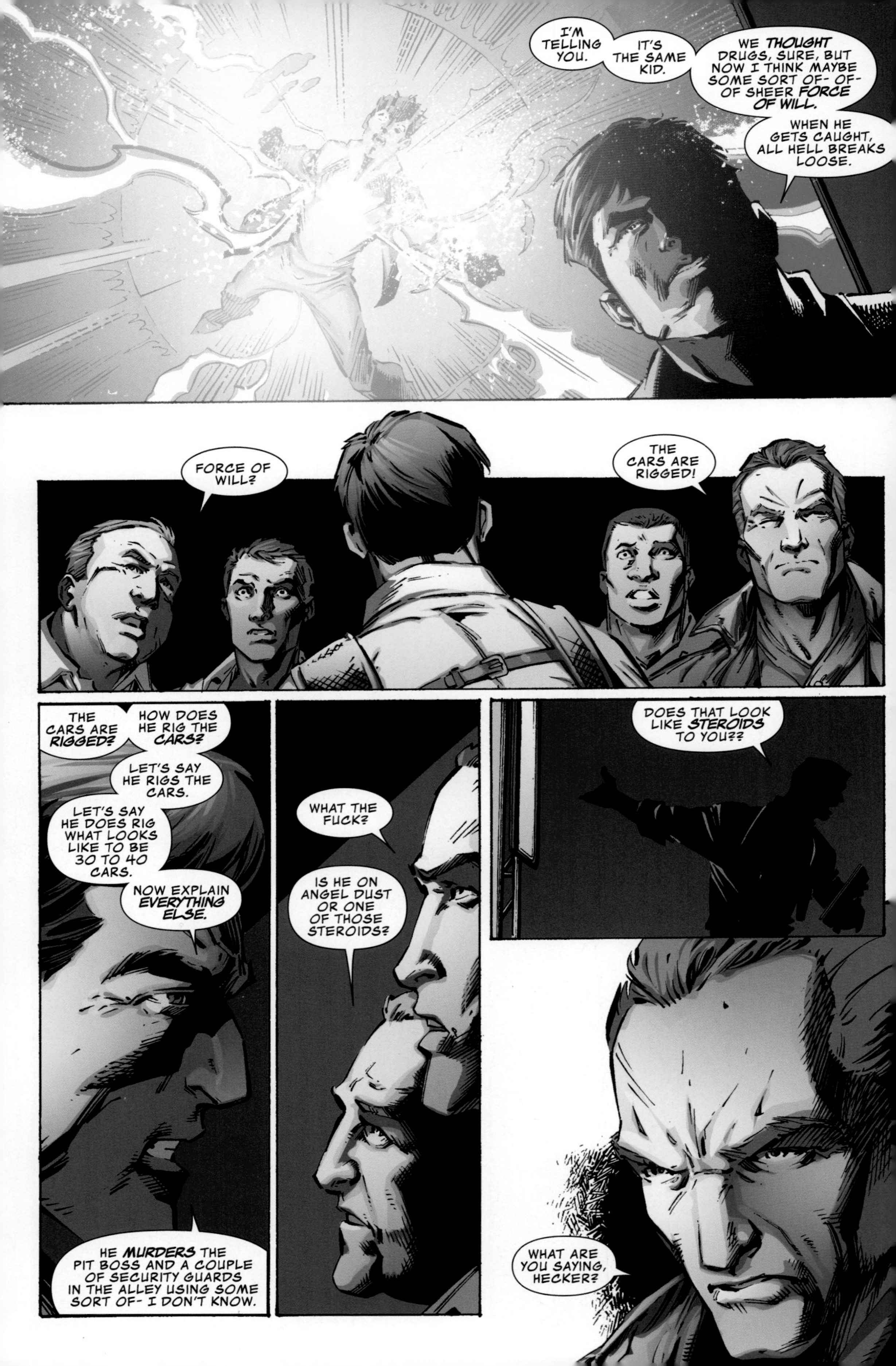
I'M TELLING YOU.
IT'S THE SAME KID.
WE THOUGHT DRUGS, SURE, BUT NOW I THINK MAYBE SOME SORT OF- OF- OF SHEER FORCE OF WILL.
WHEN HE GETS CAUGHT, ALL HELL BREAKS LOOSE.
FORCE OF WILL?
THE CARS ARE RIGGED!
THE CARS ARE RIGGED?
HOW DOES HE RIG THE CARS?
LET'S SAY HE RIGS THE CARS.
LET'S SAY HE DOES RIG WHAT LOOKS LIKE TO BE 30 TO 40 CARS.
NOW EXPLAIN EVERYTHING ELSE.
HE MURDERS THE PIT BOSS AND A COUPLE OF SECURITY GUARDS IN THE ALLEY USING SOME SORT OF- I DON'T KNOW.
WHAT THE FUCK?
IS HE ON ANGEL DUST OR ONE OF THOSE STEROIDS?
DOES THAT LOOK LIKE STEROIDS TO YOU??
WHAT ARE YOU SAYING, HECKER?

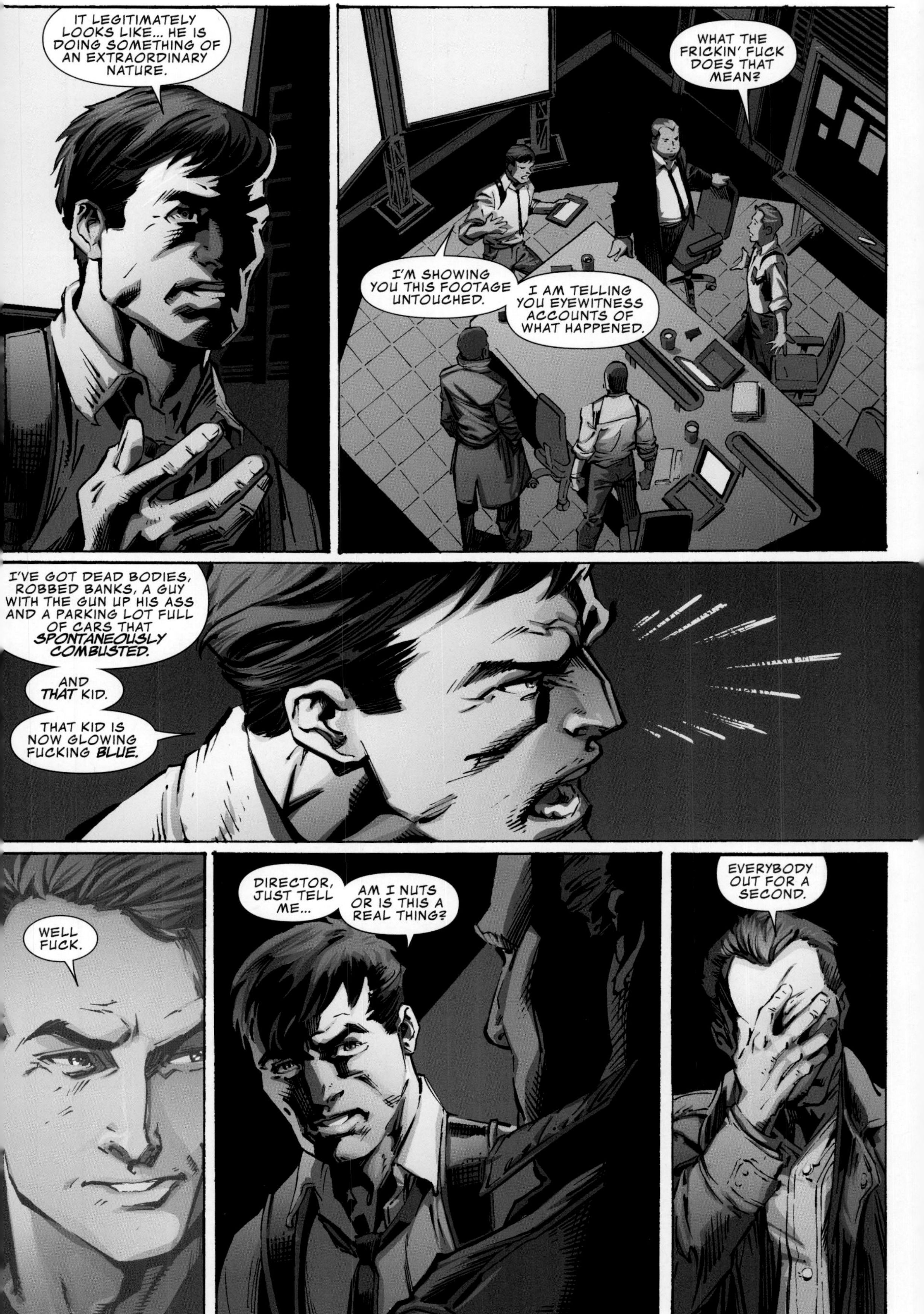
IT LEGITIMATELY LOOKS LIKE... HE IS DOING SOMETHING OF AN EXTRAORDINARY NATURE.
WHAT THE FRICKIN' FUCK DOES THAT MEAN?
I'M SHOWING YOU THIS FOOTAGE UNTOUCHED.
I AM TELLING YOU EYEWITNESS ACCOUNTS OF WHAT HAPPENED.
I'VE GOT DEAD BODIES, ROBBED BANKS, A GUY WITH THE GUN UP HIS ASS AND A PARKING LOT FULL OF CARS THAT SPONTANEOUSLY COMBUSTED.
AND THAT KID.
THAT KID IS NOW GLOWING FUCKING BLUE.
WELL FUCK.
DIRECTOR, JUST TELL ME...
AM I NUTS OR IS THIS A REAL THING?
EVERYBODY OUT FOR A SECOND.

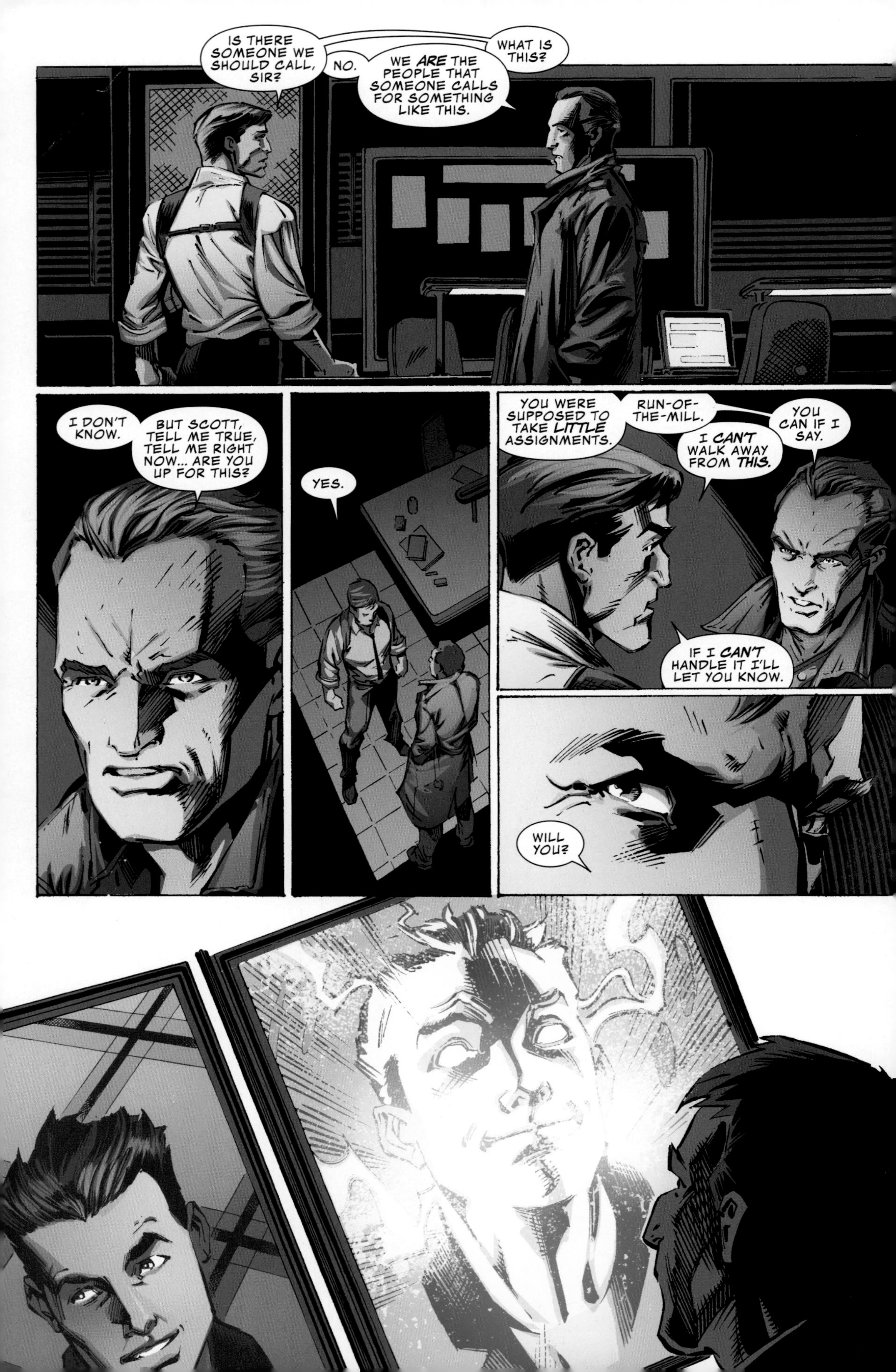
IS THERE SOMEONE WE SHOULD CALL, SIR?
WHAT IS THIS?
NO.
WE ARE THE PEOPLE THAT SOMEONE CALLS FOR SOMETHING LIKE THIS.
I DON'T KNOW.
BUT SCOTT, TELL ME TRUE, TELL ME RIGHT NOW... ARE YOU UP FOR THIS?
YES.
YOU WERE SUPPOSED TO TAKE LITTLE ASSIGNMENTS.
RUN-OF-THE-MILL.
I CAN'T WALK AWAY FROM THIS.
YOU CAN IF I SAY.
IF I CAN'T HANDLE IT I'LL LET YOU KNOW.
WILL YOU?

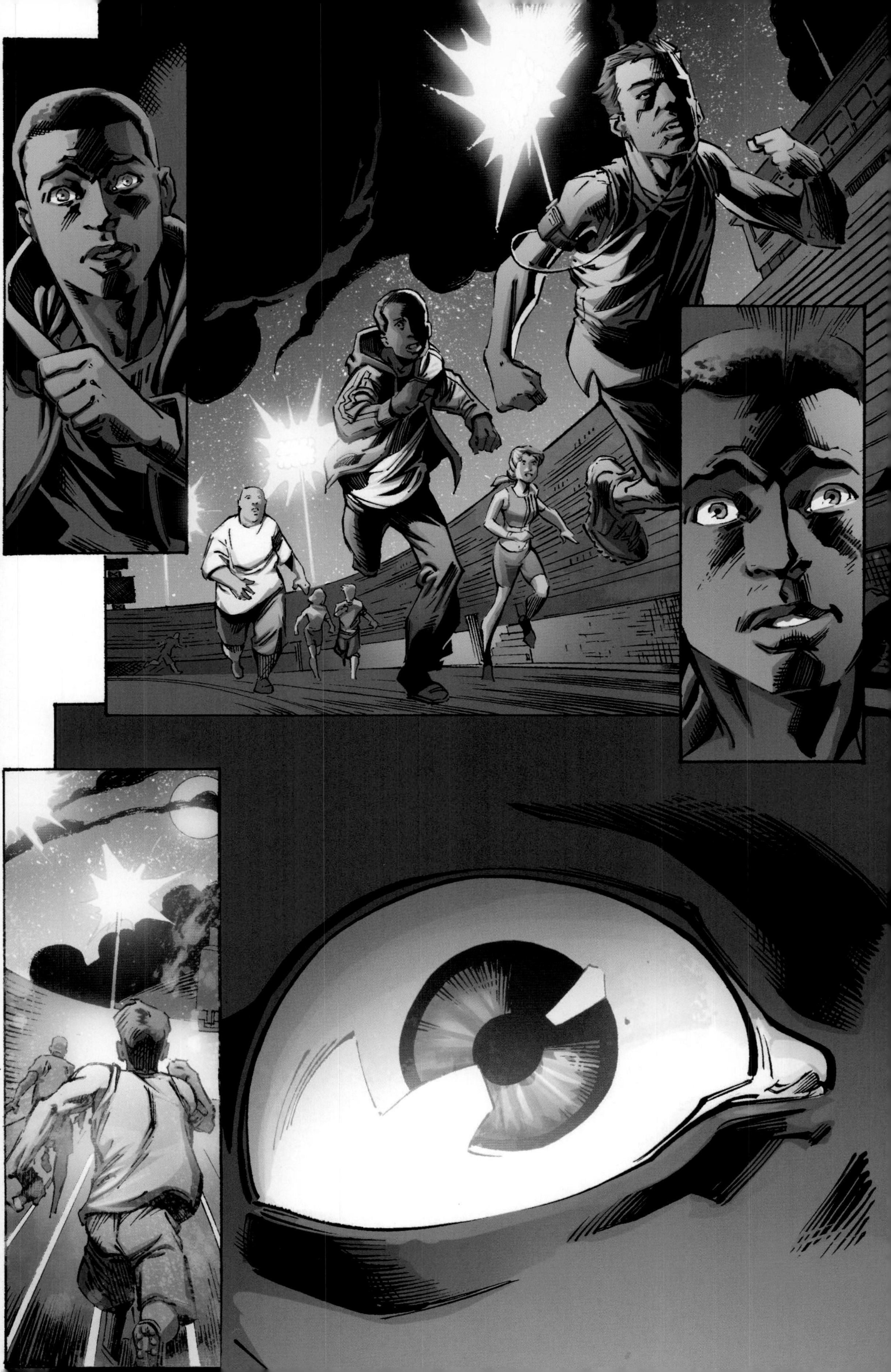

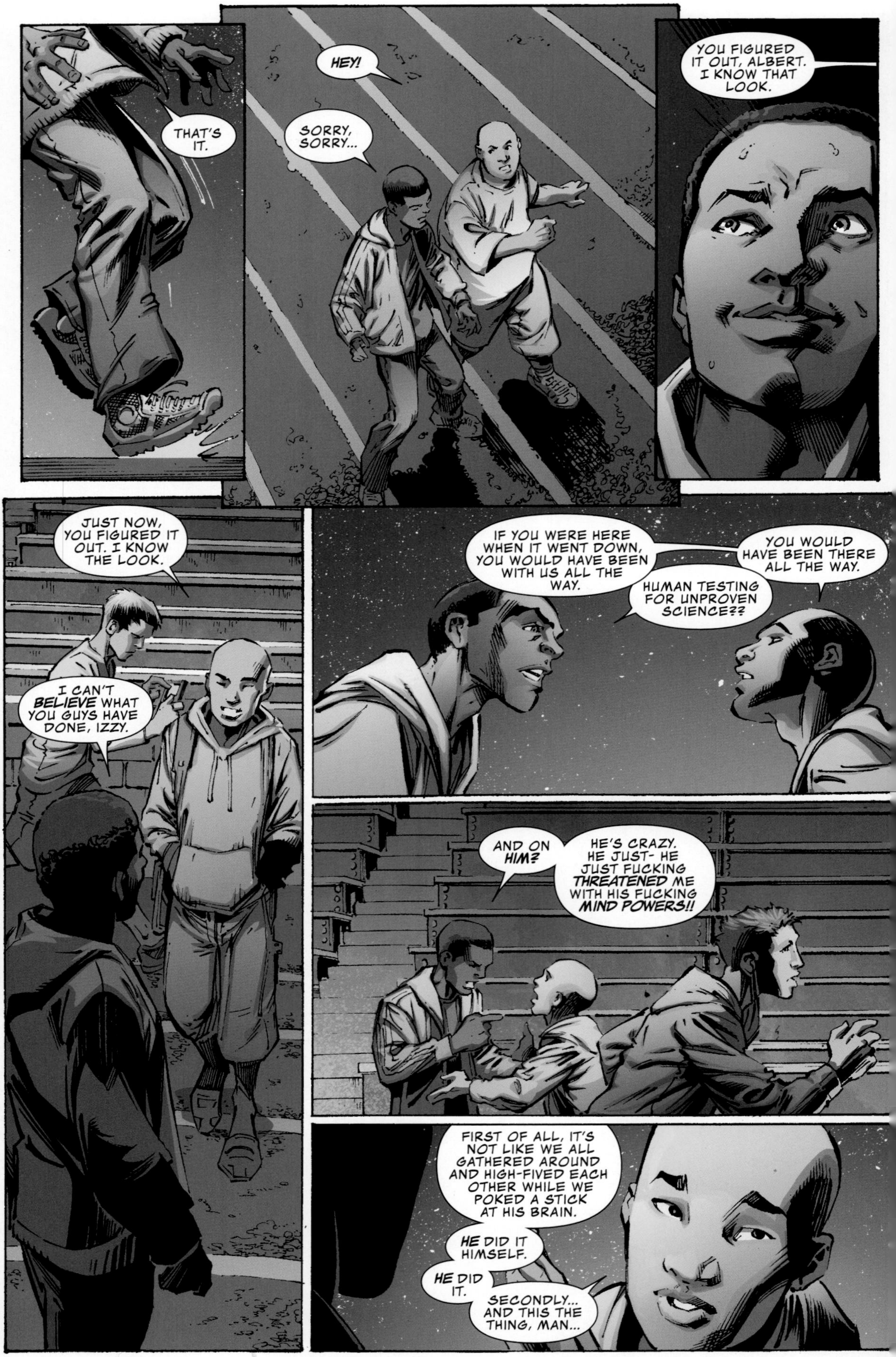
THAT'S IT.
HEY!
SORRY, SORRY...
YOU FIGURED IT OUT, ALBERT. I KNOW THAT LOOK.
JUST NOW, YOU FIGURED IT OUT. I KNOW THE LOOK.
I CAN'T BELIEVE WHAT YOU GUYS HAVE DONE, IZZY.
IF YOU WERE HERE WHEN IT WENT DOWN, YOU WOULD HAVE BEEN WITH US ALL THE WAY.
YOU WOULD HAVE BEEN THERE ALL THE WAY.
HUMAN TESTING FOR UNPROVEN SCIENCE??
AND ON HIM?
HE'S CRAZY. HE JUST- HE JUST FUCKING THREATENED ME WITH HIS FUCKING MIND POWERS!!
FIRST OF ALL, IT'S NOT LIKE WE ALL GATHERED AROUND AND HIGH-FIVED EACH OTHER WHILE WE POKED A STICK AT HIS BRAIN.
HE DID IT HIMSELF.
HE DID IT.
SECONDLY... AND THIS THE THING, MAN...

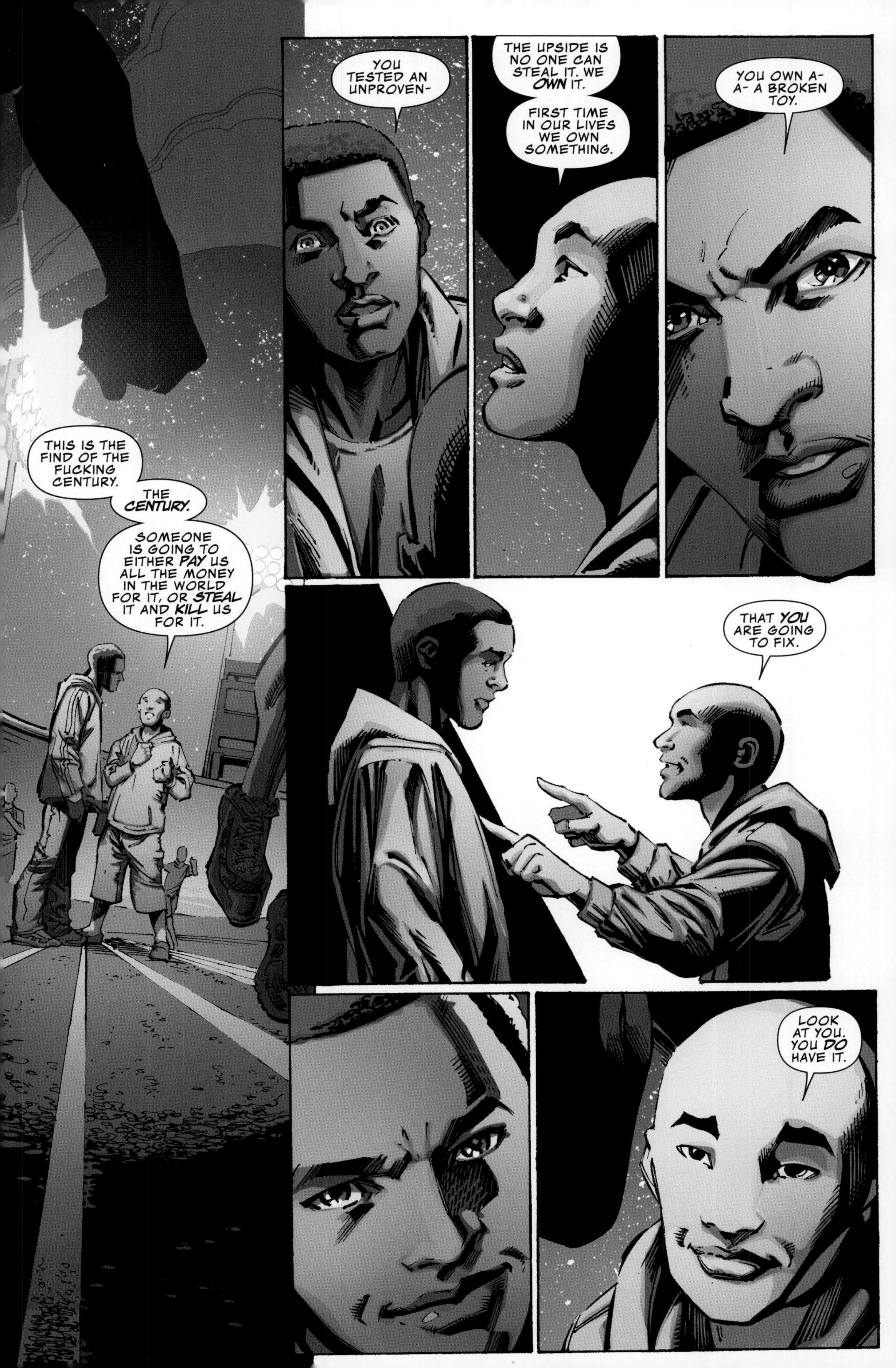
THIS IS THE FIND OF THE FUCKING CENTURY.
THE CENTURY.
SOMEONE IS GOING TO EITHER PAY US ALL THE MONEY IN THE WORLD FOR IT, OR STEAL IT AND KILL US FOR IT.
YOU TESTED AN UNPROVEN-
THE UPSIDE IS NO ONE CAN STEAL IT. WE OWN IT.
FIRST TIME IN OUR LIVES WE OWN SOMETHING.
YOU OWN A- A- A BROKEN TOY.
THAT YOU ARE GOING TO FIX.
LOOK AT YOU. YOU DO HAVE IT.

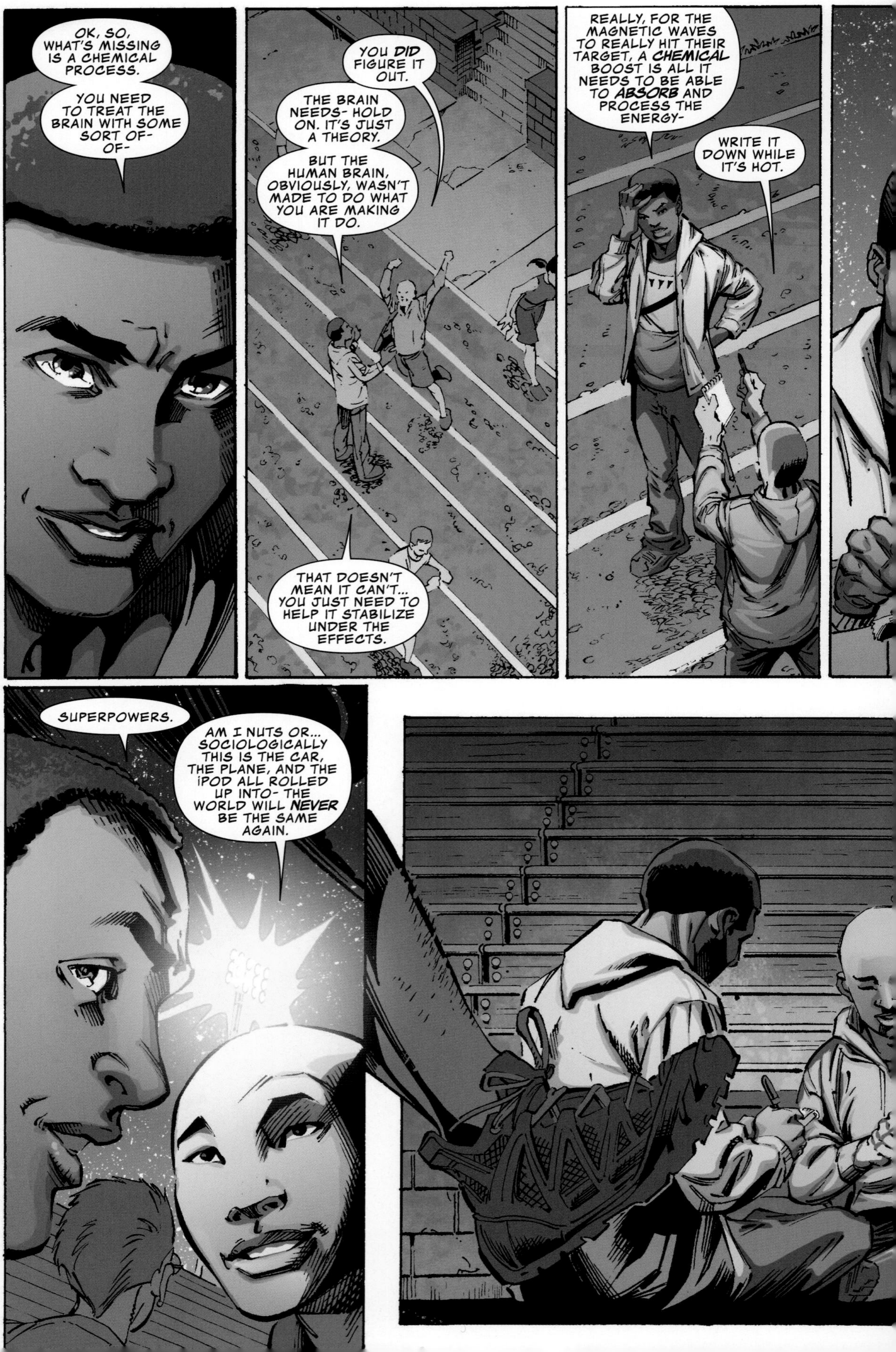
OK, SO, WHAT'S MISSING IS A CHEMICAL PROCESS.
YOU NEED TO TREAT THE BRAIN WITH SOME SORT OF- OF-
YOU DID FIGURE IT OUT.
THE BRAIN NEEDS- HOLD ON. IT'S JUST A THEORY.
BUT THE HUMAN BRAIN, OBVIOUSLY, WASN'T MADE TO DO WHAT YOU ARE MAKING IT DO.
THAT DOESN'T MEAN IT CAN'T... YOU JUST NEED TO HELP IT STABILIZE UNDER THE EFFECTS.
REALLY, FOR THE MAGNETIC WAVES TO REALLY HIT THEIR TARGET, A CHEMICAL BOOST IS ALL IT NEEDS TO BE ABLE TO ABSORB AND PROCESS THE ENERGY-
WRITE IT DOWN WHILE IT'S HOT.
SUPERPOWERS.
AM I NUTS OR... SOCIOLOGICALLY THIS IS THE CAR, THE PLANE, AND THE iPOD ALL ROLLED UP INTO- THE WORLD WILL NEVER BE THE SAME AGAIN.

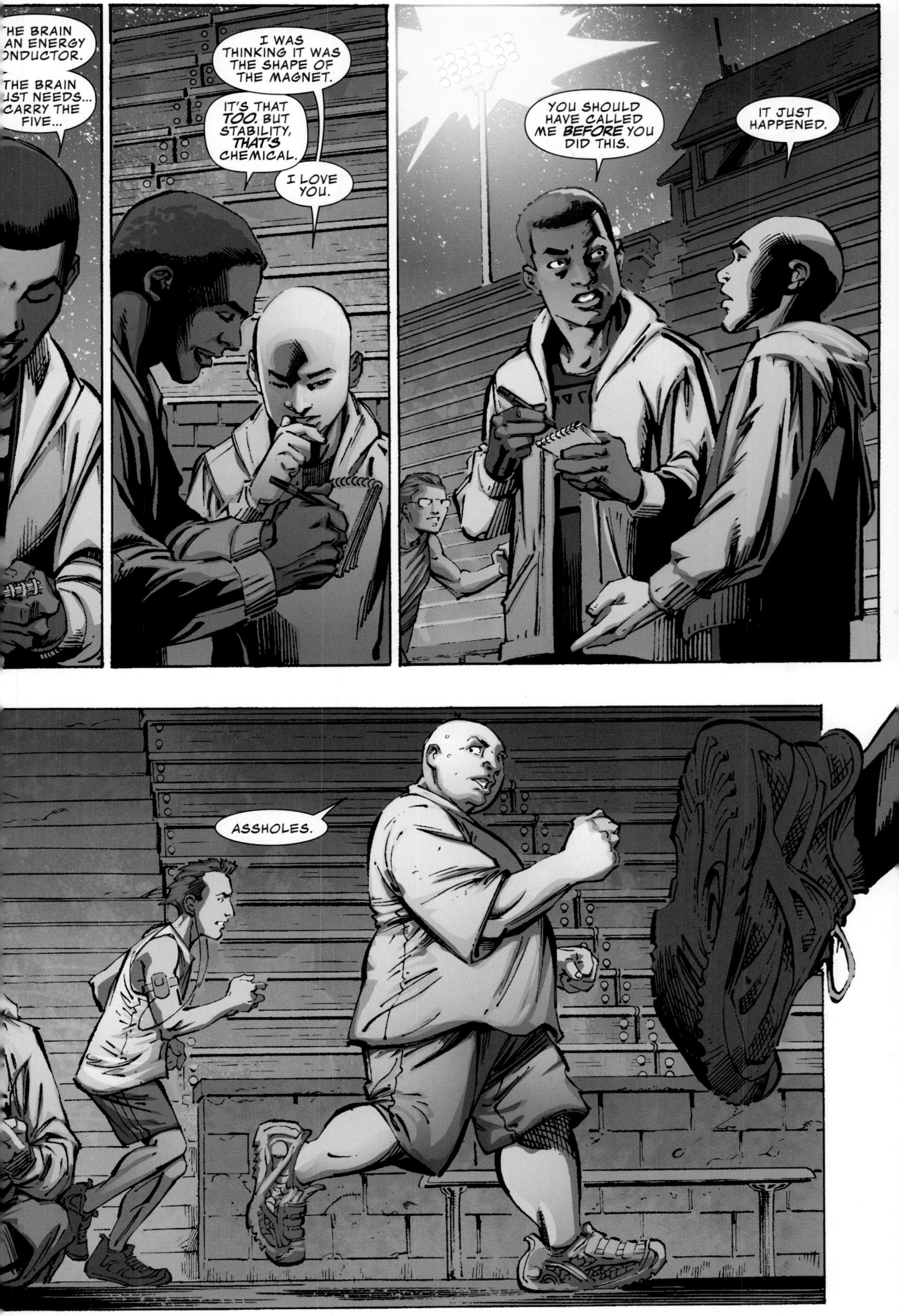
THE BRAIN AN ENERGY ONDUCTOR.
THE BRAIN UST NEEDS... CARRY THE FIVE...
I WAS THINKING IT WAS THE SHAPE OF THE MAGNET.
IT'S THAT TOO. BUT STABILITY, THAT'S CHEMICAL.
I LOVE YOU.
YOU SHOULD HAVE CALLED ME BEFORE YOU DID THIS.
IT JUST HAPPENED.
ASSHOLES.

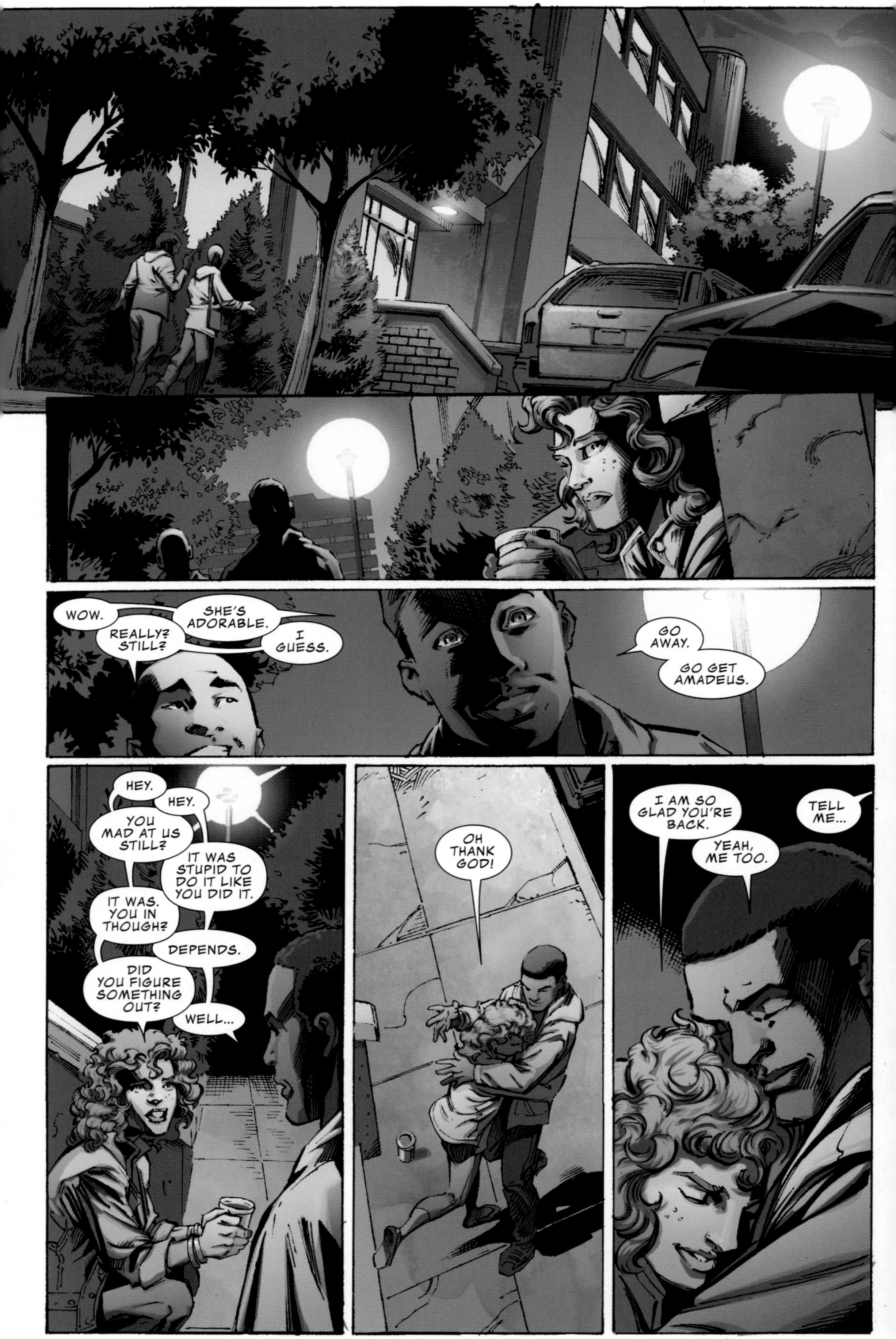
WOW.
SHE'S ADORABLE.
REALLY? STILL?
I GUESS.
GO AWAY.
GO GET AMADEUS.
HEY.
HEY.
YOU MAD AT US STILL?
IT WAS STUPID TO DO IT LIKE YOU DID IT.
IT WAS. YOU IN THOUGH?
DEPENDS.
DID YOU FIGURE SOMETHING OUT?
WELL...
OH THANK GOD!
I AM SO GLAD YOU'RE BACK.
YEAH, ME TOO.
TELL ME...

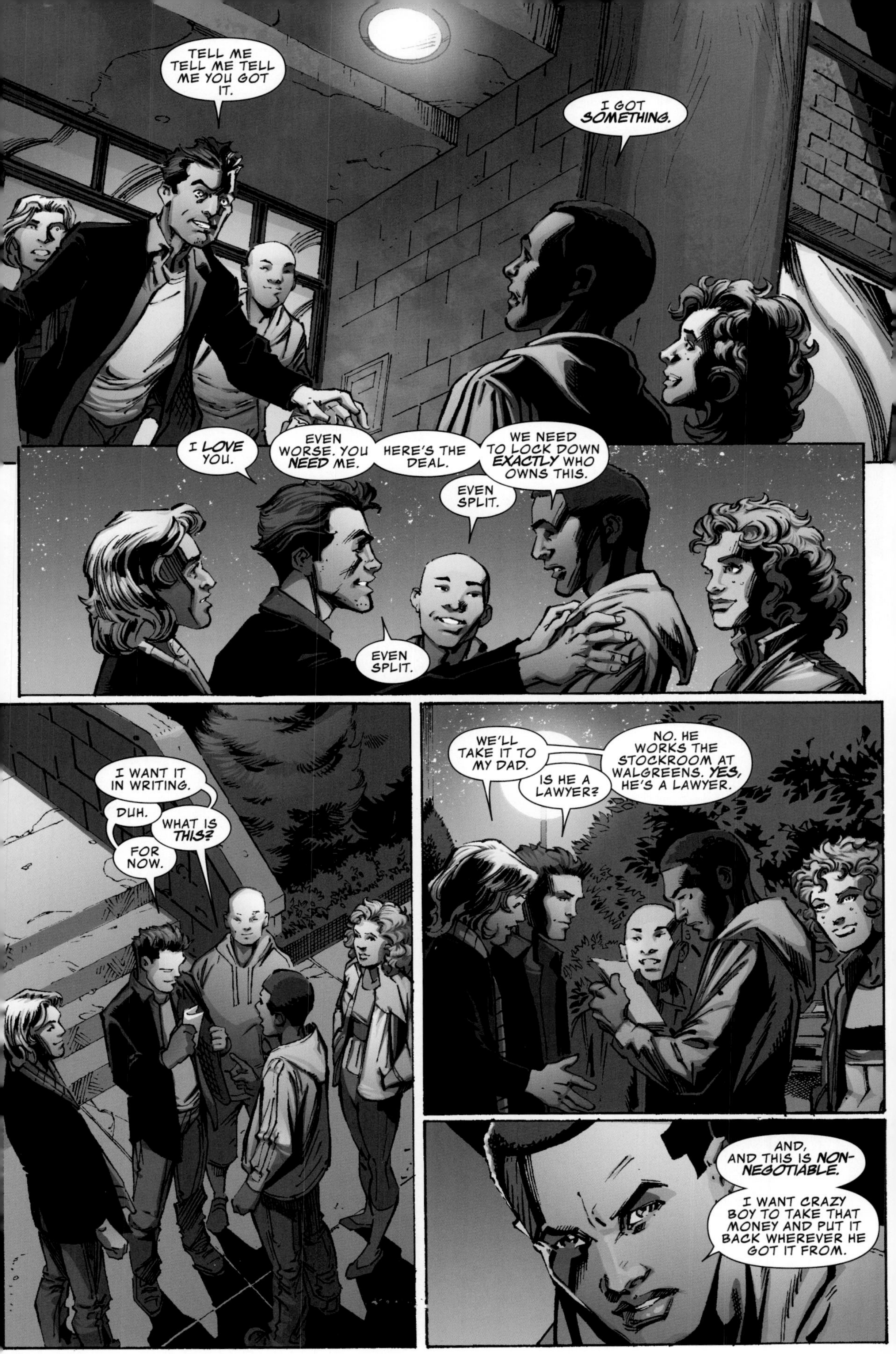
TELL ME TELL ME TELL ME YOU GOT IT.
I GOT SOMETHING.
I LOVE YOU.
EVEN WORSE. YOU NEED ME.
HERE'S THE DEAL.
WE NEED TO LOCK DOWN EXACTLY WHO OWNS THIS.
EVEN SPLIT.
EVEN SPLIT.
I WANT IT IN WRITING.
DUH.
WHAT IS THIS?
FOR NOW.
WE'LL TAKE IT TO MY DAD.
IS HE A LAWYER?
NO. HE WORKS THE STOCKROOM AT WALGREENS. YES, HE'S A LAWYER.
AND, AND THIS IS NON-NEGOTIABLE.
I WANT CRAZY BOY TO TAKE THAT MONEY AND PUT IT BACK WHEREVER HE GOT IT FROM.

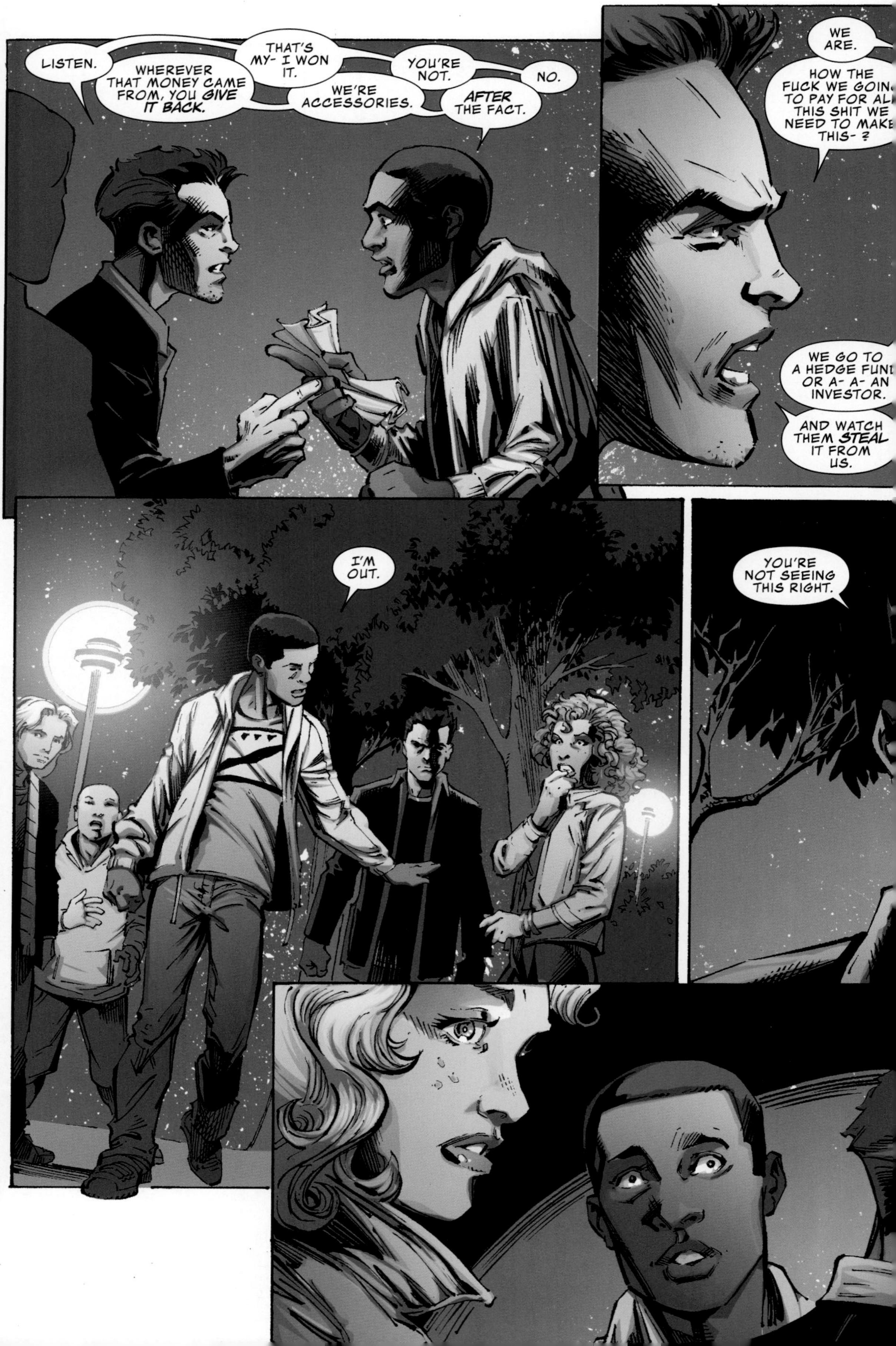

LISTEN.
WHEREVER THAT MONEY CAME FROM, YOU GIVE IT BACK.
THAT'S MY- I WON IT.
WE'RE ACCESSORIES.
YOU'RE NOT.
AFTER THE FACT.
NO.
WE ARE.
HOW THE FUCK WE GOIN TO PAY FOR AL THIS SHIT WE NEED TO MAKE THIS- ?
WE GO TO A HEDGE FUN OR A- A- AN INVESTOR.
AND WATCH THEM STEAL IT FROM US.
I'M OUT.
YOU'RE NOT SEEING THIS RIGHT.

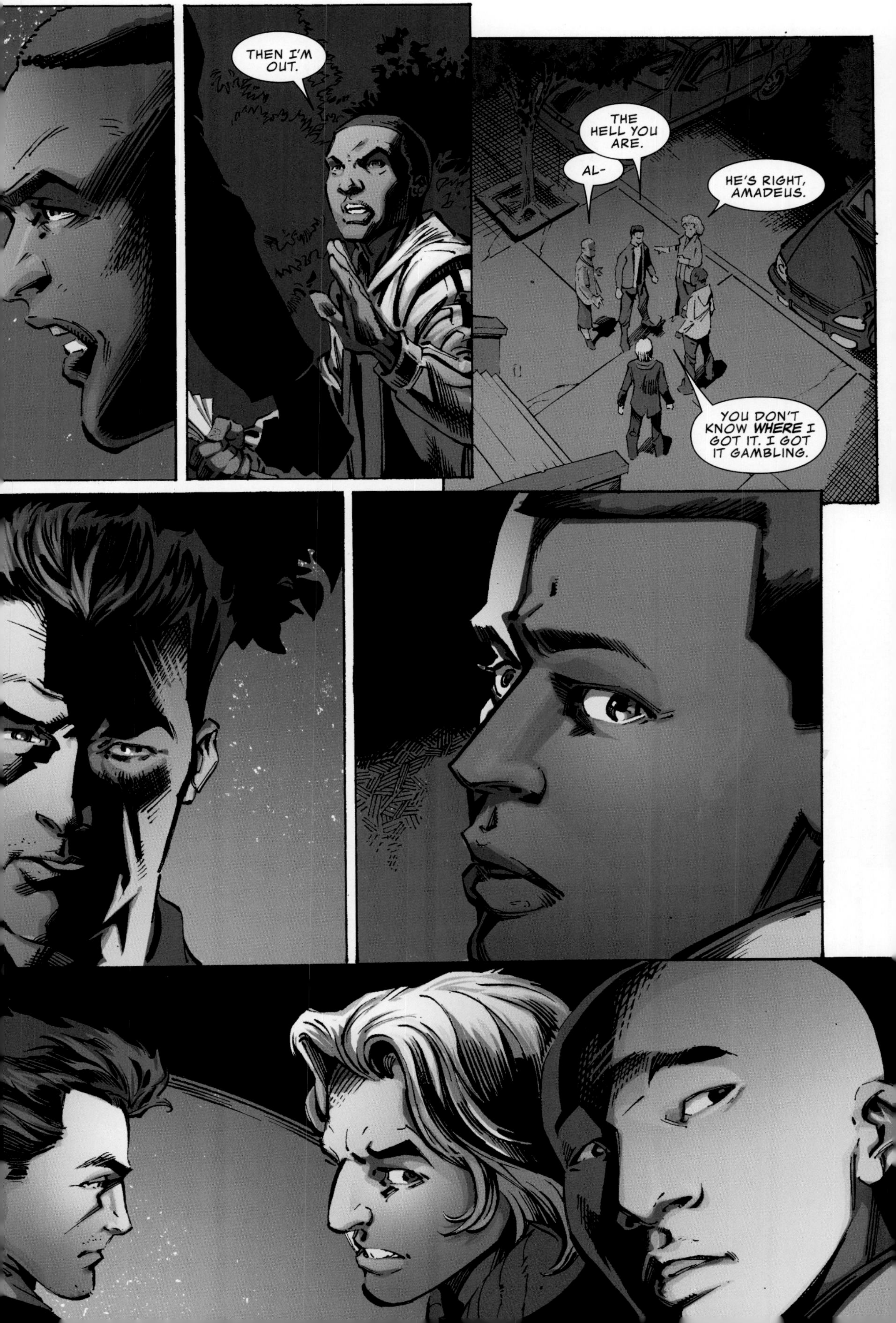
THEN I'M OUT.
AL-
THE HELL YOU ARE.
HE'S RIGHT, AMADEUS.
YOU DON'T KNOW WHERE I GOT IT. I GOT IT GAMBLING.

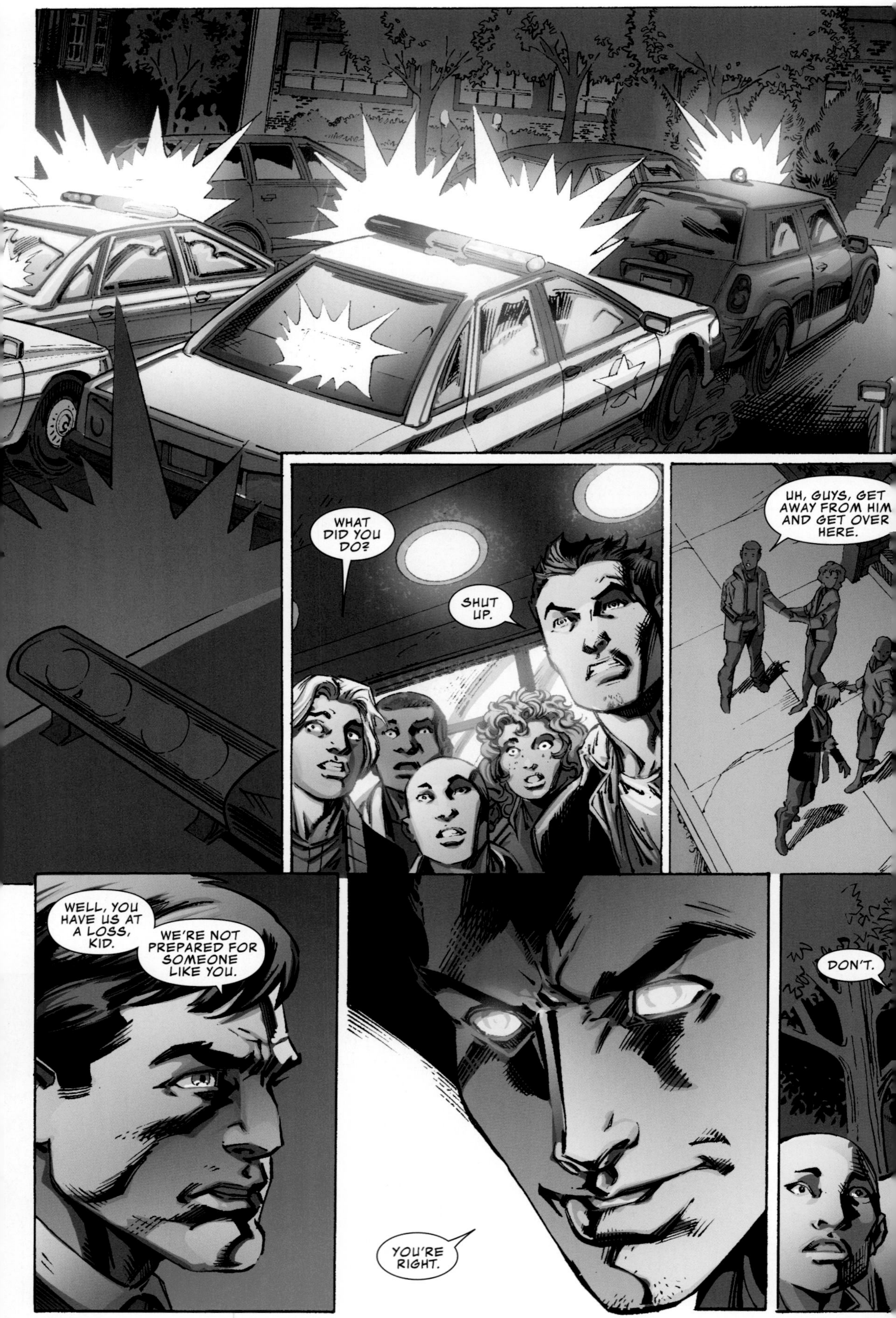
WHAT DID YOU DO?
SHUT UP.
UH, GUYS, GET AWAY FROM HIM AND GET OVER HERE.
WELL, YOU HAVE US AT A LOSS, KID.
WE'RE NOT PREPARED FOR SOMEONE LIKE YOU.
YOU'RE RIGHT.
DON'T.

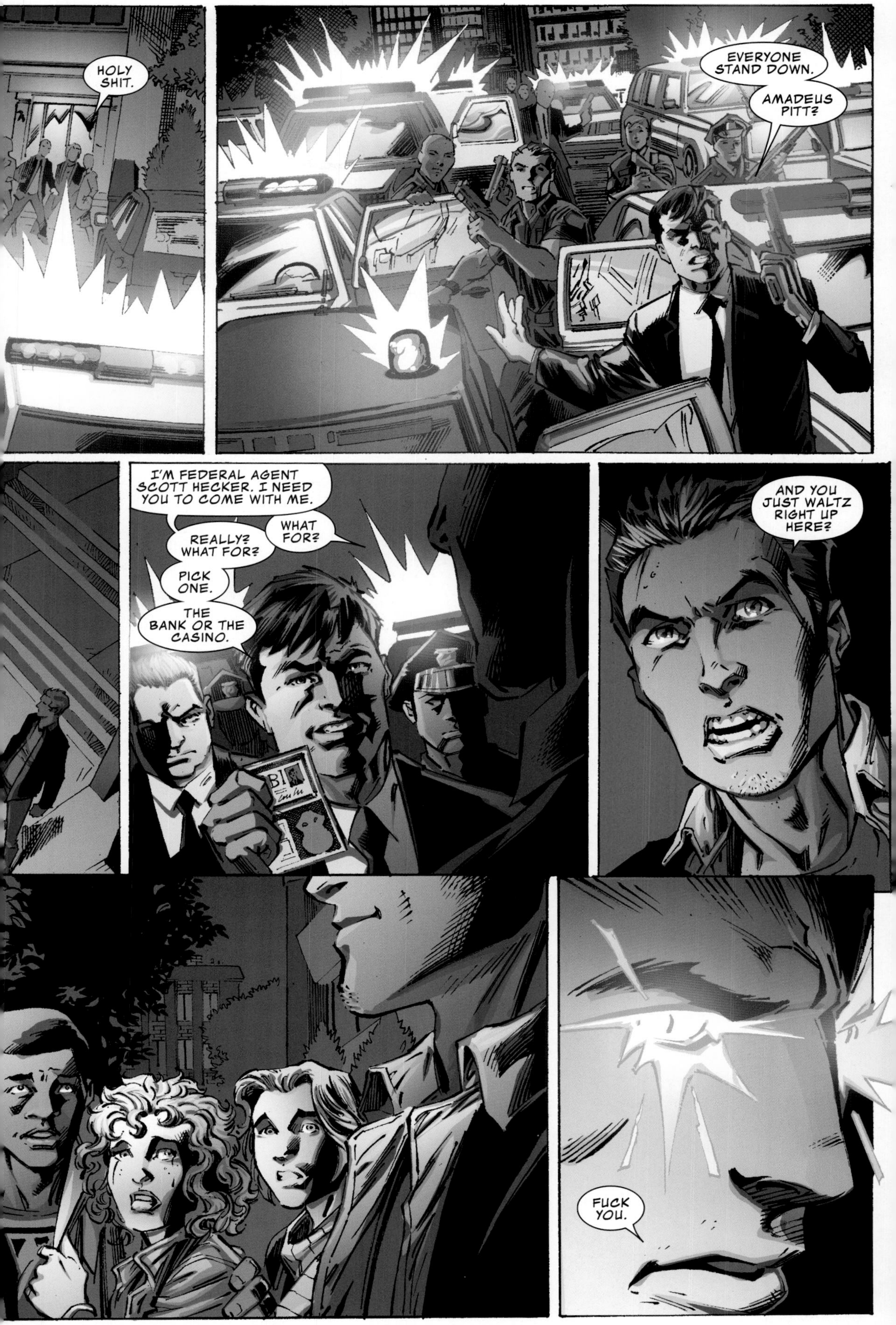
HOLY SHIT.
EVERYONE STAND DOWN.
AMADEUS PITT?
I'M FEDERAL AGENT SCOTT HECKER. I NEED YOU TO COME WITH ME.
WHAT FOR?
REALLY? WHAT FOR?
PICK ONE.
THE BANK OR THE CASINO.
AND YOU JUST WALTZ RIGHT UP HERE?
FUCK YOU.

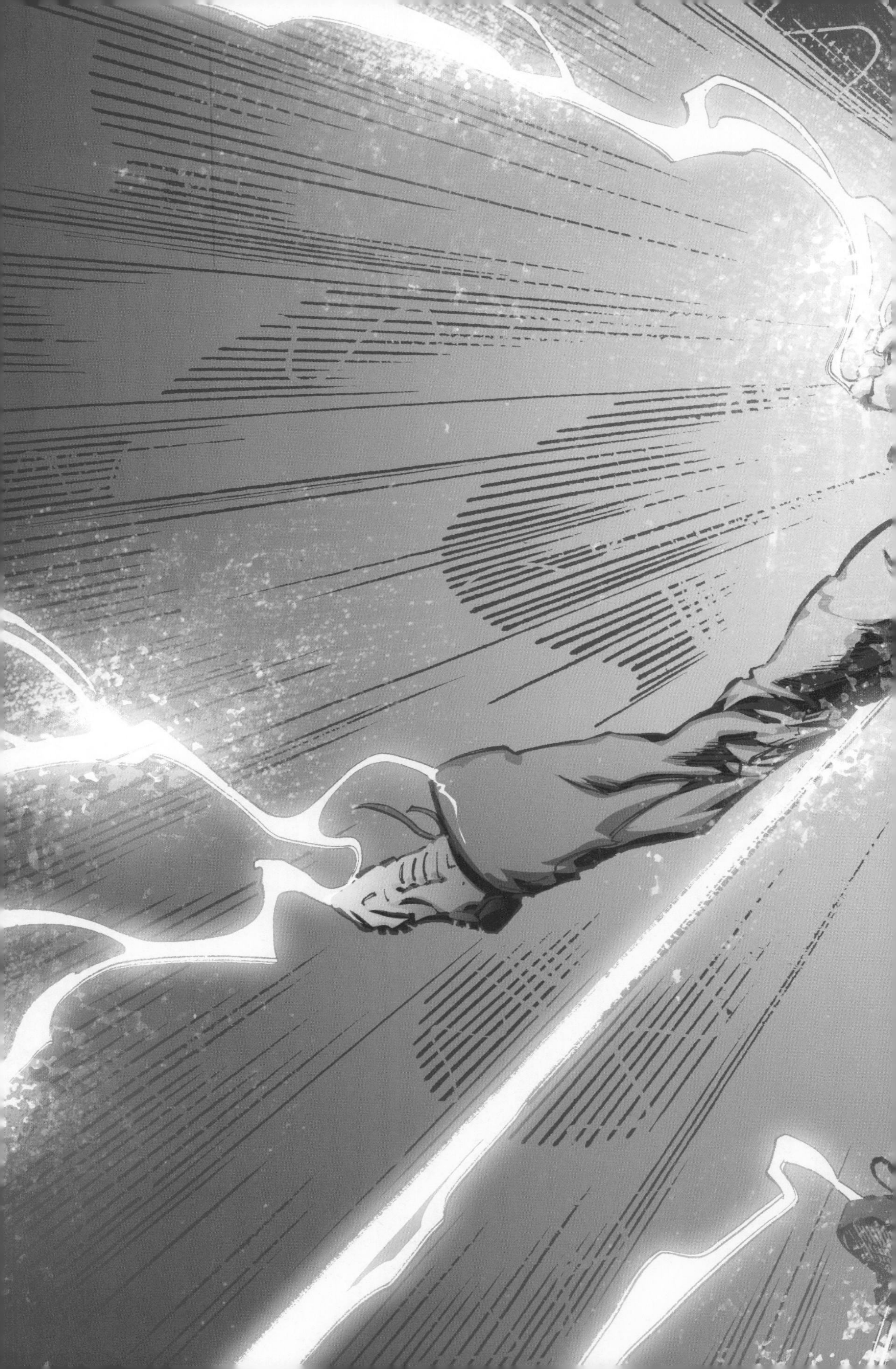

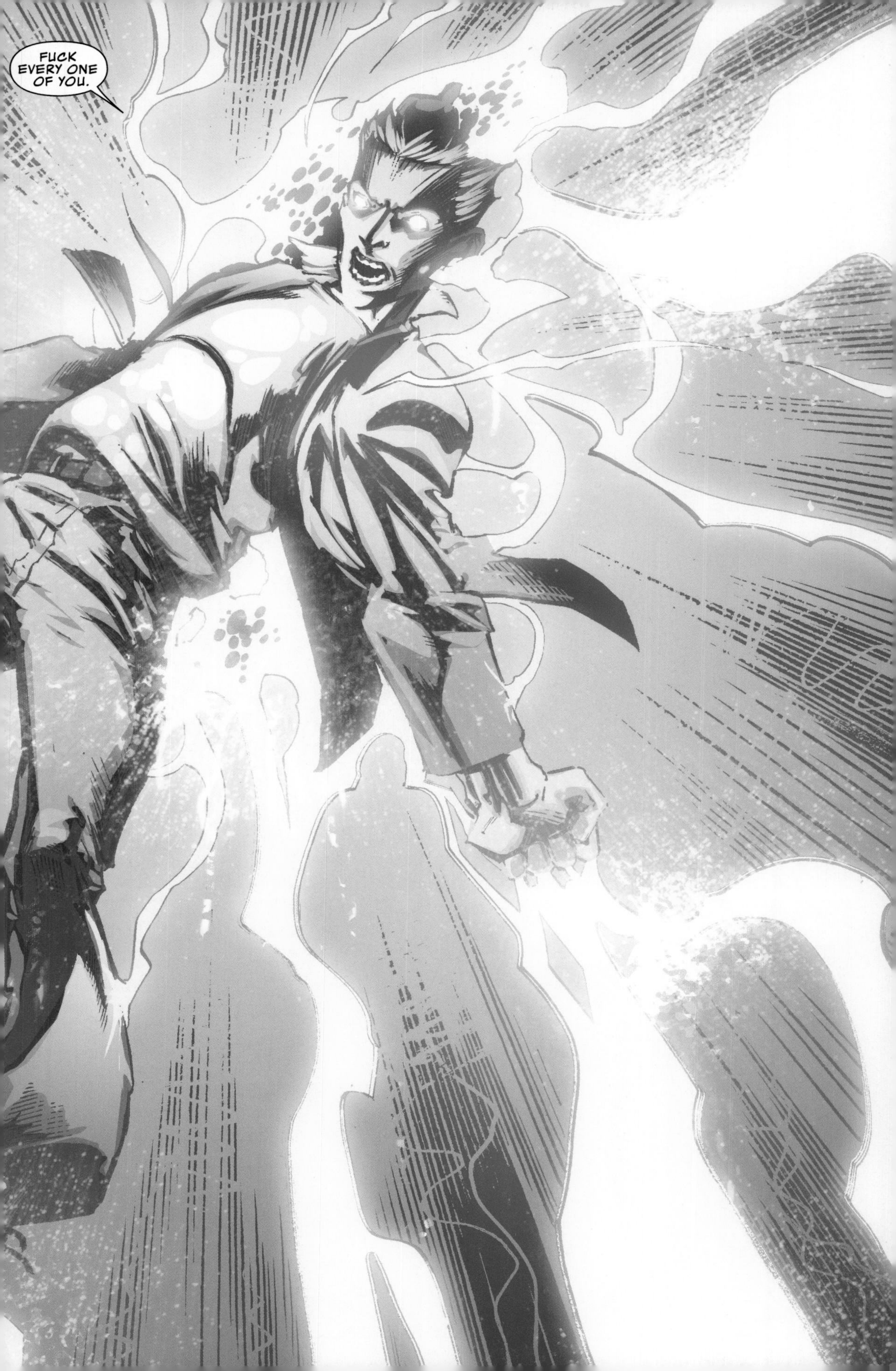
FUCK EVERY ONE OF YOU.

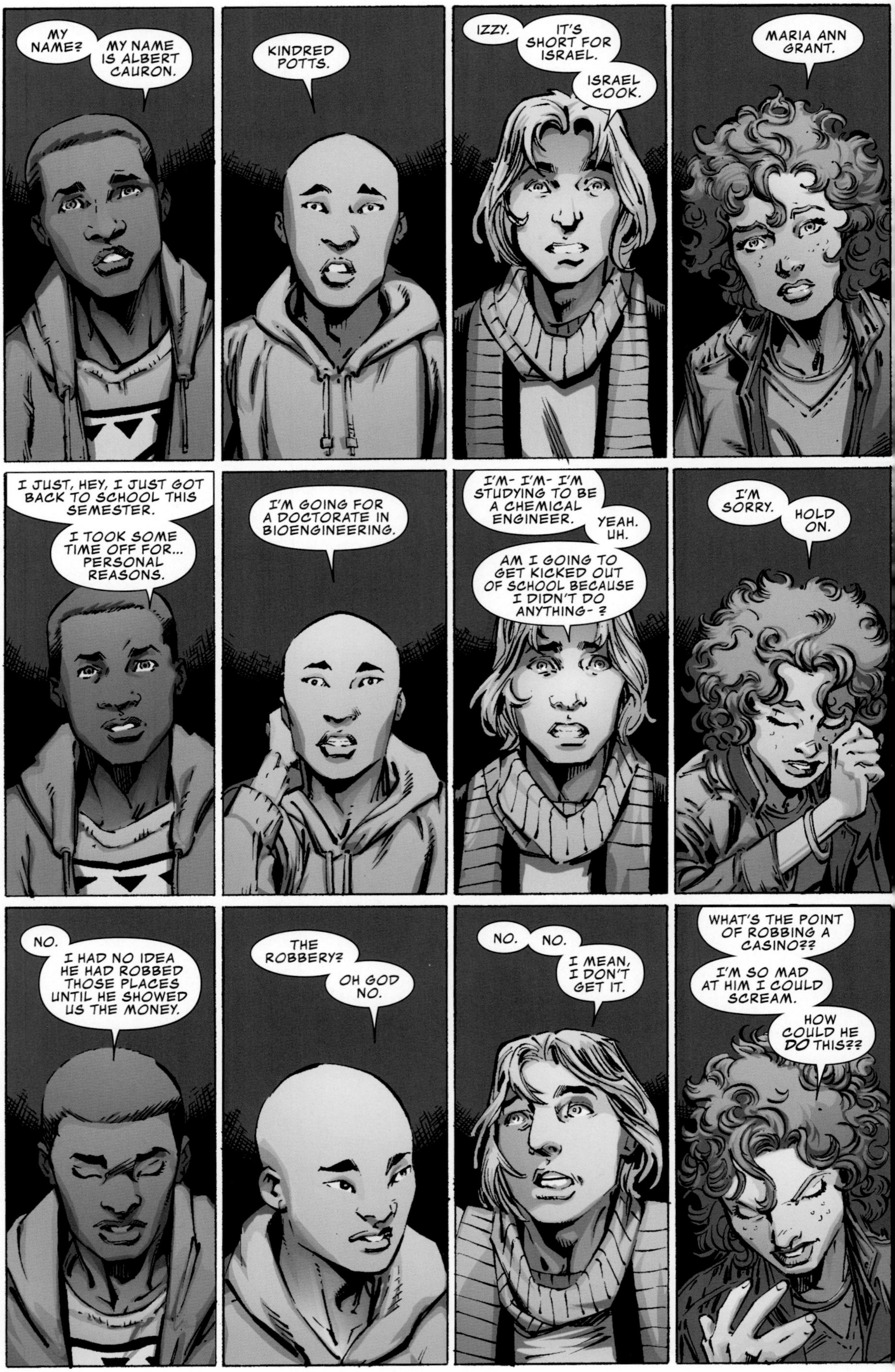
MY NAME?
MY NAME IS ALBERT CAURON.
KINDRED POTTS.
IZZY.
IT'S SHORT FOR ISRAEL.
ISRAEL COOK.
MARIA ANN GRANT.
I JUST, HEY, I JUST GOT BACK TO SCHOOL THIS SEMESTER.
I TOOK SOME TIME OFF FOR... PERSONAL REASONS.
I'M GOING FOR A DOCTORATE IN BIOENGINEERING.
I'M- I'M- I'M STUDYING TO BE A CHEMICAL ENGINEER.
YEAH. UH.
AM I GOING TO GET KICKED OUT OF SCHOOL BECAUSE I DIDN'T DO ANYTHING- ?
I'M SORRY.
HOLD ON.
NO.
I HAD NO IDEA HE HAD ROBBED THOSE PLACES UNTIL HE SHOWED US THE MONEY.
THE ROBBERY?
OH GOD NO.
NO.
NO.
I MEAN, I DON'T GET IT.
WHAT'S THE POINT OF ROBBING A CASINO??
I'M SO MAD AT HIM I COULD SCREAM.
HOW COULD HE DO THIS??

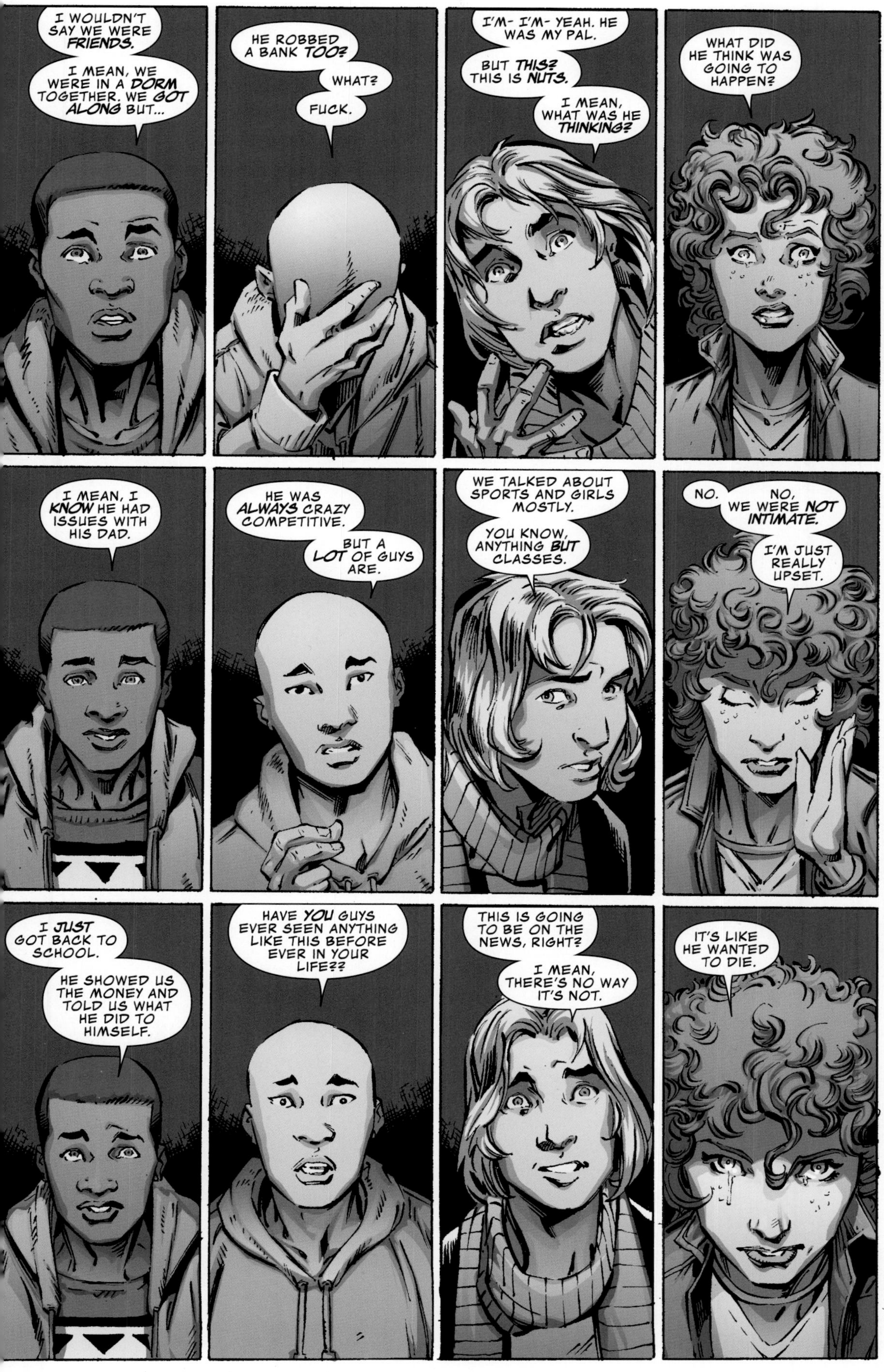
I WOULDN'T SAY WE WERE FRIENDS.
I MEAN, WE WERE IN A DORM TOGETHER. WE GOT ALONG BUT...
HE ROBBED A BANK TOO?
WHAT?
FUCK.
I'M- I'M- YEAH. HE WAS MY PAL.
BUT THIS? THIS IS NUTS.
I MEAN, WHAT WAS HE THINKING?
WHAT DID HE THINK WAS GOING TO HAPPEN?
I MEAN, I KNOW HE HAD ISSUES WITH HIS DAD.
HE WAS ALWAYS CRAZY COMPETITIVE.
BUT A LOT OF GUYS ARE.
WE TALKED ABOUT SPORTS AND GIRLS MOSTLY.
YOU KNOW, ANYTHING BUT CLASSES.
NO.
NO, WE WERE NOT INTIMATE.
I'M JUST REALLY UPSET.
I JUST GOT BACK TO SCHOOL.
HE SHOWED US THE MONEY AND TOLD US WHAT HE DID TO HIMSELF.
HAVE YOU GUYS EVER SEEN ANYTHING LIKE THIS BEFORE EVER IN YOUR LIFE??
THIS IS GOING TO BE ON THE NEWS, RIGHT?
I MEAN, THERE'S NO WAY IT'S NOT.
IT'S LIKE HE WANTED TO DIE.

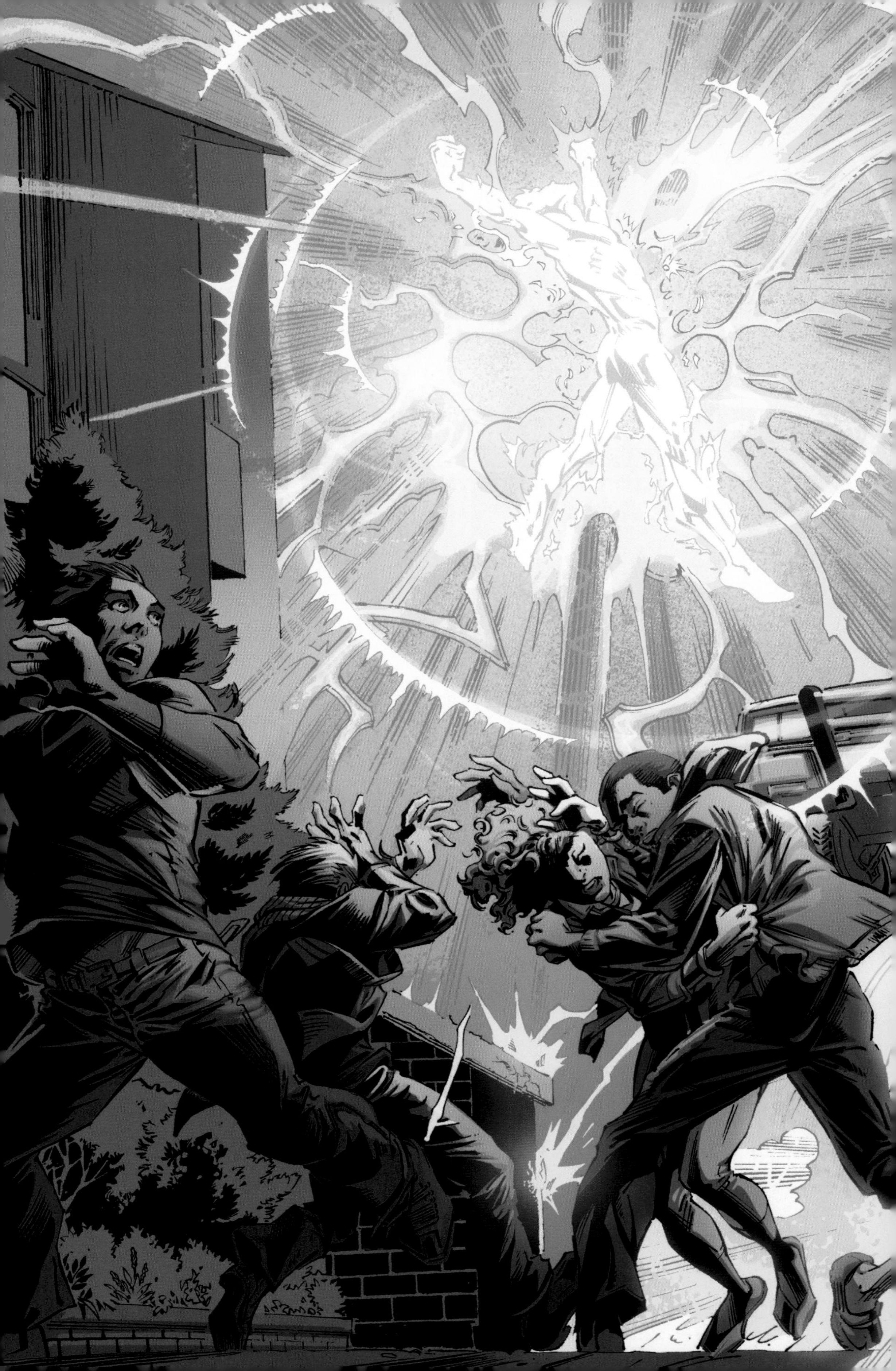

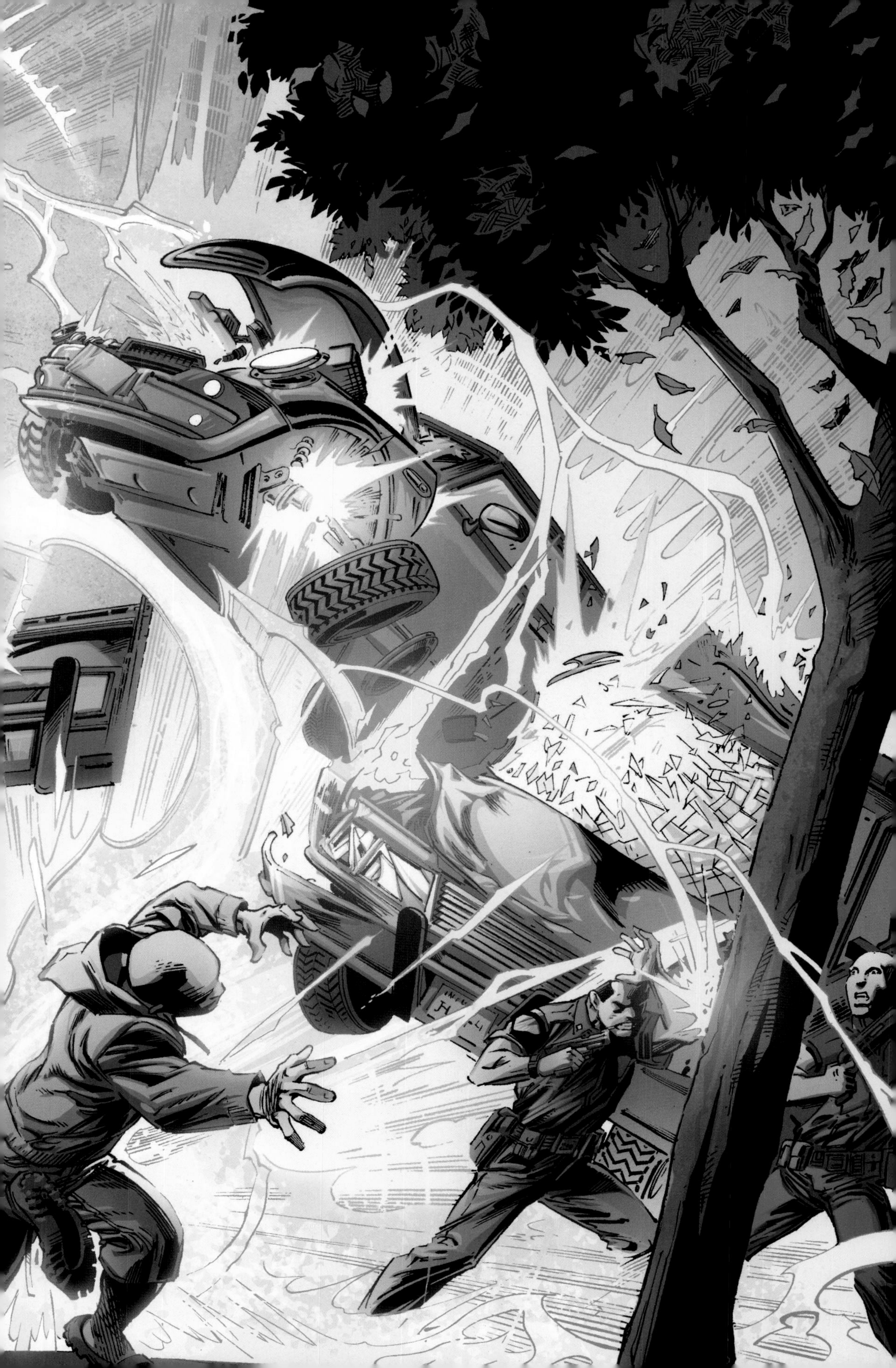

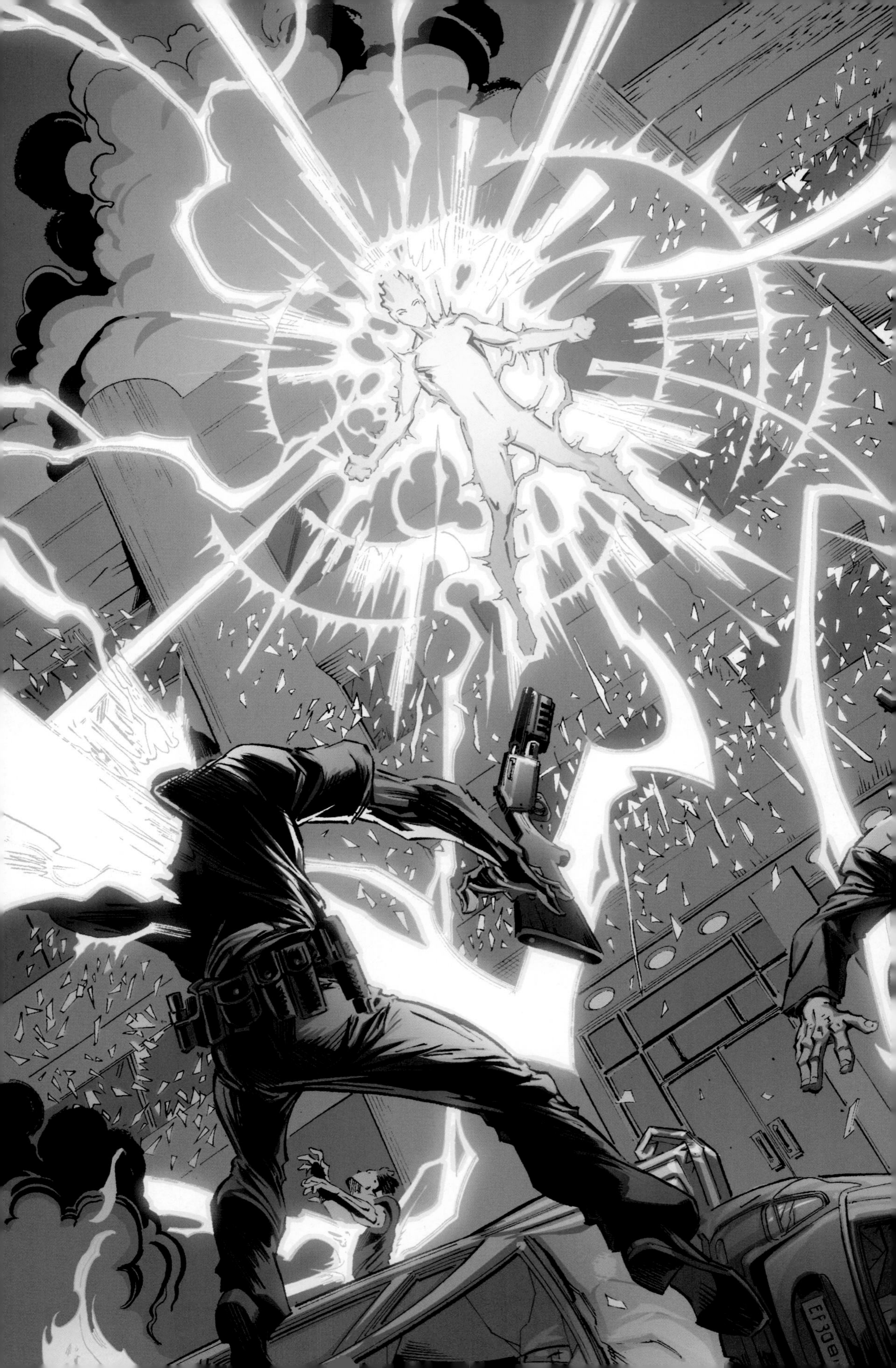

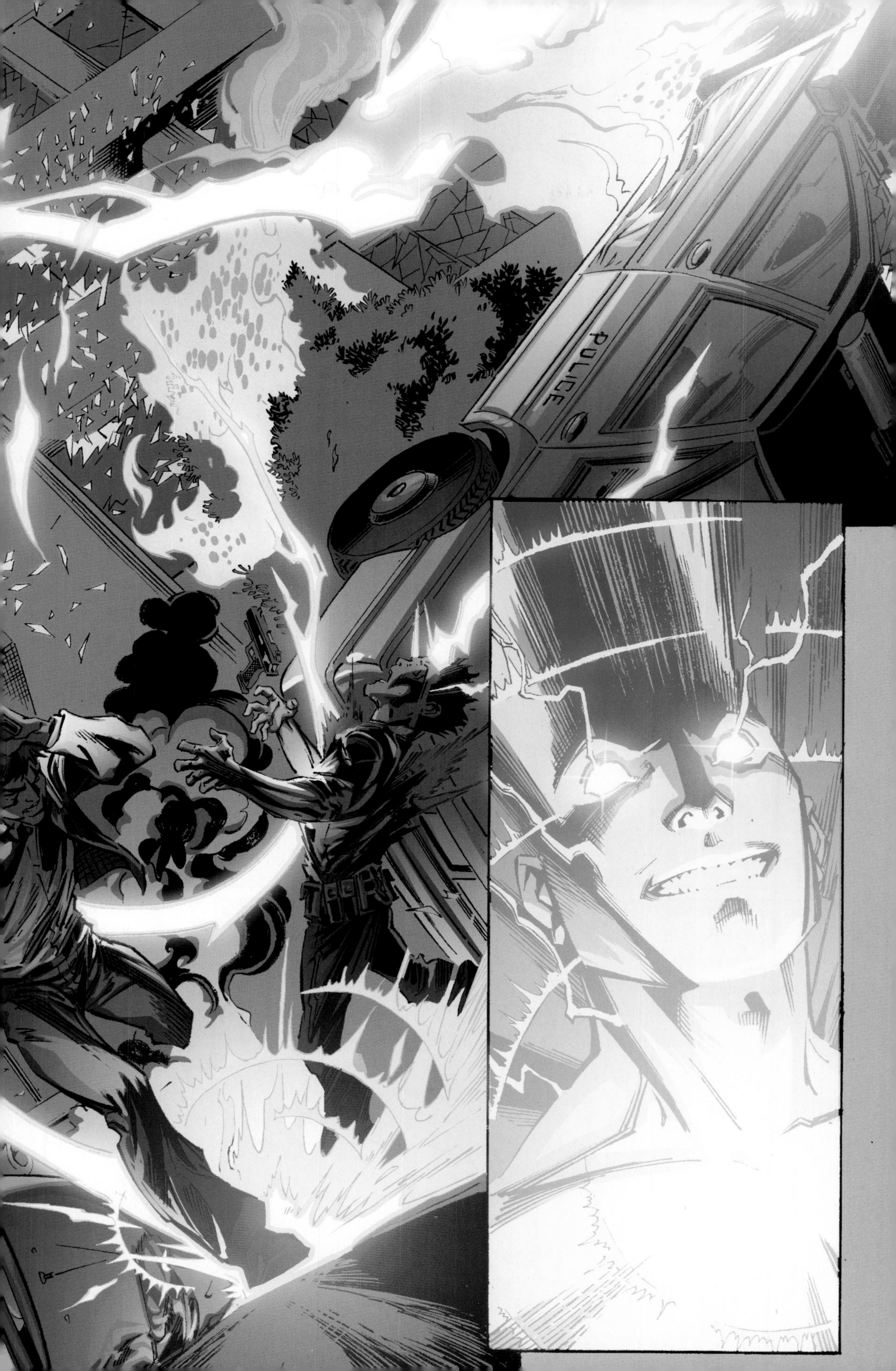
POLICE

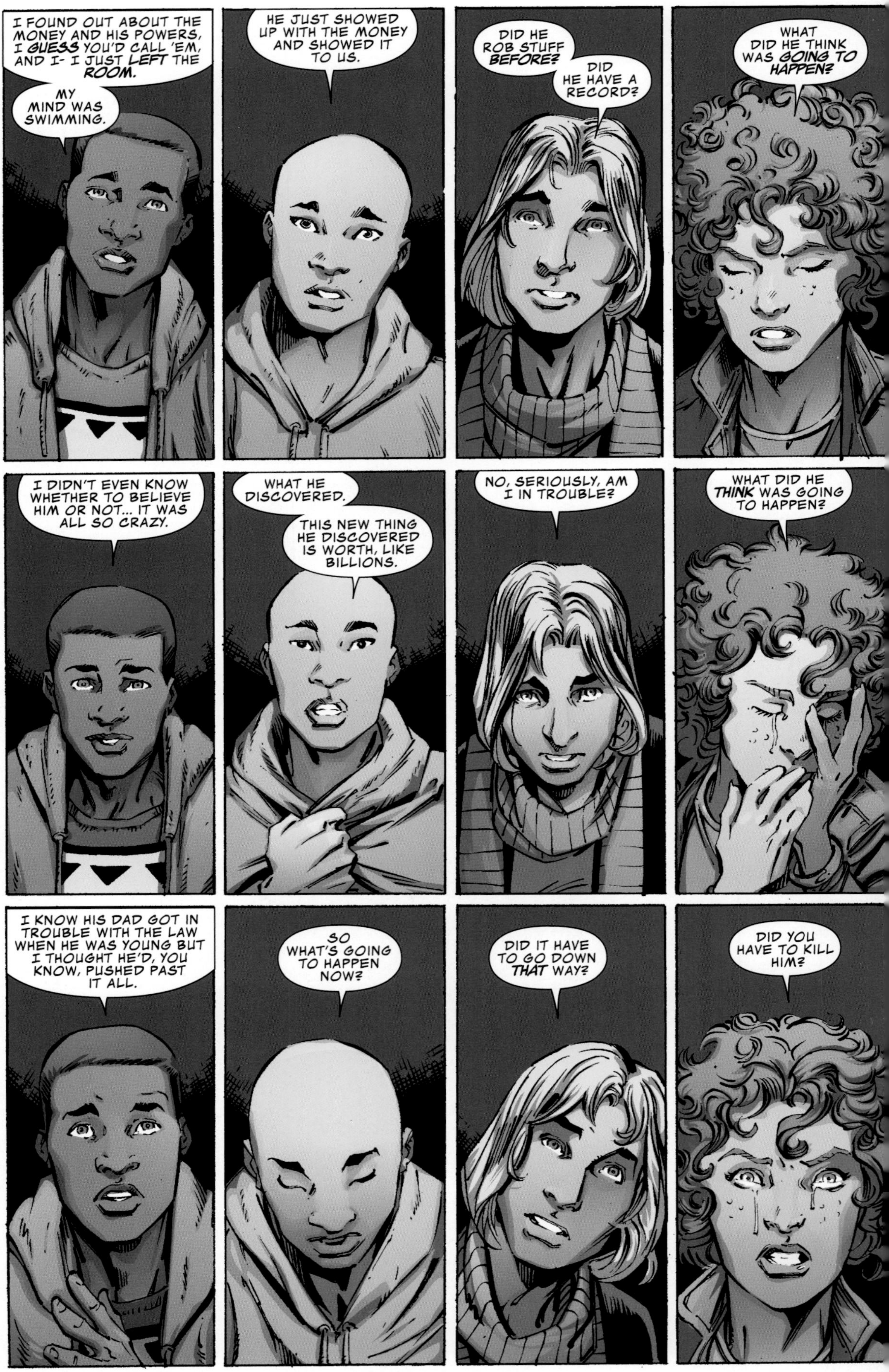
I FOUND OUT ABOUT THE MONEY AND HIS POWERS, I GUESS YOU'D CALL 'EM, AND I- I JUST LEFT THE ROOM.
MY MIND WAS SWIMMING.
HE JUST SHOWED UP WITH THE MONEY AND SHOWED IT TO US.
DID HE ROB STUFF BEFORE?
DID HE HAVE A RECORD?
WHAT DID HE THINK WAS GOING TO HAPPEN?
I DIDN'T EVEN KNOW WHETHER TO BELIEVE HIM OR NOT... IT WAS ALL SO CRAZY.
WHAT HE DISCOVERED.
THIS NEW THING HE DISCOVERED IS WORTH, LIKE BILLIONS.
NO, SERIOUSLY, AM I IN TROUBLE?
WHAT DID HE THINK WAS GOING TO HAPPEN?
I KNOW HIS DAD GOT IN TROUBLE WITH THE LAW WHEN HE WAS YOUNG BUT I THOUGHT HE'D, YOU KNOW, PUSHED PAST IT ALL.
SO WHAT'S GOING TO HAPPEN NOW?
DID IT HAVE TO GO DOWN THAT WAY?
DID YOU HAVE TO KILL HIM?

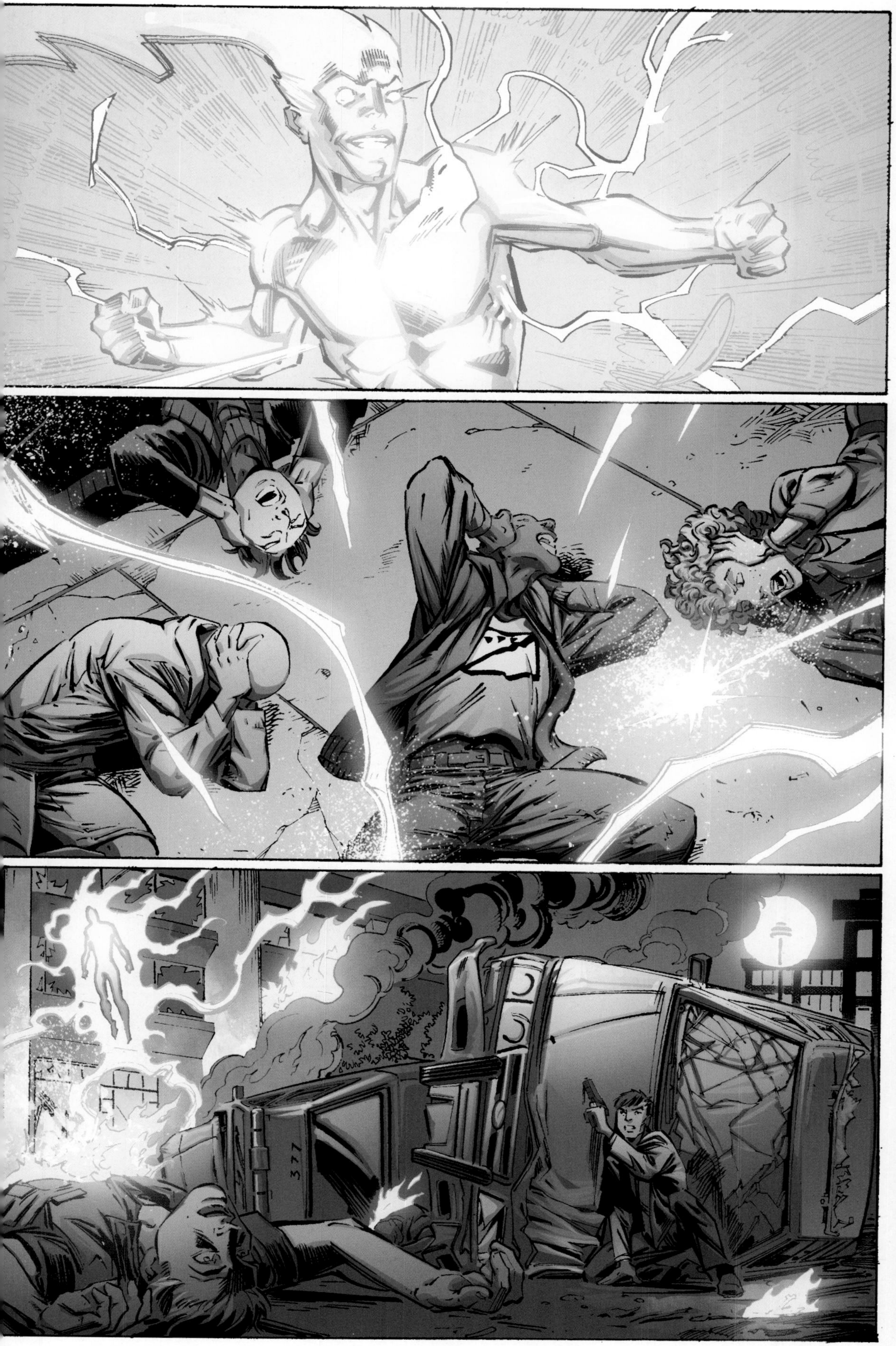
377

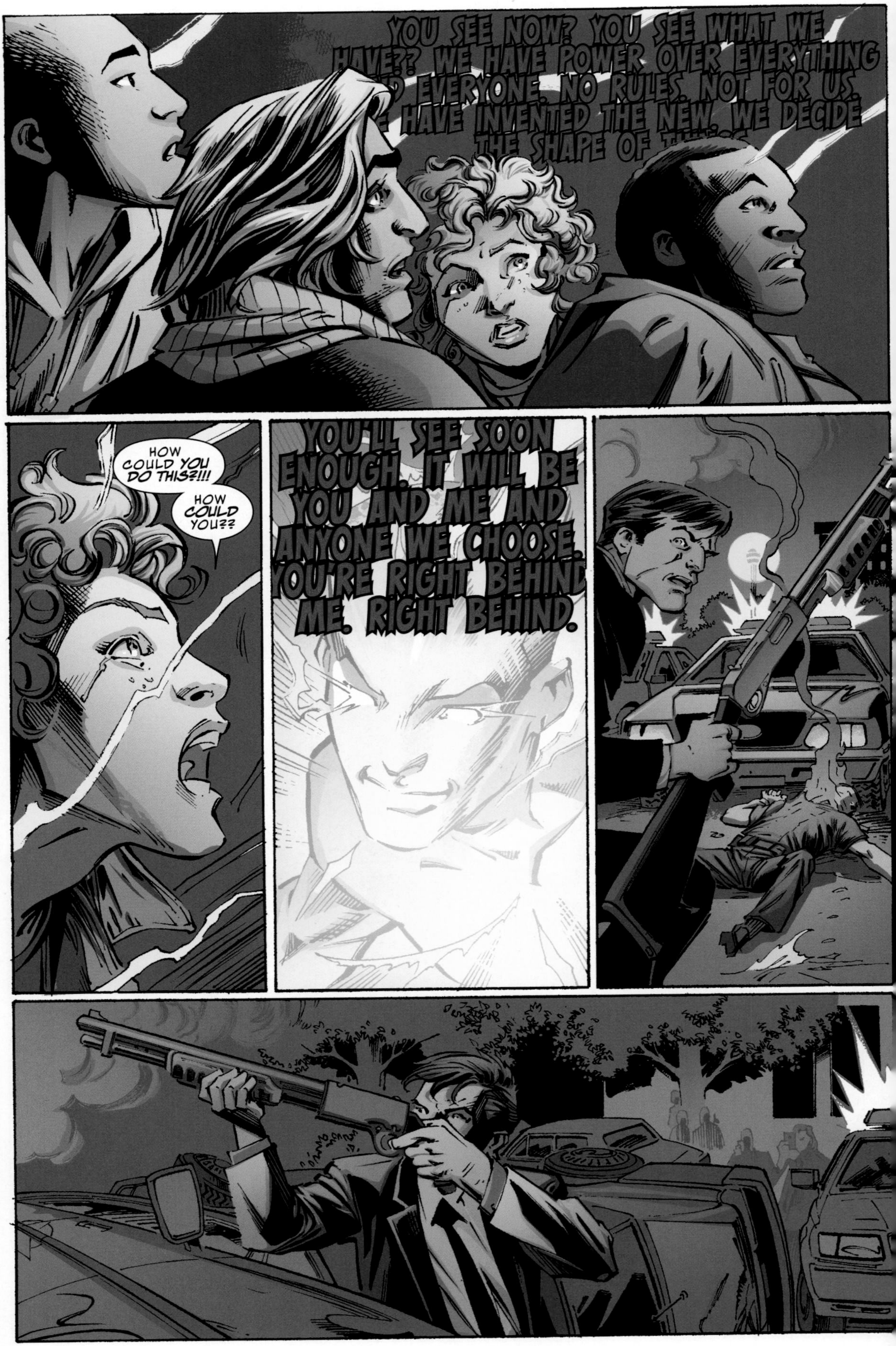
YOU SEE NOW? YOU SEE WHAT WE HAVE?? WE HAVE POWER OVER EVERYTHING AND EVERYONE. NO RULES. NOT FOR US. WE HAVE INVENTED THE NEW. WE DECIDE THE SHAPE OF THINGS.
HOW COULD YOU DO THIS?!!!
HOW COULD YOU??
YOU'LL SEE SOON ENOUGH. IT WILL BE YOU AND ME AND ANYONE WE CHOOSE. YOU'RE RIGHT BEHIND ME. RIGHT BEHIND.

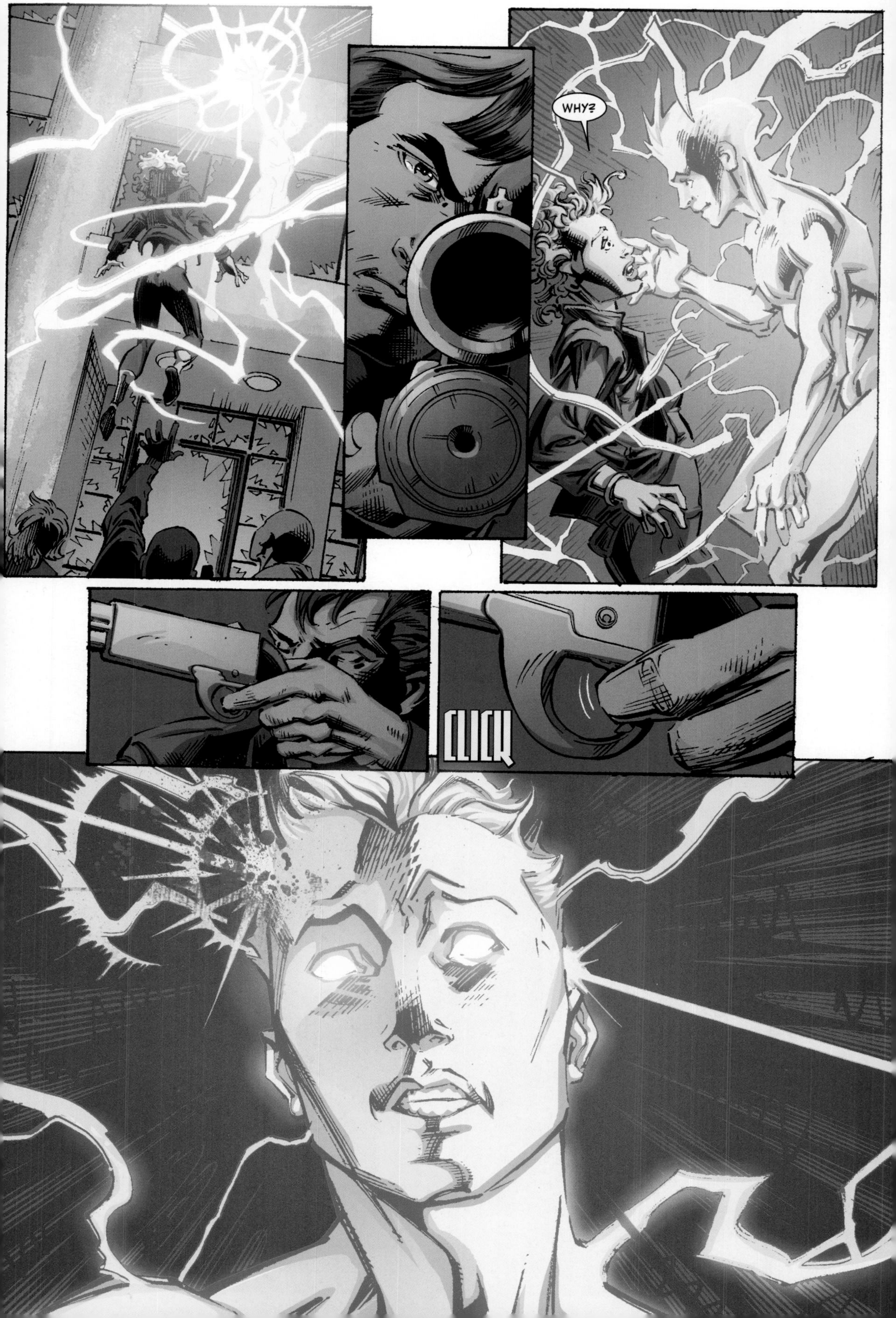
WHY?
CLICK

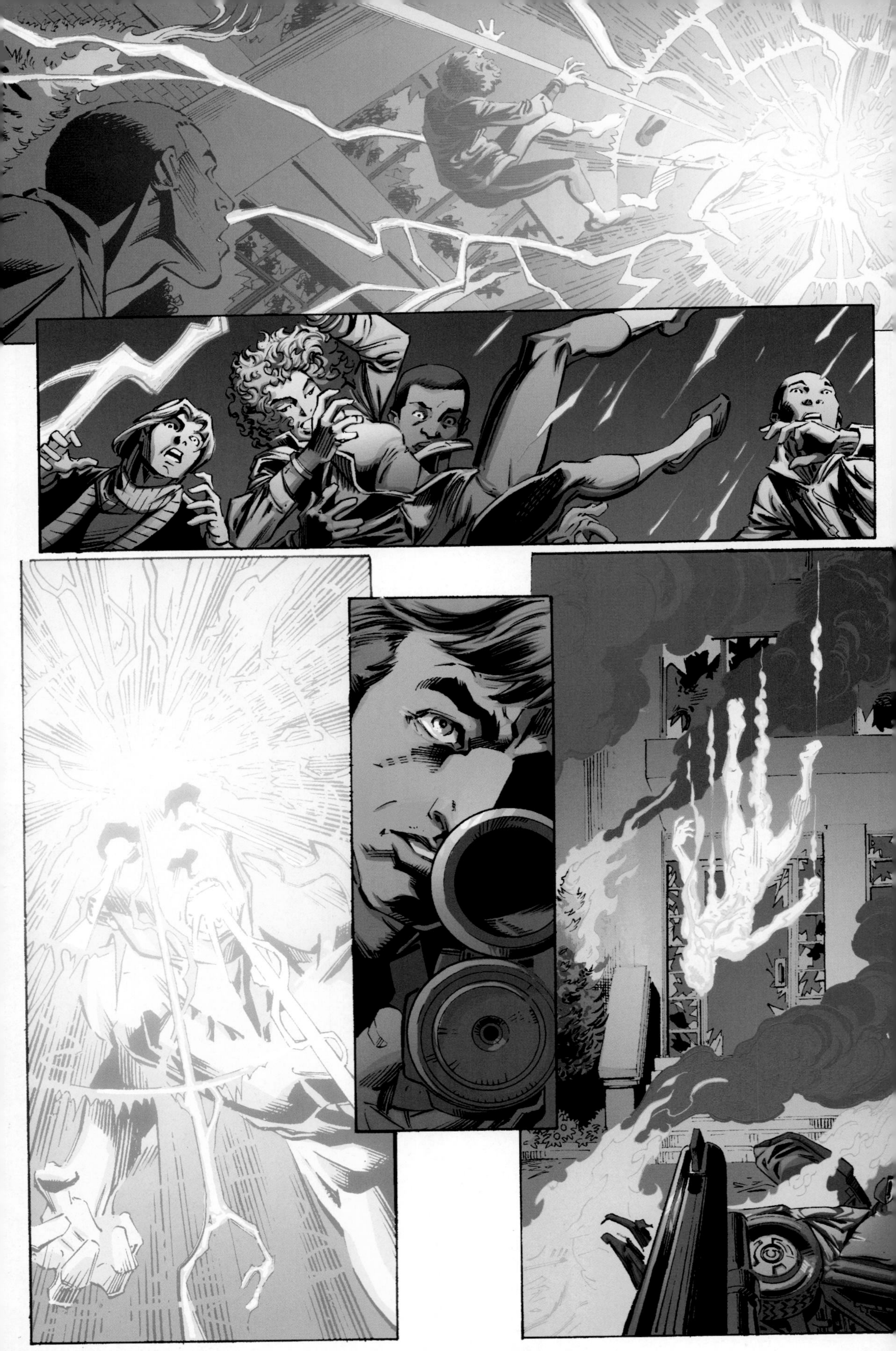

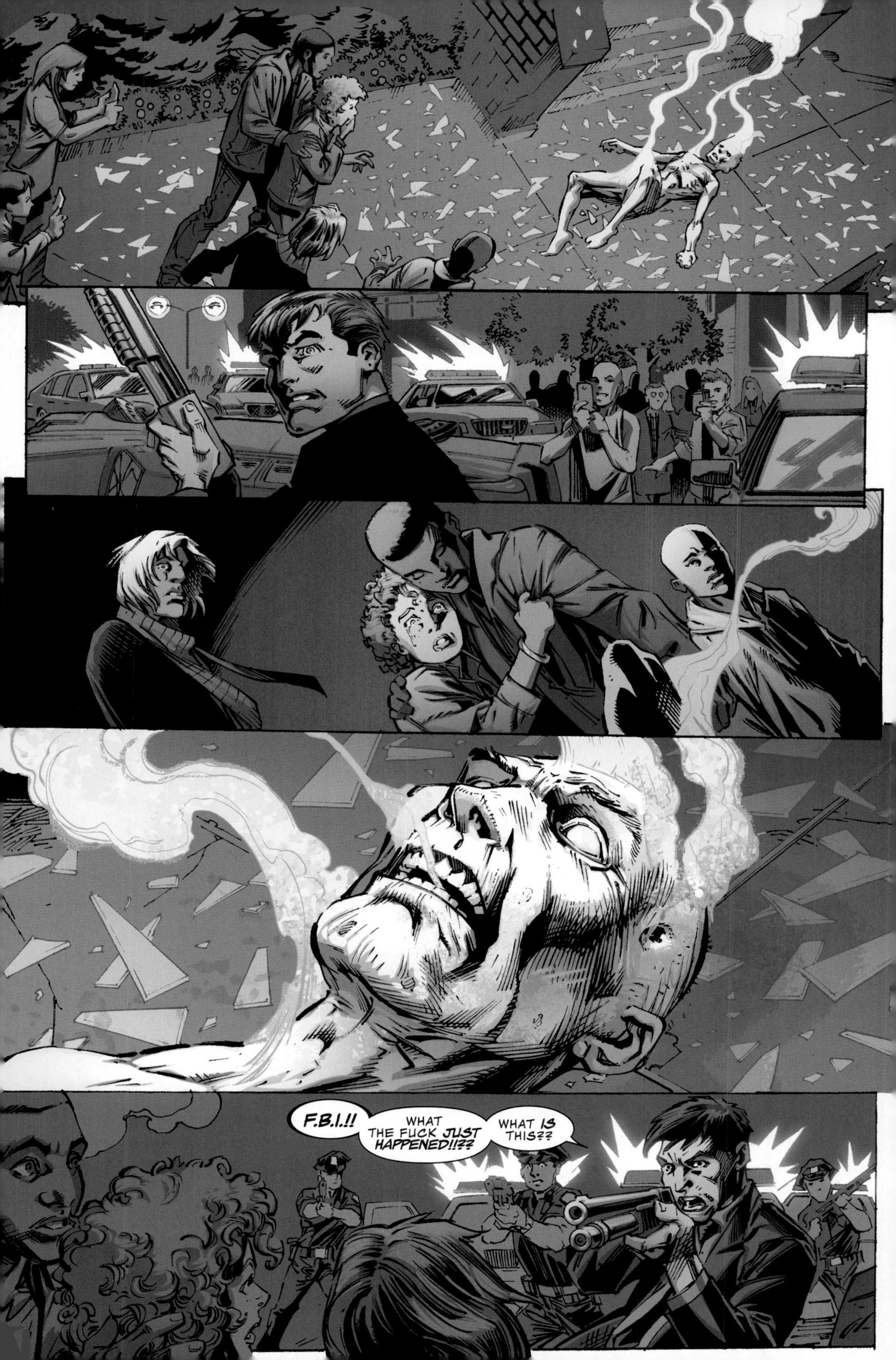
F.B.I.!!
WHAT THE FUCK JUST HAPPENED!!??
WHAT IS THIS??

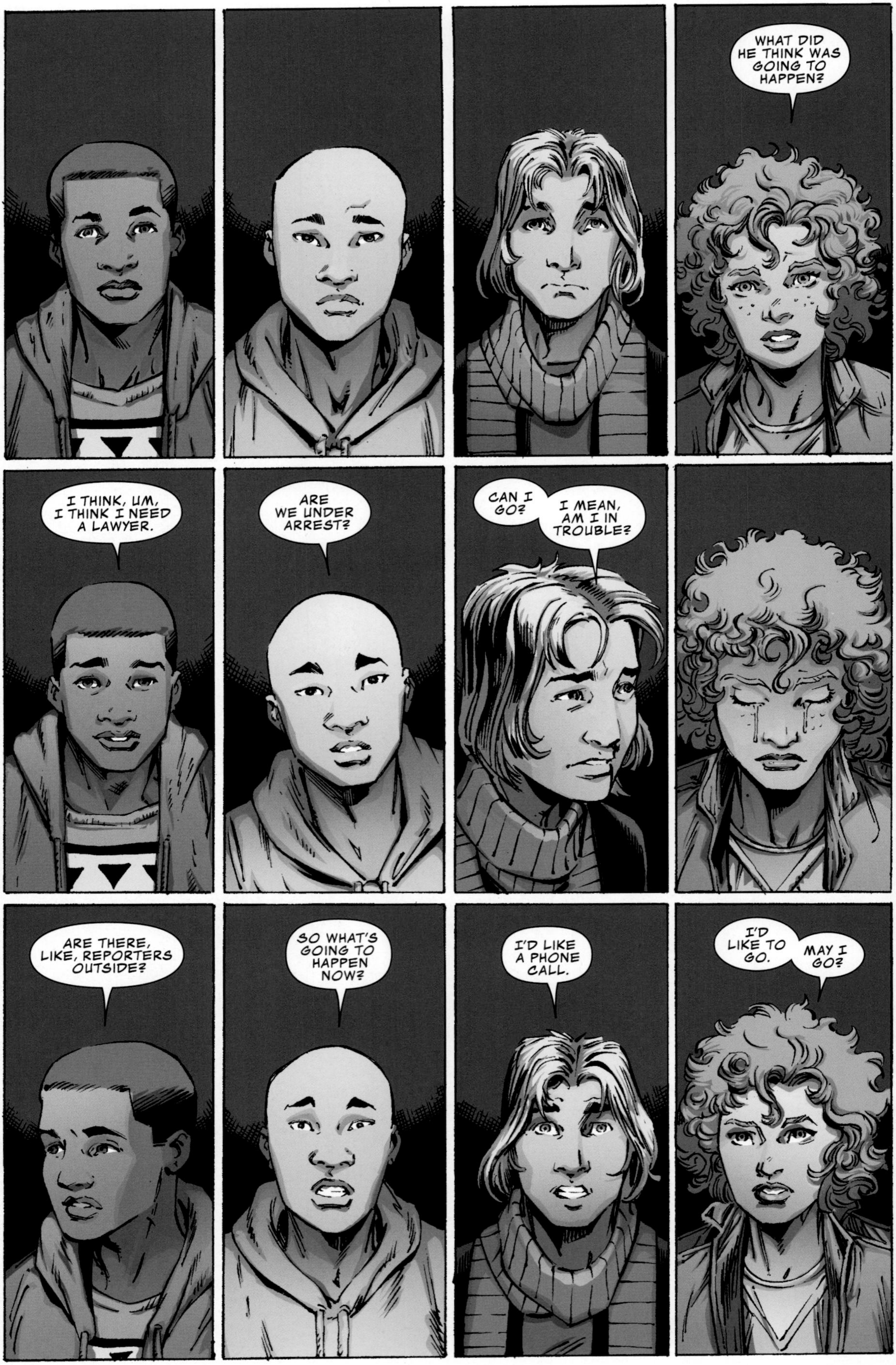
WHAT DID HE THINK WAS GOING TO HAPPEN?
I THINK, UM, I THINK I NEED A LAWYER.
ARE WE UNDER ARREST?
CAN I GO?
I MEAN, AM I IN TROUBLE?
ARE THERE, LIKE, REPORTERS OUTSIDE?
SO WHAT'S GOING TO HAPPEN NOW?
I'D LIKE A PHONE CALL.
I'D LIKE TO GO.
MAY I GO?

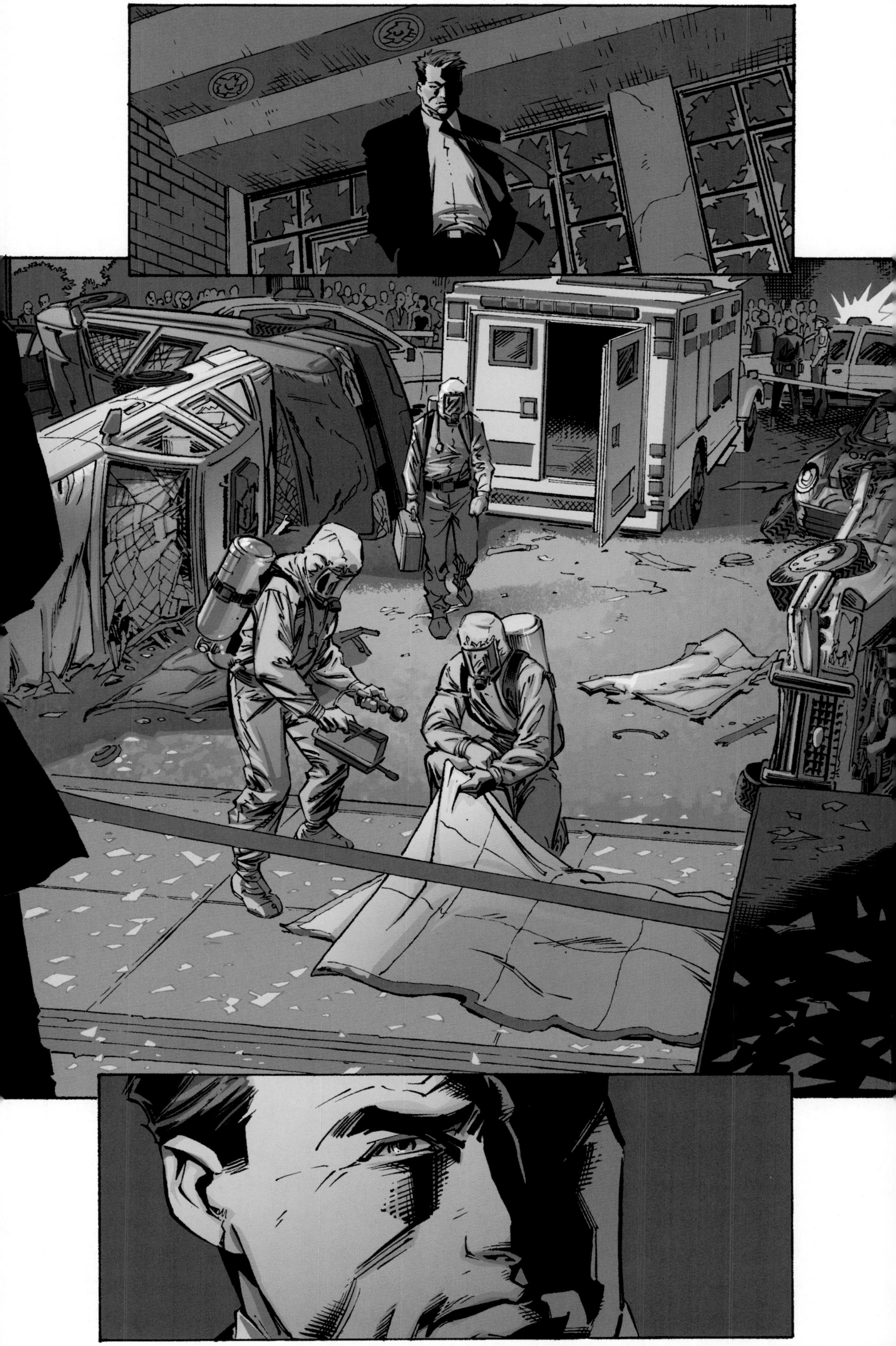

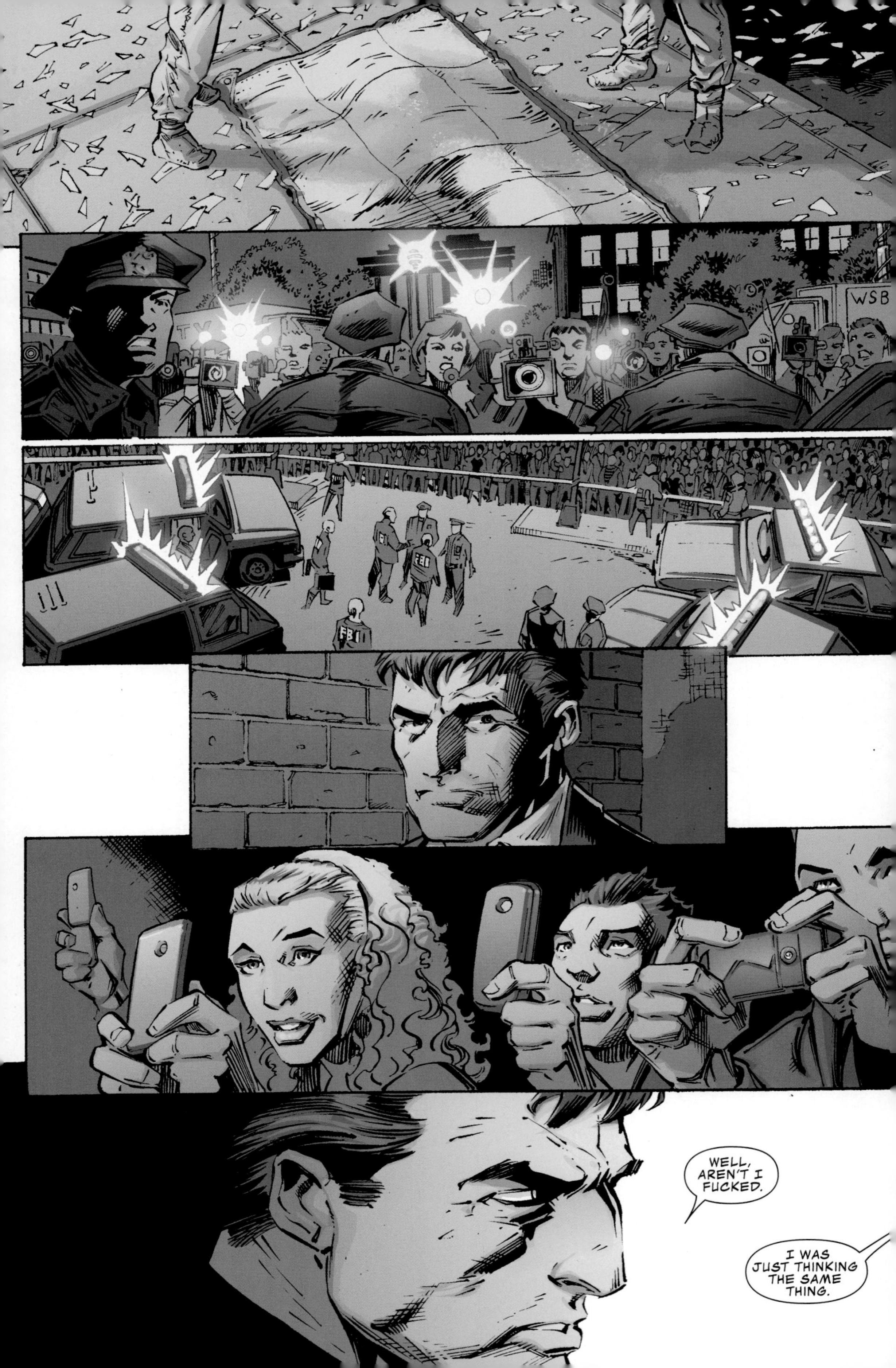
TV
WSB
FBI
FBI
FBI
WELL, AREN'T I FUCKED.
I WAS JUST THINKING THE SAME THING.

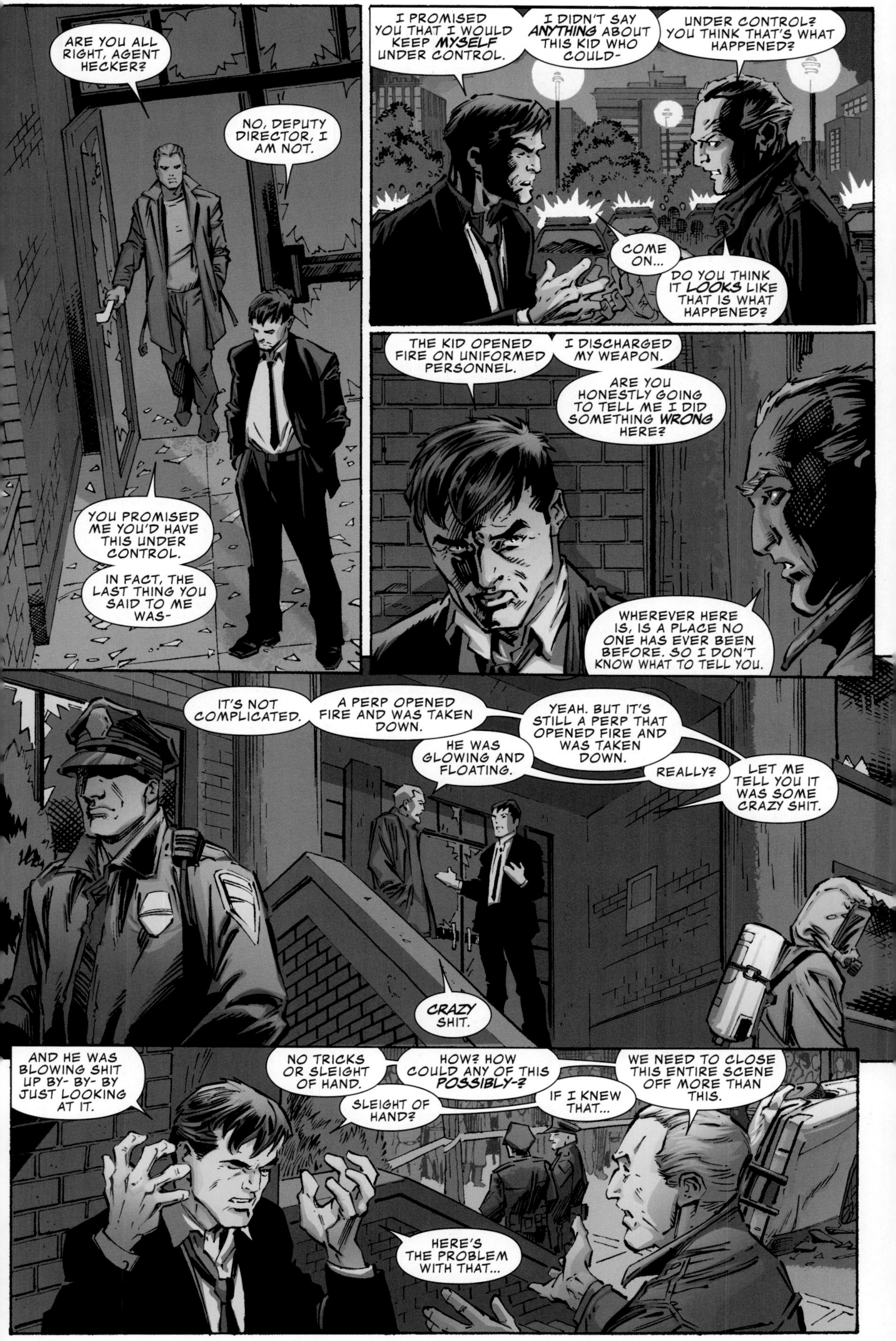
ARE YOU ALL RIGHT, AGENT HECKER?
NO, DEPUTY DIRECTOR, I AM NOT.
YOU PROMISED ME YOU'D HAVE THIS UNDER CONTROL.
IN FACT, THE LAST THING YOU SAID TO ME WAS-
I PROMISED YOU THAT I WOULD KEEP MYSELF UNDER CONTROL.
I DIDN'T SAY ANYTHING ABOUT THIS KID WHO COULD-
UNDER CONTROL? YOU THINK THAT'S WHAT HAPPENED?
COME ON...
DO YOU THINK IT LOOKS LIKE THAT IS WHAT HAPPENED?
THE KID OPENED FIRE ON UNIFORMED PERSONNEL.
I DISCHARGED MY WEAPON.
ARE YOU HONESTLY GOING TO TELL ME I DID SOMETHING WRONG HERE?
WHEREVER HERE IS, IS A PLACE NO ONE HAS EVER BEEN BEFORE. SO I DON'T KNOW WHAT TO TELL YOU.
IT'S NOT COMPLICATED.
A PERP OPENED FIRE AND WAS TAKEN DOWN.
YEAH. BUT IT'S STILL A PERP THAT OPENED FIRE AND WAS TAKEN DOWN.
HE WAS GLOWING AND FLOATING.
REALLY?
LET ME TELL YOU IT WAS SOME CRAZY SHIT.
CRAZY SHIT.
AND HE WAS BLOWING SHIT UP BY- BY- BY JUST LOOKING AT IT.
NO TRICKS OR SLEIGHT OF HAND.
SLEIGHT OF HAND?
HOW? HOW COULD ANY OF THIS POSSIBLY-?
IF I KNEW THAT...
WE NEED TO CLOSE THIS ENTIRE SCENE OFF MORE THAN THIS.
HERE'S THE PROBLEM WITH THAT...

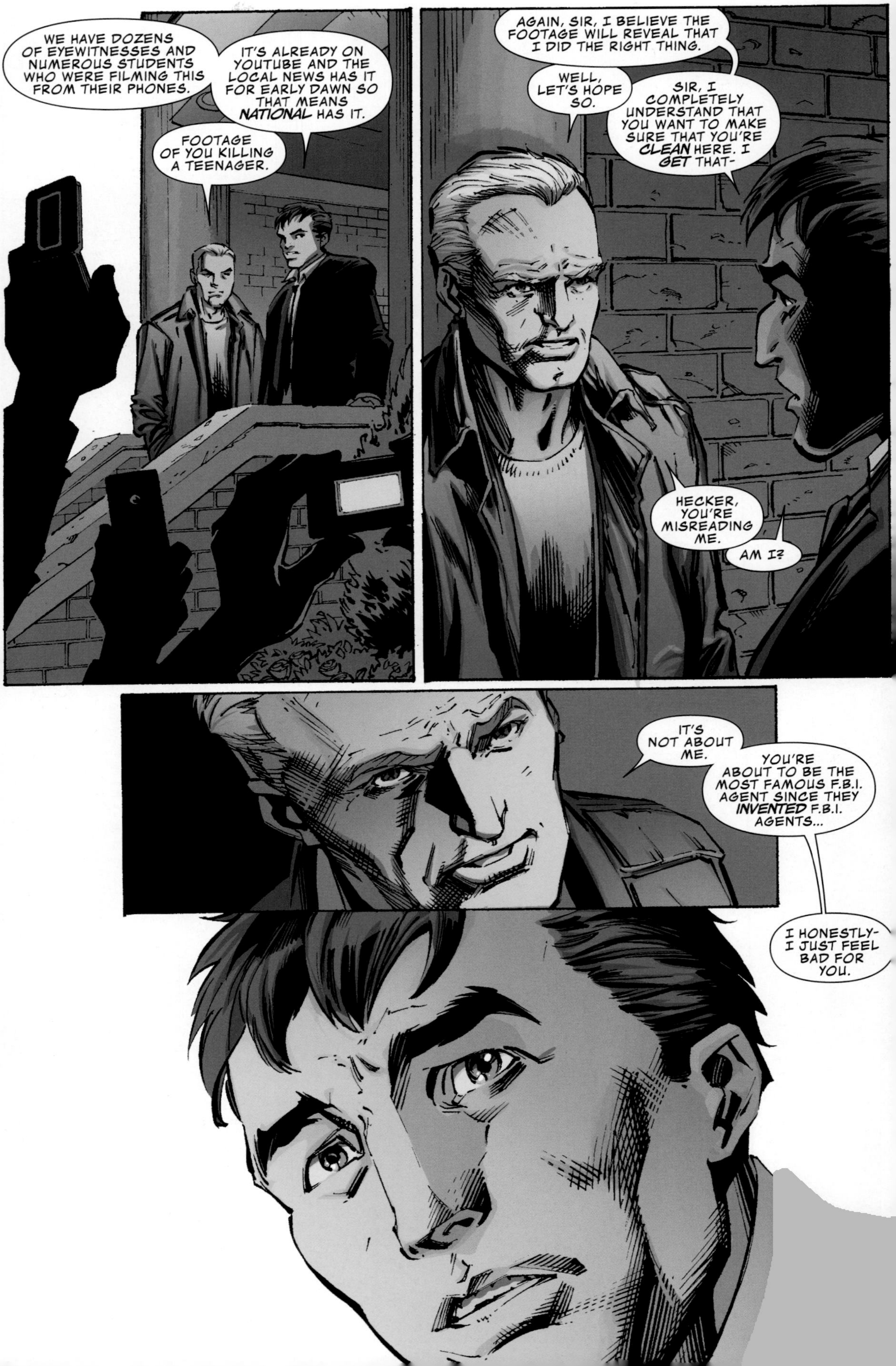

WE HAVE DOZENS OF EYEWITNESSES AND NUMEROUS STUDENTS WHO WERE FILMING THIS FROM THEIR PHONES.
IT'S ALREADY ON YOUTUBE AND THE LOCAL NEWS HAS IT FOR EARLY DAWN SO THAT MEANS NATIONAL HAS IT.
FOOTAGE OF YOU KILLING A TEENAGER.
AGAIN, SIR, I BELIEVE THE FOOTAGE WILL REVEAL THAT I DID THE RIGHT THING.
WELL, LET'S HOPE SO.
SIR, I COMPLETELY UNDERSTAND THAT YOU WANT TO MAKE SURE THAT YOU'RE CLEAN HERE. I GET THAT-
HECKER, YOU'RE MISREADING ME.
AM I?
IT'S NOT ABOUT ME.
YOU'RE ABOUT TO BE THE MOST FAMOUS F.B.I. AGENT SINCE THEY INVENTED F.B.I. AGENTS...
I HONESTLY- I JUST FEEL BAD FOR YOU.

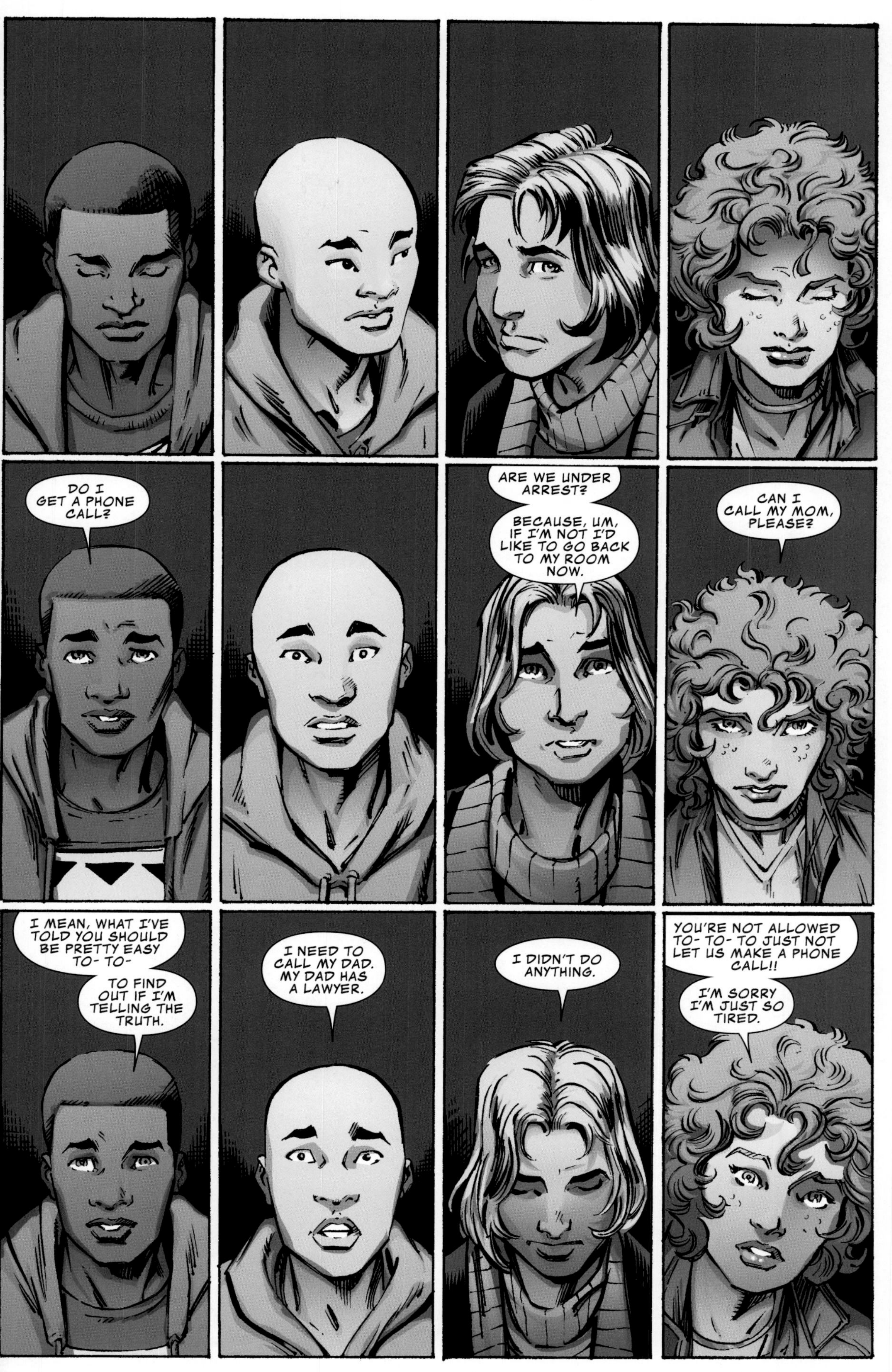
DO I GET A PHONE CALL?
ARE WE UNDER ARREST?
BECAUSE, UM, IF I'M NOT I'D LIKE TO GO BACK TO MY ROOM NOW.
CAN I CALL MY MOM, PLEASE?
I MEAN, WHAT I'VE TOLD YOU SHOULD BE PRETTY EASY TO- TO-
TO FIND OUT IF I'M TELLING THE TRUTH.
I NEED TO CALL MY DAD. MY DAD HAS A LAWYER.
I DIDN'T DO ANYTHING.
YOU'RE NOT ALLOWED TO- TO- TO JUST NOT LET US MAKE A PHONE CALL!!
I'M SORRY I'M JUST SO TIRED.

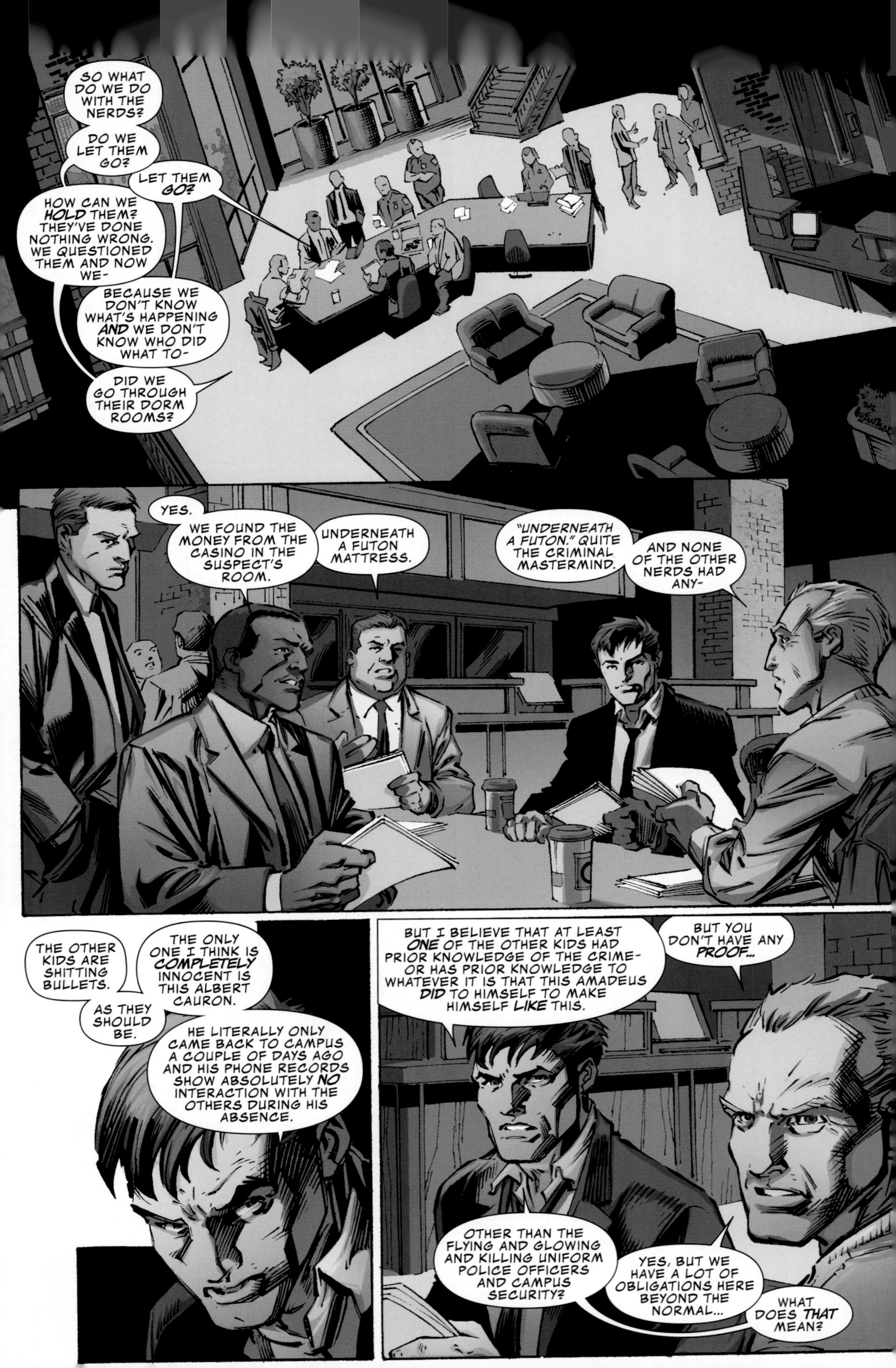

SO WHAT DO WE DO WITH THE NERDS?
DO WE LET THEM GO?
LET THEM GO?
HOW CAN WE HOLD THEM? THEY'VE DONE NOTHING WRONG. WE QUESTIONED THEM AND NOW WE-
BECAUSE WE DON'T KNOW WHAT'S HAPPENING AND WE DON'T KNOW WHO DID WHAT TO-
DID WE GO THROUGH THEIR DORM ROOMS?
YES.
WE FOUND THE MONEY FROM THE CASINO IN THE SUSPECT'S ROOM.
UNDERNEATH A FUTON MATTRESS.
"UNDERNEATH A FUTON." QUITE THE CRIMINAL MASTERMIND.
AND NONE OF THE OTHER NERDS HAD ANY-
THE OTHER KIDS ARE SHITTING BULLETS.
AS THEY SHOULD BE.
THE ONLY ONE I THINK IS COMPLETELY INNOCENT IS THIS ALBERT CAURON.
HE LITERALLY ONLY CAME BACK TO CAMPUS A COUPLE OF DAYS AGO AND HIS PHONE RECORDS SHOW ABSOLUTELY NO INTERACTION WITH THE OTHERS DURING HIS ABSENCE.
BUT I BELIEVE THAT AT LEAST ONE OF THE OTHER KIDS HAD PRIOR KNOWLEDGE OF THE CRIME- OR HAS PRIOR KNOWLEDGE TO WHATEVER IT IS THAT THIS AMADEUS DID TO HIMSELF TO MAKE HIMSELF LIKE THIS.
BUT YOU DON'T HAVE ANY PROOF...
OTHER THAN THE FLYING AND GLOWING AND KILLING UNIFORM POLICE OFFICERS AND CAMPUS SECURITY?
YES, BUT WE HAVE A LOT OF OBLIGATIONS HERE BEYOND THE NORMAL...
WHAT DOES THAT MEAN?

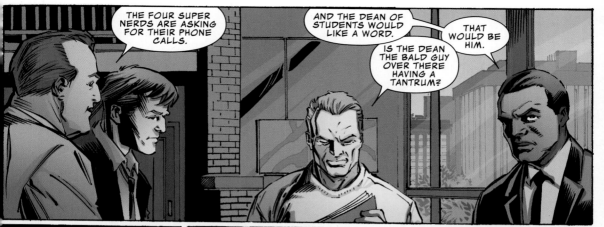

THE FOUR SUPER NERDS ARE ASKING FOR THEIR PHONE CALLS.

AND THE DEAN OF STUDENTS WOULD LIKE A WORD.

THAT WOULD BE HIM.

IS THE DEAN THE BALD GUY OVER THERE HAVING A TANTRUM?

NOT INTERESTED.

IT'S YOUR JOB, AGENTS, TO KEEP THE NOISE LEVEL AROUND ME DOWN TO A LOW ROAR WHILE WE FIGURE THIS OUT.

WE NEED TO SCOUR THOSE KIDS' COMPUTERS.

KIDS? THEY'RE ALL IN THEIR TWENTIES.

WE NEED TO SCOUR THOSE SUPER NERDS' COMPUTERS.

FOR?

FOR INTEL ON WHAT THEY WERE WORKING ON THAT TURNED THAT KID INTO *THAT*.

THESE NERDS' SCHOLASTIC RECORDS ARE CRAZY. LITTLE GENIUSES IN THEIR CHOSEN FIELDS.

WE NEED TO GET SOME EXPERTS IN HERE AND TRY TO FIGURE OUT WHAT THEY FIGURED OUT.

SO YOU THINK THESE KIDS INVENTED SOMETHING THAT TURNED THAT KID IN TO WHATEVER HE TURNED INTO?

WHAT OTHER OPTIONS ARE WE CONSIDERING?

THAT HE WAS *BORN* THAT WAY.

I DON'T CONSIDER THAT AN OPTION.

I THINK WE DO THIS...

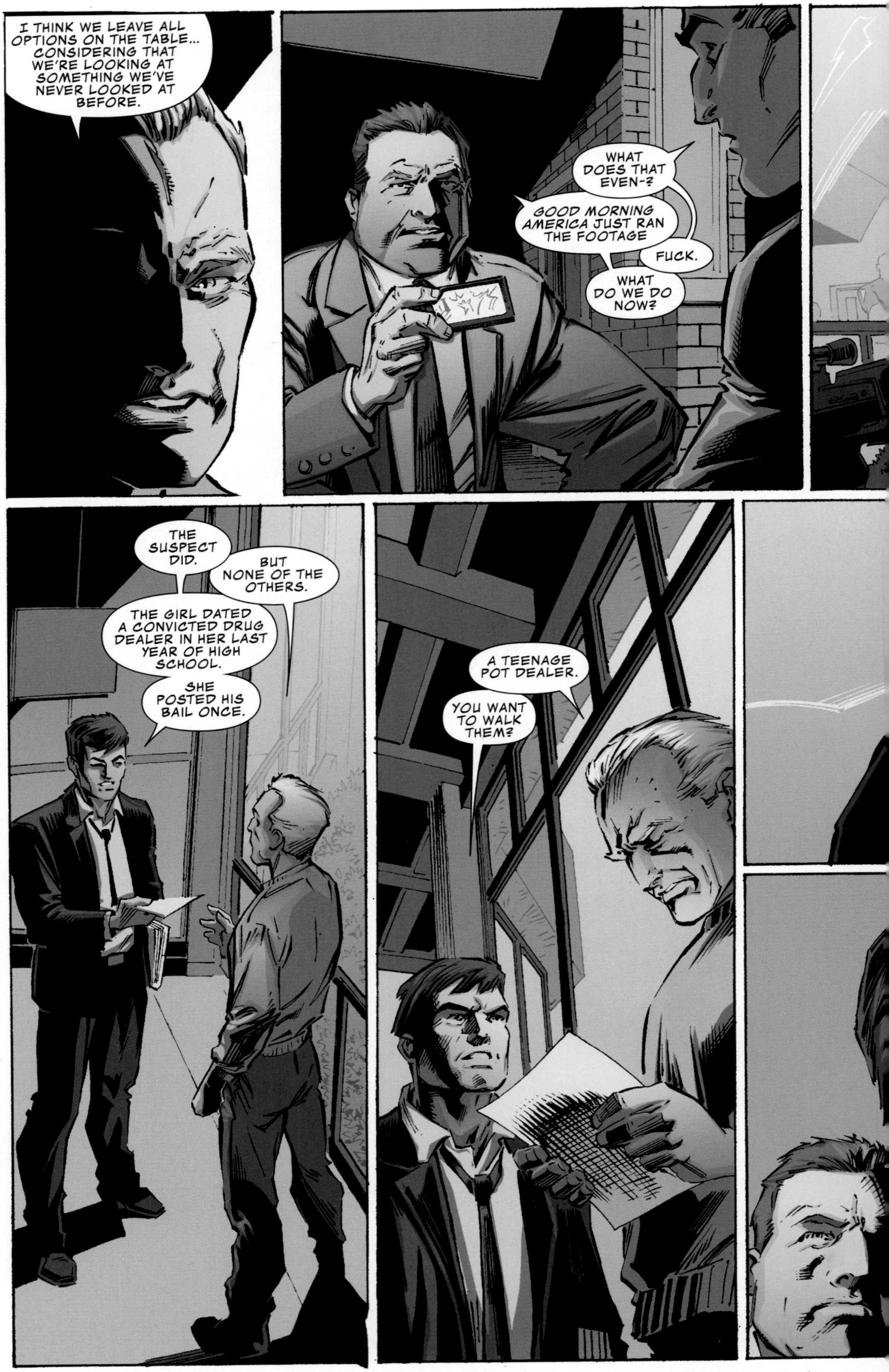
I THINK WE LEAVE ALL OPTIONS ON THE TABLE... CONSIDERING THAT WE'RE LOOKING AT SOMETHING WE'VE NEVER LOOKED AT BEFORE.
WHAT DOES THAT EVEN-?
GOOD MORNING AMERICA JUST RAN THE FOOTAGE
FUCK.
WHAT DO WE DO NOW?
THE SUSPECT DID.
BUT NONE OF THE OTHERS.
THE GIRL DATED A CONVICTED DRUG DEALER IN HER LAST YEAR OF HIGH SCHOOL.
SHE POSTED HIS BAIL ONCE.
A TEENAGE POT DEALER.
YOU WANT TO WALK THEM?

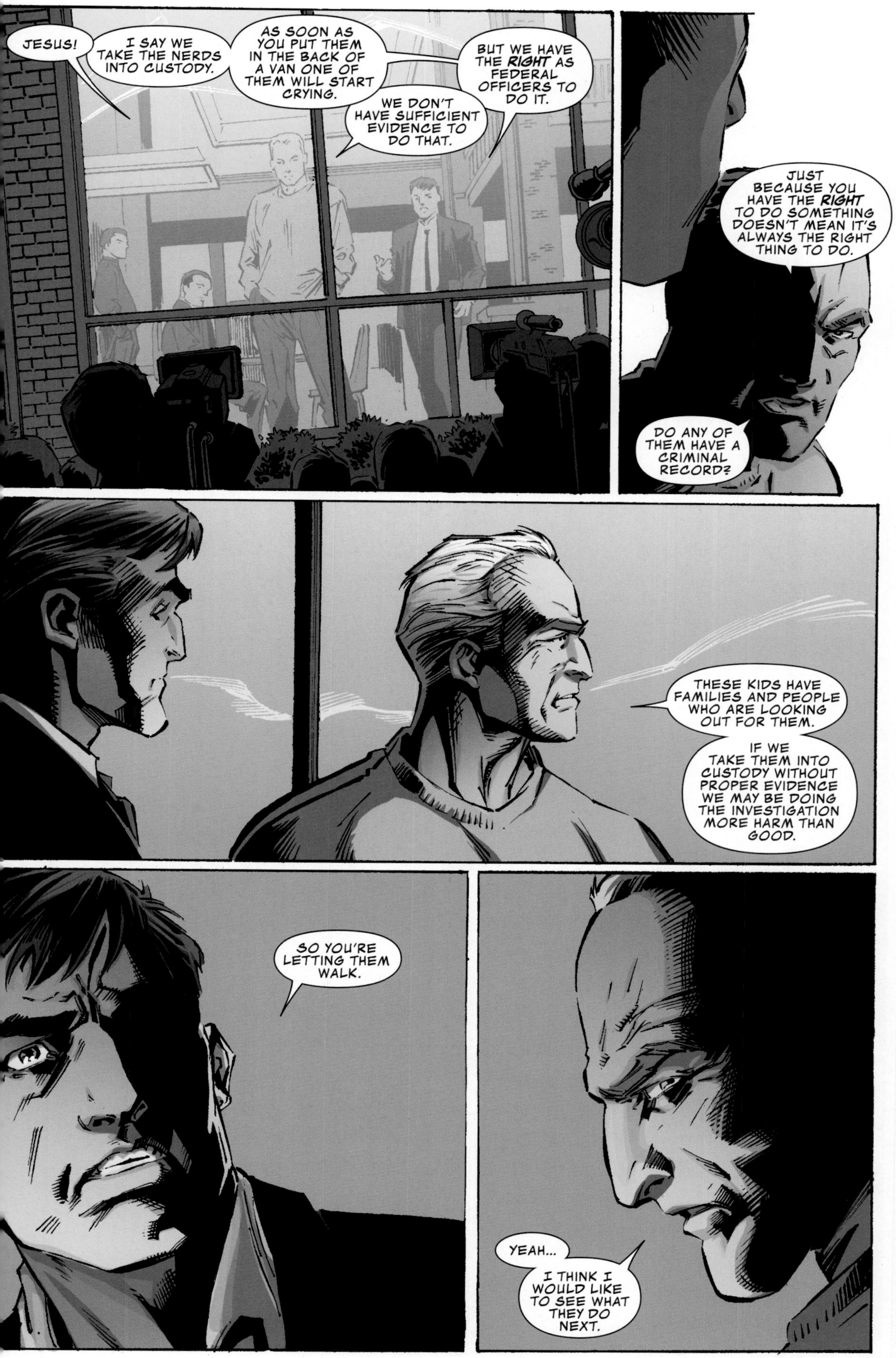
JESUS!
I SAY WE TAKE THE NERDS INTO CUSTODY.
AS SOON AS YOU PUT THEM IN THE BACK OF A VAN ONE OF THEM WILL START CRYING.
WE DON'T HAVE SUFFICIENT EVIDENCE TO DO THAT.
BUT WE HAVE THE RIGHT AS FEDERAL OFFICERS TO DO IT.
JUST BECAUSE YOU HAVE THE RIGHT TO DO SOMETHING DOESN'T MEAN IT'S ALWAYS THE RIGHT THING TO DO.
DO ANY OF THEM HAVE A CRIMINAL RECORD?
THESE KIDS HAVE FAMILIES AND PEOPLE WHO ARE LOOKING OUT FOR THEM.
IF WE TAKE THEM INTO CUSTODY WITHOUT PROPER EVIDENCE WE MAY BE DOING THE INVESTIGATION MORE HARM THAN GOOD.
SO YOU'RE LETTING THEM WALK.
YEAH...
I THINK I WOULD LIKE TO SEE WHAT THEY DO NEXT.

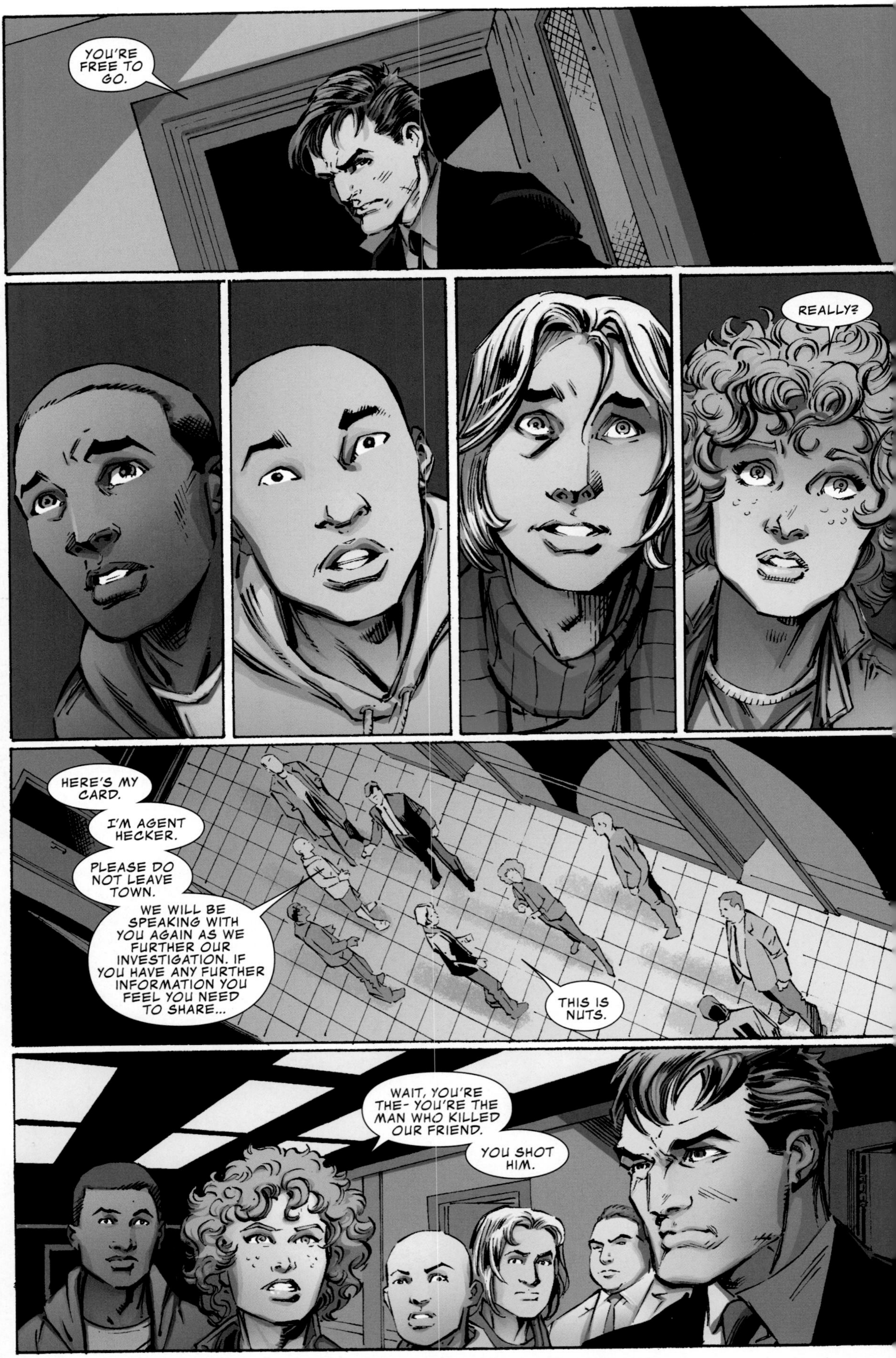
YOU'RE FREE TO GO.
REALLY?
HERE'S MY CARD.
I'M AGENT HECKER.
PLEASE DO NOT LEAVE TOWN.
WE WILL BE SPEAKING WITH YOU AGAIN AS WE FURTHER OUR INVESTIGATION. IF YOU HAVE ANY FURTHER INFORMATION YOU FEEL YOU NEED TO SHARE...
THIS IS NUTS.
WAIT, YOU'RE THE- YOU'RE THE MAN WHO KILLED OUR FRIEND.
YOU SHOT HIM.

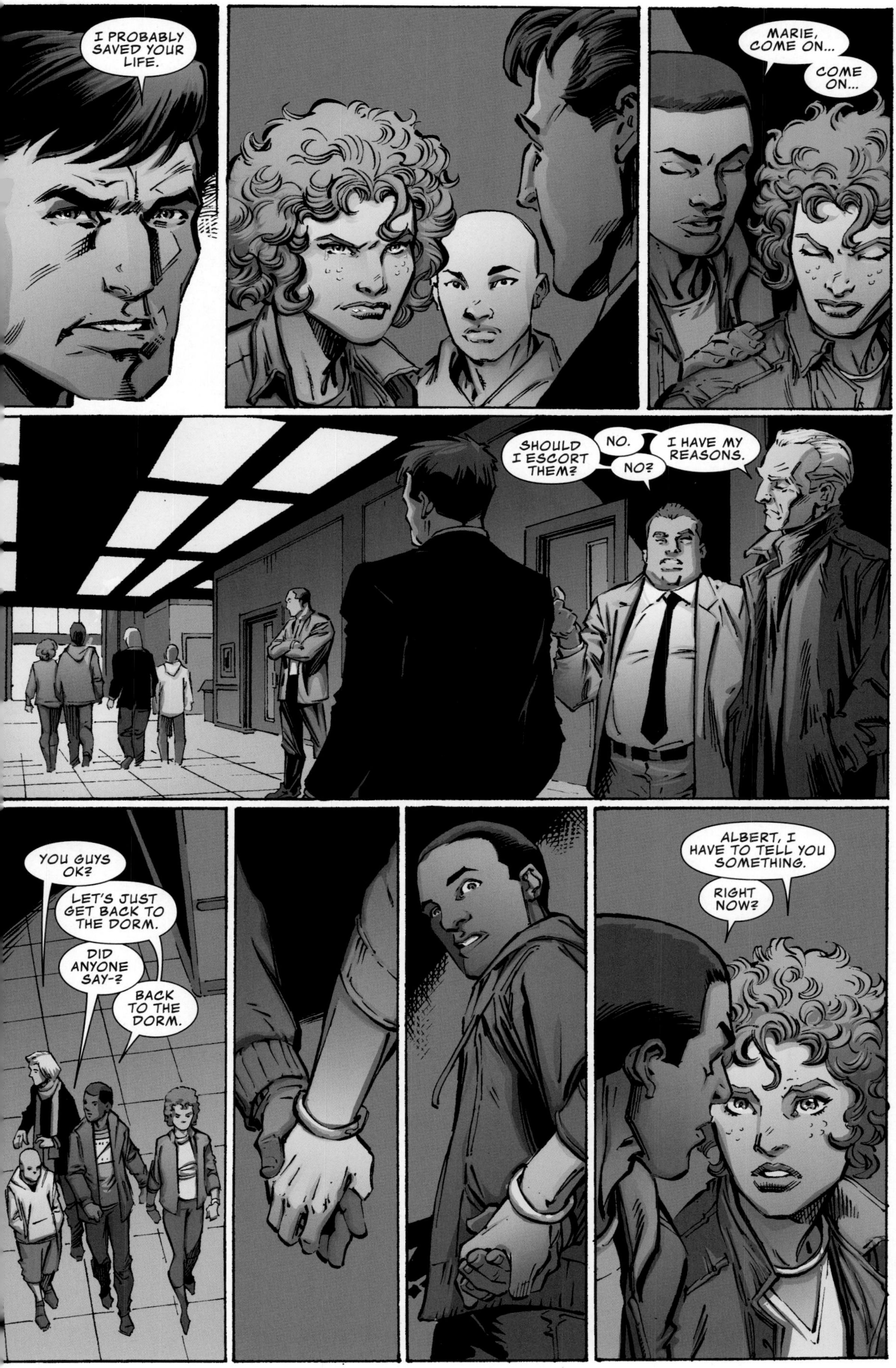

I PROBABLY SAVED YOUR LIFE.
MARIE, COME ON...
COME ON...
SHOULD I ESCORT THEM?
NO.
NO?
I HAVE MY REASONS.
YOU GUYS OK?
LET'S JUST GET BACK TO THE DORM.
DID ANYONE SAY--?
BACK TO THE DORM.
ALBERT, I HAVE TO TELL YOU SOMETHING.
RIGHT NOW?

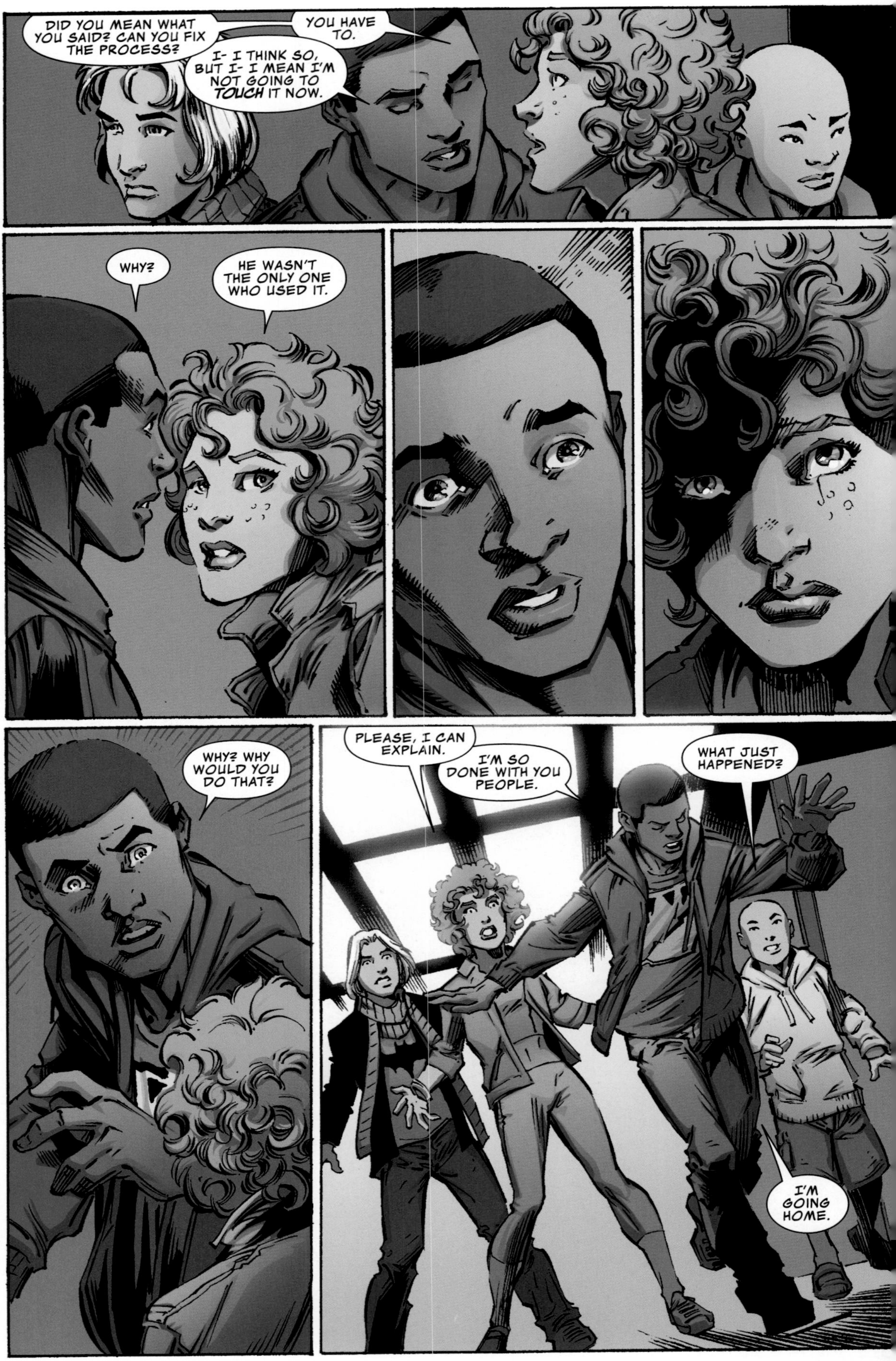
DID YOU MEAN WHAT YOU SAID? CAN YOU FIX THE PROCESS?
YOU HAVE TO.
I- I THINK SO, BUT I- I MEAN I'M NOT GOING TO *TOUCH* IT NOW.
WHY?
HE WASN'T THE ONLY ONE WHO USED IT.
WHY? WHY WOULD YOU DO THAT?
PLEASE, I CAN EXPLAIN.
I'M SO DONE WITH YOU PEOPLE.
WHAT JUST HAPPENED?
I'M GOING HOME.

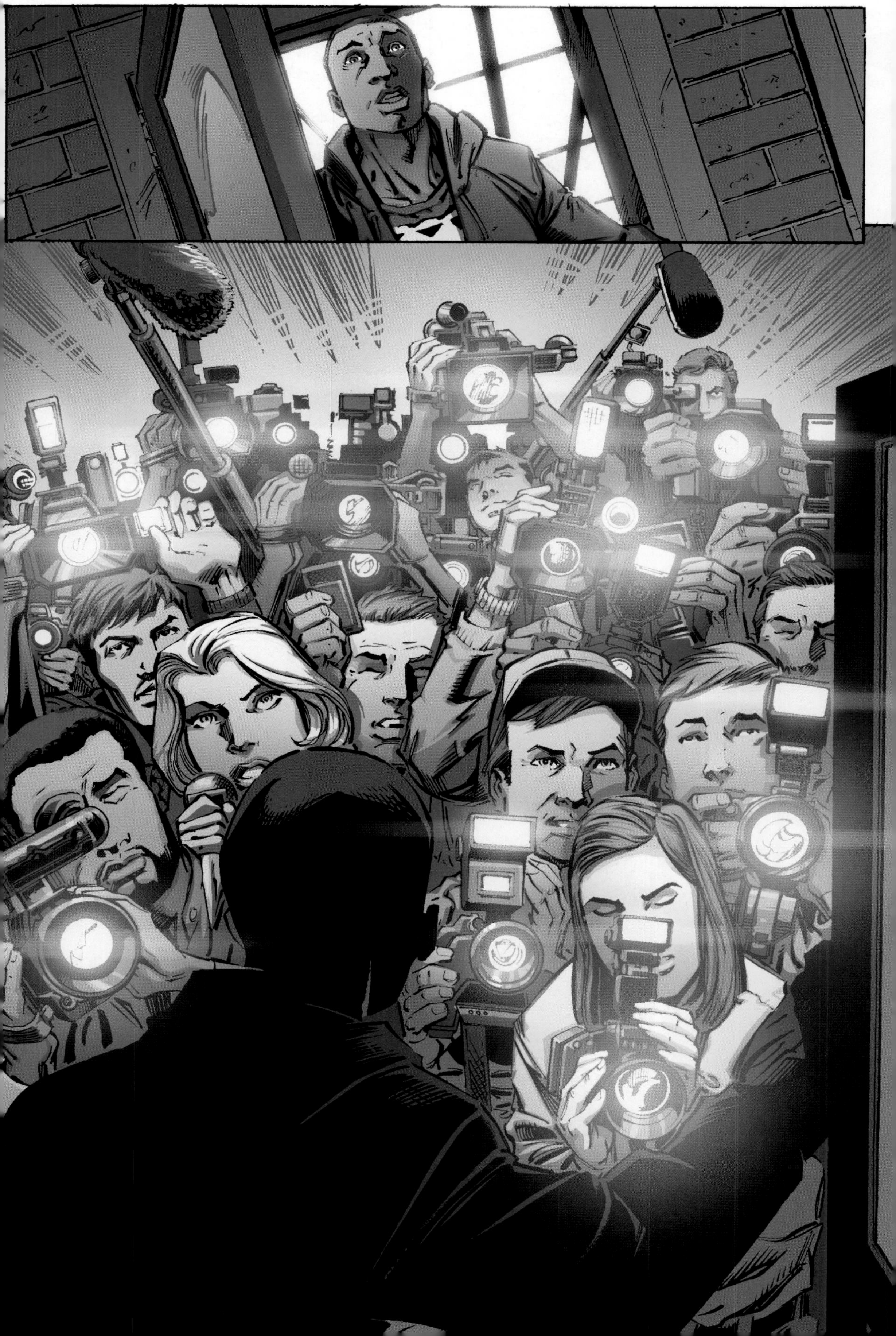

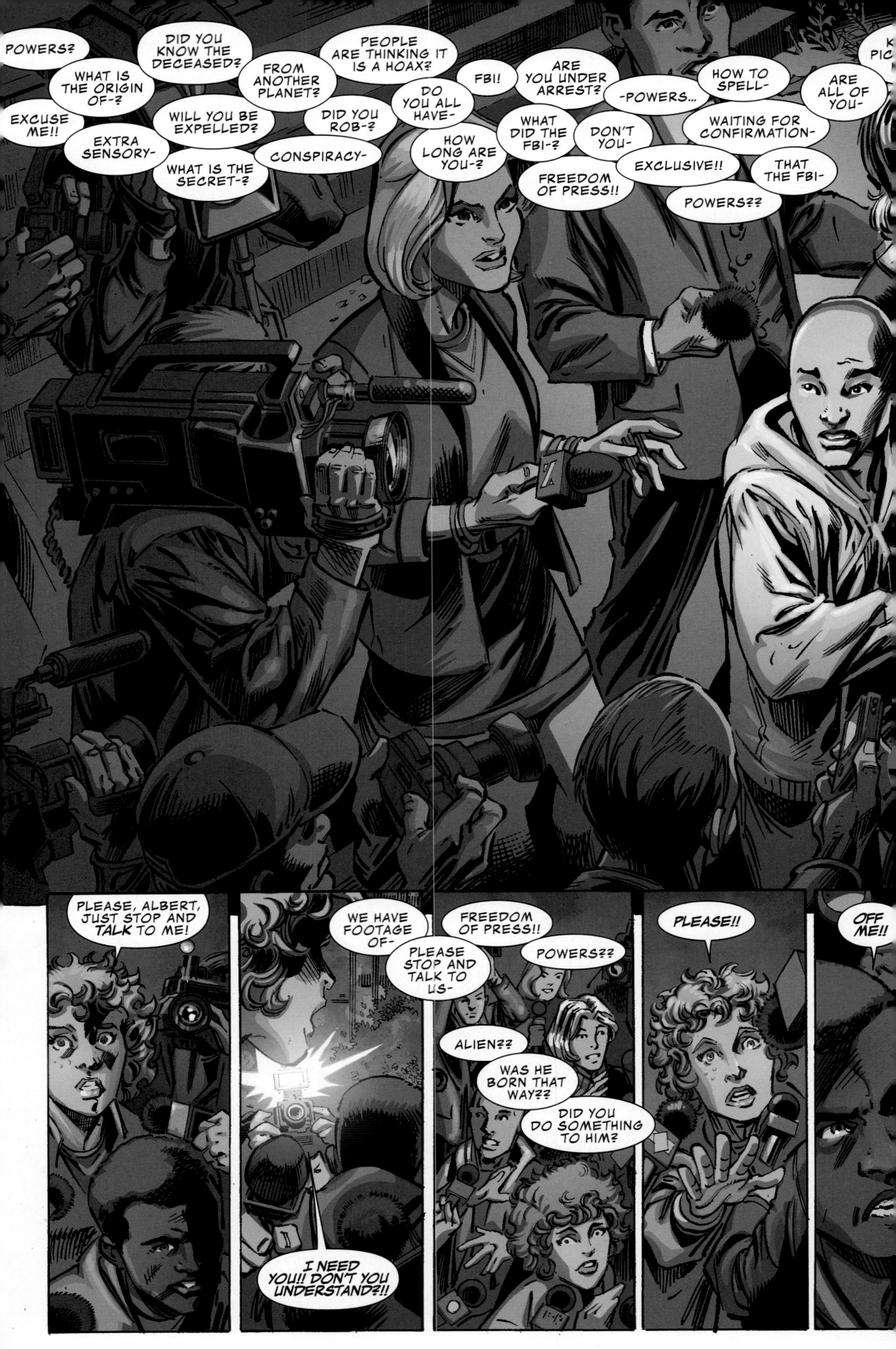
POWERS?
WHAT IS THE ORIGIN OF-?
EXCUSE ME!!
DID YOU KNOW THE DECEASED?
WILL YOU BE EXPELLED?
EXTRA SENSORY-
WHAT IS THE SECRET-?
FROM ANOTHER PLANET?
PEOPLE ARE THINKING IT IS A HOAX?
DID YOU ROB-?
CONSPIRACY-
DO YOU ALL HAVE-
HOW LONG ARE YOU-?
FBI!
ARE YOU UNDER ARREST?
WHAT DID THE FBI-?
DON'T YOU-
FREEDOM OF PRESS!!
-POWERS...
HOW TO SPELL-
WAITING FOR CONFIRMATION-
EXCLUSIVE!!
POWERS??
THAT THE FBI-
ARE ALL OF YOU-
PLEASE, ALBERT, JUST STOP AND TALK TO ME!
WE HAVE FOOTAGE OF-
I NEED YOU!! DON'T YOU UNDERSTAND?!!
FREEDOM OF PRESS!!
PLEASE STOP AND TALK TO US-
POWERS??
ALIEN??
WAS HE BORN THAT WAY??
DID YOU DO SOMETHING TO HIM?
PLEASE!!
OFF ME!!

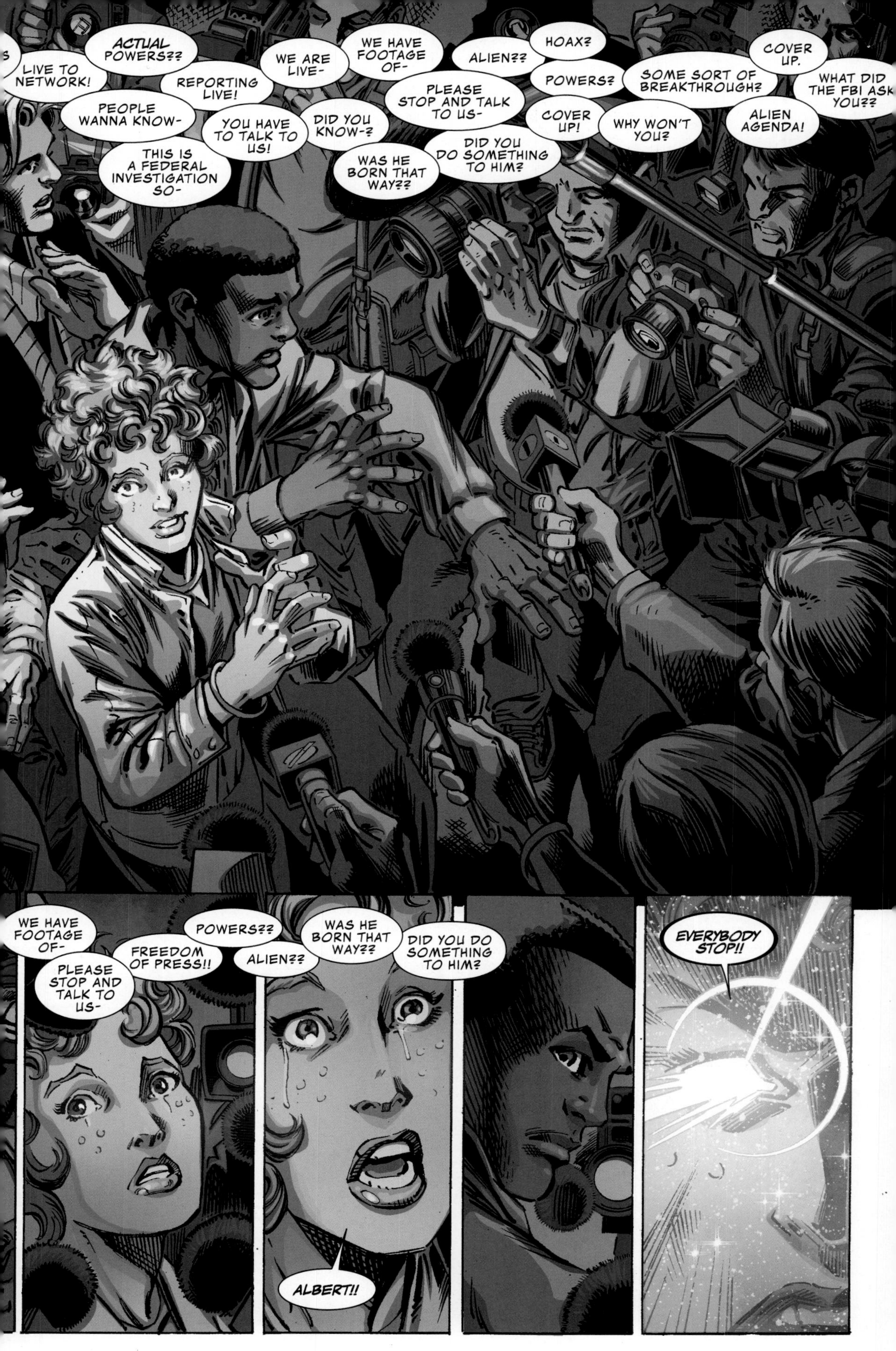
LIVE TO NETWORK!
ACTUAL POWERS??
REPORTING LIVE!
PEOPLE WANNA KNOW-
THIS IS A FEDERAL INVESTIGATION SO-
YOU HAVE TO TALK TO US!
WE ARE LIVE-
WE HAVE FOOTAGE OF-
DID YOU KNOW-?
PLEASE STOP AND TALK TO US-
WAS HE BORN THAT WAY??
DID YOU DO SOMETHING TO HIM?
ALIEN??
HOAX?
POWERS?
COVER UP!
WHY WON'T YOU?
SOME SORT OF BREAKTHROUGH?
COVER UP.
ALIEN AGENDA!
WHAT DID THE FBI ASK YOU??
WE HAVE FOOTAGE OF-
PLEASE STOP AND TALK TO US-
FREEDOM OF PRESS!!
POWERS??
ALIEN??
WAS HE BORN THAT WAY??
DID YOU DO SOMETHING TO HIM?
ALBERT!!
EVERYBODY STOP!!

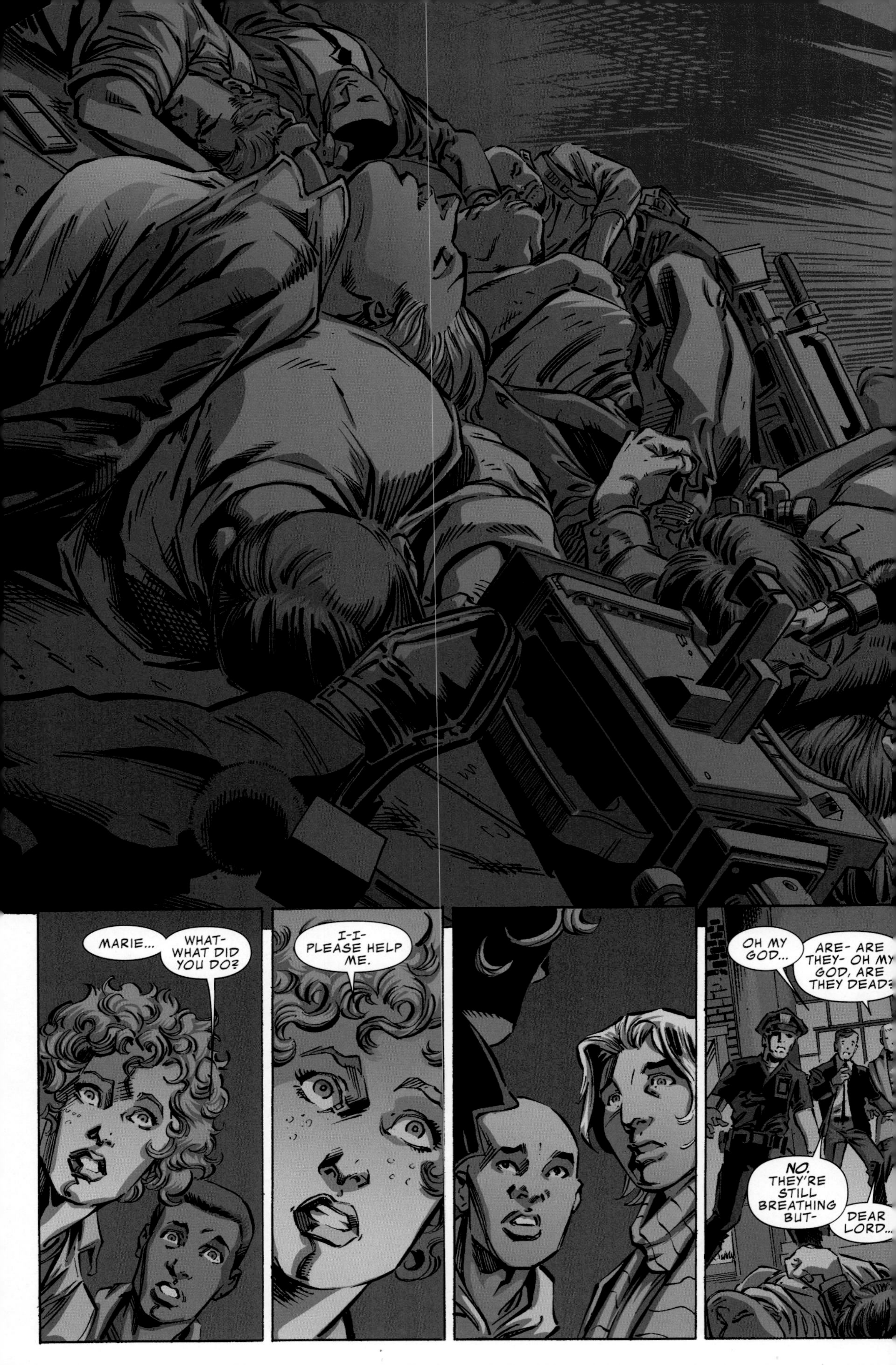
MARIE...
WHAT-WHAT DID YOU DO?
I-I-PLEASE HELP ME.
OH MY GOD...
ARE- ARE THEY- OH MY GOD, ARE THEY DEAD?
NO. THEY'RE STILL BREATHING BUT-
DEAR LORD...

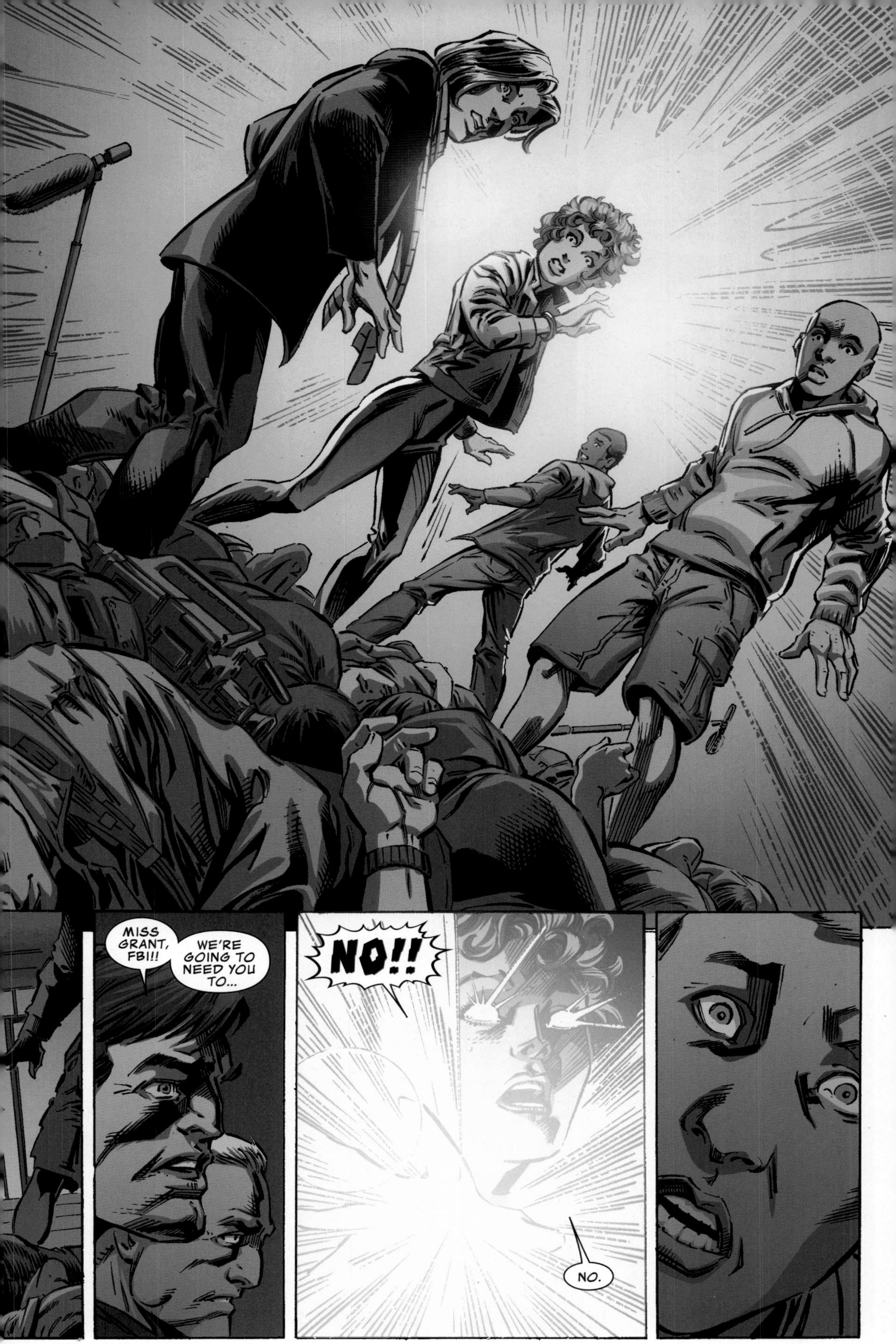
MISS GRANT, FBI!!
WE'RE GOING TO NEED YOU TO...
NO!!
NO.

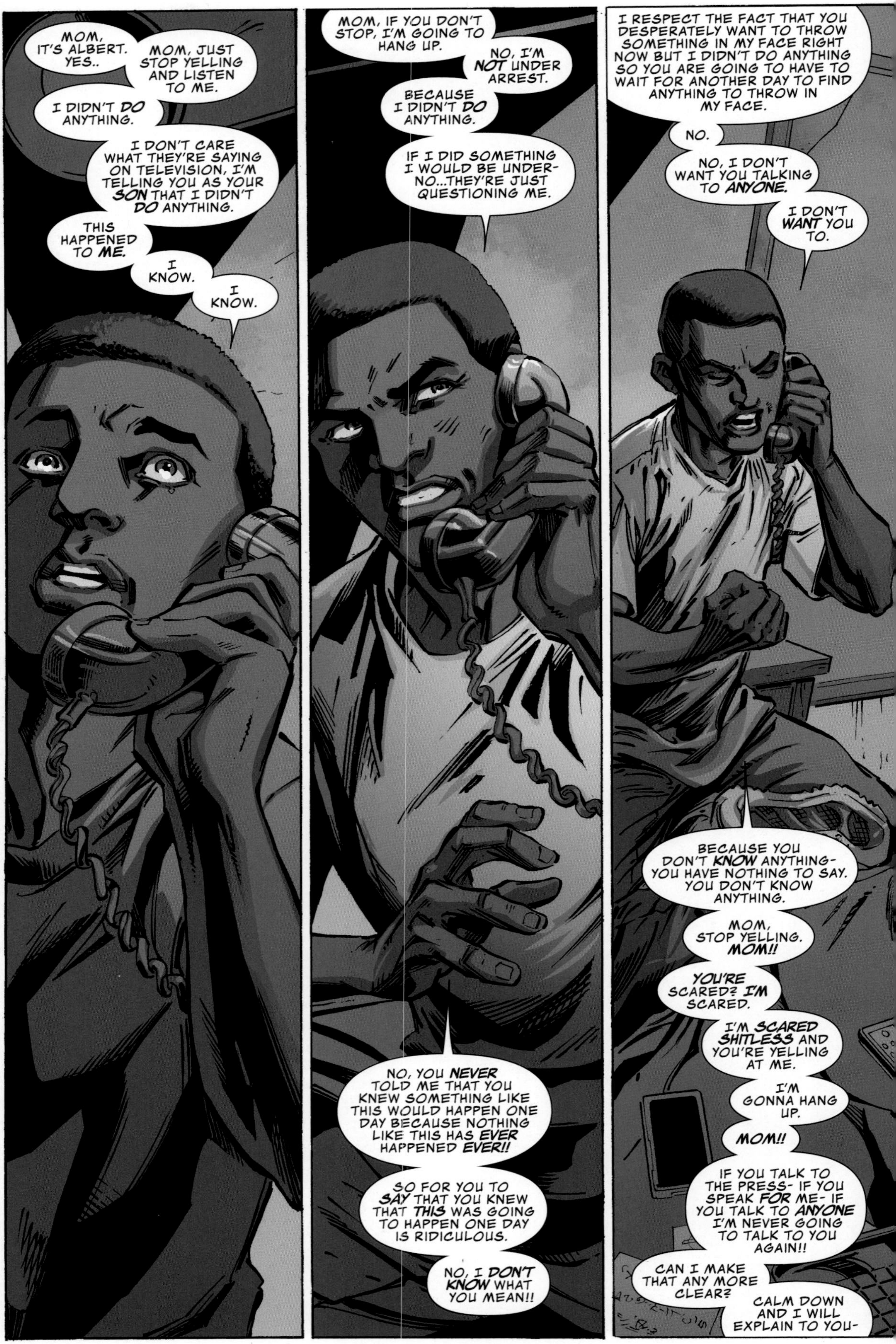
MOM, IT'S ALBERT. YES..
MOM, JUST STOP YELLING AND LISTEN TO ME.
I DIDN'T DO ANYTHING.
I DON'T CARE WHAT THEY'RE SAYING ON TELEVISION, I'M TELLING YOU AS YOUR SON THAT I DIDN'T DO ANYTHING.
THIS HAPPENED TO ME.
I KNOW.
I KNOW.
MOM, IF YOU DON'T STOP, I'M GOING TO HANG UP.
NO, I'M NOT UNDER ARREST.
BECAUSE I DIDN'T DO ANYTHING.
IF I DID SOMETHING I WOULD BE UNDER- NO...THEY'RE JUST QUESTIONING ME.
NO, YOU NEVER TOLD ME THAT YOU KNEW SOMETHING LIKE THIS WOULD HAPPEN ONE DAY BECAUSE NOTHING LIKE THIS HAS EVER HAPPENED EVER!!
SO FOR YOU TO SAY THAT YOU KNEW THAT THIS WAS GOING TO HAPPEN ONE DAY IS RIDICULOUS.
NO, I DON'T KNOW WHAT YOU MEAN!!
I RESPECT THE FACT THAT YOU DESPERATELY WANT TO THROW SOMETHING IN MY FACE RIGHT NOW BUT I DIDN'T DO ANYTHING SO YOU ARE GOING TO HAVE TO WAIT FOR ANOTHER DAY TO FIND ANYTHING TO THROW IN MY FACE.
NO.
NO, I DON'T WANT YOU TALKING TO ANYONE.
I DON'T WANT YOU TO.
BECAUSE YOU DON'T KNOW ANYTHING- YOU HAVE NOTHING TO SAY. YOU DON'T KNOW ANYTHING.
MOM, STOP YELLING. MOM!!
YOU'RE SCARED? I'M SCARED.
I'M SCARED SHITLESS AND YOU'RE YELLING AT ME.
I'M GONNA HANG UP.
MOM!!
IF YOU TALK TO THE PRESS- IF YOU SPEAK FOR ME- IF YOU TALK TO ANYONE I'M NEVER GOING TO TALK TO YOU AGAIN!!
CAN I MAKE THAT ANY MORE CLEAR?
CALM DOWN AND I WILL EXPLAIN TO YOU-

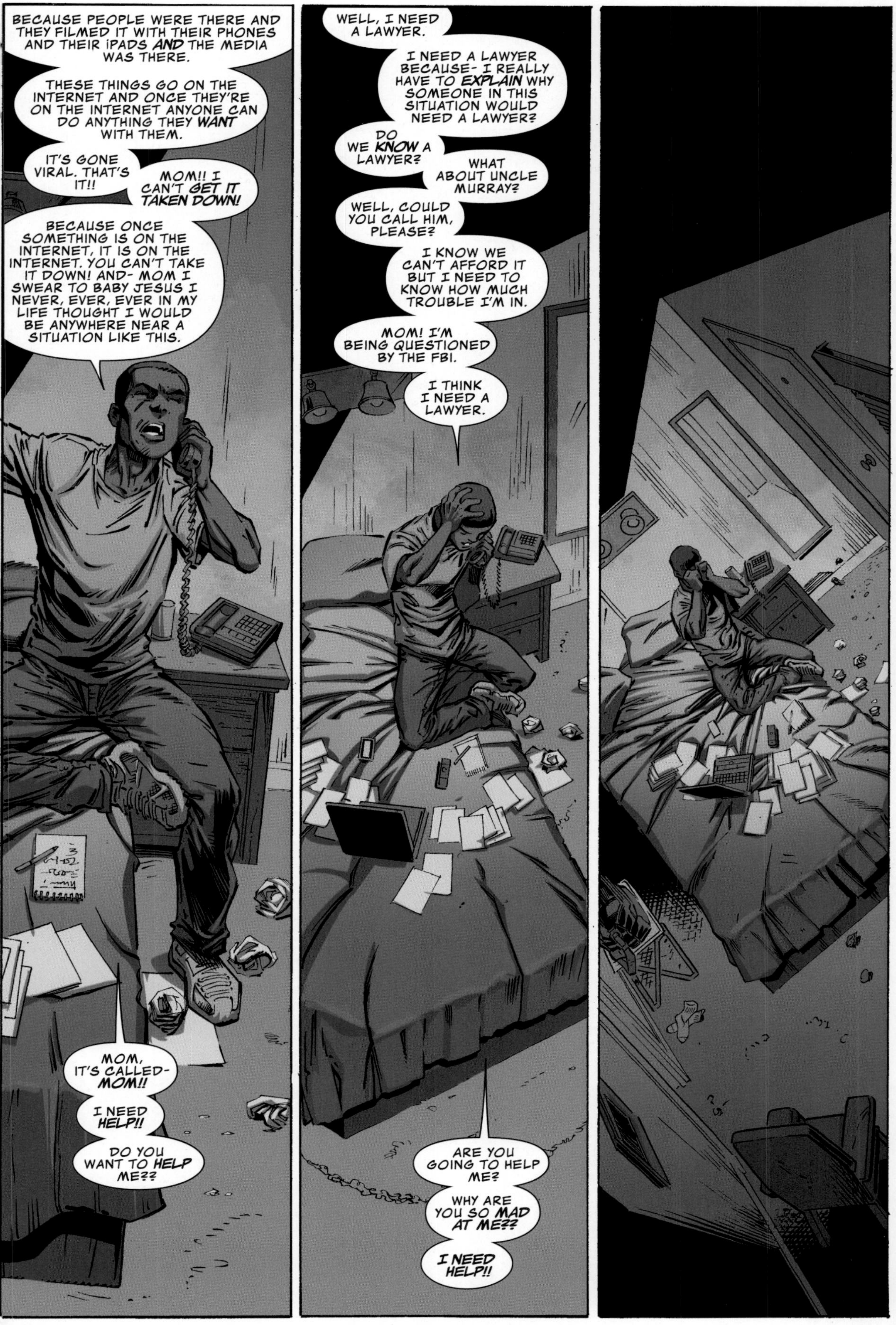
BECAUSE PEOPLE WERE THERE AND THEY FILMED IT WITH THEIR PHONES AND THEIR iPADS AND THE MEDIA WAS THERE.
THESE THINGS GO ON THE INTERNET AND ONCE THEY'RE ON THE INTERNET ANYONE CAN DO ANYTHING THEY WANT WITH THEM.
IT'S GONE VIRAL. THAT'S IT!!
MOM!! I CAN'T GET IT TAKEN DOWN!
BECAUSE ONCE SOMETHING IS ON THE INTERNET, IT IS ON THE INTERNET. YOU CAN'T TAKE IT DOWN! AND- MOM I SWEAR TO BABY JESUS I NEVER, EVER, EVER IN MY LIFE THOUGHT I WOULD BE ANYWHERE NEAR A SITUATION LIKE THIS.
MOM, IT'S CALLED- MOM!!
I NEED HELP!!
DO YOU WANT TO HELP ME??
WELL, I NEED A LAWYER.
I NEED A LAWYER BECAUSE- I REALLY HAVE TO EXPLAIN WHY SOMEONE IN THIS SITUATION WOULD NEED A LAWYER?
DO WE KNOW A LAWYER?
WHAT ABOUT UNCLE MURRAY?
WELL, COULD YOU CALL HIM, PLEASE?
I KNOW WE CAN'T AFFORD IT BUT I NEED TO KNOW HOW MUCH TROUBLE I'M IN.
MOM! I'M BEING QUESTIONED BY THE FBI.
I THINK I NEED A LAWYER.
ARE YOU GOING TO HELP ME?
WHY ARE YOU SO MAD AT ME??
I NEED HELP!!

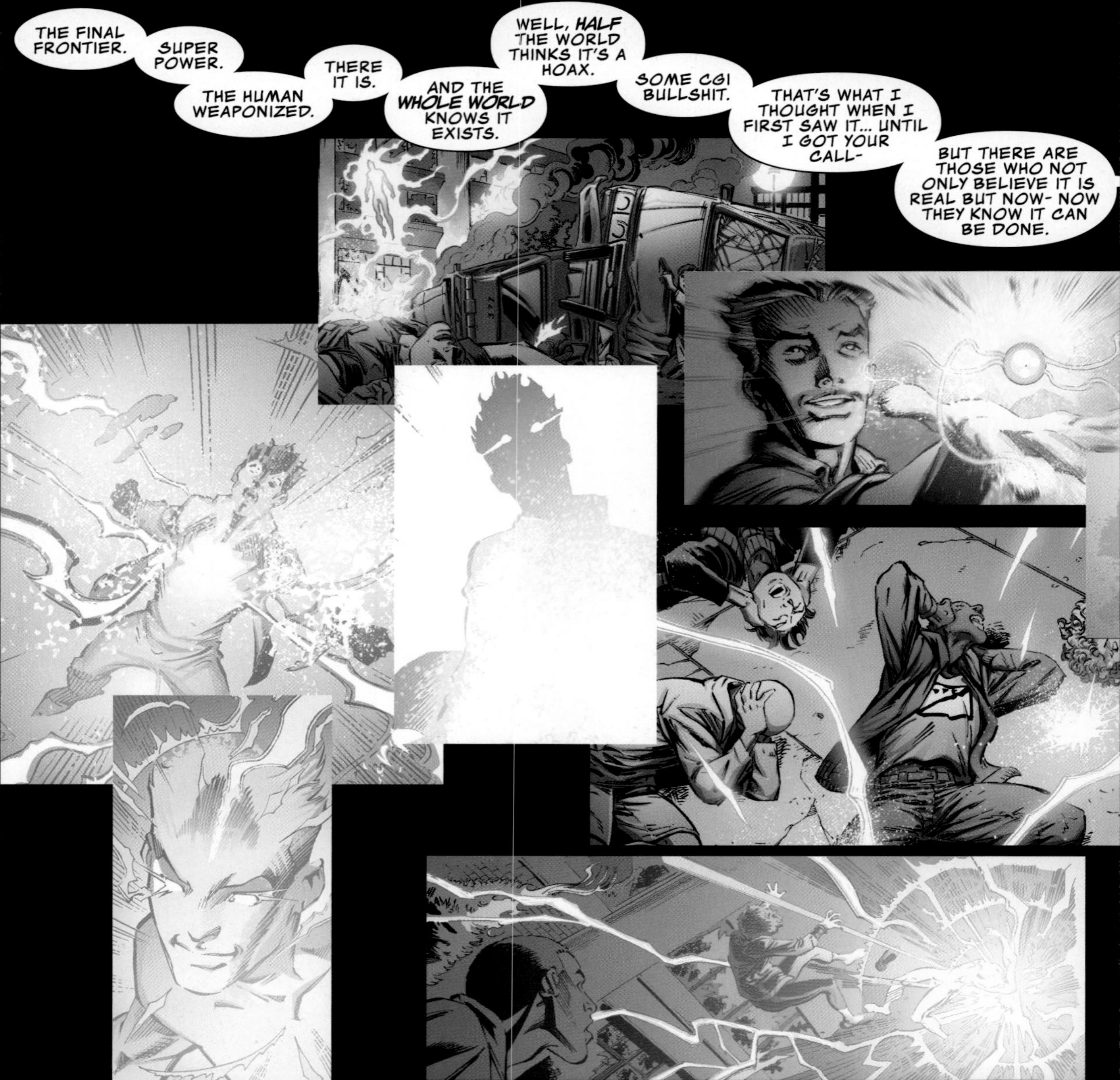
THE FINAL FRONTIER.
SUPER POWER.
THE HUMAN WEAPONIZED.
THERE IT IS.
AND THE WHOLE WORLD KNOWS IT EXISTS.
WELL, HALF THE WORLD THINKS IT'S A HOAX.
SOME CGI BULLSHIT.
THAT'S WHAT I THOUGHT WHEN I FIRST SAW IT... UNTIL I GOT YOUR CALL-
BUT THERE ARE THOSE WHO NOT ONLY BELIEVE IT IS REAL BUT NOW- NOW THEY KNOW IT CAN BE DONE.

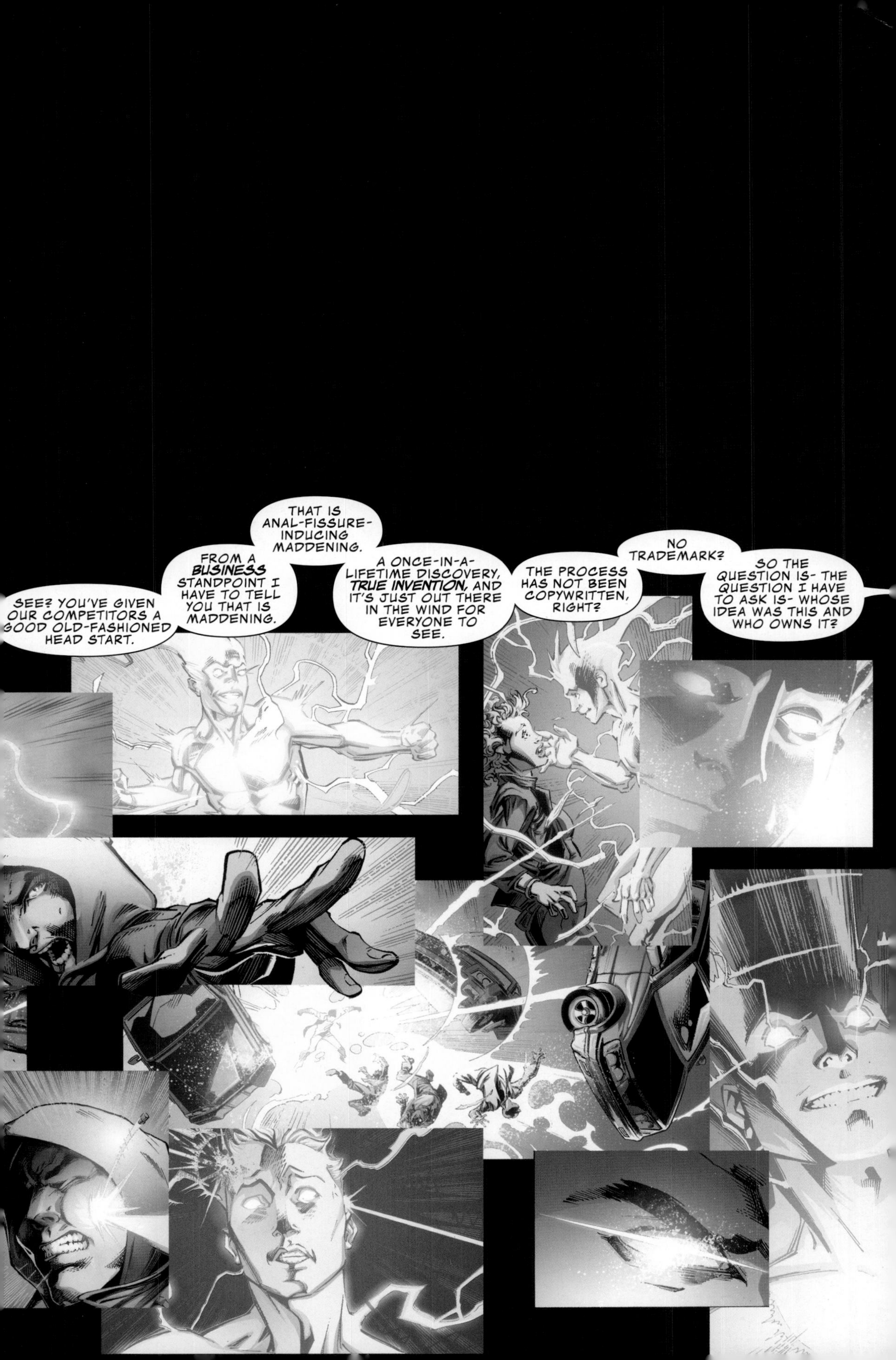
SEE? YOU'VE GIVEN OUR COMPETITORS A GOOD OLD-FASHIONED HEAD START.
FROM A BUSINESS STANDPOINT I HAVE TO TELL YOU THAT IS MADDENING.
THAT IS ANAL-FISSURE-INDUCING MADDENING.
A ONCE-IN-A-LIFETIME DISCOVERY, TRUE INVENTION, AND IT'S JUST OUT THERE IN THE WIND FOR EVERYONE TO SEE.
THE PROCESS HAS NOT BEEN COPYWRITTEN, RIGHT?
NO TRADEMARK?
SO THE QUESTION IS- THE QUESTION I HAVE TO ASK IS- WHOSE IDEA WAS THIS AND WHO OWNS IT?

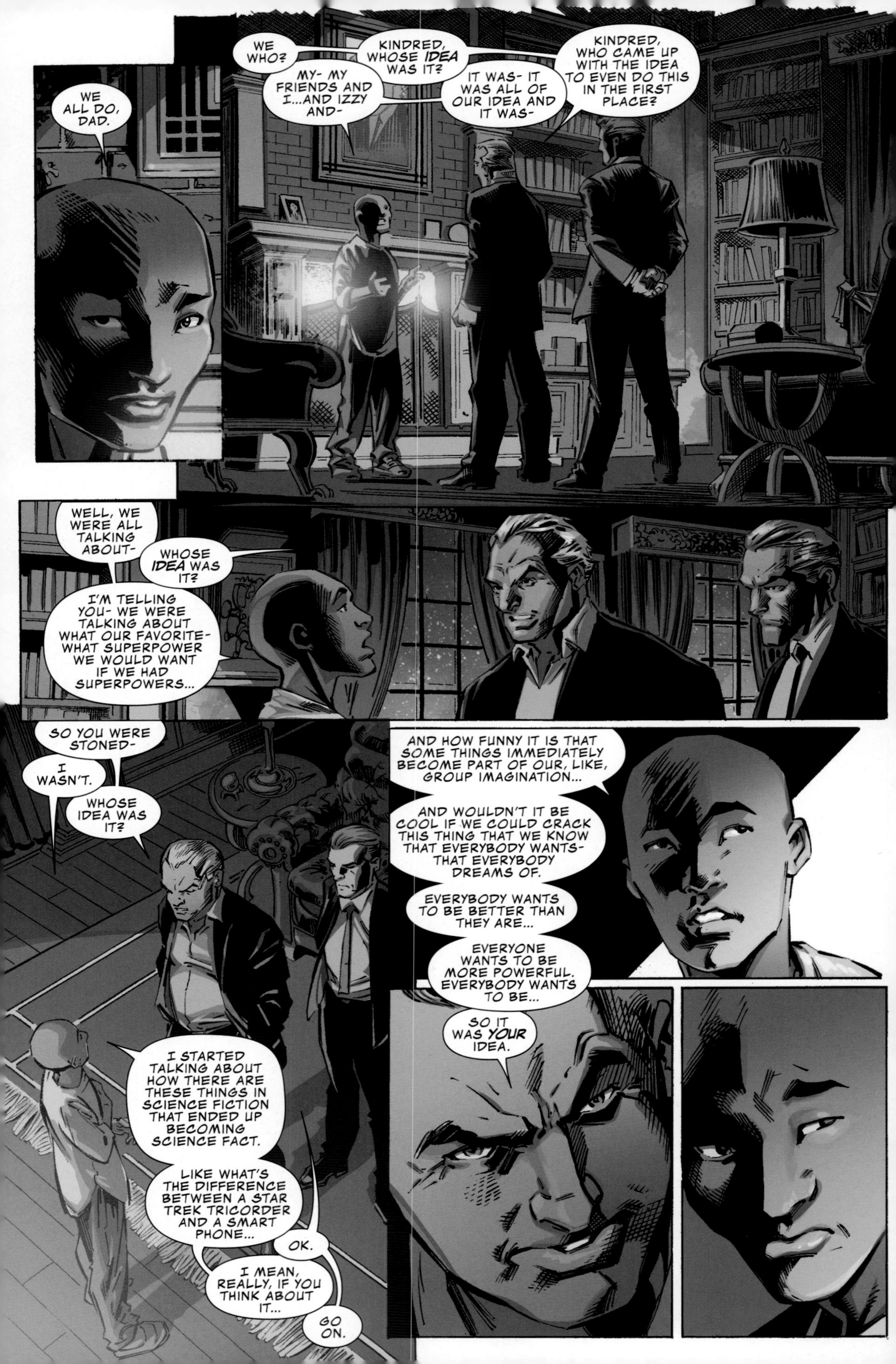
WE ALL DO, DAD.
WE WHO?
KINDRED, WHOSE IDEA WAS IT?
MY- MY FRIENDS AND I...AND IZZY AND-
IT WAS- IT WAS ALL OF OUR IDEA AND IT WAS-
KINDRED, WHO CAME UP WITH THE IDEA TO EVEN DO THIS IN THE FIRST PLACE?
WELL, WE WERE ALL TALKING ABOUT-
WHOSE IDEA WAS IT?
I'M TELLING YOU- WE WERE TALKING ABOUT WHAT OUR FAVORITE- WHAT SUPERPOWER WE WOULD WANT IF WE HAD SUPERPOWERS...
SO YOU WERE STONED-
I WASN'T.
WHOSE IDEA WAS IT?
I STARTED TALKING ABOUT HOW THERE ARE THESE THINGS IN SCIENCE FICTION THAT ENDED UP BECOMING SCIENCE FACT.
LIKE WHAT'S THE DIFFERENCE BETWEEN A STAR TREK TRICORDER AND A SMART PHONE...
OK.
I MEAN, REALLY, IF YOU THINK ABOUT IT...
GO ON.
AND HOW FUNNY IT IS THAT SOME THINGS IMMEDIATELY BECOME PART OF OUR, LIKE, GROUP IMAGINATION...
AND WOULDN'T IT BE COOL IF WE COULD CRACK THIS THING THAT WE KNOW THAT EVERYBODY WANTS- THAT EVERYBODY DREAMS OF.
EVERYBODY WANTS TO BE BETTER THAN THEY ARE...
EVERYONE WANTS TO BE MORE POWERFUL. EVERYBODY WANTS TO BE...
SO IT WAS YOUR IDEA.

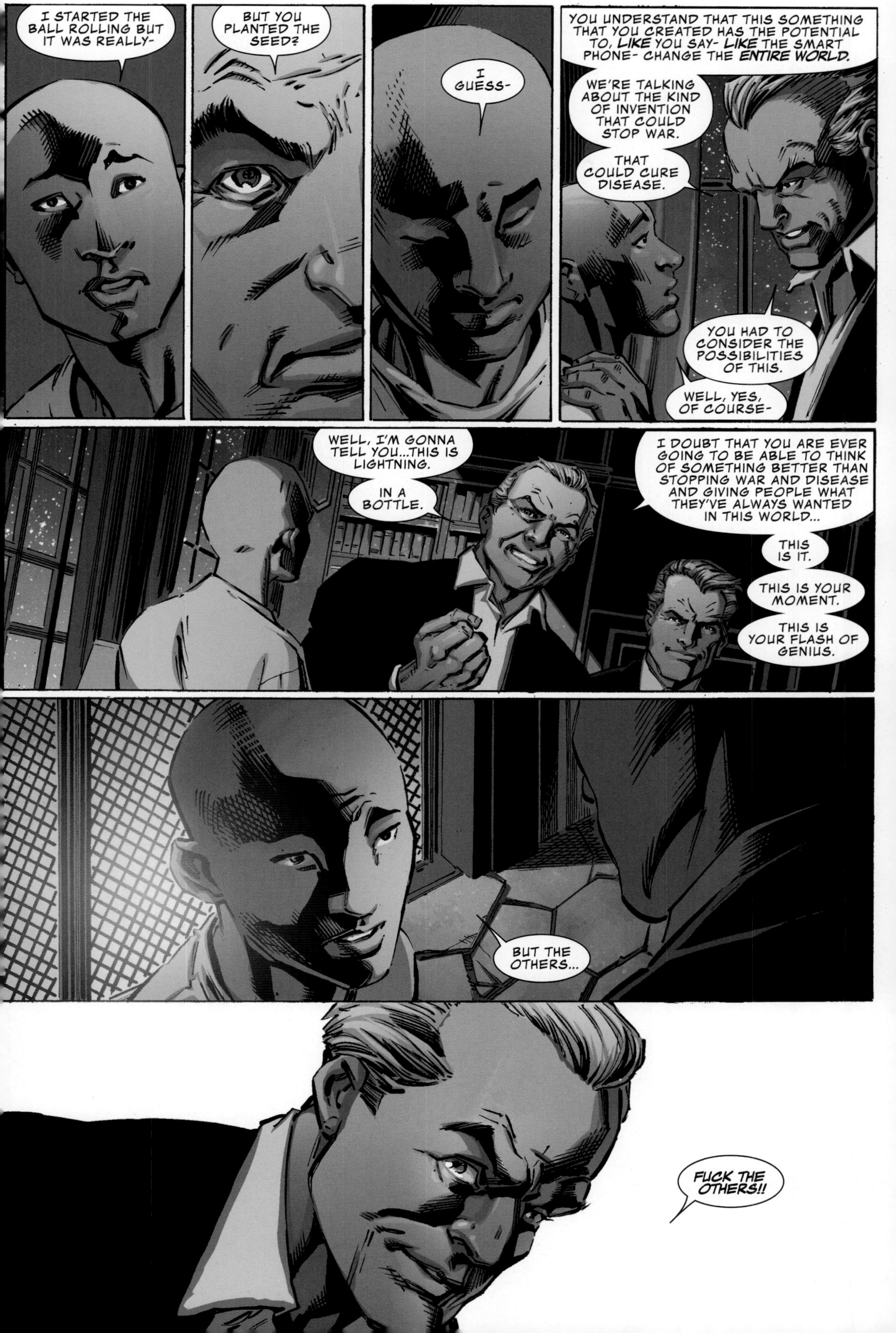
I STARTED THE BALL ROLLING BUT IT WAS REALLY-
BUT YOU PLANTED THE SEED?
I GUESS-
YOU UNDERSTAND THAT THIS SOMETHING THAT YOU CREATED HAS THE POTENTIAL TO, LIKE YOU SAY- LIKE THE SMART PHONE- CHANGE THE ENTIRE WORLD.
WE'RE TALKING ABOUT THE KIND OF INVENTION THAT COULD STOP WAR.
THAT COULD CURE DISEASE.
YOU HAD TO CONSIDER THE POSSIBILITIES OF THIS.
WELL, YES, OF COURSE-
WELL, I'M GONNA TELL YOU...THIS IS LIGHTNING.
IN A BOTTLE.
I DOUBT THAT YOU ARE EVER GOING TO BE ABLE TO THINK OF SOMETHING BETTER THAN STOPPING WAR AND DISEASE AND GIVING PEOPLE WHAT THEY'VE ALWAYS WANTED IN THIS WORLD...
THIS IS IT.
THIS IS YOUR MOMENT.
THIS IS YOUR FLASH OF GENIUS.
BUT THE OTHERS...
FUCK THE OTHERS!!

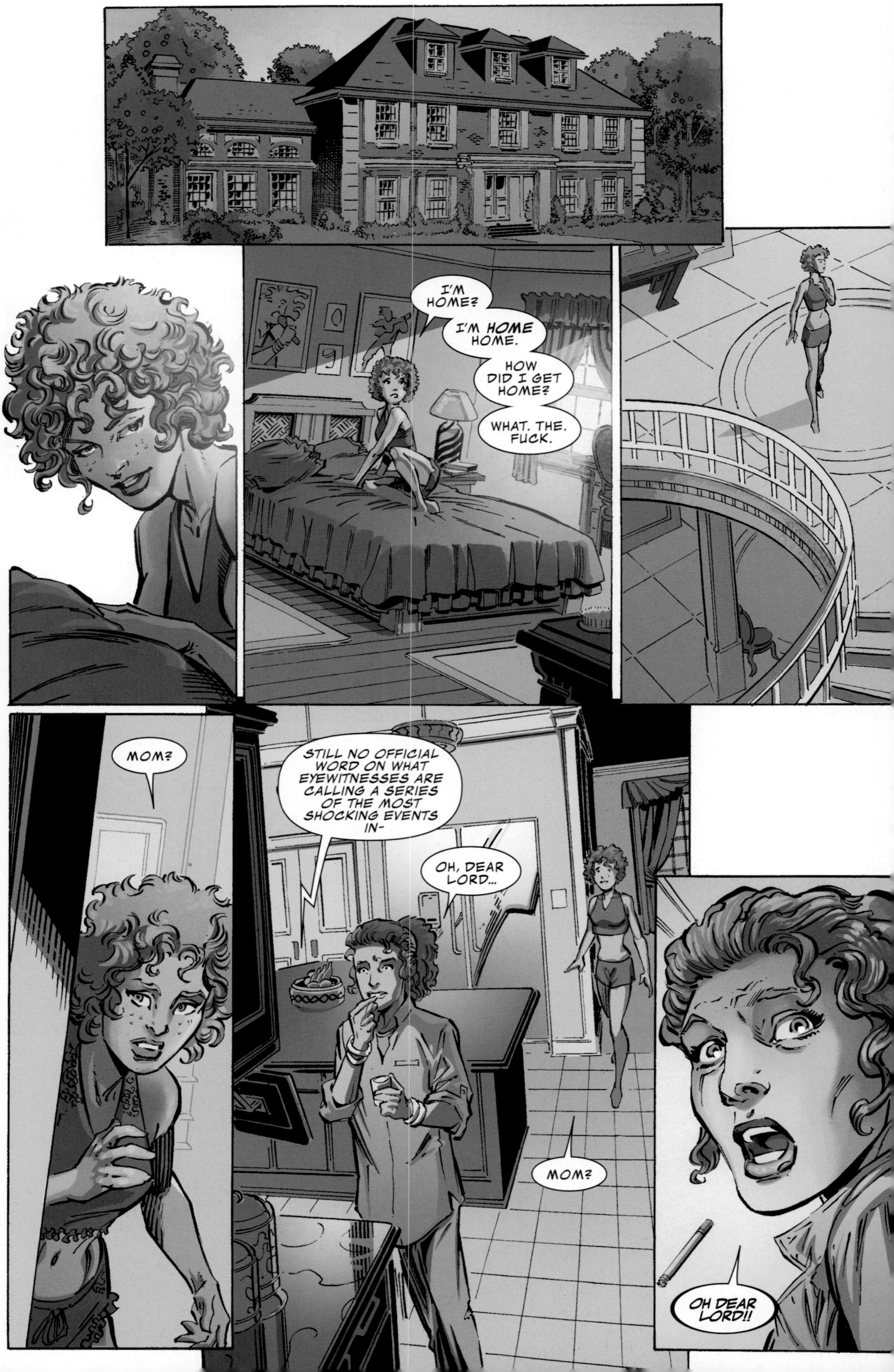
I'M HOME?
I'M HOME HOME.
HOW DID I GET HOME?
WHAT. THE. FUCK.
MOM?
STILL NO OFFICIAL WORD ON WHAT EYEWITNESSES ARE CALLING A SERIES OF THE MOST SHOCKING EVENTS IN-
OH, DEAR LORD...
MOM?
OH DEAR LORD!!

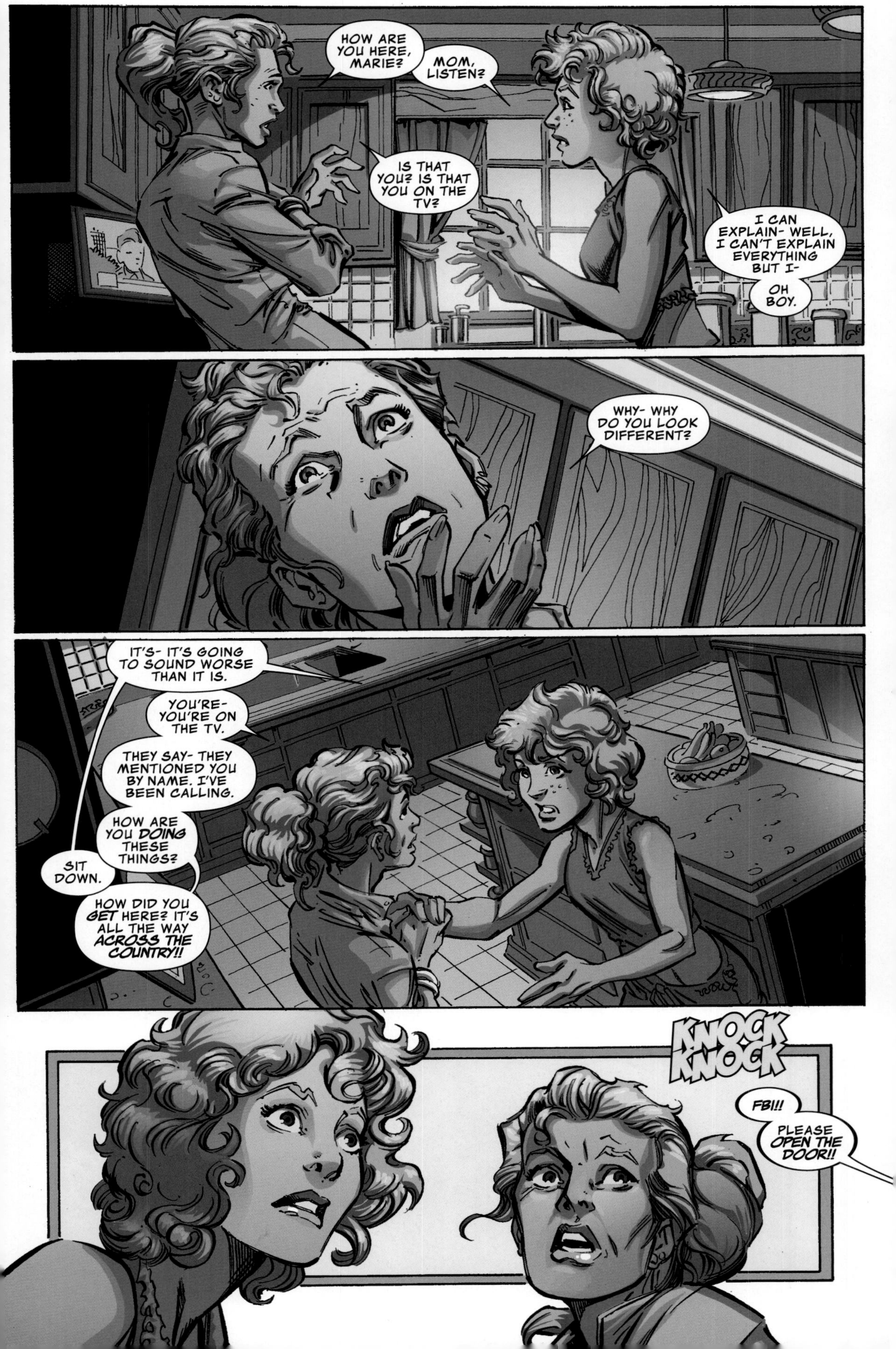
HOW ARE YOU HERE, MARIE?
MOM, LISTEN?
IS THAT YOU? IS THAT YOU ON THE TV?
I CAN EXPLAIN- WELL, I CAN'T EXPLAIN EVERYTHING BUT I-
OH BOY.
WHY- WHY DO YOU LOOK DIFFERENT?
IT'S- IT'S GOING TO SOUND WORSE THAN IT IS.
YOU'RE- YOU'RE ON THE TV.
THEY SAY- THEY MENTIONED YOU BY NAME. I'VE BEEN CALLING.
HOW ARE YOU DOING THESE THINGS?
SIT DOWN.
HOW DID YOU GET HERE? IT'S ALL THE WAY ACROSS THE COUNTRY!!
KNOCK KNOCK
FBI!!
PLEASE OPEN THE DOOR!!

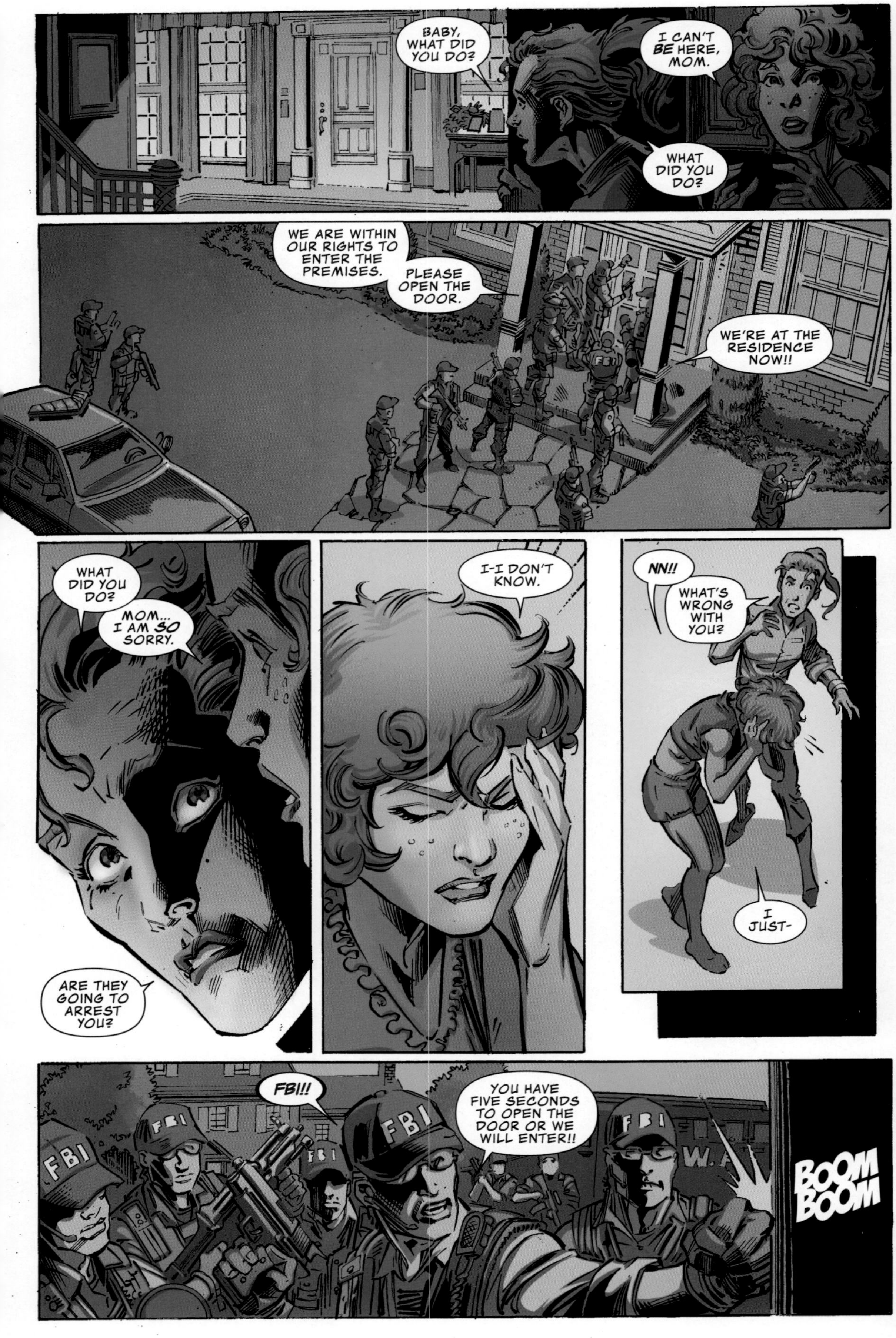
BABY, WHAT DID YOU DO?
I CAN'T BE HERE, MOM.
WHAT DID YOU DO?
WE ARE WITHIN OUR RIGHTS TO ENTER THE PREMISES.
PLEASE OPEN THE DOOR.
WE'RE AT THE RESIDENCE NOW!!
WHAT DID YOU DO?
MOM... I AM SO SORRY.
ARE THEY GOING TO ARREST YOU?
I-I DON'T KNOW.
NN!!
WHAT'S WRONG WITH YOU?
I JUST-
FBI!!
YOU HAVE FIVE SECONDS TO OPEN THE DOOR OR WE WILL ENTER!!
BOOM BOOM

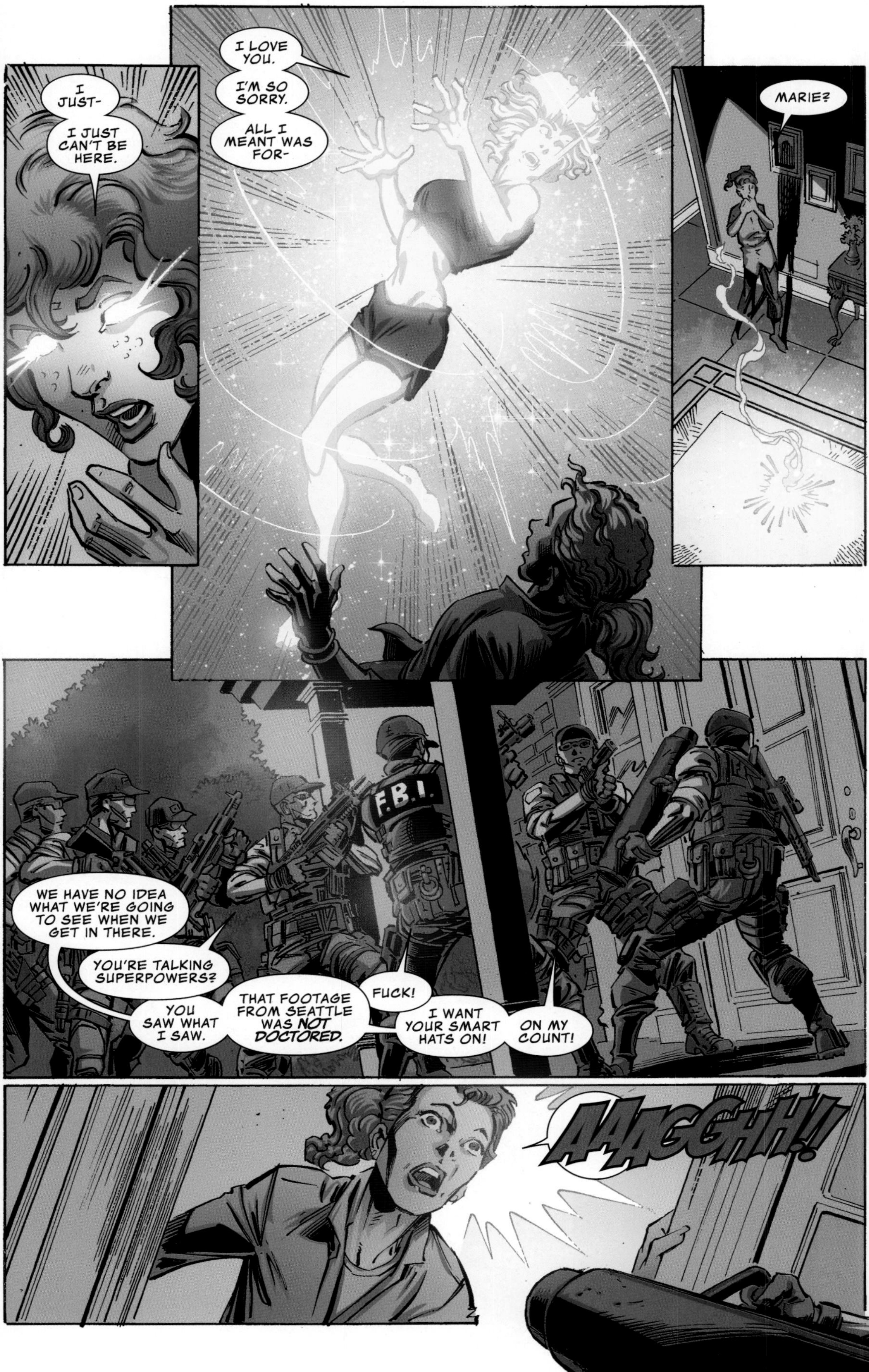
I JUST-
I JUST CAN'T BE HERE.
I LOVE YOU.
I'M SO SORRY.
ALL I MEANT WAS FOR-
MARIE?
WE HAVE NO IDEA WHAT WE'RE GOING TO SEE WHEN WE GET IN THERE.
YOU'RE TALKING SUPERPOWERS?
YOU SAW WHAT I SAW.
THAT FOOTAGE FROM SEATTLE WAS NOT DOCTORED.
FUCK!
I WANT YOUR SMART HATS ON!
ON MY COUNT!
AAAGGH!!

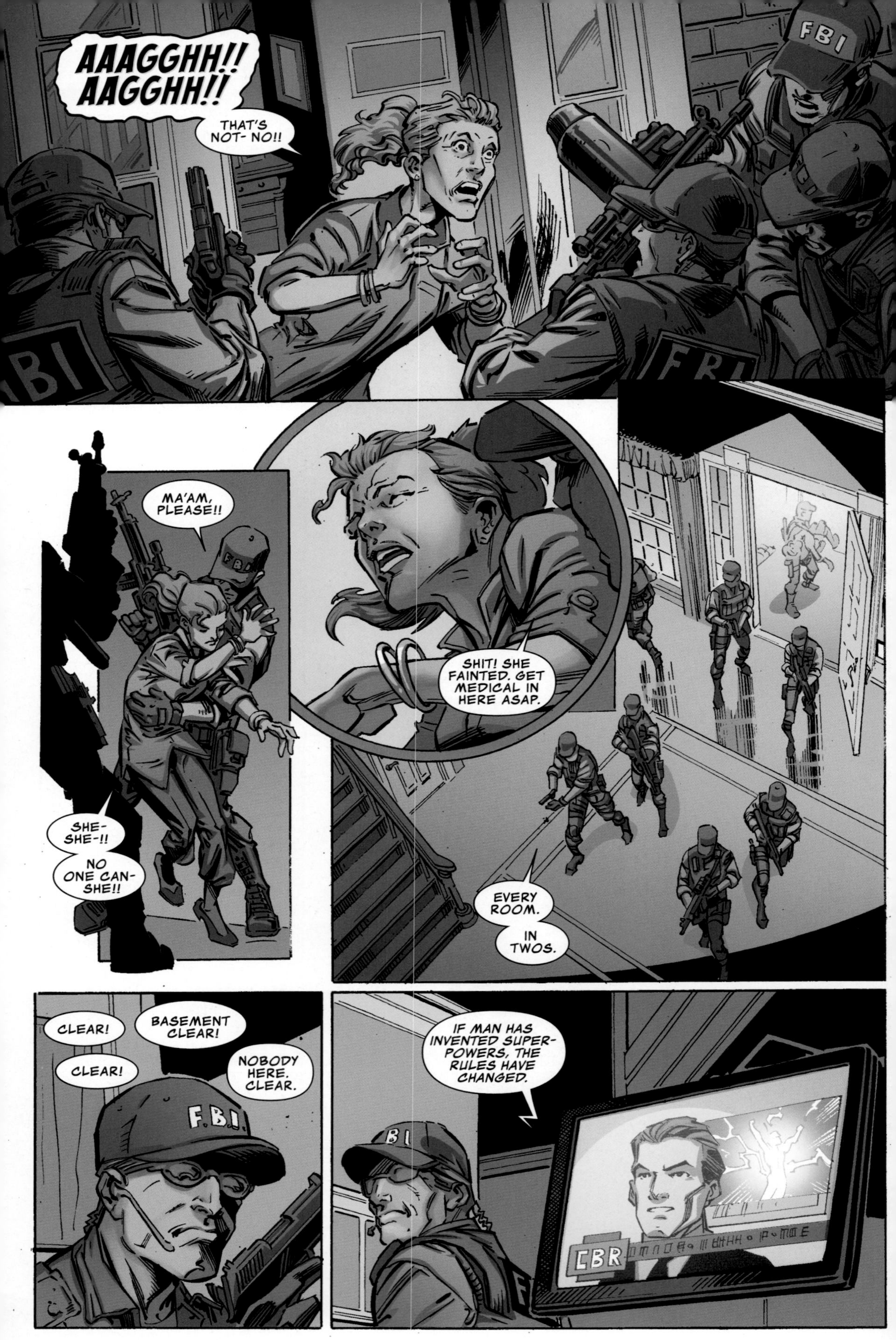
AAAGGHH!!
AAGGHH!!
THAT'S NOT- NO!!
MA'AM, PLEASE!!
SHE- SHE-!!
NO ONE CAN- SHE!!
SHIT! SHE FAINTED. GET MEDICAL IN HERE ASAP.
EVERY ROOM.
IN TWOS.
CLEAR!
BASEMENT CLEAR!
CLEAR!
NOBODY HERE. CLEAR.
IF MAN HAS INVENTED SUPER-POWERS, THE RULES HAVE CHANGED.
CBR

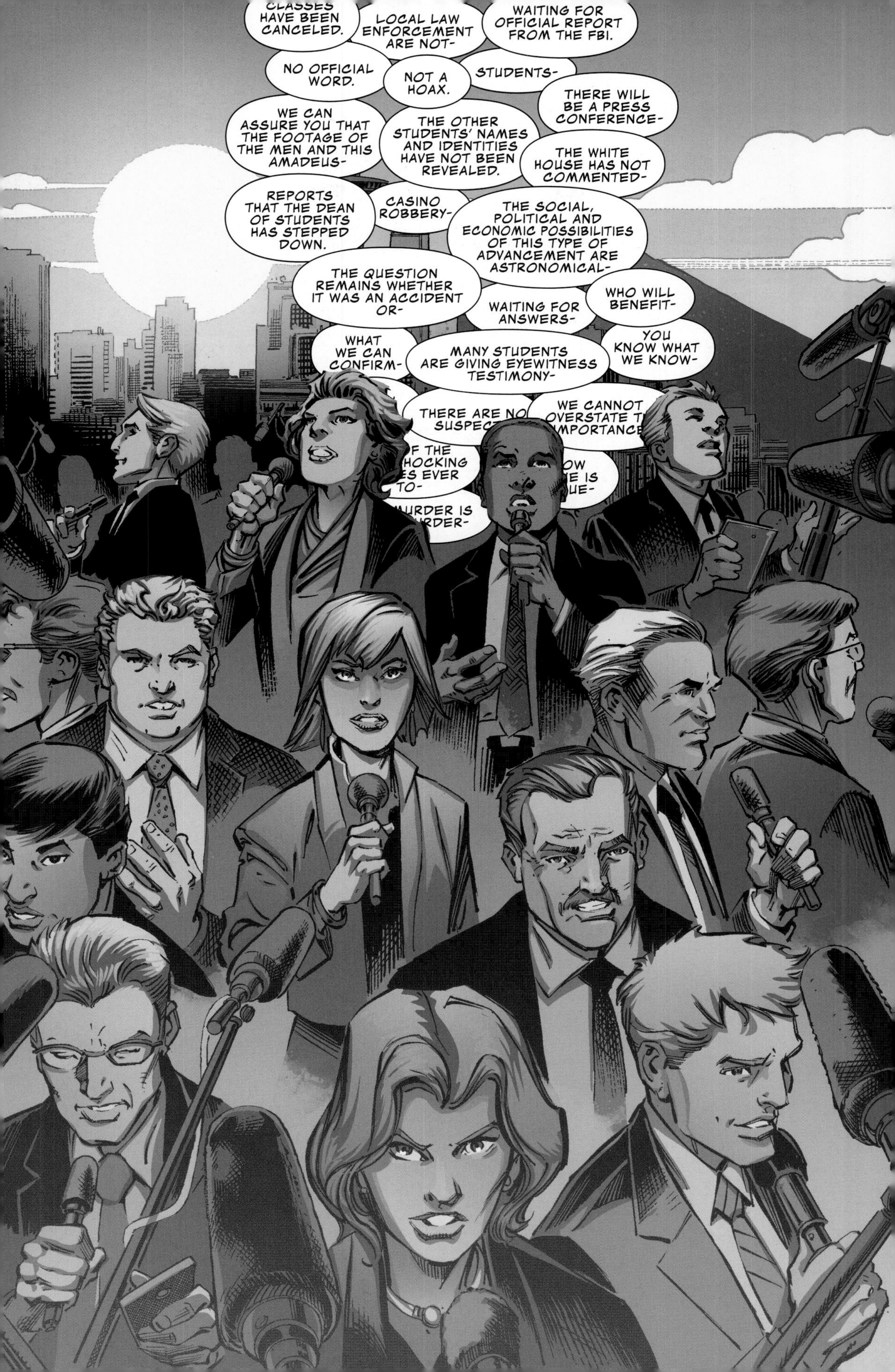

CLASSES HAVE BEEN CANCELED.
LOCAL LAW ENFORCEMENT ARE NOT-
WAITING FOR OFFICIAL REPORT FROM THE FBI.
NO OFFICIAL WORD.
NOT A HOAX.
STUDENTS-
THERE WILL BE A PRESS CONFERENCE-
WE CAN ASSURE YOU THAT THE FOOTAGE OF THE MEN AND THIS AMADEUS-
THE OTHER STUDENTS' NAMES AND IDENTITIES HAVE NOT BEEN REVEALED.
THE WHITE HOUSE HAS NOT COMMENTED-
REPORTS THAT THE DEAN OF STUDENTS HAS STEPPED DOWN.
CASINO ROBBERY-
THE SOCIAL, POLITICAL AND ECONOMIC POSSIBILITIES OF THIS TYPE OF ADVANCEMENT ARE ASTRONOMICAL-
THE QUESTION REMAINS WHETHER IT WAS AN ACCIDENT OR-
WAITING FOR ANSWERS-
WHO WILL BENEFIT-
WHAT WE CAN CONFIRM-
MANY STUDENTS ARE GIVING EYEWITNESS TESTIMONY-
YOU KNOW WHAT WE KNOW-
THERE ARE NO
WE CANNOT OVERSTATE
MURDER IS

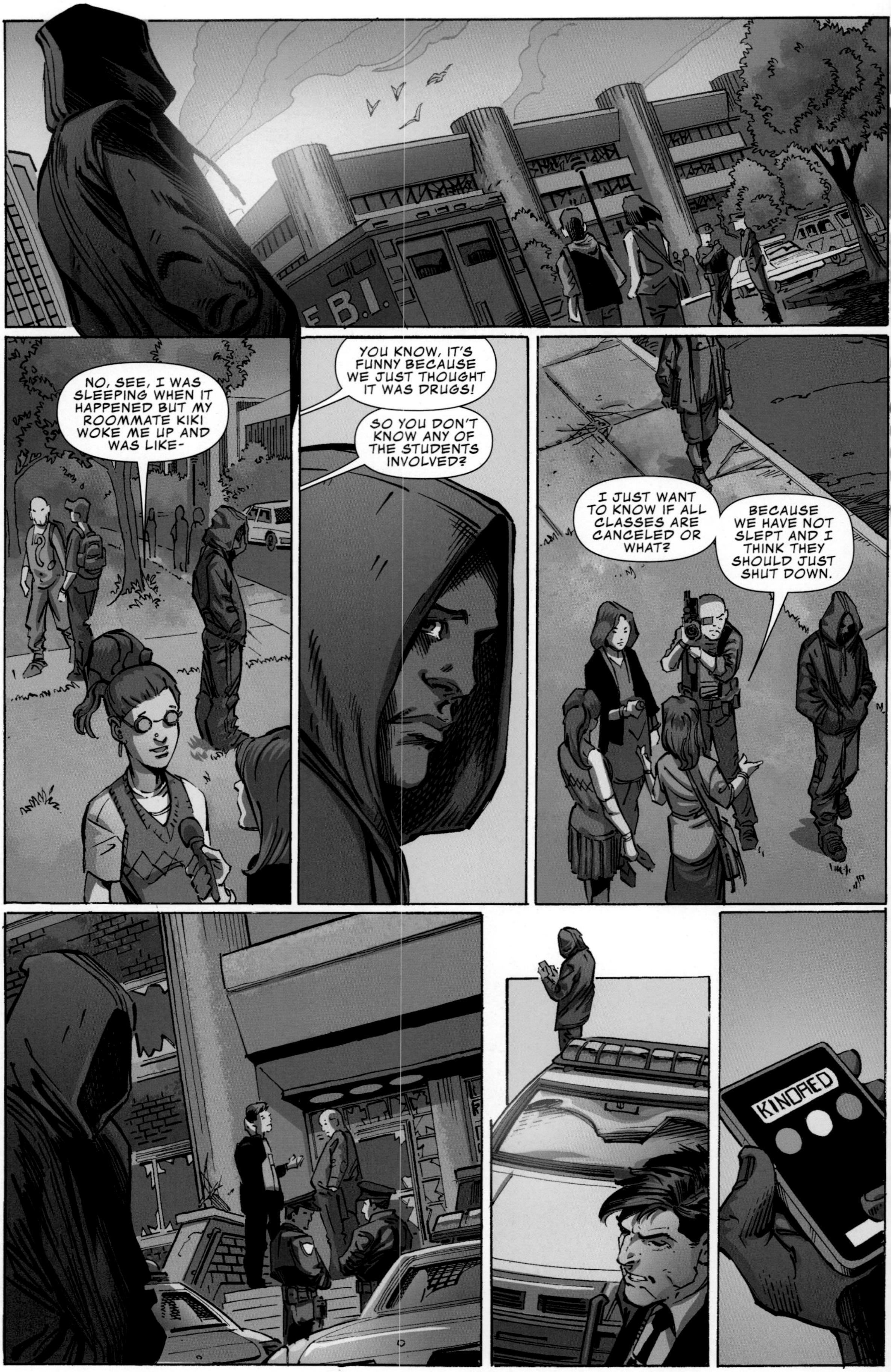
F.B.I.
NO, SEE, I WAS SLEEPING WHEN IT HAPPENED BUT MY ROOMMATE KIKI WOKE ME UP AND WAS LIKE-
YOU KNOW, IT'S FUNNY BECAUSE WE JUST THOUGHT IT WAS DRUGS!
SO YOU DON'T KNOW ANY OF THE STUDENTS INVOLVED?
I JUST WANT TO KNOW IF ALL CLASSES ARE CANCELED OR WHAT?
BECAUSE WE HAVE NOT SLEPT AND I THINK THEY SHOULD JUST SHUT DOWN.
KINDRED

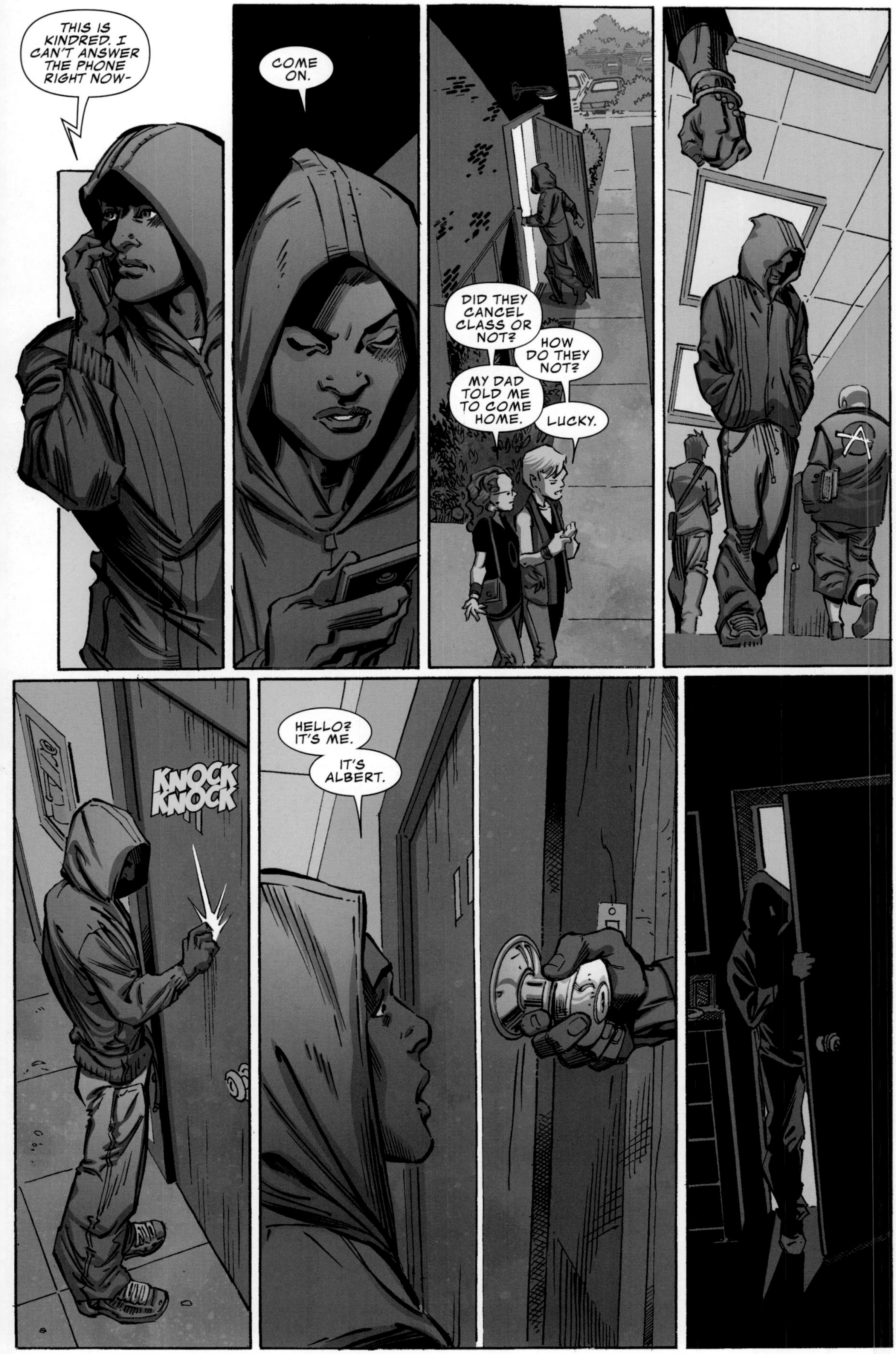
THIS IS KINDRED. I CAN'T ANSWER THE PHONE RIGHT NOW-
COME ON.
DID THEY CANCEL CLASS OR NOT?
HOW DO THEY NOT?
MY DAD TOLD ME TO COME HOME.
LUCKY.
KNOCK KNOCK
HELLO? IT'S ME.
IT'S ALBERT.

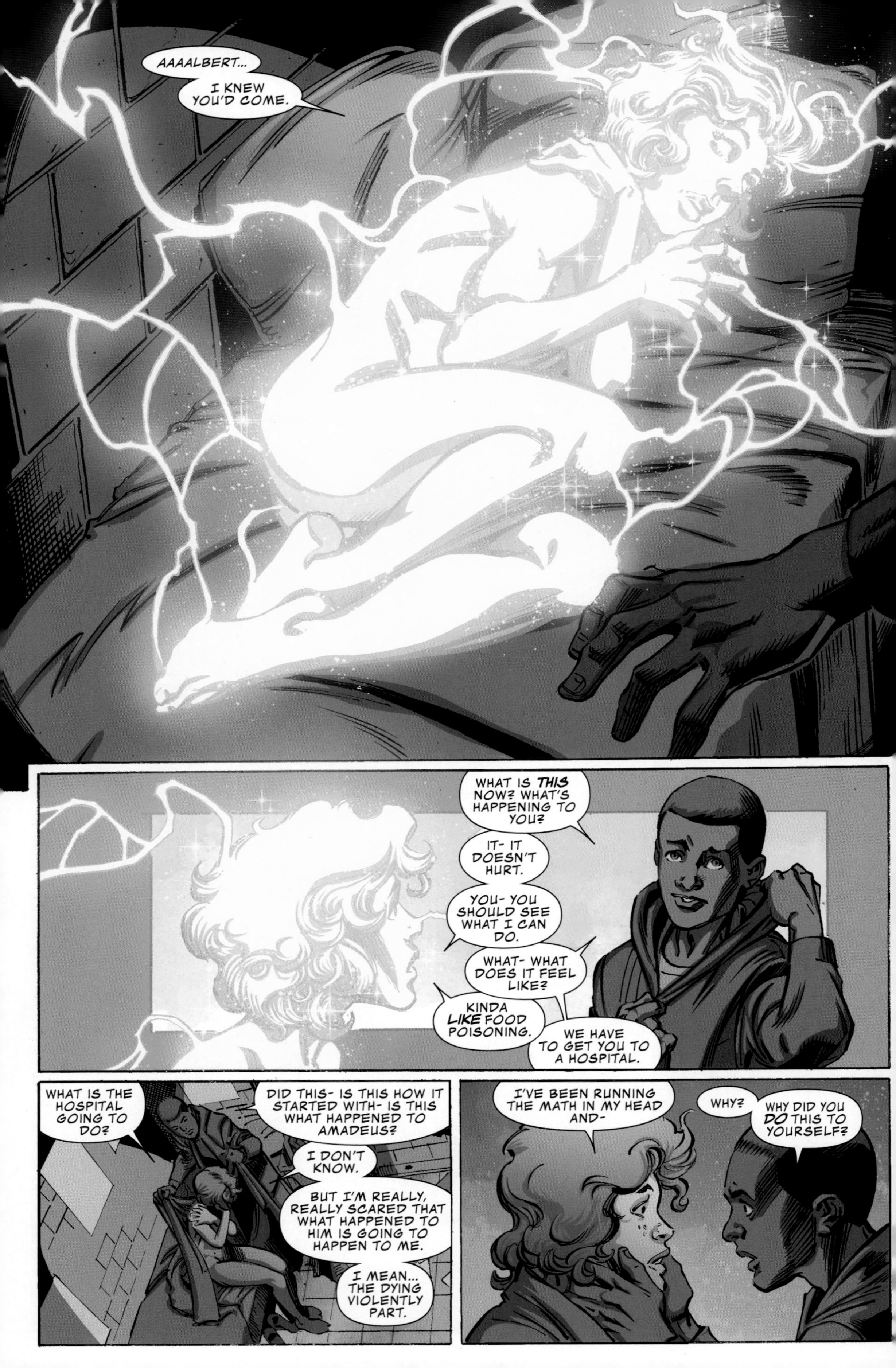
AAAALBERT...
I KNEW YOU'D COME.
WHAT IS **THIS** NOW? WHAT'S HAPPENING TO YOU?
IT- IT DOESN'T HURT.
YOU- YOU SHOULD SEE WHAT I CAN DO.
WHAT- WHAT DOES IT FEEL LIKE?
KINDA **LIKE** FOOD POISONING.
WE HAVE TO GET YOU TO A HOSPITAL.
WHAT IS THE HOSPITAL GOING TO DO?
DID THIS- IS THIS HOW IT STARTED WITH- IS THIS WHAT HAPPENED TO AMADEUS?
I DON'T KNOW.
BUT I'M REALLY, REALLY SCARED THAT WHAT HAPPENED TO HIM IS GOING TO HAPPEN TO ME.
I MEAN... THE DYING VIOLENTLY PART.
I'VE BEEN RUNNING THE MATH IN MY HEAD AND-
WHY?
WHY DID YOU **DO** THIS TO YOURSELF?

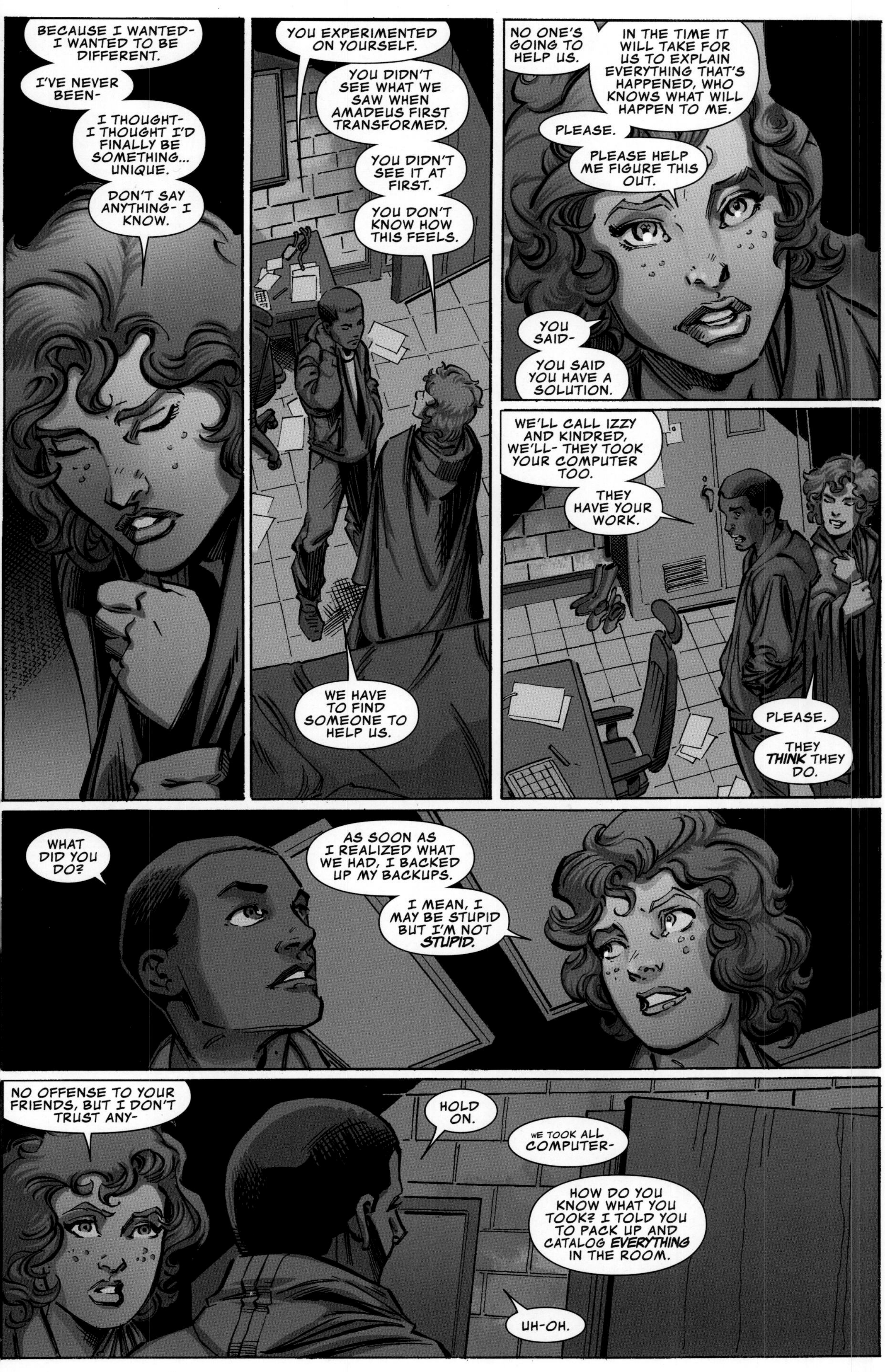

BECAUSE I WANTED- I WANTED TO BE DIFFERENT.
I'VE NEVER BEEN-
I THOUGHT- I THOUGHT I'D FINALLY BE SOMETHING... UNIQUE.
DON'T SAY ANYTHING- I KNOW.
YOU EXPERIMENTED ON YOURSELF.
YOU DIDN'T SEE WHAT WE SAW WHEN AMADEUS FIRST TRANSFORMED.
YOU DIDN'T SEE IT AT FIRST.
YOU DON'T KNOW HOW THIS FEELS.
WE HAVE TO FIND SOMEONE TO HELP US.
NO ONE'S GOING TO HELP US.
IN THE TIME IT WILL TAKE FOR US TO EXPLAIN EVERYTHING THAT'S HAPPENED, WHO KNOWS WHAT WILL HAPPEN TO ME.
PLEASE.
PLEASE HELP ME FIGURE THIS OUT.
YOU SAID-
YOU SAID YOU HAVE A SOLUTION.
WE'LL CALL IZZY AND KINDRED, WE'LL- THEY TOOK YOUR COMPUTER TOO.
THEY HAVE YOUR WORK.
PLEASE.
THEY *THINK* THEY DO.
WHAT DID YOU DO?
AS SOON AS I REALIZED WHAT WE HAD, I BACKED UP MY BACKUPS.
I MEAN, I MAY BE STUPID BUT I'M NOT *STUPID.*
NO OFFENSE TO YOUR FRIENDS, BUT I DON'T TRUST ANY-
HOLD ON.
WE TOOK ALL COMPUTER-
HOW DO YOU KNOW WHAT YOU TOOK? I TOLD YOU TO PACK UP AND CATALOG *EVERYTHING* IN THE ROOM.
UH-OH.

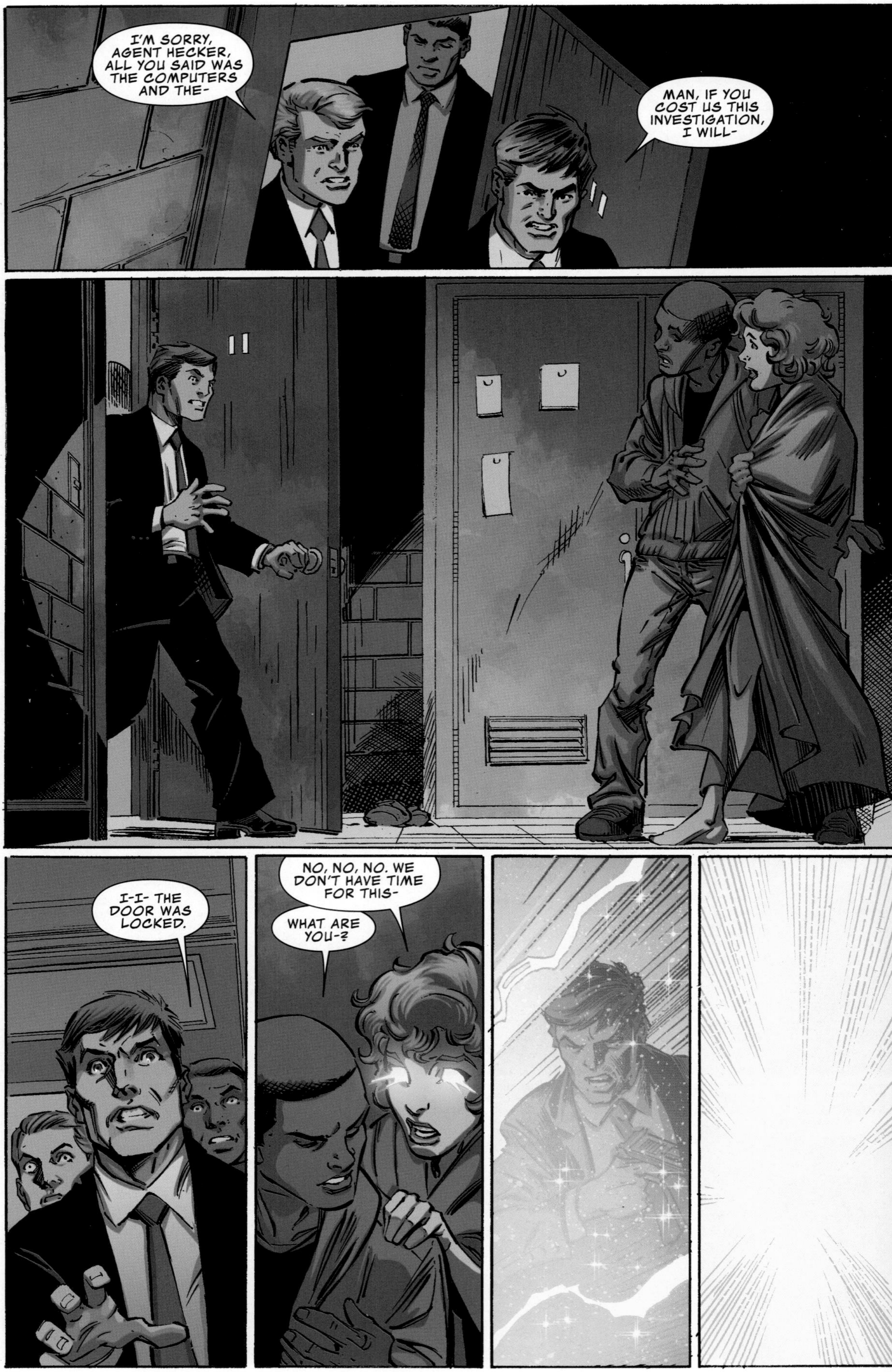
I'M SORRY, AGENT HECKER, ALL YOU SAID WAS THE COMPUTERS AND THE-
MAN, IF YOU COST US THIS INVESTIGATION, I WILL-
I-I- THE DOOR WAS LOCKED.
NO, NO, NO. WE DON'T HAVE TIME FOR THIS-
WHAT ARE YOU-?

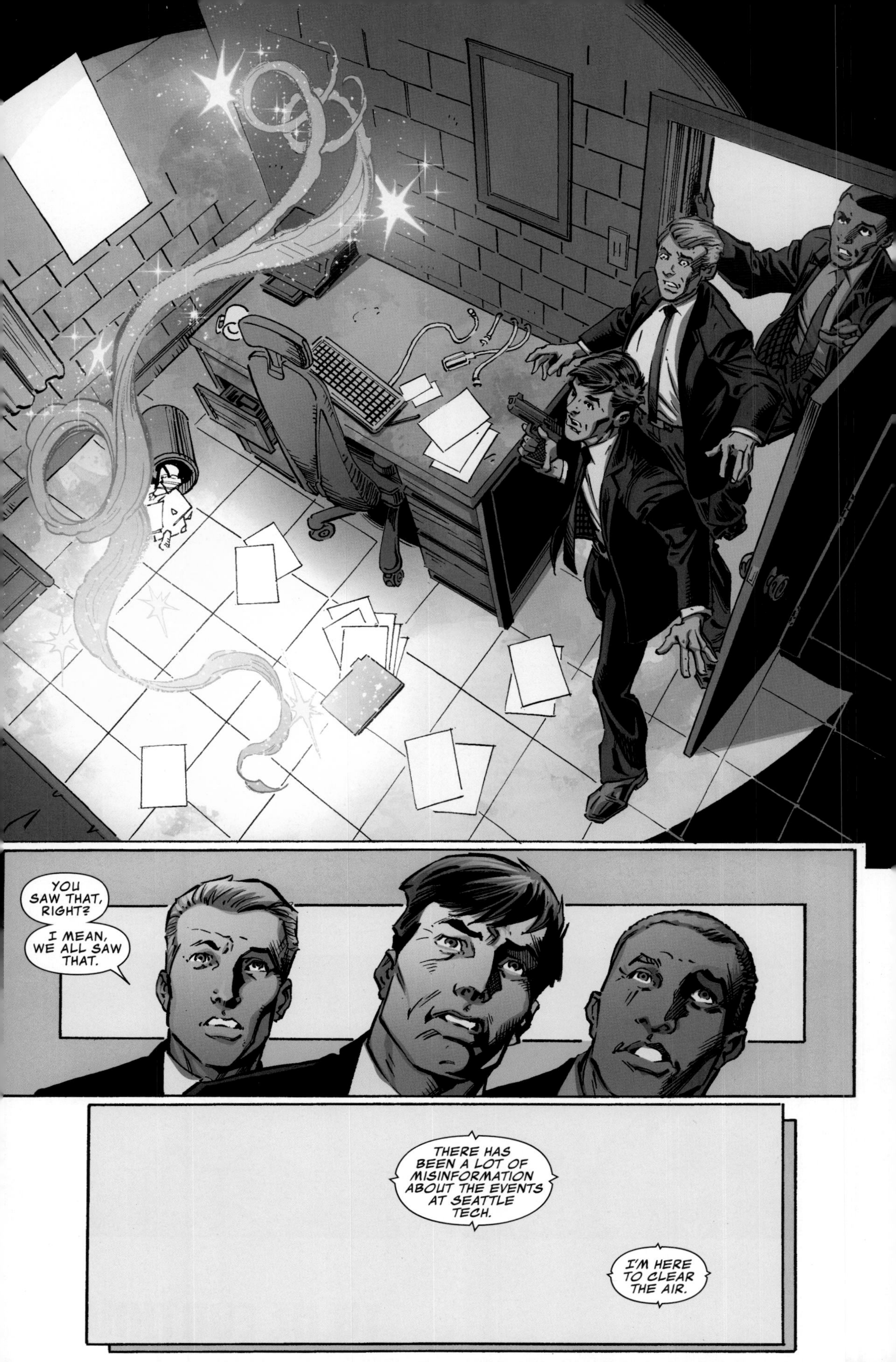
YOU SAW THAT, RIGHT?
I MEAN, WE ALL SAW THAT.
THERE HAS BEEN A LOT OF MISINFORMATION ABOUT THE EVENTS AT SEATTLE TECH.
I'M HERE TO CLEAR THE AIR.

I APPRECIATE YOU GIVING US THIS OPPORTUNITY.

MY SON, A TRUE SCIENCE PRODIGY, HAS BEEN SECRETLY DEVELOPING ONE OF THE BIGGEST BREAKTHROUGHS IN HUMAN GENEALOGY.

HE HAS INVENTED A PROCESS IN WHICH MAN CAN TAP INTO POWERS AND ABILITIES THAT WE DID NOT KNOW WE WERE CAPABLE OF.

THINGS THAT WE, AS A SOCIETY, HAD ONLY FANTASIZED.

EXCLUSIVE! Woodrow Potts, CEO of Potts Technologies

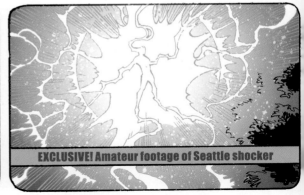

EXCLUSIVE! Amateur footage of Seattle shocker

THE TRAGEDY AT SEATTLE TECH HAPPENED BECAUSE ONE OF HIS—WELL, I DON'T WANT TO SAY FRIENDS, BUT AN ACQUAINTANCE OF MY SON ATTEMPTED TO STEAL THE PROCESS BEFORE IT WAS PERFECTED AND WITHOUT ANY KNOWLEDGE OF HOW TO USE IT.

EXCLUSIVE! Woodrow Potts, CEO of Potts Technologies

EVEN THOUGH THAT EVENT WAS TRAGIC, IT CERTAINLY SHOWS THAT MY SON IS A GENIUS WHO IS ON THE CUSP OF ONE OF THE GREATEST BREAKTHROUGHS IN THE HISTORY OF MANKIND.

MY SON HAS BROUGHT THIS TO ME AND MY COMPANY AND WE WILL BE DEVELOPING IT AND PERFECTING IT.

EXCLUSIVE! Kindred Potts: the brains behind the Seattle s

AND HOPEFULLY WE ARE JUST MONTHS AWAY FROM BEING ABLE TO APPLY OUR FINDINGS IN A MEANINGFUL WAY.

SO YOU'RE SAYING YOUR SON HAS INVENTED SUPERPOWERS.

EXCLUSIVE! Woodrow Potts, CEO of Potts Technologies

I'M SAYING HE, AND HE ALONE, HAS MADE THIS AMAZING BREAKTHROUGH.

AND I HAVE NEVER BEEN MORE PROUD.

EXCLUSIVE! Kindred Potts: the brains behind the Seattle s

TO BE CONTINUED...

COVER GALLERY

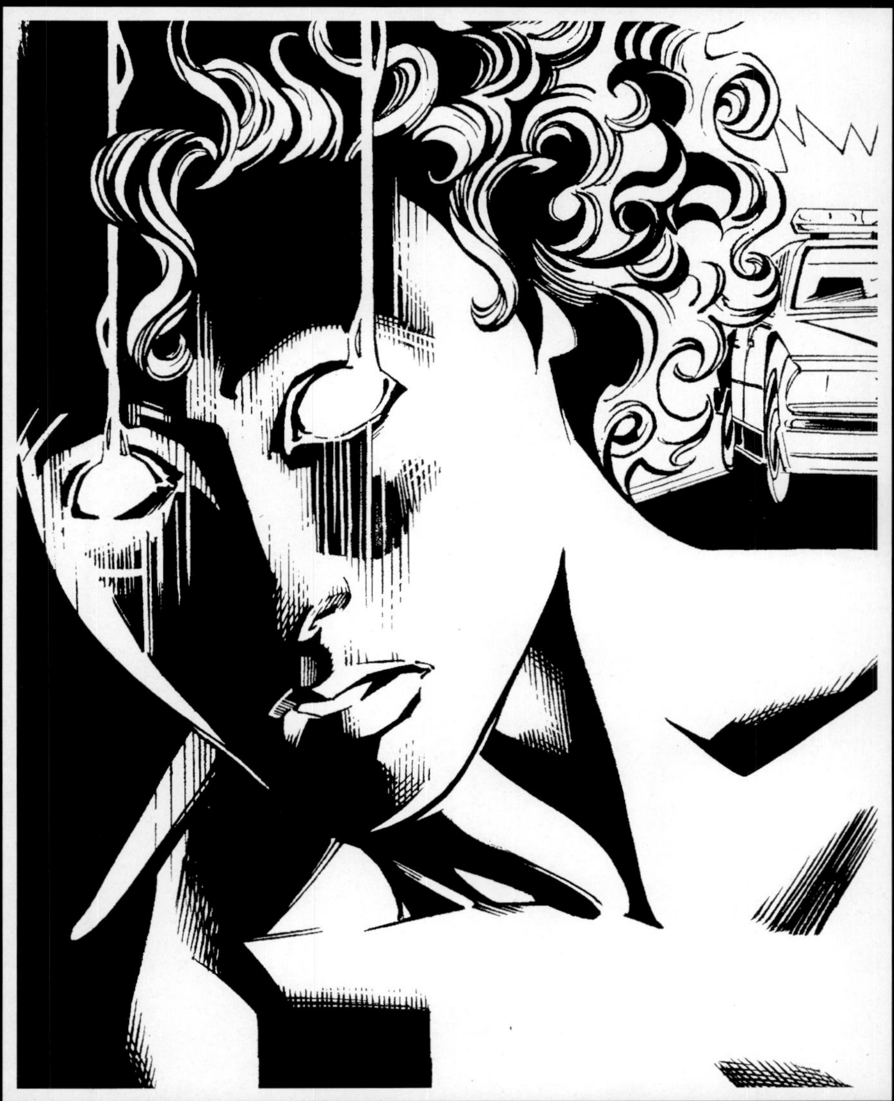

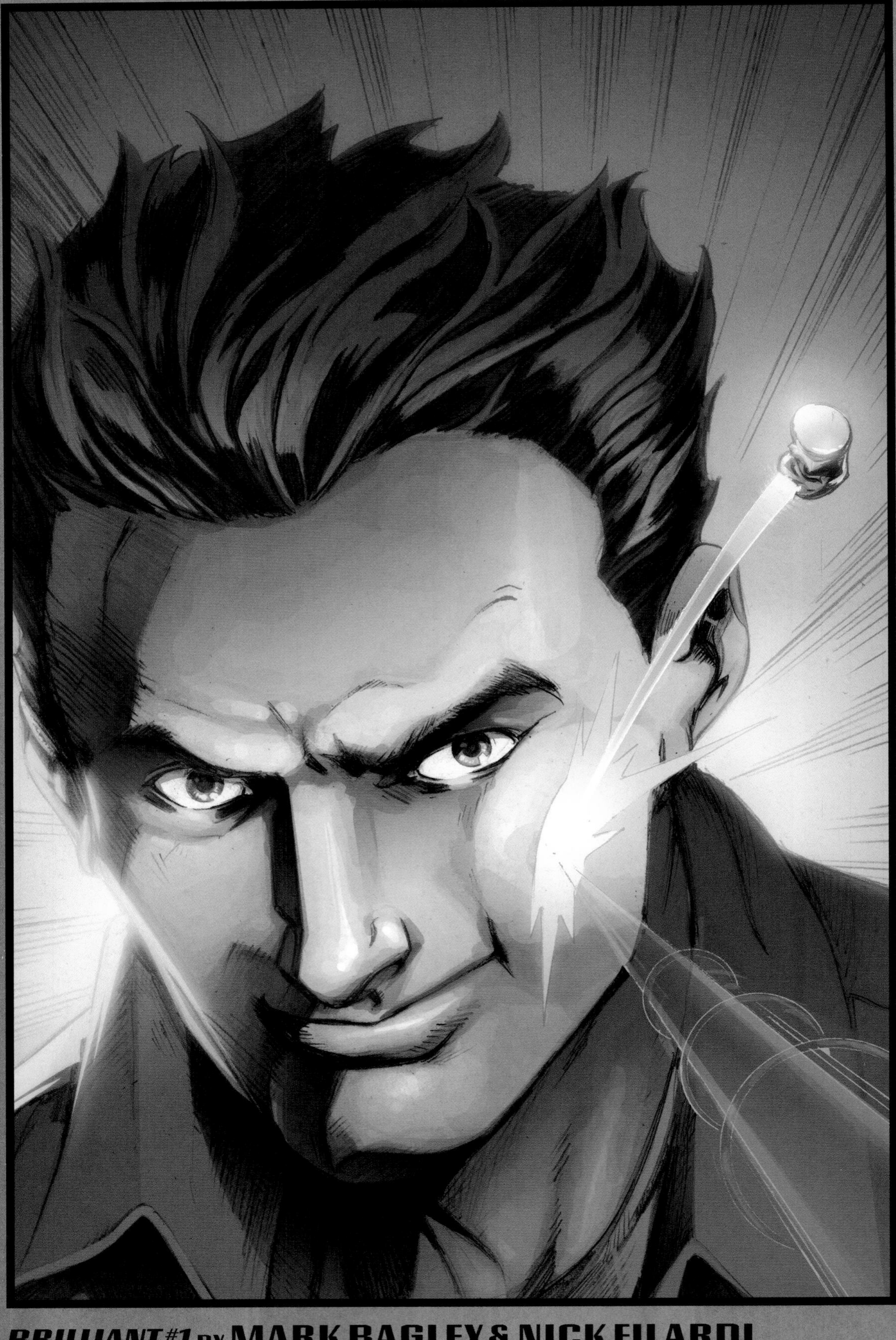

BRILLIANT #1 BY **MARK BAGLEY & NICK FILARDI**

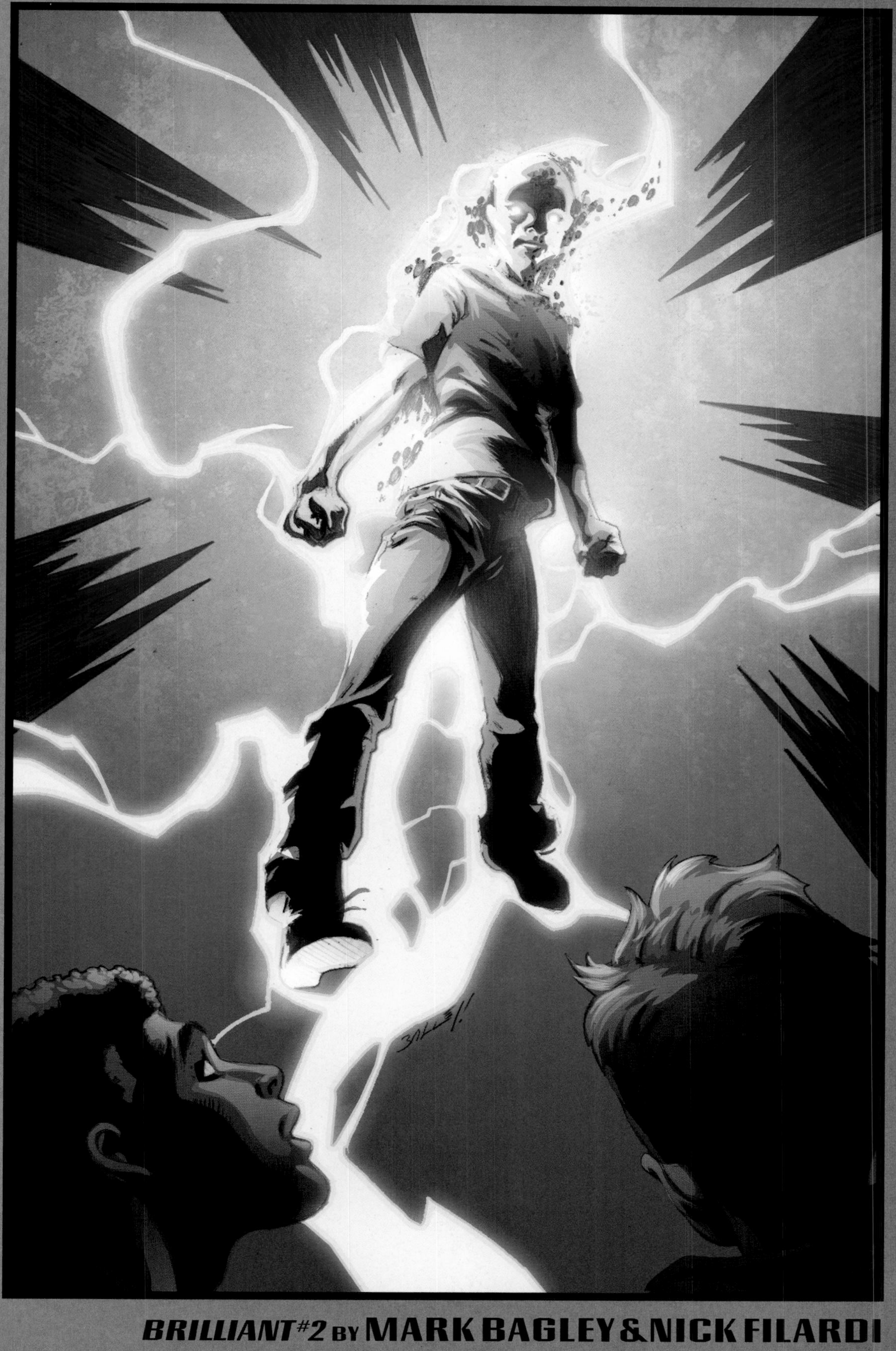

***BRILLIANT* #2 BY MARK BAGLEY & NICK FILARDI**

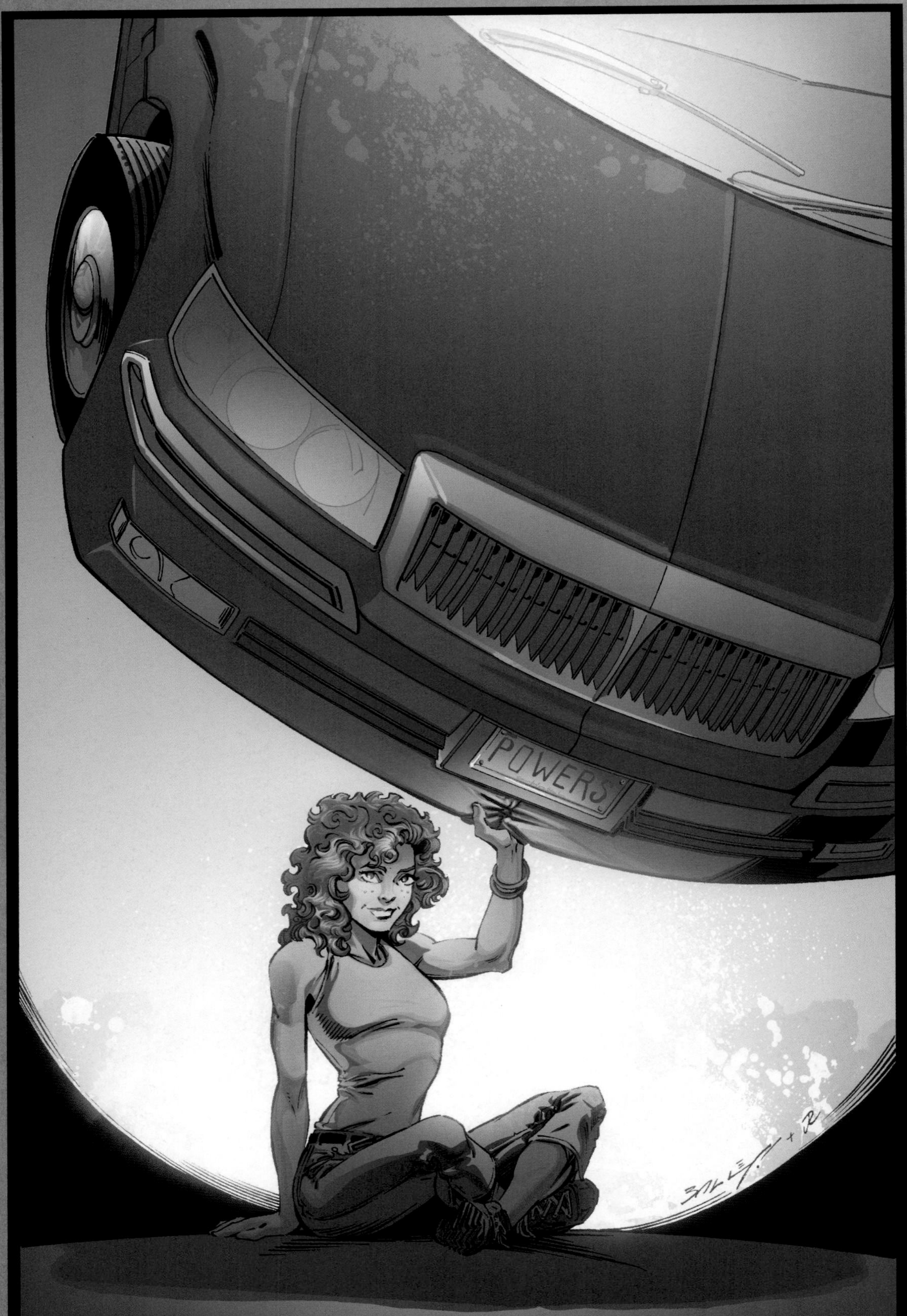
POWERS

***BRILLIANT* #3 BY MARK BAGLEY & NICK FILARDI**

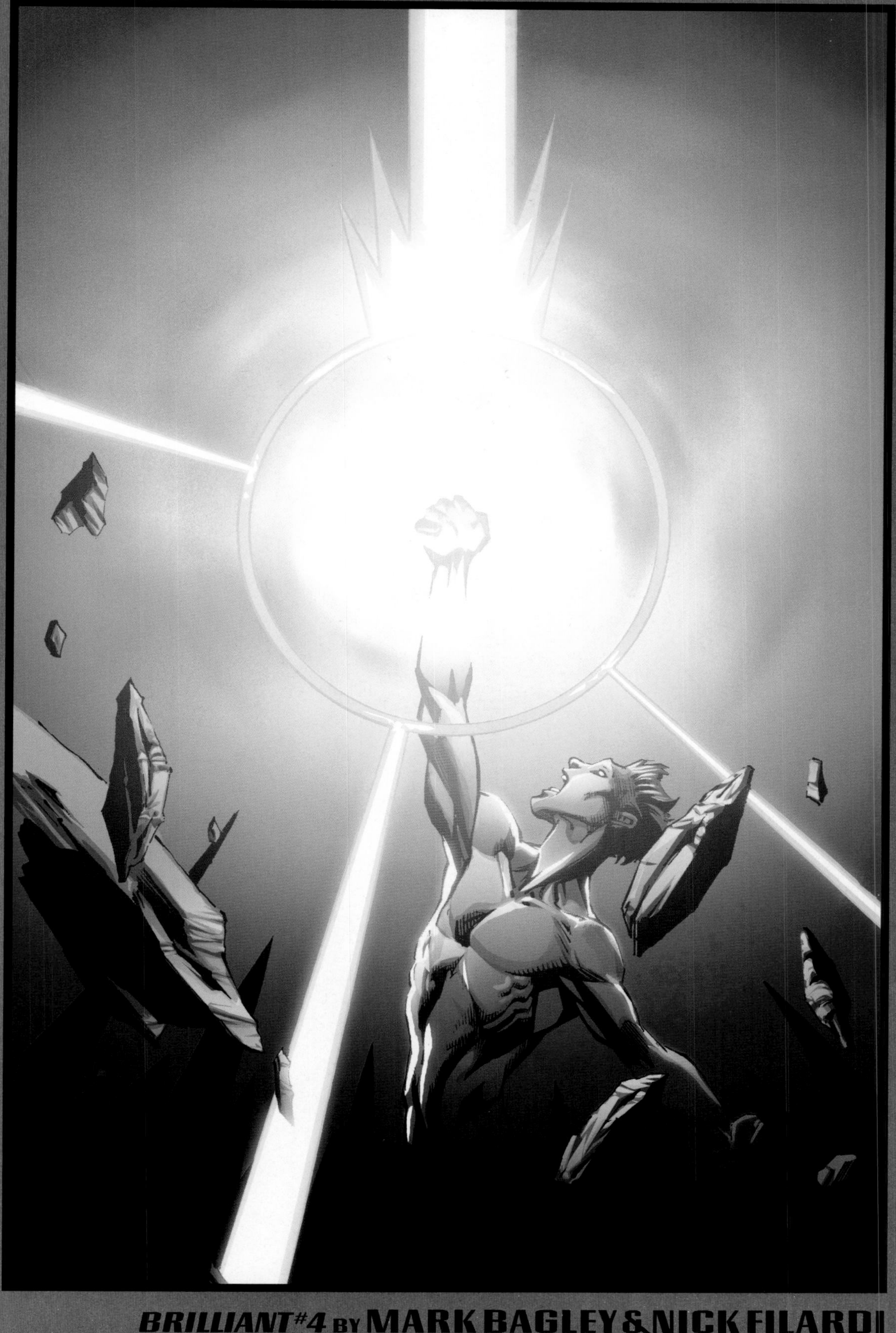

BRILLIANT #4 BY MARK BAGLEY & NICK FILARDI

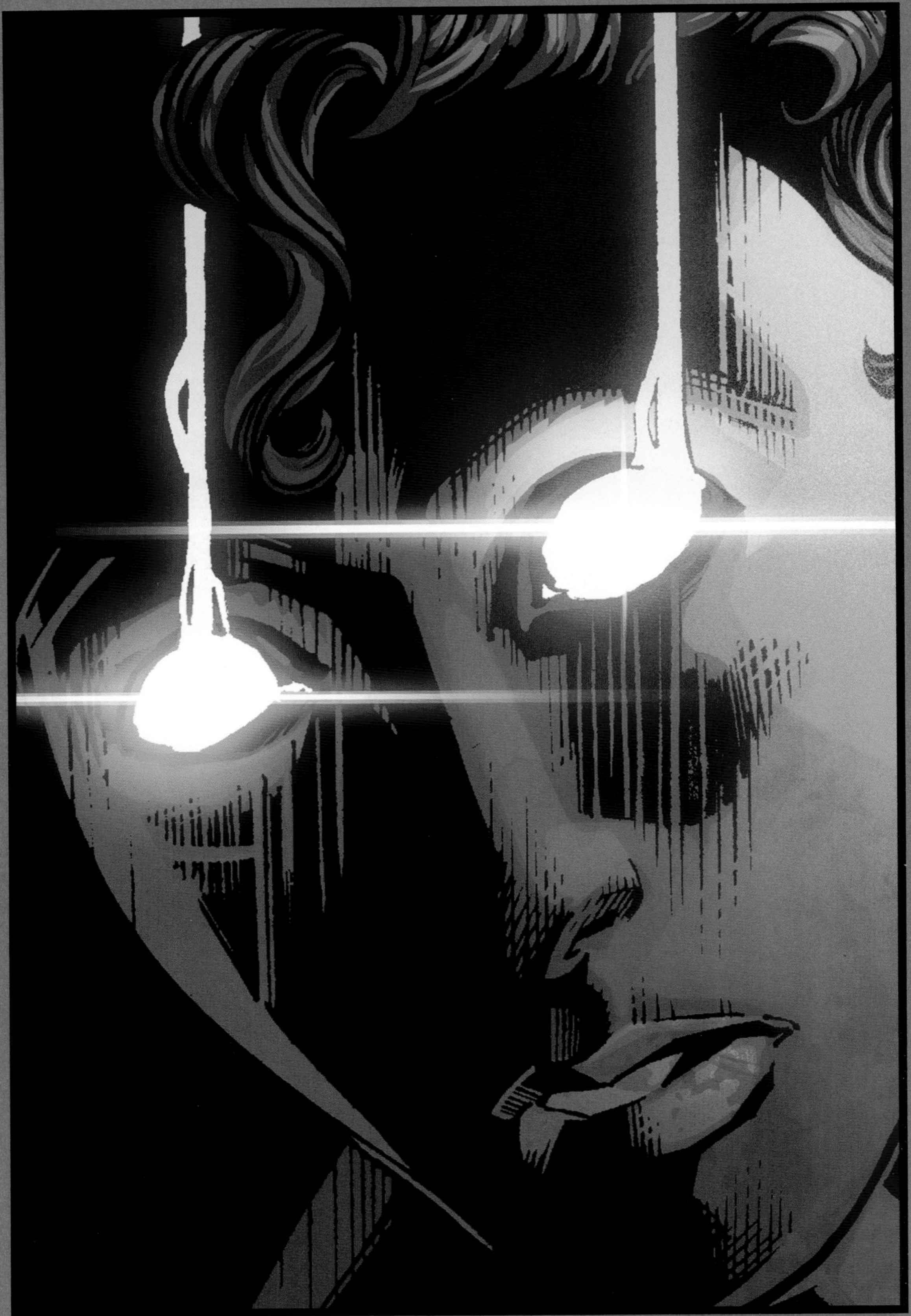

BRILLIANT #5 BY MARK BAGLEY & NICK FILARDI

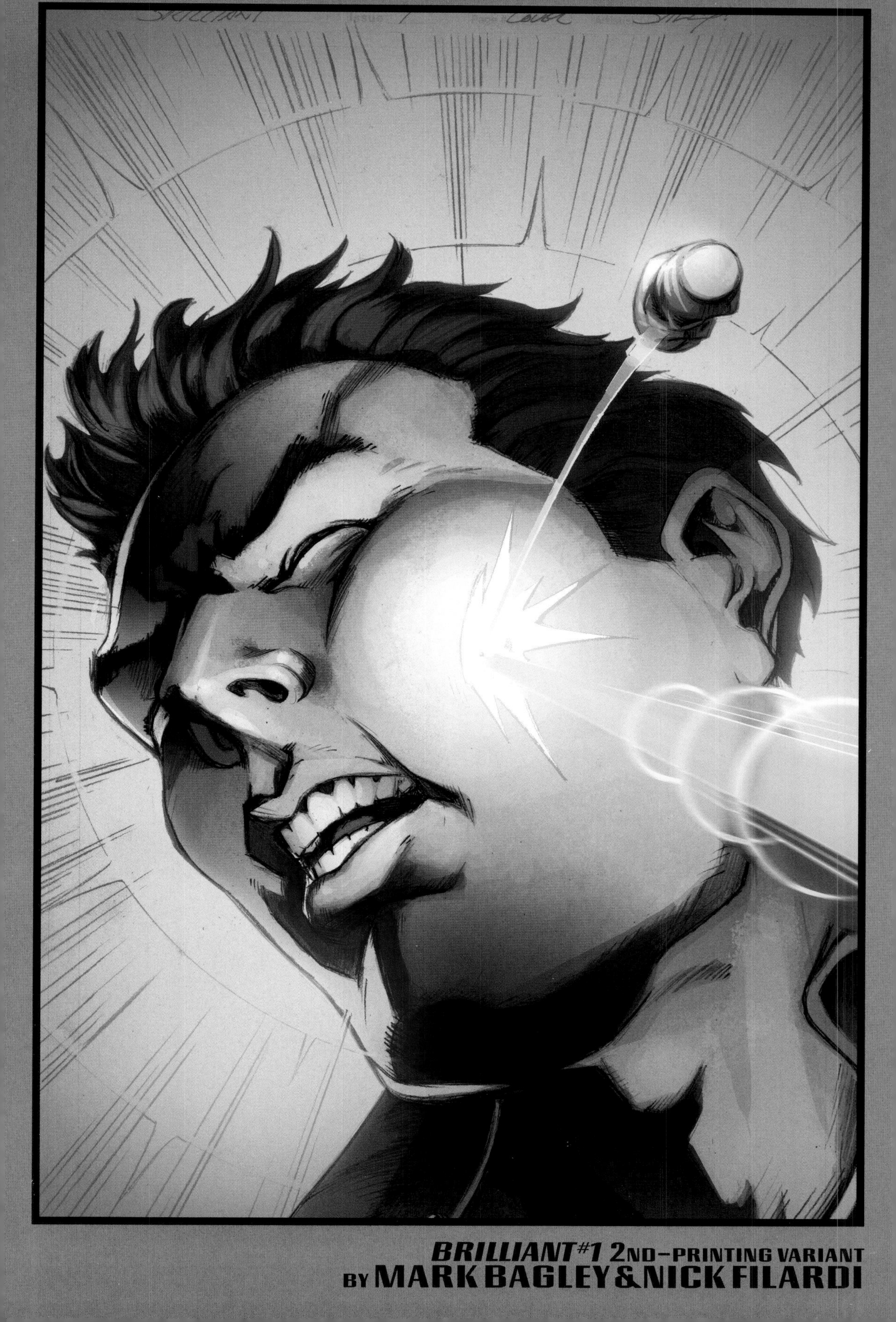

BRILLIANT **#1 2ND-PRINTING VARIANT**
BY MARK BAGLEY & NICK FILARDI

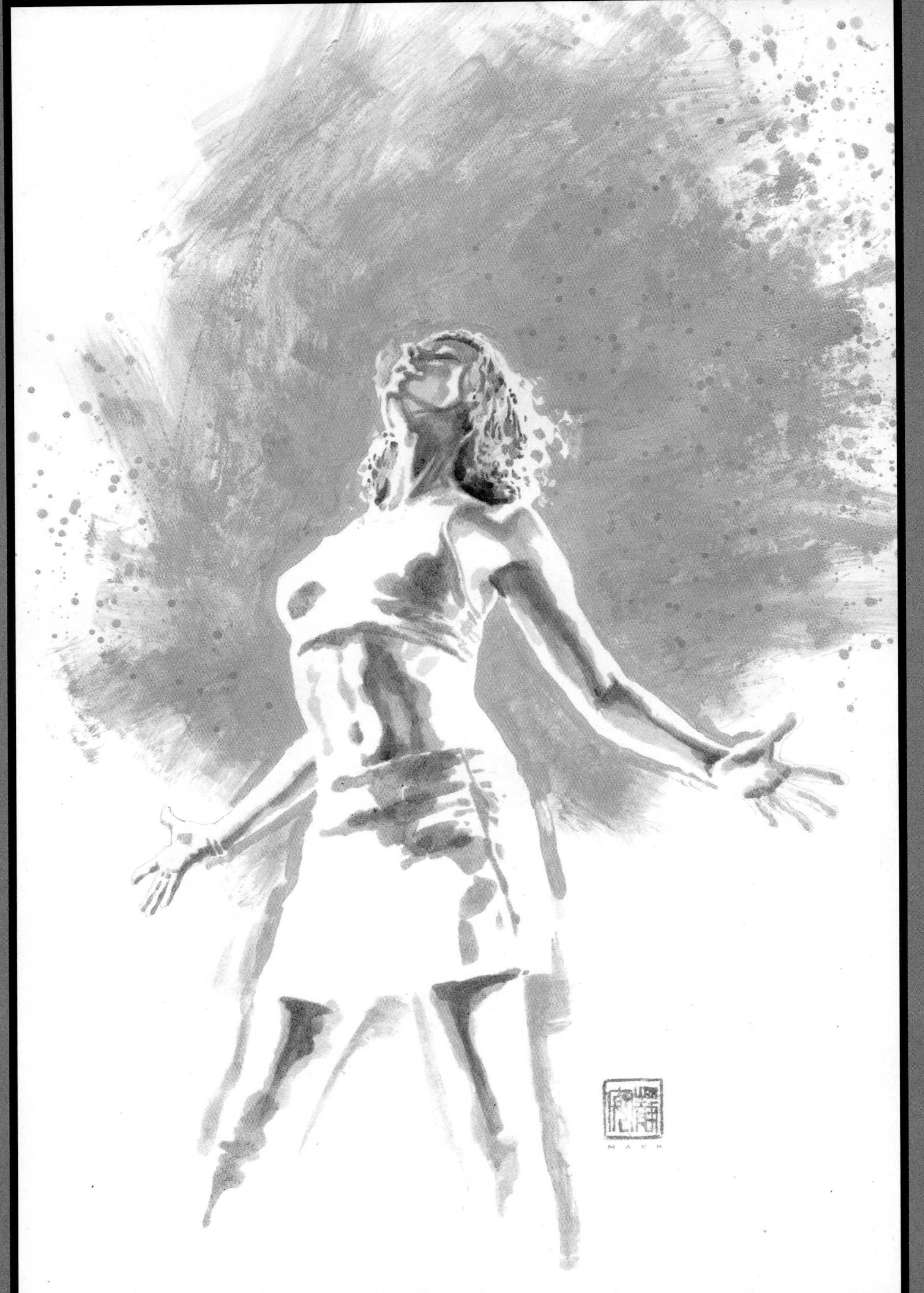
MACK

BRILLIANT #1 VARIANT BY **DAVID MACK**

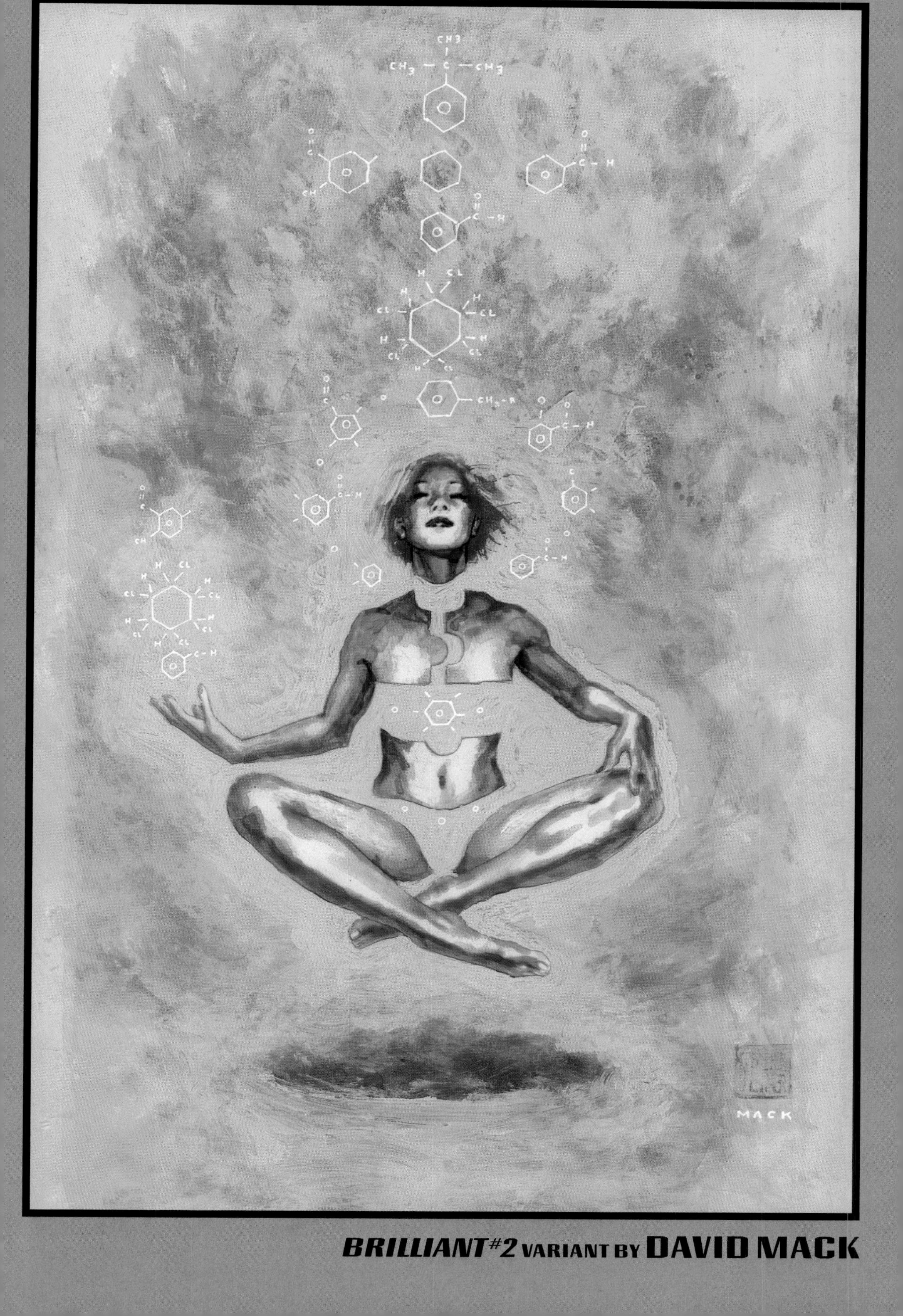
CH3
CH3 — C — CH3
C—H
CH2-R
MACK

BRILLIANT #2 VARIANT BY DAVID MACK

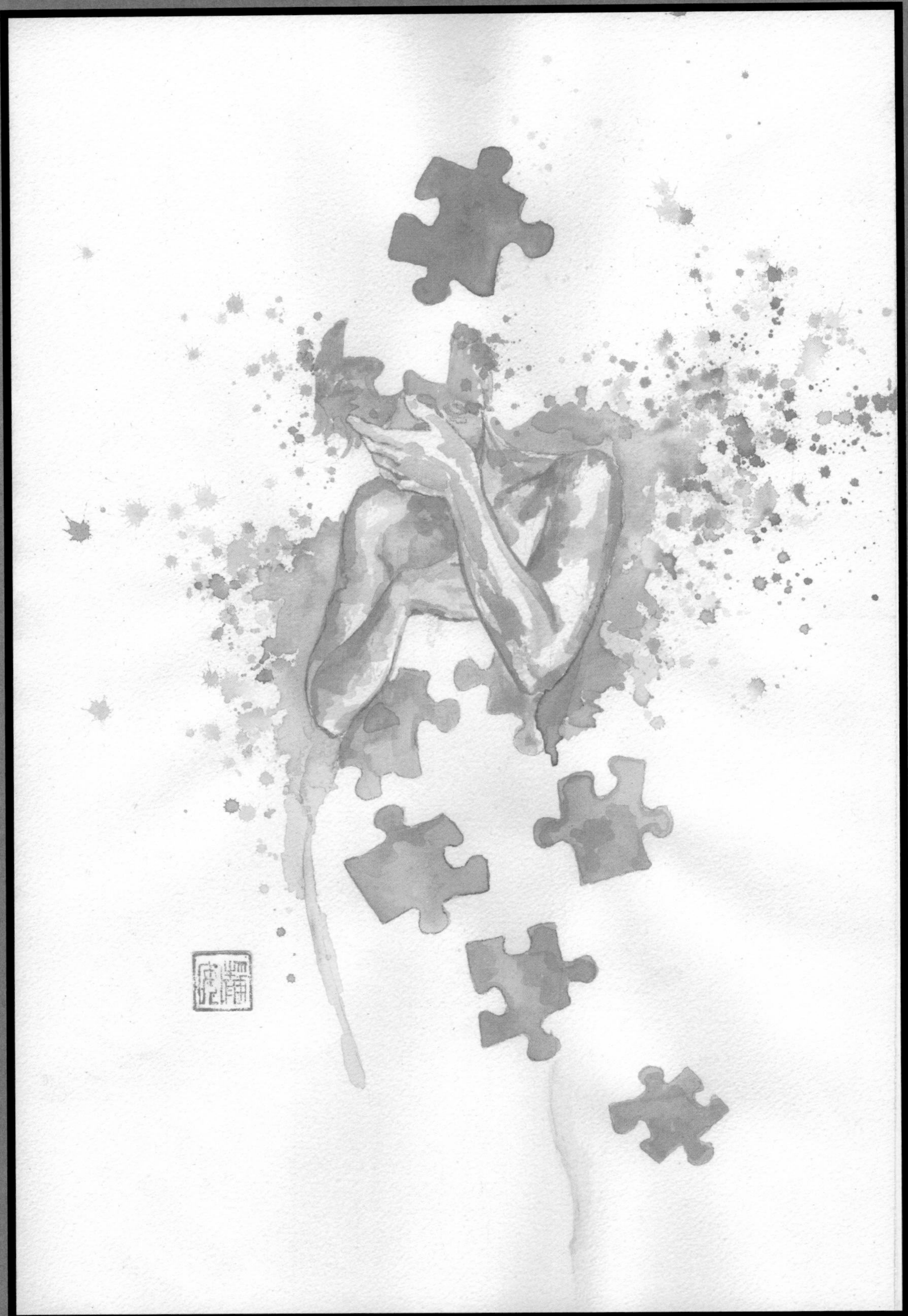

BRILLIANT #3 VARIANT BY DAVID MACK

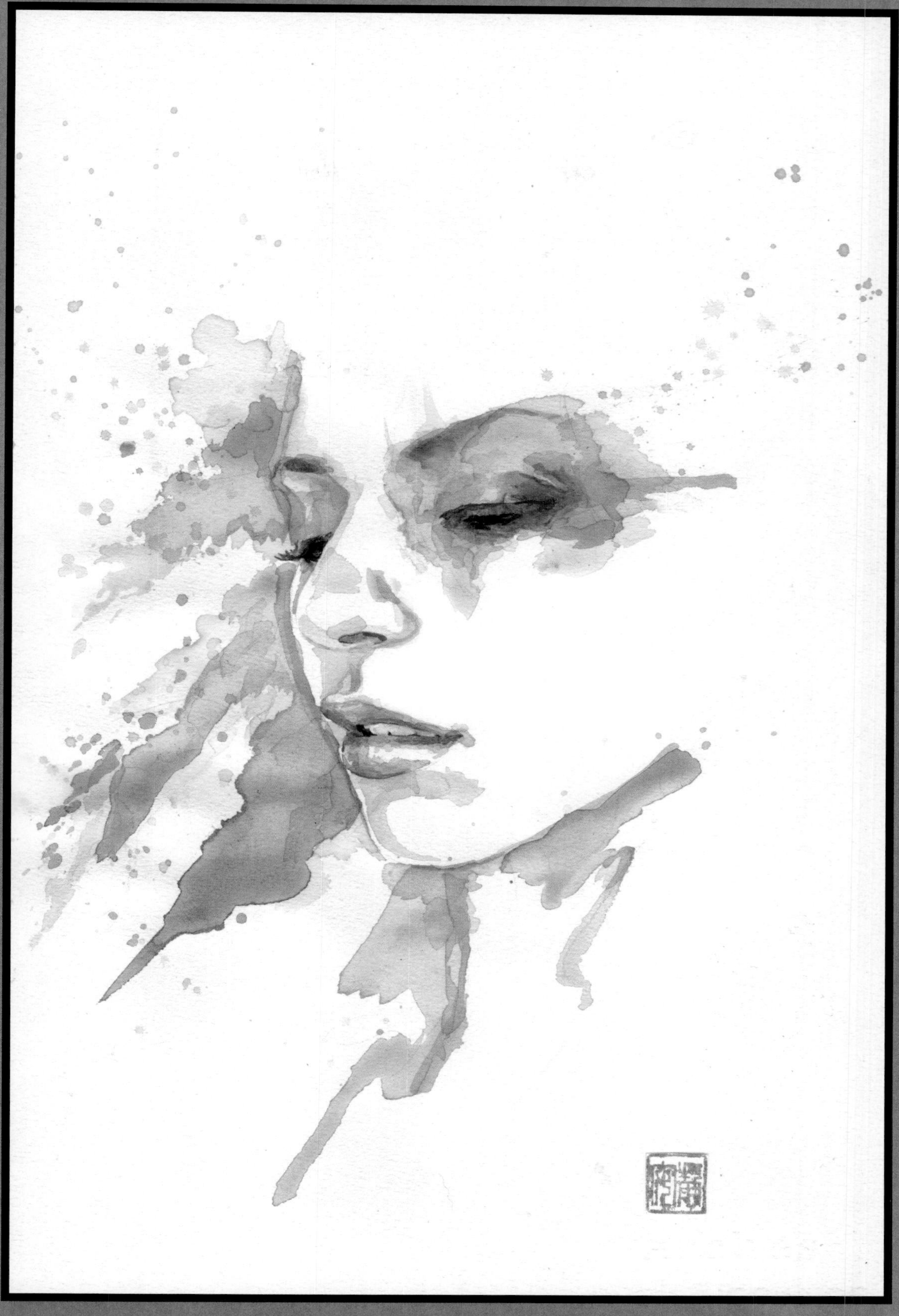

BRILLIANT #4 VARIANT BY DAVID MACK

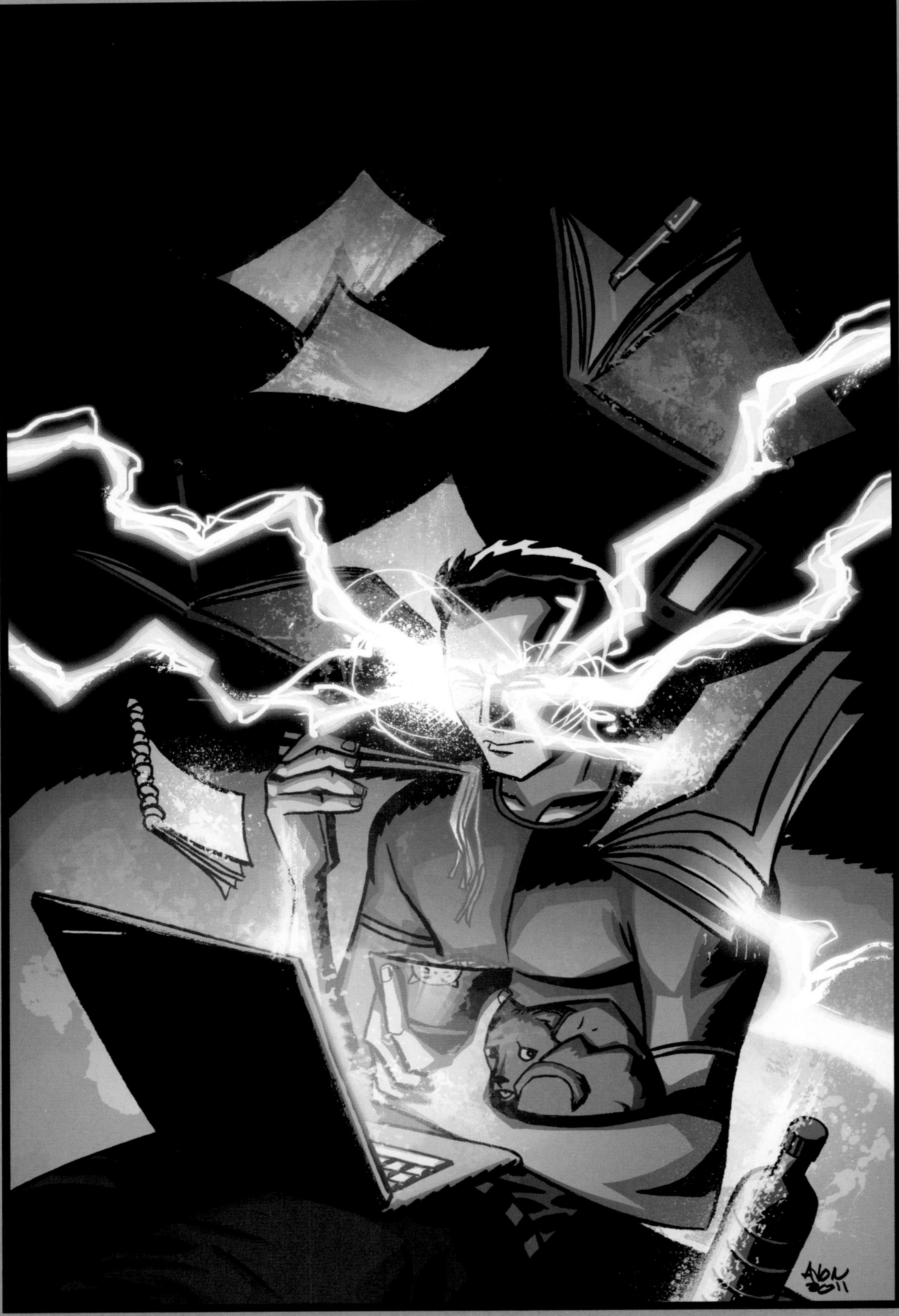
AVON 2011

***BRILLIANT* #1 VARIANT**
BY MICHAEL AVON OEMING & NICK FILARDI

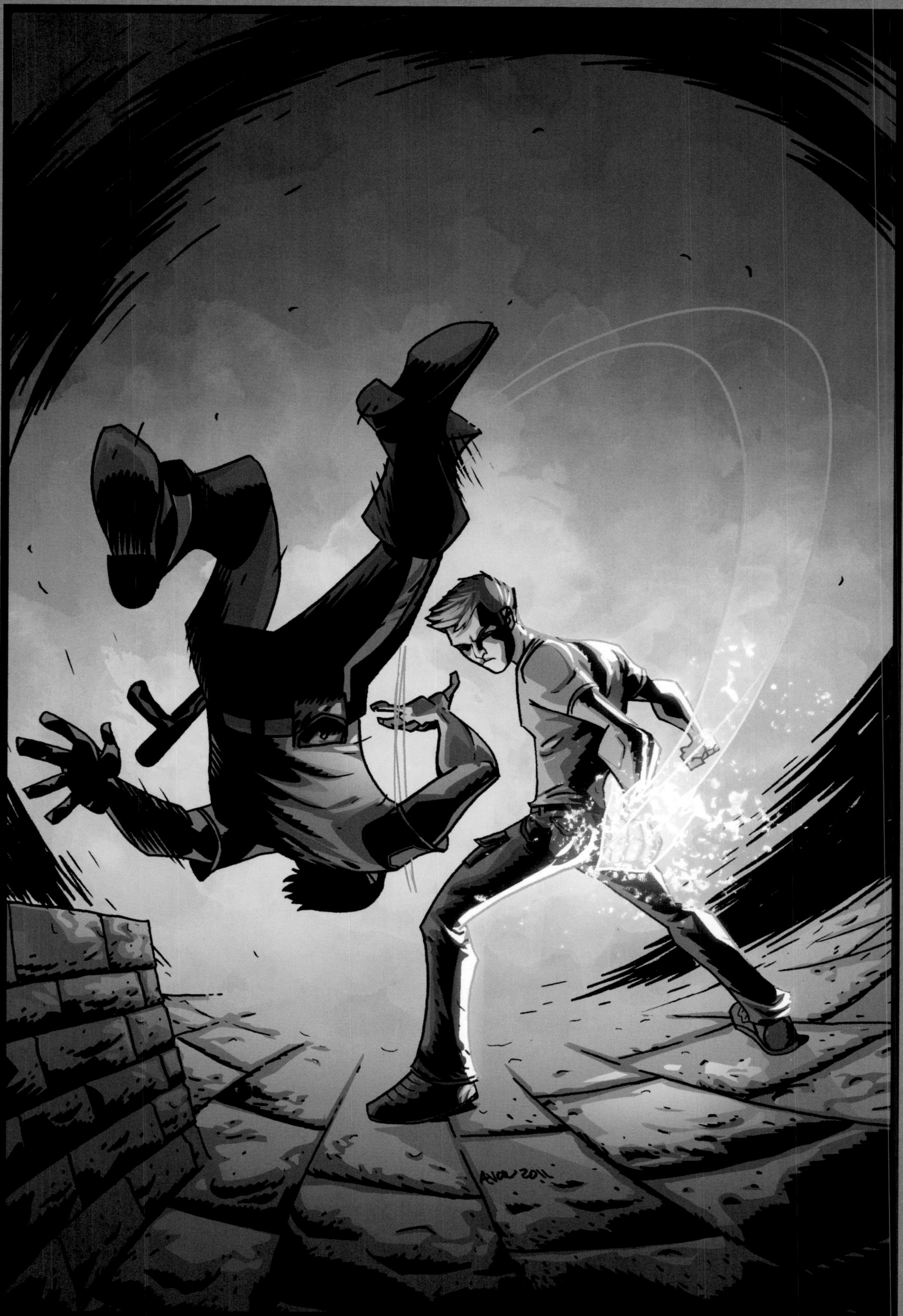

***BRILLIANT* #2 VARIANT**
BY MICHAEL AVON OEMING & NICK FILARDI

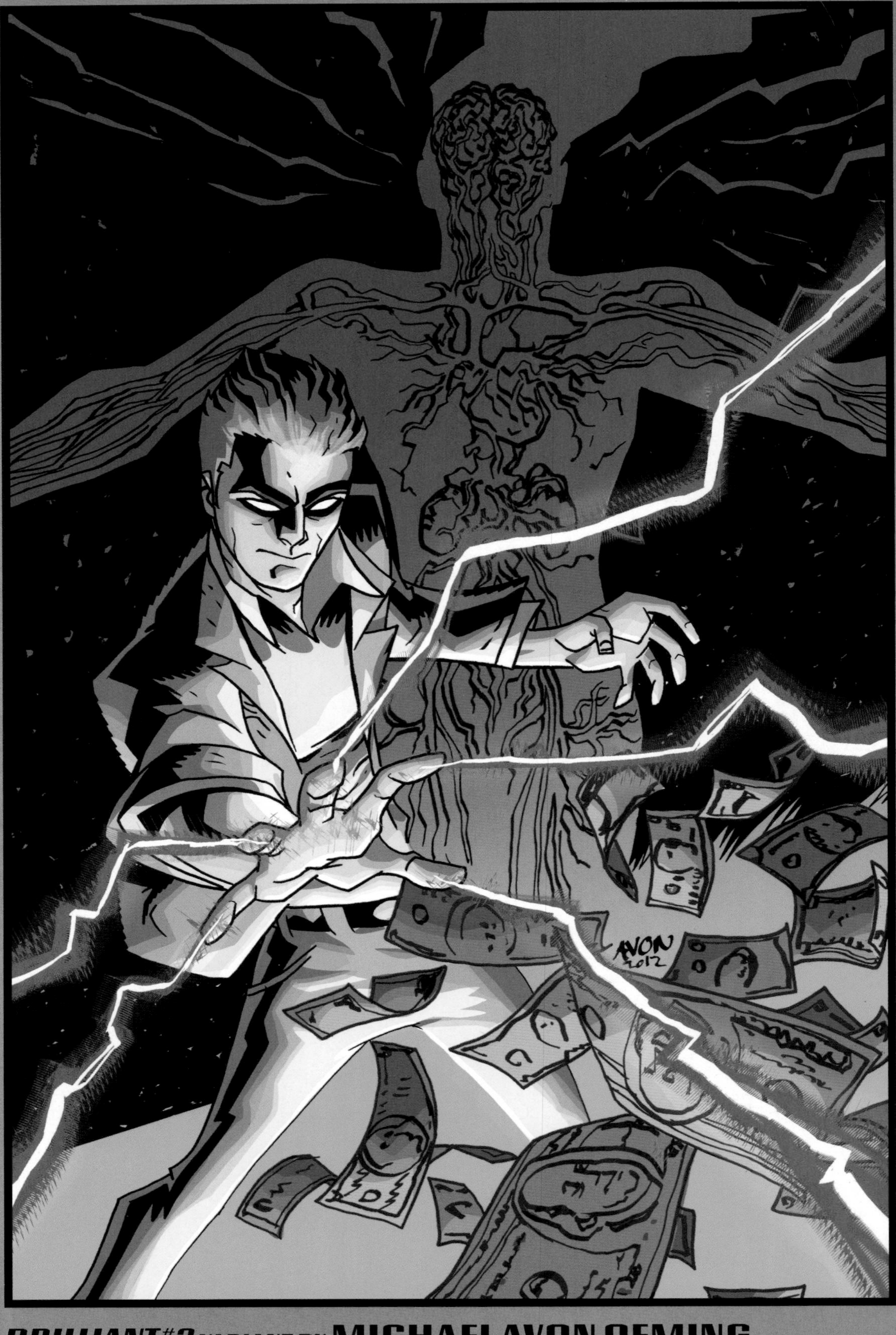
AVON
2012

***BRILLIANT*#3** VARIANT BY **MICHAEL AVON OEMING**

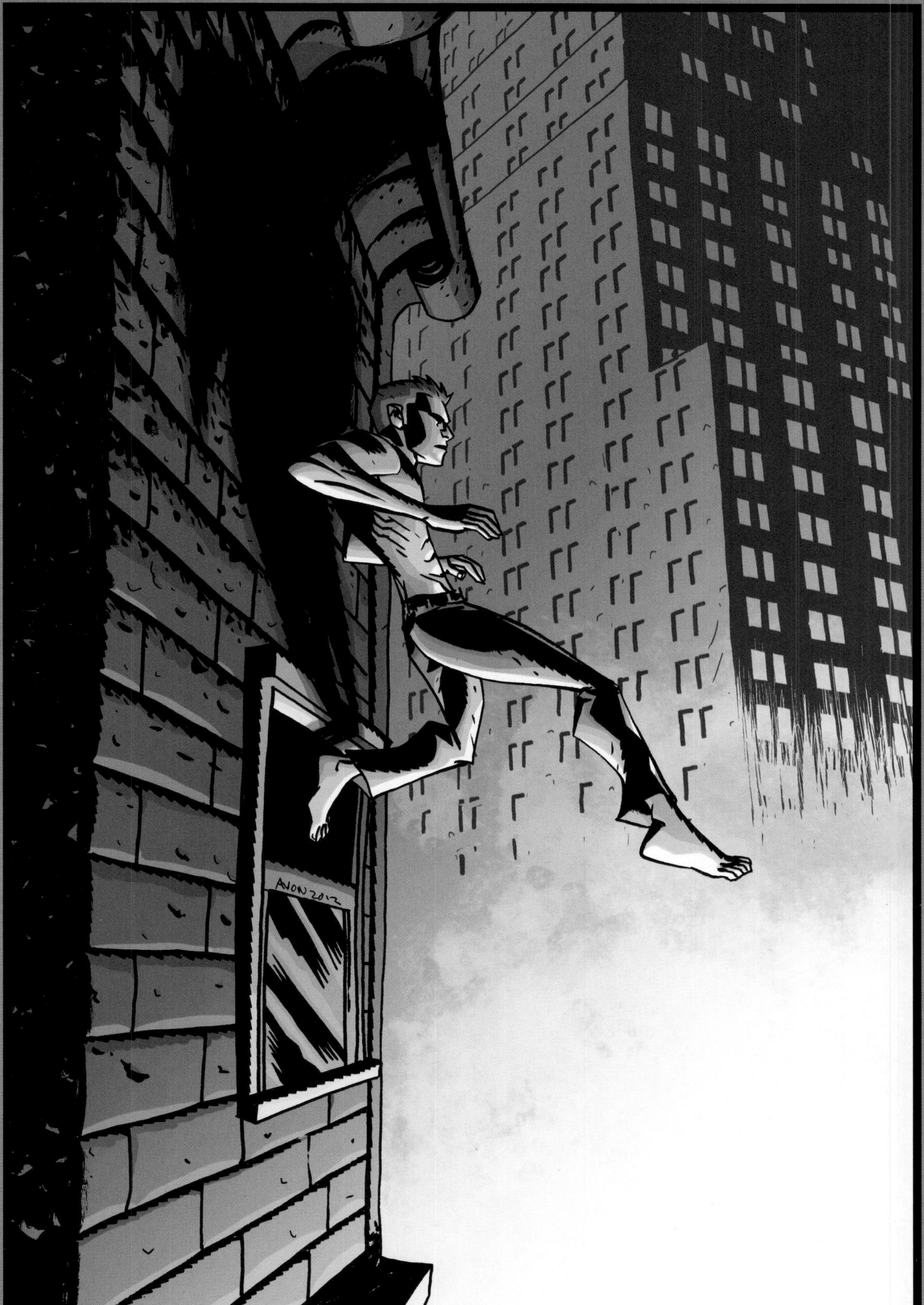
AVON 2012

***BRILLIANT* #4 VARIANT BY MICHAEL AVON OEMING**

CHARACTER SKETCHES

BY MARK BAGLEY

AMADEUS ?

ALBERT

ALBERT ?

BACH?

IZZY!

MARIE-
SORT
JENNIFER
CONNELLY
(PRESERVERY)

BRILLIANT SCRIPT

ISSUE 1

BY BRIAN MICHAEL BENDIS AND MARK BAGLEY

Mark- as described privately this is the story of young geniuses who invent... SUPERPOWERS. These are the men who make science fiction into science fact. Just ádevices this kind of thing has happened over and over again in our society. A genius turns fiction into fact.

The students that we are introducing are all physically normal people so it's going to be up to you to design characters that are very engaging and very recognizable without giving them anything ridiculous.

Though the story will have a superpower element it is not a superhero story and probably never will be. It's more like a political thriller. This will be more like The Firm than Superman.

This is about what would happen in the real world if the secret of the untapped nature of the human condition was unleashed in our corporatized world. There are literally dozens of stories we could tell with this premise so I'm hoping we will be able to go back to these characters in this idea as often as you want to be on this quote unquote origin story.

I know we have a shorthand for working together all the years but this is a different kind of animal. These characters are our babies and we are their parents and we need to birth them, raise them and protect them in a different way than we do the Marvel characters because the Marvel characters do have people protecting them and watching them for us. Think about who they are and why they are and where they came from, I will help you with this in any way shape or form that you need.

The other thing to remember is that this is a creator owned book and with that comes freedom. Now because of our place in the comic book industry we are allowed certain freedoms that we may take for granted. We are bold and masterful with our storytelling on a regular basis. But subconsciously we know we have people to answer to... editors and Marvel and audience expectations. But with a book like this we don't have anyone to answer to but ourselves. So if there are design elements that you think you want to explore... things that you haven't tried yet... this is the place to do it. Think about what these pages are really about... futurists, frustration, paranoia, youth... and design the page anyway you see fit.

I have been waiting to do this with you for years so excuse my enthusiasm.

PAGE 1

1- Ext. Seattle

Establishing shot. The city in all it's glory.

> **READS: SEATTLE**

2- Ext. Street- day

Waist shot. AMADEUS (22, lanky, white) in a very trendy slacker outfit and a very nice haircut is standing by the opening of an alley. He is just standing there, looking, observing. A back pack over one shoulder.

> **READS: AMADEUS**

3- Over Amadeus' shoulder, It's mid day in Seattle. Lunch time. Perfectly normal. Across the street is a normal, average corner bank.

4- Tighter. Amadeus is watching intently. Thinking. Deciding to go for it.

> **AMADEUS**
>> Do it.

PAGE 2-3

Double page spread

1- Over Amadeus' shoulder, he is walking across the street to the bank. Walking in between passing cars.

2- Int. Chase manhattan bank- day

Amadeus walks into the bank. a smattering of people walking around. He looks like he is not trying excited and nervous. The balloons just float. Overheard conversation.

> **VOICE**
>> That's what your Mortgage lender is for-

Brilliant #1 — Page 1 Pencils

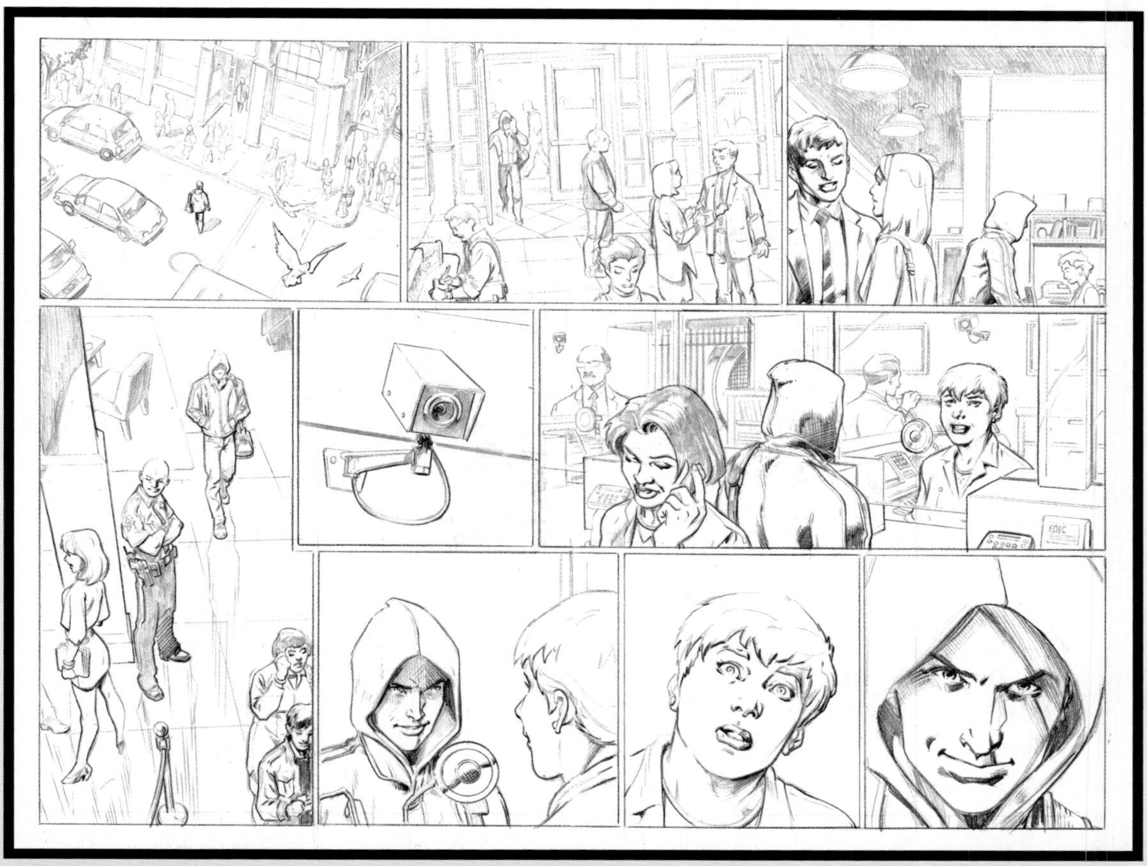

Brilliant #1 — Page 2-3 Pencils

VOICE

I had my ATM card stolen.

VOICE

When will the funds be made available-

VOICE

I need to open a money market account but I have no idea-

VOICE

-need a better job-

3- Over Amadeus' shoulder, the manager is talking to customers. All silent so it is all in the gestures.

4- Over Amadeus' other shoulder, The security guard is leering at a couple of tellers. Living in his fantasy world.

5- The security cameras on the ceiling...

6- From behind the female bank teller looking out past the thick glass- Amadeus, adjusting his glasses, tries not to look nervous as he approaches her. The busy bank all around and behind them.

TELLER

Next in line!

AMADEUS

Hi.

I'm having trouble with my ATM card...

TELLER

What kind of problem, sir?

AMADEUS

It won't give me my money.

7- From behind Amadeus, the teller eyes the man and almost laughs at the silly sounding request.

> **TELLER**
>> *Let me see what we can...*

> **AMADEUS**
>> *Just give me all the money you can.*

> **TELLER**
>> *All the money in the entire.*

8- The teller looks up. Her smile drops. Something is wrong with her. She is being controlled. She is stunned. But for now we're not sure if she is just scared or what?

9- Amadeus looks at her. Intently. Working on her psychically.

> **AMADEUS**
>> *Thank you.*

PAGE 4

1- Over Amadeus' shoulder, the teller, stunned, dazed, comes back with a messy pile of cash. More than she can carry.

More than any teller is allowed to handle without approval. The assistant bank manager, behind her, at a copy machine, is just turning to see this odd sight. Are they being robbed?

The poor teller is struggling. The power of suggestion is compelling her but every muscle in her body is trying to stop herself from doing this.

> **TELLER**
>> *Nnn...*

2- The teller is shaking and shoving bricks of money into the thick, glass teller door.

The assistant manager is behind her and is completely shocked. He has no idea what to do. He is about to touch her but doesn't want to. The teller can't stop herself and is crying as she does it.

> **ASSISTANT MANAGER**
>> *Is everything ok Corey?*

> **TELLER**
>> *Nnn...*

> **ASSISTANT MANAGER**
>> *Excuse me? Corey!!*
>>
>> *You don't have that kind of authori-*

3- Amadeus is shovelling the money in his bag. Quickly.

> **ASSISTANT MANAGER**
>> *Corey!! Stop!*
>>
>> *Corey you need to-!!!*

4- Amadeus's p.o.v The assistant manager grabs Corey by the arms and stops her from giving the money over. But she is fighting him all the way.

> **ASSISTANT MANAGER**
>> *Corey, stop!!*

5- Same. Corey screams in crazy horror. Her mind is seizing. She is having a crazy attack.

The assistant manager cowers at it but doesn't let go of her.

> **TELLER**
>> *Aaaaaiiieeeeeee!!!!*

PAGE 5

1- Wide of the bank. In the foreground, Amadeus turns away from the teller and towards us. He has a back pack full of money. Some of it on the floor.

Behind him, Corey is screaming and convulsing in the manager's arms. The security guard is hopping to and the other customers and employees are shocked. No one knows what is going on.

Is it the teller? Are they being robbed?

ASSISTANT MANAGER
> *Help!!*

TELLER
> *Aaaaaiiieeeaaaa!!*

ASSISTANT MANAGER
> *Stop him!*
> *Stop that man!!*

2- The portly security guard comes right up on Amadeus. Wrestling with his gun.

SECURITY
> *Hey You!!*

3- Amadeus turns around and holds out his hand with purpose. The security guard seems to suddenly lose control of his body. He starts to faint on the spot.

SECURITY
> *Ggkkksss!*

BYSTANDER
> *What's happening?*
> *What's going on??*

4- Amadeus keeps going towards us as the security guard falls on his face, dead asleep.

ASSISTANT MANAGER
> *Someone!!*

5- Amadeus is at the door and turns to see if he getting away with it. The sun glints off of his smile and glasses.

6- A gun is raised and fires. Angle on the barrel.
> *SPX: BAM*

PAGE 6-7

Double page spread

1- Amadeus turns and a bullet hits his cheek. It doesn't tear the skin. It bounces off. Ever so slightly.

But the impact. The force of it, winces his face and his skin bounces a little from it.

Amadeus is shocked by it. He didn't expect it or ever experience it. He just stopped a bullet with his face!!

2- Over another security guards' shoulder, the man who fired the gun, Amadeus holds his face and winces in pain. Stomping his foot like he got poked in the eye.

> **AMADEUS**
> *Son of a bitch!! Ow!! Damn that hurt!!*

3- Slightly low looking up, The security guard, gun up, and a couple of bank employees on the other side of the bank stare at this insane sight in open mouthed shock.

> **AMADEUS**
> *Ow!!*

4- Angle on the bullet that has fallen on the floor near Amadeus' money bag.
> SPX: TINK

5- Amadeus lets go of his cheek. It's fine. But Amadeus is pissed and pointing at the security guard.

> **AMADEUS**
> *You fuck!!*
>
> *Stick that gun up your ass, why don'tcha!!??*

6- Amadeus is spinning on his heal and taking his money and heading out. He is all smiles. He took a bullet and survived it.

Behind him, the security guard is trying to shove a gun up his own ass as the others try to stop him.

> **SECURITY**
> *Help me!! Help me!!*

> **WOMAN**
> *What is this?? What are you doing??*

> **SECURITY**
> *Aaggh!!*

7- Ext. Bank

Amadeus slinks out of the bank and into the innocent lunch crowd. Lunch time. Perfectly normal.

In the background. The cops are on their way. Amadeus looks shocked and almost orgasmicly delighted to have done what he just did.
> SPX: WWEEEEOOOEEEEEOOOO

8- Big panel. Same but wider. Wider shot of the bedlam outside the bank. Amadeus has slinked into the crowd as the police have descended on the scene.

The crowd reacts accordingly. People are getting out of the way or coming to see what is up.

One of the tellers has come out of the bank and is looking around in amazement to see if she can find the insane mystery robber.

But she can't.

PAGE 8

1- Ext. Seattle institute of technology campus- night

A beat up station wagon filled with a lifetime of belongings, pulls up to the quiet dorm parking lot of a large modern campus.

This is a made up institution. Think of a new wave of ivy league.

2- Albert (21, African American, skinny, tall) stumbles out of his car and stretches. It was a long drive. It's a quiet night on campus.

> ***READS: ALBERT***

3- Albert settles down and is surprised to see...

ALBERT

Hey.

4- Over Albert's shoulder, Bach (21, head shaved, Korean) sits on the steps to the dorm reading a huge text book. The high beam security lights to the dorm bathe him.

READS: BACH

BACH

Hey to you.

5- Albert stands there. Bach doesn't get up. These good friends need to say some things to each other. Some ice needs to be broken. They tease. That's what they do.

ALBERT

Were you sitting out here waiting for me?

BACH

Just needed the fresh air.

ALBERT

You WERE sitting out here waiting for me.

That's so cute and creepy.

BACH

So, how did she take it?

ALBERT

My mom?

6- Bach smiles sarcastically.

BACH

Yeah, all of a sudden I care about your mom.

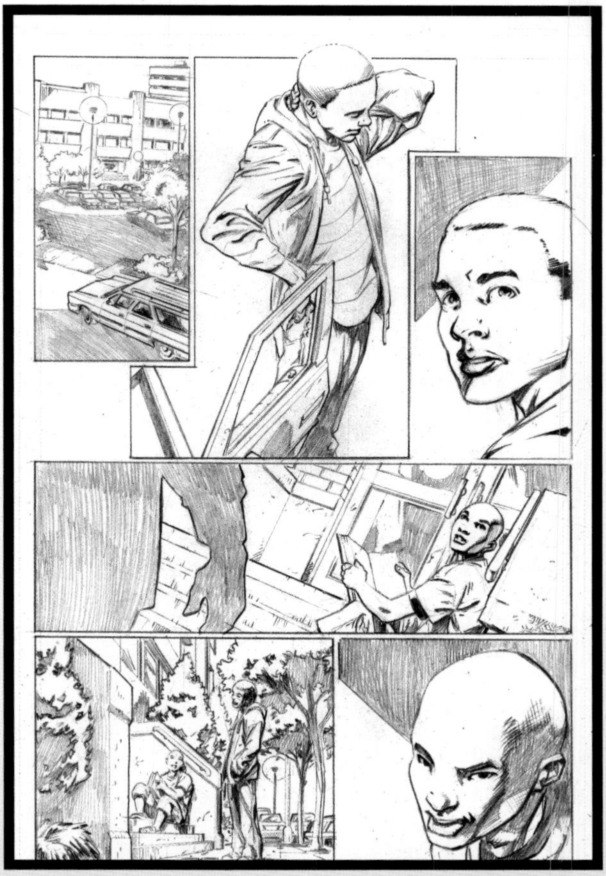

Brilliant #1 — Page 8-9 Pencils

PAGE 9

1- Albert opens his trunk and is about to unload his little life back into his dorm.

He unconsciously sighs at the sight of his entire life shoved into the back of a car.

ALBERT

You were right.

BACH

I know.

But, boy, do I want to hear you say it.

ALBERT

We broke up.

BACH

No!!

ALBERT

Stop it.

2- Bach pulls a box out of Albert's trunk with a smile. Helping. Bach is going to bust his balls.

BACH

Well at least you didn't make the mistake of skipping the entire semester to find out.

ALBERT

That's not why I took the semester off.

BACH

Sure it is.

ALBERT

Stop.

BACH

Absolutely not.

3- Albert looks to his friend and deflates his ego and says... Bach lets it all go.

ALBERT

I'm sorry I didn't call more.

BACH

What am I? Your bitch of an ex girlfriend?

ALBERT

Ok. Now stop.

BACH

Hey, we missed your birthday.

4- Albert waves it away. Bach lets him step ahead and on to the dorm stairs.

ALBERT

My birthday? What am I? 6?

BACH

Twenty one.

You're a man. It's a big one.

ALBERT

"Big one."

BACH

It is.

5- Albert is at the door and opening it.

ALBERT

Believe me, it's ok.

Is there food?

I just want to sit and-

PAGES 10-11

Double page spread

1- Int. Dorm rec room- same

Huge panel across both pages. PARTY!! The entire dorm and a smattering of campus friends have come out for a big surprise party. Decorations, a keg, plastic cups raised high.

The Walmart generic birthday banner. The keg on tap. A kid's plastic swimming pool full of spiked punch in the middle of the room.

But this is the nerd dorm. This is the tech nerds at play.

EVERYONE

Surprise!!!

2- Bach takes Albert's duffle bag away so some of the girls can hug him. Albert looks at Bach. His old friends got him.

DORM GIRL

Ooohhh!!

We missed you.

DORM GUY

Dude, I can't believe you came back to Shawshank.

3- Three people try to hand Albert a drink as Albert hugs his dormmate IZZY.

Izzy (21, white man's Afro) seems to have really missed Albert and hugs him low. Longer than Albert was prepared for.

READS: IZZY

IZZY

Oh, man, thank god you're back.

ALBERT

Hey, Izzy.

IZZY

Seriously, man. I was callin' you.

ALBERT

I know, I'm sorry...

IZZY

I missed our talks.

4- Izzy shuffles back into the crowd. Bach and Albert toast each other.

ALBERT

When did me and him have TALKS?

BACH

He's very emotional.

MARIE

(drunk, off panel)

Oh my god, Albert! Albert!!

KINDRED

Here we go...

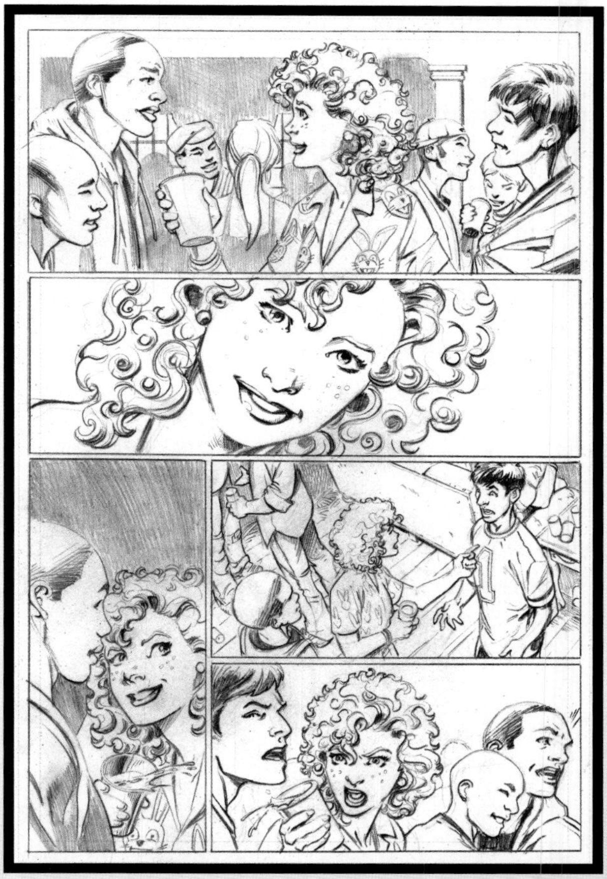

Brilliant #1 — Page 12 Pencils

PAGE 12

1- Marie (20, a burst of red hair) wearing bunny pajamas, pushes through the crowd and almost spills a little of her drink on Albert in her quest to get to him.

READS: MARIE

ALBERT

Hi Marie.

MARIE

That kind of devotion from a boyfriend.

ALBERT

I didn't--

MARIE

How are you?

2- She yells in Albert's ear, we imagine over the music, as she pulls her wide-eyed boyfriend around by his shirt like a pet.

ALBERT

I'm ok.

It's ALL ok.

MARIE

No really?

ALBERT

Really.

MARIE

Did they talk to you yet?

ALBERT

About what?

3- Marie turns to her date as if it just occurred to her that she hates him.

> **MARIE**
>> Hey, you know WHAT, man? We're DONE.

> **BOYFRIEND**
>> WHAT?

> **MARIE**
>> You would never give up a semester for me.
>> NEVER!!
>> I don't need YOU!! I need real commitment.

> **BOYFRIEND**
>> This is our FIFTH DATE.

4- Kindred and Albert turn away from the ugly scene, trying to push through the growing crowd. We imagine the DJ music gets louder. Mash ups.

Albert seems crazy happy to see someone off panel.

> **MARIE**
>> You're not HALF THE MAN this man is!!

> **BOYFRIEND**
>> Oh my GOD.

> **KINDRED**
>> Well, that was a hallmark moment.

> **ALBERT**
>> Amadeus, Amadeus, Amadeus!

Brilliant #1 — Page 13 Pencils

PAGE 13

1- They turn and bump into AMADEUS. Amadeus is not as dapper as he was in the first scene. He looks rough around the edges. In need of sleep and a shave. a bruise on his cheek. A little one. From the bullet.

Whatever caused the amazing opening scene doesn't seem to be there now. He seems like he's crashing. But he is happy to see his old friend.

> **AMADEUS**
>> My man...
>> How is she?

> **ALBERT**
>> She's ok.

> **AMADEUS**
>> How are you?

> **ALBERT**
>> I'm fine.

2- Amadeus and Albert hug hard. The hug of men who play sports together. Very sincere.

> **AMADEUS**
>> No really, man.
>> For real. How are you?

> **ALBERT**
>> I'm good.

> **AMADEUS**
>> Sorry to hear about your phone.

3- Albert pushes off the hug and smiles at the never ending ball-busting. Kindred smiles too but has an eye on Amadeus.

ALBERT
> Yeah, ok. I get it.

AMADEUS
> I heard your phone broke.

ALBERT
> Ok, I get it.

4- Amadeus presents Albert with his birthday present with a knowing smile...

ALBERT (CONT'D)
> What is this?

4- Albert opens the package. It's a brand new iPhone or something close. Amadeus barks the last bit of ball-busting into his face.

AMADEUS
> I assumed your phone must be broken so I GOT YOU THIS FOR YOUR BIRTHDAY.

ALBERT
> Amadeus...

AMADEUS
> Now you can RETURN A FUCKING PHONE CALL!!

5- Everyone laughs and applauds the "funny because it's true" gift. Albert is startled by the generosity.

ALBERT
> I can't accept--

AMADEUS
> It's a present.

ALBERT
> This is really...
>
> Where'd you get the money?

PAGE 14

1- Amadeus theatrically kisses him on the cheek and smiles. Very glad Albert is back.

AMADEUS
> I gotta go.
>
> Tell these fuckers not to touch any of my shit.

2- Amadeus grabs Kindred by the shoulder and whispers in his ear. Albert sees this but can't hear it. Something is up. Secrets.

KINDRED (small font)
> Yeah.
>
> No.
>
> I know.

3- Albert stares at the iphone. It may be the nicest present he has ever received.

In the background, Amadeus is pushing through the crowd and out of the party.

ALBERT
> What the fuck?
>
> KINDRED
>
> I'll take it.

ALBERT
> (singing, smiling)
>
> Fuck the hell off, you will!
>
> 8- The party grows and grows. Beer. Lots of beer. A couple is sloppily making out behind the couch.

PAGE 15

1- Int. Dorm ROOM- same

Izzy is nervously chasing a couple of partying intruders out of his dorm room. a room shared by Kindred and Amadeus.

They were clearly looking for somewhere to make out but Izzy caught them before it was too late.

The room is crazy cluttered with books and unfinished tech projects and clothes and the center of it is his handmade computer terminal.

> **IZZY**
>> No. No! Out!
>>
>> Out of this room. Not THIS room.

> **DORM GUY**
>> We're just chillin'.

> **PARTY GIRL**
>> Where's the john?

> **IZZY**
>> Not in HERE!

2- The dorm guy points to an odd contraption on Izzy's desk. Izzy has a homemade Lego robot-hand that is programmed to work the mouse of his computer mining some kind of World's of Warcraft MMO and is very anxious about anyone touching it.

> **DORM GUY**
>> What is THAT?

> **IZZY**
>> This-- this is MY business.

> **DORM GUY**
>> It's a Lego robot hand. Did you MAKE that?

> **IZZY**
>> That-- that I INVENTED.

> **DORM GUY**
>> What IS it?

3- Izzy is blocking his computer station. The couple are confused and amused. The girl is. The guy just wants to get laid.

> **DORM GIRL**
>> Is it using the computer?

> **IZZY**
>> It's mining my MMO for me. It's mining.

> **DORM GUY**
>> Mining?

4- Izzy is a uber genius nerd. Gesturing to his creation like he has one a prize.

> **IZZY**
>> For gold.
>>
>> I then sell that gold on the net and pay my bills.
>>
>> So please.
>>
>> Ok.

5- They just blankly stare at Izzy like he is an alien.

> **PARTY GIRL**
>> I don't understand a WORD he just said.

> **DORM GUY**
>> Consider it a good thing.

PARTY GIRL

Uh-huh.

VOICE OUTSIDE

Ladies and gentlemen!!

PAGE 16

1- Int. Dorm rec room- same

From behind Albert, across the crowd, Kindred holds out his hands and gets everyone's attention. Albert chills back and waits for whatever this nonsense is going to be.

KINDRED

Ladies and gentlemen!!

If you please!!

For years this ENTIRE campus has been locked in intense debate,

A debate started by my life-long friend and birthday boy, Albert!

2- Albert rolls his eyes, what is this now? And Marie hangs on him drunk. All eyes on Kindred off panel.

KINDRED

A debate that has inspired heated dialogue among you, the greatest scientific minds of this and the next generation of nerd.

3- Kindred gestures for the lights.

KINDRED

But TONIGHT!!

FINALLY!

Here!

The question will be answered.

4- Kindred steps aside as The lights dim. A couple of desk lamps are used as spotlights on a hanging bedsheet.

KINDRED

Ladies and gentlemen, I ask you...

PAGE 17-18

Double-page spread

1- Big panel. Two party nerds dressed up in handmade foam core Robocop and Halo's Master Chief outfits present themselves.

But we can't call them that or make them look like that so make a parody of them. Just two looking goofballs in transformer/ robot/ gamer cosplay.

Way too much time was spent making these barely holding together costumes.

KINDRED (CONT'D)

"Who will win in a fight between Roboformer and The Tech??!!"

2- The crowd goes wild. Albert laughs to himself. This is as good as he has felt in months.

ALBERT

Oh my god!!

3- Roboformer and The tech take fighting stances. They circle each other. Kindred is the ringmaster.

Brilliant #1 — Page 17 Pencils

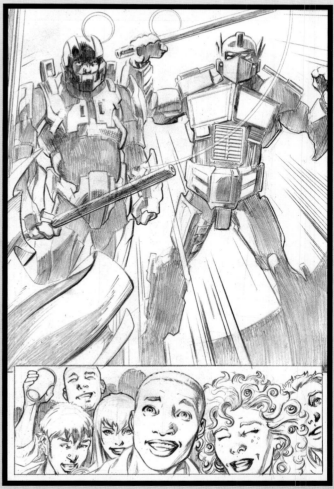

KINDRED

Prepare to die, shitty sequel movie maker!!

4- Then... they battle!! The two robo foam cores smash into each other and The crowd goes insane. Beer spills. The costumes already start to break!!

ROBOFORMER

Have at thee!!

5- Albert laughs. The crowd goes crazy.

PAGE 19

1- Izzy blocks his doorway with his life as the pretend battle rolls down the hallway. Crashing into everything and everybody. Everyone laughing and diving out of the way

IZZY

Oh god!

2- The foam core robots knock over everything and everyone in their path. The audience cheers and dives out of the way.

ROBOFORMER

Agh!!

     SPX: CRAASH

IZZY

Outside!!

3- Robocop falls into the pool of spiked punch.

     SPX: SSPLAASSHH

ROBOFORMER

You will not-- agh!!

TECH

Ha ha!!!

4- Ext. Parking lot

The chaos and party noise builds to a crescendo as the warriors fall out the front door. Everyone on the street is seeing this party spill out on them.

     SPX: CRAAASHH

ROBOFORMER

Hey, I'm wet!!

I'm hysterical and I'm wet!!

TECH

Give up then!!

ROBOFORMER

You're a cheater!

5- The battle and its audience pour out into the parking lot. Roboformer and the Tech's costumes break apart as they fall onto the grass.

DORM GUY

Fifty on Roboformer.

DORM GUY 2

Done.

ROBOFORMER

Dude!! This took me all day!

TECH

Waagghh!!

Brilliant #1 — Page 18 Pencils

Brilliant #1 — Page 19 Pencils

6- Campus security swoops in. Albert and Kindred hang back with their drinks and watch the party break up. The security vehicle is one of those electric cars. Very specific design. Make it a point. Its a plot point.

CAMPUS SECURITY

Ok people.

That's enough!!

Hey!!

PAGE 20

1- People scatter. Roboformer in his broken costume, in his underwear, declares his victory as he is escorted away by obnoxious campus security.

Everyone is laughing and having a good time. The tech is almost naked. Using foam core to cover his bits.

ROBOFORMER

I declare victory in the name of the Tyrell corporation.

KINDRED

Wrong movie.

ALBERT

That's Bladerunner.

ROBOFORMER

Whatever.

Brilliant #1 — Page 20 Pencils

2- Albert tries to casually calm the very annoyed security guard down. The security guard is all adrenaline and shrugs off Albert with a sneer.

ALBERT

Hey man, it's ok. We'll put him to bed.

CAMPUS SECURITY

He damaged CAMPUS PROPERTY!! A report HAS to filed!!

The authorities have to be involved.

ALBERT

Come on man, it's just...

CAMPUS SECURITY

Hey!! BACK OFF!!

3- Kindred, Albert and Izzy give each other looks. Incredulous at this overzealous security guard who thinks he controls the universe.

Behind them, Party's over. Everyone goes back to their dorms.

KINDRED

Well...

He told you.

ALBERT

Really.

4- Same. Marie comes up to Albert and gives him a sincere peck on the cheek.

MARIE

Very glad you're back, Albert.

5- Same. Albert gives Kindred a look. A kiss? Marie is walking away in the background.

ALBERT

She's glad I'm back.

KINDRED

Batter up.

ALBERT

> Who? Me or her?

KINDRED

> I don't know.
>
> I'm terrible at sports metaphors.

ALBERT

> What now?

6- Kindred clearly has a mischievous idea.

KINDRED

> After party.
>
> I'll call Amadeus.

PAGE 21-22

Double page spread

1- Ext. Campus rooftop- night

It's a much quieter outdoors after party. Kindred, Albert, Izzy, Amadeus and a few others drink beer while working on a mystery project.

It's not clear exactly where they are or what they are doing. Smudges of oil and dirt on their clothes indicate that they have been doing it for a while. There are pieces of tech all over the place.

A difficult page to design because we are revealing what they're working on and where they are as the punchline.

You could have a lot of fun with circular or broken panel designs. As if we are doing a lot of quick cuts among the guys.

ALBERT

> Hey, where was Anthony tonight?

AMADEUS

> Anthony no longer attends this fine institution.

ALBERT

> He's gone?

2- Amadeus points his wrench.

AMADEUS

> He said, and I quote: "I don't even like Astrophysics."
>
> Packed up his shit... and left.

3- Albert sits back against the rooftop ledge with his beer. Stunned.

ALBERT

> Fuck.

4- Izzy gestures with a screw driver. A piece of a motor in his hand.

> *IZZY*
>
> Leonardo left too.
>
> Got a job.

5- Albert and Kindred sit back and take a break.

Brilliant #1 — Page 21 Pencils

Brilliant #1 — Page 22 Pencils

ALBERT

Leonardo got a job?

KINDRED

With a brokerage firm. Supposedly it's money.

Real money.

ALBERT

Doing what?

KINDRED

Whatever they do.

6- Albert looks genuinely disappointed...

ALBERT

I thought he was going to be an economist.

Huh.

Good for him, I guess.

7- Amadeus smiles to himself as he works. A piece of a motor in his hand.

AMADEUS

That sounded sincere.

8- Albert shrugs. Kindred never gets the references...

ALBERT

He has an AMAZING mind and now his aspiration in life-- his GOAL now is to be, I don't know, Bud Fox?

KINDRED

Who?

ALBERT

Charlie Sheen in Wall Street.

KINDRED

So just say: "Charlie Sheen in Wall Street."

9- Albert sits with his beer and thinks. Amadeus and Izzy are building something. Kindred sees Albert has fallen into a funk.

KINDRED

What?

ALBERT

I think... I think I HATE biophysics.

KINDRED

You HATE it?

ALBERT

I think I ALWAYS hated it.

KINDRED

Well, tough shit about it being your major.

10- Albert gestures... Kindred sits back stunned.

ALBERT

I'm good at it, so I do it.

But I don't think I like it.

11- Kindred and Amadeus give each other a look as they work on their project.

KINDRED

Wow.

12- Kindred turns back and looks at the confused and a little depressed Albert. A piece of a motor in his hand.

ALBERT

I know.

KINDRED

> We're rounding third on our academic career.

ALBERT

> I am aware.

13- Amadeus, working with tools, smiles to himself as he eavesdrops on this semi-private conversation.

AMADEUS

> There's always football.
>
> Oh wait, you throw like a girl.

PAGE 23

1- Albert sits back with a beer. Kindred approaches him out of the earshot of the others. All whispers.

KINDRED

> Dude, you just got back.
>
> You-- you know what you need. You need a goal.
>
> A project.

ALBERT

> A project?

KINDRED

> Something to lock onto.

2- Albert takes the new iPhone out of his pocket and looks at it. All whispers.

ALBERT

> (whispers)
>
> Hey, where did Amadeus get the money for this?

KINDRED

> It's nice.

ALBERT

> It's real nice.
>
> My point is he's not that nice.

KINDRED

> Guy's, uh, flush lately.

ALBERT

> Flush??
>
> You're in the Rat Pack now? If he has money, why doesn't he move out of the damn dorm?

3- Kindred crouches down, leans in and whispers. A little excited to be getting in to this with his friend.

KINDRED

> Are you back?

ALBERT

> What do you MEAN?

KINDRED

> Are you staying?
>
> Or are you looking around and deciding whether or not to.

ALBERT

> I'm here. I'm back.
>
> I just-- I don't know why.

KINDRED

> We need you back.

Brilliant #1 — Page 23 Pencils

4- Albert doesn't understand what this conversation is about.

> **ALBERT**
>> You NEED me back?
>>
>> For what?

5- Amadeus looks up from the project and gives the boys a silent nod. It is time to bring him IN.

> **AMADEUS**
>> Bring him in.

PAGE 24

1- Over Albert's shoulder, Kindred leans in and tries to gently tell him what's going on. All the while the others still working on the project that we still can't tell what it is.

> **KINDRED**
>> We've been working on something.

> **ALBERT**
>> Who?

> **KINDRED**
>> Us.
>>
>> And Marie.

> **ALBERT**
>> What?

2- Amadeus works on his mystery project. A piece of a motor in his hand. Smiling to himself.

> **AMADEUS**
>> Something better than being Bud Fox from Wall Street.

3- Albert's interest is peaked. Almost laughing. What could this be?

> **ALBERT**
>> What's going on?

4- Amadeus works...

> **AMADEUS**
>> Do you know who Jack Parsons was?

5- Albert sifts through his mind.

> **ALBERT**
>> No.

6- Amadeus looks up and says it. Izzy behind him.

> **AMADEUS**
>> He was one of the founders of the jet propulsion laboratory.

> **IZZY**
>> He invented the rocket.

7- Kindred interjects.

> **KINDRED**
>> He was also a crazy devil-worshiper.

8- Izzy is insulted by the simplification. A piece of a motor in his hand.

> **IZZY**
>> Occultist.

9- Amadeus adds. Izzy behind him.

> **AMADEUS**
>> The guy was a genius.

Brilliant #1 — Page 24 Pencils

IZZY

    MAD genius.

AMADEUS

    And what's interesting is, at least to me...

Brilliant #1 — Page 25 Pencils

Brilliant #1 — Page 26 Pencils

PAGE 25-26

Double page spread

1- Amadeus keeps working on the mystery project. A hint of a tire.

AMADEUS

    That this man of science fact often found himself surrounded by what ended up being the great voices of science fiction.

2- Kindred turns to Albert as if to impress him. Albert pinches his nose.

KINDRED

    L. Ron Hubbard.

ALBERT

    I thought you said great.

KINDRED

    Isaac Asimov, Robert Heinlein...

3- Amadeus points his oily wrench.

AMADEUS

    Philip K. Dick.

AMADEUS

    The point is there was this magic moment in history where science fiction and science fact lived in the same universe and fed off of each other...

4- Kindred offers...

4- Albert doesn't understand what this conversation is about.

> **ALBERT**
>
> *You NEED me back?*
>
> *For what?*

5- Amadeus looks up from the project and gives the boys a silent nod. It is time to bring him IN.

> **AMADEUS**
>
> *Bring him in.*

PAGE 24

1- Over Albert's shoulder, Kindred leans in and tries to gently tell him what's going on. All the while the others still working on the project that we still can't tell what it is.

> **KINDRED**
>
> *We've been working on something.*

> **ALBERT**
>
> *Who?*

> **KINDRED**
>
> *Us.*
>
> *And Marie.*

> **ALBERT**
>
> *What?*

2- Amadeus works on his mystery project. A piece of a motor in his hand. Smiling to himself.

> **AMADEUS**
>
> *Something better than being Bud Fox from Wall Street.*

3- Albert's interest is peaked. Almost laughing. What could this be?

> **ALBERT**
>
> *What's going on?*

4- Amadeus works...

> **AMADEUS**
>
> *Do you know who Jack Parsons was?*

5- Albert sifts through his mind.

> **ALBERT**
>
> *No.*

6- Amadeus looks up and says it. Izzy behind him.

> **AMADEUS**
>
> *He was one of the founders of the jet propulsion laboratory.*

> **IZZY**
>
> *He invented the rocket.*

7- Kindred interjects.

> **KINDRED**
>
> *He was also a crazy devil-worshiper.*

8- Izzy is insulted by the simplification. A piece of a motor in his hand.

> **IZZY**
>
> *Occultist.*

9- Amadeus adds. Izzy behind him.

> **AMADEUS**
>
> *The guy was a genius.*

Brilliant #1 — Page 24 Pencils

IZZY

    MAD genius.

AMADEUS

    And what's interesting is, at least to me...

Brilliant #1 — Page 25 Pencils

Brilliant #1 — Page 26 Pencils

PAGE 25-26
Double page spread

1- Amadeus keeps working on the mystery project. A hint of a tire.

AMADEUS

    That this man of science fact often found himself surrounded by what ended up being the great voices of science fiction.

2- Kindred turns to Albert as if to impress him. Albert pinches his nose.

KINDRED

    L. Ron Hubbard.

ALBERT

    I thought you said great.

KINDRED

    Isaac Asimov, Robert Heinlein…

3- Amadeus points his oily wrench.

AMADEUS

    Philip K. Dick.

AMADEUS

    The point is there was this magic moment in history where science fiction and science fact lived in the same universe and fed off of each other...

4- Kindred offers...

KINDRED

Ideas that Jack Parsons was working through became the fodder for all these writers.

5- Amadeus gestures as he bolts something.

AMADEUS

Exactly.

They fed off each other.

And no one will ever really know exactly how and from who and why these ideas burst into the world except for those who were there.

But when you start to think about how much brain power was at work...

Ugh!

MM!!

6- Albert cannot figure this out. Dry.

ALBERT

Did you all become devil-worshipers while I was gone?

7- Kindred and Amadeus look at him and smile. They are going to tell him.

AMADEUS

We're talking about brain power.

KINDRED

Inspiration.

8- Albert doesn't understand what's going on.

ALBERT

What?

9- Over Albert's shoulder, Kindred turns and offers...

KINDRED

What is the one piece of science fiction that has not become science fact yet?

10- Same as 8.

ALBERT

Barbarella?

11- Amadeus looks right at us. The punchline.

AMADEUS

Superpowers.

12- Albert is confused. What is this?

PAGE 27

1- Over Albert's shoulder, Kindred turns and looks his friend right in the eye.

KINDRED

We may have-- we may have cracked it.

2- Albert is stunned. Not sure if this is real.

ALBERT

You invented... SUPERpowers?

3- Amadeus smiles. Izzy behind him.

AMADEUS

We got something.

But honestly... We need another set of eyes.

IZZY

And now YOU'RE back.

4- Albert is confused. Looking at Kindred for some sort of clue. Kindred is all smiles.

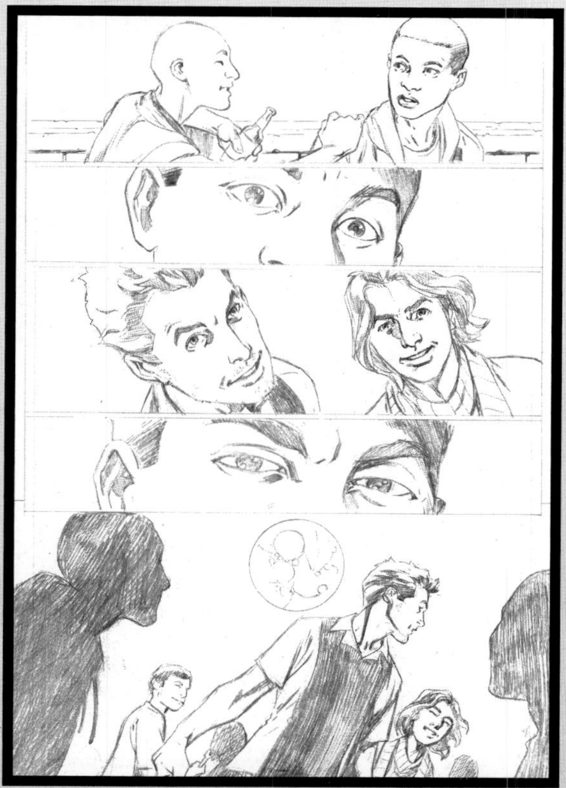

Brilliant #1 — Page 27 Pencils

ALBERT

SHOW me.

5- Amadeus, satisfied, stands up and wipes his hands. Smiling to himself

AMADEUS

All right…

Guys.

Wipe it down.

We're done.

Let's go.

PAGE 28

Full page spread

Wide of the entire roof. Albert and Kindred join the others as they scramble off from what we now reveal to be a campus rooftop. They are climbing down the roof ladder.

The boys have spent the entire night dismantling and rebuilding the campus security car onto the roof of one of the buildings.

A prank only a handful of geniuses could pull off.

The campus buildings all around them.

TO BE CONTINUED…

Brilliant #1 — Page 28 Pencils